Cultural Flow Between China and Outside World Throughout History

Shen Fuwei

FOREIGN LANGUAGES PRESS   BEIJING

First Edition   1996
Second Printing   1997

Translated by Wu Jingshu

ISBN 7-119-00431-X
© Foreign Languages Press, Beijing, 1996
Published by Foreign Languages Press
24 Baiwanzhuang Road, Beijing 100037, China

Printed by Beijing Foreign Languages Printing House
19 Chegongzhuang Xilu, Beijing 100044, China

Distributed by China International Book Trading
Corporation
35 Chegongzhuang Xilu, Beijing 100044, China
P. O. Box 399, Beijing, China

Printed in the People's Republic of China

Bodhisattva entertainers (in part) in Cave 7 of the Thousand-Buddha Caves of Kizir in Baicheng of Xinjiang.

Vault ceiling mural painting in Cave 21 of the Thousand-Buddha Caves of Kumutula in Kuqa of Xinjiang.

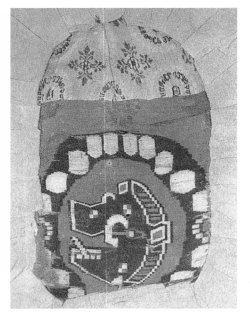

Tang Dynasty silk brocade with stringed beads and pig's head pattern, unearthed in Turpan of Xinjiang.

Gilded silver kettle of Sassanian Persia, unearthed from the Northern Zhou Dynasty tomb of Li Xian in Guyuan of Ningxia.

Part of the late Tang Dynasty copy of "Mahaparinirvana Sutra," unearthed from the Thousand-Buddha Caves of Bazikrik in Xinjiang.

Jean de Wavrin's Chroniques d'Angleterre, 15th century. An assault on a castle during the Hundred Years' War (Paris, Bibliothèque nationale).

Part of the painting of "Hundred Stallions" by Giuseppe Castiglione.

A mural painting in the Dunhuang Grottoes.

Flying deer on a stone tomb arch in an Eastern Han Dynasty painting, unearthed from Zengjiabao of Chengdu in Sichuan Province.

The Eastern Han Dynasty silk with double-rhombus and four-beast pattern, unearthed in Syria.

A winged angel (woodcut unearthed from Loulan ruins of Xinjiang).

A coloured bodhisattva bust unearthed from Yanqi.

Relief pattern of deer on the pedestal of a buddha statue in Lashao Temple of Wushui in Gansu Province.

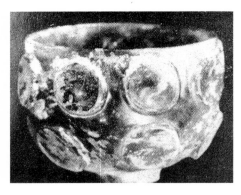

Sassanian Persian glass bowl with embossed ringed pattern, unearthed from the Northern Zhou Dynasty tomb of Li Xian in Guyuan of Ningxia.

Islamic glass vase, unearthed from the Northern Song Dynasty Huiguang Pagoda in Rui'an of Zhejiang Province.

A blue-floral patterned porcelain pot of the Ming Dynasty's Zhengde period, unearthed from a Ming Dynasty tomb in Dongyin Village, Beijing.

Portrait of Xu Guangqi.

Portrait of Joannes Adam Schall von Bell.

The orrery made by Rich Glnne Fecit of England in the 18th century.

Haiyan Hall in the Changchunyuan (Park of Everlasting Spring).

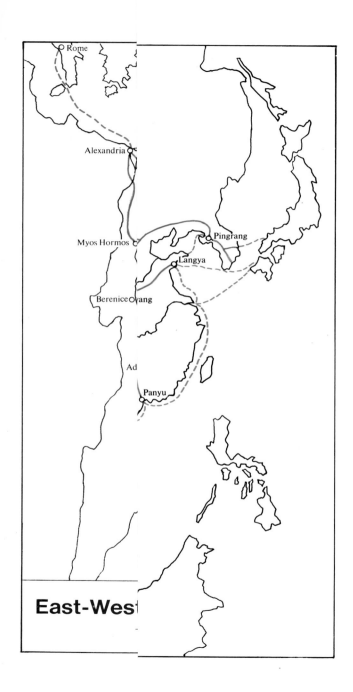

Rome

Alexandria

Myos Hormos

Pingrang

Langya

Berenice○yang

Ad

Panyu

East-Wes

ead of China's
entions

Xativa
1150

Acheng copper pistol
1287

utai paper
110

Fez
1100

Ding Kiln
800-1368

Bianjing
970

Luoyang paper
105

n

ingdezhen Kiln
900-1840

Yue Kiln
800-1150

Yuzhang
(today Nanchang)
904

Longquan Kiln
1050-1450

Guangzhou
1000

● ....
■ ....
◆ ....
▲ ....
★ ....

Contents

PART ONE
Cultural Intercourse Between China and The Western
 Regions   1

Chapter One
The Earliest Contact Between China and The Western Re-
 gions Before the Qin Dynasty   3
  I The Western Regions as Described in Ancient Chinese
    History   3
    1. The Origins of Chinese Culture   3
    2. The Ancient Chinese Legend About Xiwangmu
      (Western Queen Mother) and Its Relations with
      the Western Regions   5
  II The Origin of Chinese Civilization   8
    1. Various Hypotheses on the Origin of Chinese
      Civilization   8
    2. The Yangshao Culture of Painted Pottery and Its
      Introduction to the West   10
  III Convergence of the Hua Xia Culture and the Eura-
    sian Steppe Culture   13
    1. The Northward Advance of the Bronze Culture of
      the Shang and Zhou Dynasties   13
    2. The Westward Migration of Jichuo and Westward
      Expedition of the Zhou Dynasty's King Mu   18
  IV Nomadic Travellers and the Silk Trade   21
    1. Silk—the Earliest Link Between China and Greece   21
    2. Silk Fabrics Make China Known Throughout the
      World   23
    3. The Route of Glass and Gem Trade   25
    4. The Animal Style in the Northern Chinese Art

Designs   28

Chapter Two
Opening of the Sino-Western Communications During the
  Han Dynasty   31
  I An Open Society and Smooth Traffic   31
  II Parthia and the Monopoly of Silk Trade   35
  III China and the Oriental Trade of the Roman Empire   38
    1. The Biggest Customer of Chinese Silk   38
    2. The Proposed Diplomatic Relations Between China
      and Rome   41
    3. The Voyage of Chinese Sailing Ships to Port Adulis   43
    4. The Acclaimed "Land of Treasures"   45
  IV Earliest Cultural Exchanges Between China and
    India   47
    1. The Origin of Buddhism and Its Introduction to
      the East   47
    2. The Bridge Between China and Egypt   50

Chapter Three
The Introduction of Culture and Art from the Western
  Regions During the Han and Tang Dynasties   53
  I The Steppe Empire and East-West Cultural Exchange   53
  II The Influx of Art from the Western Regions   56
    1. The Buddhist Art in Inland China   56
    2. Popularity of the Xiyu Theme in Art Style   59
    3. Paintings and Sculptures of the Graeco-Roman
      Genre   64
    4. The Gandhara Buddhist Art of North China   66
    5. Fine Arts of Sassanian-Persian Style   71
  III Music of the Western Regions   74
    1. The Introduction of Persian Musical Instruments
      and Songs During the Han Dynasty   74
    (A) *Konghou*   75
    (B) *Pipa*   78
    (C) *Bili*   80
    (D) Drum and Cymbal Music and Songs   81

2. The Collation and Promotion of Xiyu Music During the Northern Zhou, Sui and Tang Dynasties   82

IV   The Xiyu Dances and Acrobatics   86

   1. The Xiyu Music and Dance Boom During the Sui and Tang Dynasties   86

   2. The Hu Drama of the Tang Dynasty   89

   3. Introduction of Xiyu's Acrobatics and Magic Arts   91

V   The Introduction of Foreign Folk Arts and Games   94

   1. Puppet Shows and India   94

   2. Indian Chess   96

   3. The Arabian *Shuangliu* Game   98

   4. The Polo Game   99

VI   The Translation of Buddhist Scripture and Its Influence on Chinese Literature   100

   1. The Inception of Buddhist Scripture in China   100

   2. The Endeavours of Masters Fa Xian and Xuan Zhuang   103

   3. A 700-Year-Long History of Translation Work   108

   4. The Indian Touch in Chinese Literary Styles   111

VII   The Introduction of Science and Technology from Egypt, Persia and Arabia   114

   1. Persian Armour Widely Adopted Across China   114

   2. Glass-Making Based on Egyptian Prescription   116

   3. The Introduction of Medicine from Arabia and Persia   120

VIII   Science and Technology Introduced from India   122

   1. The Nine-Volume Calendar and Gautama   122

   2. Indian Medicine and Longevity Drugs   124

   3. The New Creative Buddhist Architecture   125

   4. The Improvement of Sugar-Refining Skills   127

Chapter Four

Cultural Exchange During the Course of Founding a Unified Empire   130

I   The Famous Conqueror Gürkhan   130

II   The Westward Advance of Chinese Culture During the Mongolian Rule   134

   1. The Three Mongolian Expeditions to the West and the Tide of National Amalgamation   134

   2. The Khanate Golden Horde and the Northern Passage of Chinese Culture to the West   137

   3. Il-Khanate and the Southern Passage of Chinese Culture to the West   140

III The Mongolians and the Roman Catholic Church   143

   1. The Vatican Envoy's Trip to the Orient   143

   2. An Mongolian Envoys' Visit to Europe   146

IV The Arabian Culture During the Yuan Dynasty   149

Chapter Five

Cultural Communication Across the Maritime "Silk Road" During the Period from the Ninth to the Fifteenth Century   154

I Developments of Ocean Shipping in the Tang, Song and Yuan Dynasties   154

   1. Maritime "Silk Road" to the Indian Ocean   154

   2. Delegations Sent Overseas by China During the Song and Yuan Dynasties   157

II The Maritime "Silk Road" and the Communication in Materials and Culture   159

   1. Overseas Markets Opening to Chinese Silk   159

   2. The Chinese Porcelain Boom Across Three Continents   162

   3. The Influx of Spice, Rhinoceros Horns and Ivory into China   167

III The Three Famous Travellers of the Yuan Dynasty   168

   1. Marco Polo and His Trip to China   169

   2. Ibn Battutah's Tour of the Orient   176

   3. Wang Dayuan's Two Voyages Across the Indian Ocean   180

IV Zheng He's Voyages to the West and China's New Ties with the Asian and African Countries   187

   1. The Itinerary of Zheng He's Seven Voyages   187

   2. The Treasure Boat Fleet and Overseas Cultural Exchange   191

3. The Attraction of Blue-Floral-Patterned Porcelain 195

Chapter Six
Chinese Science and Culture Introduced Worldwide 199
  I The Inventor of Iron Foundry and Tunnelling Techniques 199
  II China's Sericulture Spread Overseas and Silk-Weaving Skills 203
  III Taoist Alchemy Originated in China 207
  IV The Rapid Development of Porcelain Industry 210
  V Global Tour of the Paper-Making and Printing Techniques 214
    1. Paper-Making Skills Introduced Across the Ocean 214
    2. Printing Techniques and the Renaissance of Europe 217
  VI Mariner's Compass and the Revolution of Maritime Navigation 219
  VII Historic Changes Caused by the Invention of Gunpowder and Firearms 223

PART TWO
The Development of Modern Science and the Reform of Chinese Traditional Culture 227

Chapter Seven
China's Access to Western Culture During the Ming and Qing Dynasties 229
  I Matteo Ricci and His Collaborators Xu Guangqi and Li Zhizao 229
  II Xu Guangqi's Reform of the Chinese Calendar System 237
  III Western Missionaries and Emperor Kangxi of the Qing Dynasty 242
    1. Emperor Kangxi and Western Science 242
    2. The Catholic Crisis 256
  IV A Chinese Visitor to the Original Site of the Renaissance 261

Chapter Eight
Missionaries and the Turning Point of European Culture   266
  I The Enlightenment Movement of Europe and the Political Ideology in China   266
    1. The Mode of an Open-Minded Monarch in the Orient   266
    2. The Chinese and Western Views of "Contemporary China"   269
    3. Francois Voltaire and His Play *L'Orphelin de la Chine*   272
    4. The Chinese Monarchism and the European Physiocrats   275
  II New Creations of the Western Fine Arts   277
    1. The Different Genres of Chinese and Western Fine Arts   277
    2. Samples of the Rococo Architecture   282
    3. The "Anglo-Chinese Gardens"   288
  III Sinology and the Chinese Cultural Boom in Europe   292

Chapter Nine
China's First Attempt to Understand the Western World   298
  I The New Maps and New Knowledge   298
    1. Wei Yuan and Xu Jishe, and Their Works on Knowledge of the World   298
    2. Li Shanlan and Xu Shou, and Their Cooperation with the Missionaries   301
    3. The Kiangnan Machine Building Works and Its Publications   305
  II Schools Teaching Western Sciences   308
    1. From Tongwen Institute to Military Academies   308
    2. The Missionaries and Mission Schools   312
  III The Transplanting of Modern Science and Ideology   314
    1. The Theory of Evolution by Natural Selection as Reflected in *Outlines of Astronomy* and *Principle of Geology*   314
    2. The Widespread Introduction of Darwinian and

Spencerian Theories   319
3. The Democratic Ideologies of Zheng Guanying and
   Liang Qichao   321
IV Western Democratic Politics and Its Influence on
   Chinese Revolutionaries in the Late Qing Dynasty   324
   1. Dr. Sun Yat-sen's Revolutionary Ideal and the
      Western Sciences   324
   2. Anarchism and Populism   328

Chapter Ten
An Open China and the New Culture Movement   330
I China with Wide Open Doors   330
   1. The Footpath of the Missionaries   330
   2. The Follow-Up Explorers   332
   3. The Surprising Discovery of the Dunhuang Trea-
      sures   333
   4. Havoc in the Art Caves of Xinjiang Grotto   338
II The May Fourth Literary Revolution and the Tide
   of Social Revolution   341
   1. The New Literature Movement and the Western
      Literature   341
   2. The Choice of the Socialist Ideology   345
   3. China's New Art Movement   348
   4. Introduction and Translation of Western Literature 352
      (A) Literature of the Weak and Small Nations   353
      (B) Works of the Renowned European Writers   354
      (C) The Popular Russian Writers   356
      (D) American Writers Known for Their Outspoken
          Praise for Democracy and Progress   358
III The Widely-Circulated Theories of the Western So-
    ciety   359
    1. John Dewey and His Positive Philosophy   359
    2. The Philosophies of Friedrich Wilhelm Nietzsche
       and Georg Wilhelm Friedrich Hegel   361
    3. Sociology and the Culturists   363
    4. Eugenics   364
    5. Anthropogeography   365

    6. The Culturist Trend of Comparative History   366
IV China's Modern Sciences and Its Returned Students   368
    1. The Enthusiastic Trend of Going Abroad to Study   368
    2. The Inception of China's Modern Sciences   371
    3. The Riddle of the Peking Man   374
V Chinese Culture and the Western World   377
    1. The Rediscovery of Chinese Culture   377
    2. China's Classics and Traditional Literature   380
    3. The Reevaluation of the History of Chinese Sciences   383
VI The Rejuvenation of Chinese Arts   386
    1. Dr. Mei Lanfang and the Reform of Beijing Opera   386
    2. Colour Ink Paintings and the International Popularity of Chinese Art   389

Epiloque
The Outlook of Chinese Culture   394

Index   398

PART ONE
CULTURAL INTERCOURSE BETWEEN CHINA AND THE WESTERN REGIONS

Chapter One
The Earliest Contact Between China and the Western Regions Before the Qin Dynasty

I   The Western Regions as Described in Ancient Chinese History

The two great rivers of Huanghe (Yellow River) and Changjiang (Yangtze River) flowed across the valleys and plains of East Asia towards the sea, and between them opened an extensive, fertile ground for the inception of Chinese Civilization. It was on this land that emerged the early human society and widespread culture of the Stone Age, which was followed by even more splendid cultures of the Bronze Age and Iron Age. Thereby, China has distinguished itself as the origin of one of the four ancient civilizations in the world, along with the Nile River, Mesopotamia, Indus Valley and the Maya Indians of Central America.

1. The Origins of Chinese Culture

The Xia Dynasty, which was founded during the 21st century B.C., in an area across the middle reaches of the Yellow River between its two tributaries of Yishui and Luoshui, was known as the first slavery state in Chinese history. The dynasty of Xia was succeeded by that of Shang, and later by the Zhou Dynasty. Zhou, which was originally a princedom under Shang in the area of the current northern Shaanxi Province, distinguished itself from the neighbouring ethnics by calling its nation both "Xia" and "Zhong Guo" (Middle Kingdom). The people of Zhou, claiming themselves to be the descendants of the Xia Dynasty, also called their own territory "Qu Xia" or "You Xia" or "Shi Xia" (meaning Xia territory). The name of "Zhong Guo" was used to indicate their identity as a farming community, as opposed to the nomadic tribes in the surrounding areas.

During the reign of the Xia Dynasty, whose domain was sometimes also called "Hua," its many princedoms—located in the middle and lower reaches of the Yellow River—referred to their territories as parts of "Hua Xia."

During the Spring and Autumn Period (770-476 B.C.) and the Warring States Period (475-221 B.C.), political and economic exchanges increased among the prince states in both the Yellow River and Yangtze River valleys, the territory of "Zhong Guo" also expanded as a result. It was then that people believed that this Middle Kingdom was 3,000 *li* (1,500 kilometres) in both directions, a square-shaped area surrounded by seas. This area, as described in the verses of the ancient literature *Li Ji* (*The Book of Rites*), was "extending to running sand in the west, reaching Hengshan Mountain in the south, bordering East Sea in the east and looking upon Mount Hengshan in the north." Such an area, which was already nine times bigger than the Middle Kingdom as earlier claimed in legends, became the territory of "Zhong Xia" or "Zhong Hua" in ancient history. This marked a major expansion of the original concept of Middle Kingdom, which covered just an area of approximately 500,000 square kilometres, embracing parts of the present Henan, Shanxi, Hebei, Shaanxi and Shandong provinces in North China. By the 5th century B.C., the heartland of Chinese Civilization had expanded to more than one million square kilometres in area, whose geographic size was far larger than the other ancient civilizations existing in the contemporary era.

However, despite the spectacular expansion of Chinese Civilization in area, it remained far apart, geographically, from the civilizations of Mesopotamia in the west and the Indus Valley in the southwest, by a distance of some 6,500 and 4,000 kilometres, respectively. The immense mountains and deserts that separated the East and the West, across which only some nomadic tribes drifted, had, for centuries, blocked the communication between these ancient civilizations.

2. The Ancient Chinese Legend About Xiwangmu (Western Queen Mother) and Its Relation with the Western Regions

The Warring States Period saw a rapid growth in exchange between China and other nations inhabiting the neighbouring steppe, which further broadened the world outlook of the Chinese people. As a result, Zou Yan, a scholar of the Qi State, introduced the idea, during the 4th century B.C., that the world was composed of "Great Nine Continents." The world, in Zou's idea, was much larger than the Middle Kingdom surrounded by "Four Seas." According to Zou, China, which was then known as "Chi Xian Shen Zhou" (the Red Sacred Land) to many Chinese, was a continent in itself, surrounded by the nine other continents. Each of these continents, including the central continent of China, was assumed to comprise also "nine smaller regions distinguished by their geographic features," according to Zou. The ancient book, *Master Lü's Spring and Autumn Annals*, compiled during the 3rd century B.C., held that the Great Nine Continents occupied an area of 28,000 *li* (14,000 kilometres) from east to west and 26,000 *li* (13,000 kilometres) from north to south, while the Middle Kingdom measured 3,000 *li* (1,500 kilometres) in both directions.

In geographic concept, the border of this Nine Continent world extended westward to the Kunlun Mountains or the Congling range (the Pamirs) in western Xinjiang. According to the ancient literature *Shanhaijing (Classic of Mountains and Rivers)* written during the Warring States Period, this region was illustrated, in a legendary style, as an area situated somewhere between the "Black Water" (Syr-Darya) and the "Red Water" (Yarkant River) under the Kunlun Mountains. This area, which was surrounded by "deep valleys and blazing hills," was the location of the cave-dwellings of Xiwangmu (Western Queen Mother), who was described as "adorned with hairdress, tiger's fangs and leopard's tail." And the area "had everything imaginable," according to the legend.

In a later edition of the *Classic of Mountains and Rivers*, Xiwangmu was said to live in Yushan Mountain to the east of the Congling range. This introduction symbolized the shifting of the main route, linking the West with China, from the north of the Tianshan range to its south, following growing trade activities along this route.

In fact, Xiwangmu referred to a matriarchal tribe, which then lived in China's western border area and whose totem consisted of tigers and leopards. Here, Xi stood for the Scythia nationality or a large tribe inhabiting western China. In the ancient Chinese literature *Erya* (*Literary Expositor*), Xiwangmu was used to represent the "remote West," where lived an Iranian-speaking nation called "Se" by Chinese and "Saka" by Persians. These Se people, who were said to have originated in the Qilian Mountains of Gansu, had gradually moved westward, thereby losing any real connection with the original legend of Xiwangmu. Since then, Xiwangmu had become a general term connected with "running sand" and "thin water," representing the western nation living at the place "near the sunset."

During the Eastern Han Dynasty (25-220), after trade relations had begun between China and the Roman Empire, the Chinese came to know that "running sand" (desert) and "thin water" also existed in the land of Africa beyong the Red Sea, which was, then, the western territory of the Roman Empire. In the words of the book *Hou Han Shu* (*History of the Eastern Han Dynasty*), the place was "very near to the home of Xiwangmu and almost where the sun sets down." According to the Greek historian Herodotus (484-425 B.C.), the "thin water" (where even a feather could not float) was obviously a stream of petroleum, flowing from Egypt into Ethiopia. "Running sand" referred to Nubian Desert of Africa. Xiwangmu (Western Queen Mother) could be none other than the ruling Queen Kushi of Meroe, which was the site of the court and graves of at least five ruling queens from Queen Bartare (260-250 B.C.) to Queen Amanikhatashan (62-85), besides

Kushi.[1] These female rulers thus became the "Western Queen Mother" described in the ancient Chinese books, which, originating from fascinating historic legends, later became figurative symbols of China's expanding geographic contact with, and her widening knowledge about the Western world.

Xiwangmu was first used to refer to the Se nationality living in the east of the Congling range. The Se natives were the earliest to introduce the ideals of Babylonian Jardins Suspendus (suspended garden) to the Orient. In the *Book of Huainanzi*, compiled in the early 2nd century B.C., a story told that a person could live forever if he drank the "yellow water" from a well in the garden of the Kunlun Mountains; and if he proceeded from Kunlun Mountains further to the remote "Mountain of Cool Breeze," he would become immortal. According to the story, if the person continued to climb for a distance twice as far, he would reach the Jardins Suspendus where he should be able to exercise such magic power as ordering rains or winds. Marching still farther would land him in "Heaven" as an "immortal being." Heaven was where the God lived, which showed that the Chinese Taoist ideology to seek "Ascension to Heaven" had, in part, originated from the Western mythology, and so was the subsequent Taoist ideal of "flying into Heaven with angel's wings."

While the legends of Xiwangmu lingered in China until about the 2nd century, a more realistic and geographically sound concept had begun to surface regarding the West. This first happened in the reign of Emperor Wudi (Liu Che 140-87 B.C.) of the Western Han Dynasty (206 B.C.-A.D. 24), when the opening of a westward corridor (called Hexi Corridor) along the west bank of the Yellow River gave rise to a new title for the vast territory, extending from the Qilian Mountains in the east to the Congling range in the west. The name Xiyu (Western Regions) was later applied to the entire Western world—stretching from the Congling range to the extensive area of Central, South and West Asia, Europe and Africa—following the expansion of diplomatic ties

---

[1] F. Hintze, *Studien zur meroitishen chronologie und zu den Opfertafeln aus den Pyramiden von Meroe*, Berlin, 1959, 24.

between the Han Dynasty and the nations in the area.

II   The Origin of Chinese Civilization

1. Various Hypotheses on the Origin of Chinese Civilization

The application of modern archaeological methods in China's historic research had not begun until the 1920s, when the many relics and scripts had been unearthed in several ancient cultural centres to the west of China, which enabled people to re-evaluate the ancient history from a more thorough and specific angle. However, the origin of Chinese Civilization remained ambiguous to many Western scholars and missionaries who concluded that Chinese Civilization was the result of a migration of certain civilized nations from the West to the Yellow River valley. Such theories began with the 17th century allegation of Egyptian migration to China, which was followed by reports of Babylonian migration. The theory of Egyptian migration as first suggested by the German Jesuit missionary Athanasius Kircher (1602-1680) in his book the *Oedipus Egyptiacus* published in Rome in 1654, and again in his *China Monumentis qua Sacris qua Profanis Illustrata* published in 1667 in Amsterdam. In his books, Kircher, after comparing Chinese characters with the Egyptian hieroglyphics, imagined that the Chinese were descendants of the Hamite and that Chinese culture had originated in Egypt. Kircher's hypothesis was repudiated by French scholar N. Fréret in 1718. However, later in 1759, another French scholar Joseph de Guignes suggested that ancient China had been an "Egyptian colony." This was based on his study of Egyptian script of hieroglyphics. He alleged that the year 1122 B.C. (the 13th year in the reign of King Wu of the Zhou Dynasty in ancient China) was the year of the Egyptian migration to China.[1] This theory attracted many followers at that time, including R. Cibot, a missionary then

---

[1] See *Mémoire dans Lequel on Prouve, que les Chinois sont une Colonie Egyptienne*, Paris, 1760.

visiting Beijing, the capital of the Qing Dynasty.

The theory of so-called Babylonian migration emerged still later but out of similar hypothesis, namely, attributing the origin of Chinese culture to a nearer ancient civilization of Mesopotamia. In 1882, Terrien de Lacouperie (1845-1894) of London University in England, based on his study of the ancient Chinese *Yijing* (*Book of Changes*), suggested that Babylonian script was found in *Yijin*. Then in 1894, he published his work, *Western Origin of the Early Chinese Civilization*, initiating the theory of Bak migration. He claimed that the "Baixin" (folks) of ancient China were actually the Bak nation of Babylon, that the Chinese sage Shennon (Holy Farmer) was Sargon, and that Huangdi (or the Yellow Emperor, the legendary ancestor of Chinese people) was named Youxiongshi, who was actually Kudur-Nakhunte. Such an arbitrary hypothesis had, nevertheless, won some approval at that time, when the Western colonialism was at its peak. In 1913, C.J. Ball of Oxford University also copied such theory in his *Chinese and Sumerian*.

Since the 20th century, those who supported the so-called "migration of civilization" introduced a monoism in the origin of civilization. This group, with Elliot-Smith as its representative, described Egyptian or the Mediterranean Civilization as the origin of world civilization, or described the birth of Chinese culture as having been induced by the migration of Egyptian culture—through the south of the Caspian Sea and Central Asia —to Shaanxi of China.[1] Others ascribed Chinese culture to the sphere of Greek, South Russian and Central Asian cultures.[2] A few of them even held that Western culture had been introduced to China from North and South Europe during the Neolithic Age.[3]

These hypotheses lacked reliable historic ground and were not convincing. And, following the rapid progress in the archaeological discoveries of the Stone Age relics in China, the origin of

[1] Elliot-Smith, *The Ancient Egyptian*, PP. 196-198.

[2] Michael Rostovtzeff, *Iranians and Greeks in South Russia*, Ox, 1922, PP. 181-209.

[3] Hubert Schmidt, *Prohistorisches aus Ostasien Zeitsch fur Ethnologie*, 1924.

primeval Chinese culture has become more and more clear to the world. The fact that Chinese Civilization had grown as an independent system with its own heritage is now beyond dispute.

2. The Yangshao Culture of Painted Pottery and Its Introduction to the West

The late Neolithic culture of China was first unveiled through the discovery of prehistoric relics from a site in Yangshao Village of Mianchi County, Henan Province, in 1921, by Swedish archaeologist Johan Gunnar Andersson (1874-1960). The ancient relics unearthed included stone-ware, bone-ware, ceramic-ware, and painted pottery marked for its polished outer and inner surfaces with geometric patterns. The discoveries were named painted pottery culture. In 1923, Andersson published his book, *An Early Chinese Culture*, in which he dated Yangshao culture as being around 2500 B.C. or 1,000 years after the Babylonian painted pottery era. Based on such an assumption, Andersson claimed that Yangshao culture was a result of a migratory culture from the West, with linkage to painted pottery cultures found in areas, ranging from Central Asia to such places as Italy's Sicily, Greece's Choeronia, East Europe's Glacia, Tripolije near Kiev, and Kukuteny in the lower reaches of the Danube. According to Andersson, the Yangshao painted pottery resembled relics found in Susa of Iran and Tripolije of southern Russia, and was, therefore, attributable to a cultural transition from these origins in the West, through Central Asia as the bridge.

In fact, however, Yangshao culture, despite its superficial resemblance, differed from the cultures of Central Asia or Tripolije in basic characteristics. Moreover, C14 tests have indicated that the early Yangshao cultural relics, unearthed in Banpo Village near Xi'an in 1954, dated back to 5000 to 4500 B.C. —some 2,000 years earlier than the original estimate by Andersson. In the late 1970s, another prehistoric culture of Cishan-Peiligang was discovered in Henan Province, and it dated back to as early as 6000 to 5700 B.C. Additionally, ancient relics found from the Laoguantai culture of Huaxian County, in the Wei

River valley of Shaanxi Province, bore striking resemblance to the early Yangshao culture in both their outer shape design and finish patterns; and more Yangshao cultural relics were found in strata above Laoguantai culture. The discovery indicated that the painted pottery culture of Yangshao had gone through a period of development.

It should be noted that the painted pottery cultures discovered in areas of Gansu and Xinjiang dated one to three thousand years after the Yangshao culture of Central China. Since 1957, when the ancient cultural site of Majiayao-Wajiaping was discovered in Lintao of Gansu Province, many similar colourfully-painted pottery objects were found from subsequent finds of the Majiayao and Banshanmachang cultures in Gansu, which dated between 3000 to 2000 B.C. In fact, despite the decline of painted pottery in Central China since the era of Longshan culture, it continued to flourish in Gansu and became more variegated in colour after Majiayao culture; and painted pottery was found to have existed in Gansu as late as during the Spring and Autumn and Warring States periods—long after it had vanished in Central China.

Yangshao painted pottery culture had entered Xinjiang, via Shaanxi, Gansu and Ningxia, during the prehistoric period from 5000 to 1000 B.C.; and cultural linkage between Xinjiang and the inland China had already begun during the early Neolithic Age. A culture marked by fine stone-ware had spread throughout the whole Xinjiang area, and merged itself into the fine stone-ware culture, which extended across Gansu, Qinghai, Ningxia, Inner Mongolia and Northeast China. This corroborated the course of cultural dissemination and national migration over this vast territory. Then, at about 1000 B.C., a chiefly agricultural and partly pastoral economy emerged in some areas of Xinjiang. At such sites of agricultural economy, cultural relics composed of ground stone tools and painted pottery were unearthed. These were scattered over the major oases in Barkol, Hami, Turpan and Tarim Basin, including Yanqi, Kuqa, Xinhe, Xayar, Pishan, Hotan, Qiemo and Lop Nur areas, and Ili River valley. The pottery was made of red sandy clay, with painted finish found on some unearthed jars, bowls and cups, and with black or maroon mesh or curved and geometric patterns over white or red finish found on other wares. This unearthed pottery resembled the painted pottery culture of Gansu, in both shape and pattern designs. This was evidenced by a boat-shaped pot unearthed in Barkol of Xinjiang, which was nearly identical with another such pot found at the ancient site of Beishouling of Baoji in Shaanxi—differing only in the lack of paint finish on the Barkol pot. Obviously, the Barkol pot was a copy of the Shaanxi pottery. The pottery culture found in Xinjiang's Yutain, Pishan, Xayar and the Ili River valley, which represented the farthermost of the westward transition of painted pottery culture from Central China, was dateable to as late as the Shang and Zhou dynasties.

According to the table of cultural sequences, Anno culture (Namazka culture) dated to approximately the same time as the Yangshao culture. However, the former painted pottery, which featured dark-brown painted pattern upon a reddish brown base, was coarsely finished. It had obviously descended from the Zaitun culture unearthed in southern Turkmenistan, which was dateable to 5000 to 4000 B.C. Painted pottery had been found in sites of Zaitun culture in both Zaitun and Zopan. While the pottery unearthed in Zaitun had darkish painted curved or parallel pattern on a base of uneven milky shade, the pottery found in Zopan had brown pattern of vertical curves or dotted lines on a milky or rosy painted base. Meanwhile, the painted pottery objects found in Central Asia, Iran and southern Russia were also related to each other in cultural sequence. The Tripolije culture was found by C14 tests to date just before the late Neolithic culture of Gansu, and its discovery in Ukraine happened in the 5th century B.C. Such a cultural sequence tells us that the Yangshao culture of Central China and the Zaitun culture of Central Asia were two separate centres of painted pottery culture, which spread out to their own neighbouring regions almost at the same time, particularly, in a westward orientation. This shows that the assertion by Ludwig Bachkofer that a higher culture was brought to China by the plateau inhabitants was groundless.[1] In fact, even Johan Andersson did not believe such an assertion. Another claim by L.S. Vassiliyev that the painted pottery culture emerged in inland China as a result of the immigration of inhabitants from the original site of such pottery culture was, naturally, even more unfounded.[2]

III   Convergence of the Hua Xia Culture and the Eurasian Steppe Culture

1. The Northward Advance of the Bronze Culture of the Shang and Zhou Dynasties

China's bronze culture was at its prime in the Shang Dynasty after 1388 B.C., when the Shang ruler moved its capital to Yin in northern Henan Province. Before that, its development had been sluggish. Archaeological discoveries from the Yin ruins at Xiaotun of Anyang County in Henan in 1928 had, after a few years' study, revealed that the brilliant Shang culture was composed of three principal elements, namely, cities, scripts and bronze-ware. It was also characterized in the specific style of its jade carvings, patterned white pottery, primitive porcelain and horse-drawn chariots. Since the research on Xia culture is still in its preliminary stage, the sophisticated Shang bronze culture had been used by some scholars to speculate that it was the result of a cultural transition from the West. However, the bronze casting of the Shang Dynasty was unique in its own technical and artistic style, representing the high standard of Shang culture.

The Shang bronze included ritual objects (such as those used for serving wine or food, cooking vessels and other containers), musical instruments, weapons, tools and chariots or harness, of which the ritual bronze objects were most outstanding for their

---

[1] Ludwig Bachkofer, *Bulletin of the Museum of Far Eastern Antiquities*, No. 15, 291.

[2] L.S. Vassiliyev, *The Origin of Ancient Chinese Civilization, Problems of History*, No. 12, 1974.

spectacular decor, magnificent structure and intricate design, representing the most remarkable technical achievement of ancient civilization.

Noteworthy was the Shang bronze crucible, unearthed at the Yin ruins, which was 83 centimetres in diameter and big enough to cast large bronze objects. Another example was the famous Simuwu *ding* (a cooking vessel) unearthed in Wuguan Village of Henan Province. It measured 133 centimetres high and 115 centimetres wide, weighed 875 kilogrammes and was rarely seen among the bronze vessels found in the world. Other Shang bronze vessels such as Lufang *ding* (deer square cooking vessel), Niufang *ding* (ox square cooking vessel), Siyang *zun* (four-goat wine container) and Xiang *zun* (elephant wine container) were also remarkable for their exquisite design, clear-cut lines and fanciful decor. The scale of Shang bronze casting had far surpassed that of its two predecessors in Bronze Age—Egypt and Babylon. However, the Shang bronze vessels were cast, piece by piece without using wax models, which differed markedly from the bronze casting technique of wax molding used in the Near East, West Asia, Central Asia and Siberia. Casting technique without wax modeling was first adopted in China during the early and middle the Spring and Autumn Period. Earliest bronze vessels by such technique unearthed include a wine container stand from a Chu tomb in Xichuan of Henan and a house model and a vessel from a Yue tomb in Shaoxing of Zhejiang Province. These featured both a local style and the traditional Shang-Zhou skill and were, therefore, not copies of the Western casting technique.

The growth of bronze culture in China was by no means attributable to the benefaction of a visiting foreign culture, but was due to the creative efforts of the ancient labourers inhabiting the Yellow River valley. This was a fact proven by discoveries of recent years, including the Xia culture of the Erlitou type found in Yanshi of western Henan and southern Shanxi, and the early Shang ruins unearthed at Erligang of Zhengzhou also in Henan. The Erlitou culture of Yanshi, dating from 1900 to 1600 B.C., was categorized into four successive phases, of which the first two phases were believed to be Xia culture and the last two phases were considered early Shang culture. Among the early Shang culture relics, belonging to the third phase, were not only tools and weapons but also such vessels as wine goblets. Of the early Shang bronze unearthed at the Erligang site of Zhengzhou, the largest find was the 13 bronze objects discovered in 1982. Since then, many more mid-Shang bronze ritual vessels have been unearthed in Dengfeng, Xingyang, Mixian, Zhongmou, Xinzheng, Wuzhi and Xiangcheng of Henan Province. These newly-discovered bronze relics resemble the objects of Erligang culture of the Shang Dynasty and those from the Yin ruins of Anyang in shape, further identified the history of the late Shang culture of the Yin ruins.

Bronze objects of an earlier era had been unearthed at the site of late Longshan culture in Henan, which preceded the Erlitou culture in history. The earliest relic among these finds was a green sheet of bronze, found in the fourth stage ashpit of Wangchenggang in Dengfeng of Henan in 1980. This piece of relic was verified as a bronze casting, containing 7 percent of tin, and dateable to some 3,850 years ago. Remains of a bronze smelting crucible had been found in a second-stage excavation at Meishan of Linru, and bronze casting slags were found in both Pingliangtai of Huaiyang and Niuzhai of Zhengzhou.

It can be seen from these discoveries and the ancient city, unearthed during the second-stage excavation of Dengfeng's Wangchenggang, that bronze casting had begun in China since late Longshan culture of Henan.

At the time when the Central China region entered the Bronze Age, its neighbours in the west and north were still using copper. This was shown in the discoveries of bronze daggers, knives, chisels, rings and awls from Majiayao culture and Machang culture of Gansu and Longshan culture of Inner Mongolia. The Majiayao bronze unearthed in Dongxianglinjia of Gansu in 1978 were the earliest bronze objects discovered thus far, dating back to approximately 2700 B.C.—close to the legendary age when Huangdi (the Yellow Emperor) was said to have cast a bronze cauldron with ore taken from Shoushan Mountain, while his arch foe Chiyou cast weapons with the metal. These cultures had intimate relations with those of Central China, which was evidenced by a bronze awl of Longshan culture origin, found during excavation work in Ejin Horo Banner of Inner Mongolia in 1974. The Longshan culture there was similar to that of Henan, and can be traced to a northward transition of Longshan culture from Central China, and its age corresponded to Xia culture of Central China. All these served as preliminary evidence to the fact that Chinese bronze culture of Xia and Shang dynasties had developed, independently, first in the Yellow River valley.

But Chinese bronze culture also had some links with bronze culture in other regions outside today's China. Such links were shown in the influence of external cultures—coming through the medium of northern grassland tribes—on the design of the Shang Dynasty bronze weapons. Also, the more powerful current of Shang culture surged, at about the same time, to the outer Lake Baikal region through the Ordos Grassland of Mongolia. The Minoshinsk Basin of Siberia bordering on the Altay Mountains had been a transit of the East-West traffic in 2000 B.C., and was also a centre of cultural communication from the West to China. However, there appeared only limited scale of metallurgical culture throughout the evolution in this region, including Avanashio culture (approx. 2000-1500 B.C.), Andronovo culture (approx. 1500-1200 B.C.), and Karasuc culture (approx. 1200-700 B.C.). Therefore, it was hard to believe that the bronze casting skills of the Yellow River valley had originated from this area, as was claimed by some scholars.[1]

Supporters of such a claim found evidence in the fact that European Seima culture (1600-1300 B.C.) had spread to Siberia and, through Karasuk culture, passed on their swords, axes, lance, and white jade ring to Anyang in China. It should be pointed out that Shang culture, having absorbed these Western tools and ornaments, further refined them with its own artistry, which were shown in the crude Seima axes becoming well-decorated with intricate ogre-mask patterns. Swords were found near the Great Wall in Inner Mongolia, including swords with bow-shaped backs and pommels in the shape of goat or deer head.[2]

---

[1] Max Loehr, *Chinese Bronze Age Weapons*, Ann Arbor, 1956, PP. 103-105.

[2] Namio Ekami and S. Mitsuno, *Inner Mongolia and Great Wall Area* (II), "Bronze."

After 1949, archaeologists discovered a deer-head-handled sword in Chaodaogou of Qinglong, a horse-head-handled sword in Shaanxi's Yantou Village and a dragon-head-handled sword from a Yin tomb in Henan.

This culture was found to have entered China through a channel provided by ancient nationalities living to the north of Chinese Civilization. They were Xunyu tribes in the north and Guifang or Guirong tribes in Hexi Corridor of Gansu. Guifang of the Qiang nationality played a key role in introducing bronze culture to the north. Then, in the late Shang Dynasty, Guifang tribes moved eastward across the Yellow River and began threatening the Shang Dynasty's western border, causing many clashes with troops of King Yin, Wuding, of the Shang Dynasty. Meanwhile, Xunyu, pressed by the invading Guifang, started moving northward, thereby introducing Shang culture to the Dili (Dinling) nationality living in the outer Lake Baikal region. These were indicated by the discovery of more than 30 Chinese pottery vessels in the excavations of Karasuc culture around Lake Baikal. Also found was a semicircular ornament, which was considered a typical sample of Karasuc culture but was traced to the Hetao region of the Yellow River valley. Karasuc culture in the upper reaches of Yenisey River was also found to have been directly influenced by Shang bronze culture, which was shown in the similarity between such finds as bronze swords, bronze lance and arrowheads, and bow-shaped tools unearthed there and those objects unearthed in Anyang of China. The late Shang Dynasty weapons, such as swords with handles in the shape of the deer and goat head unearthed in Hebei and Shanxi provinces, were possibly regular weapons used by Xunyu. These dagger-like bronze swords were popular in North China as well as in Mongolia and the outer Lake Baikal region. They were, however, never found in China's Liaoning or in Siberia's Minoshinsk Basin.

Later, the concave-checked swords of Karasuc culture and swords with animal-shaped handles of the first stage of Takar culture (8th-4th century B.C.) were found to resemble the willow-leave-shaped swords popularly used in Central and North China during the Western and Eastern Zhou dynasties. During the 11th century B.C., bronze swords with ring-shaped handles were introduced to western Europe from Russia. Willow-leave-shaped swords were popular in the Ordos region and used by the nomadic nationalities until the Han Dynasty. Such a sword was found also in No. 53 Tomb of the early Western Zhou in Liulihe of Fangshan near Beijing. Bronze swords belonging to European Harstadt culture (10th-5th century B.C.), unearthed in Denmark, were marked by double edges, double-ringed horn handles and half-moon or dolong hand guards. They differed completely from the traditional sword of that region.

2. The Westward Migration of Jichuo and the Westward Expedition of the Zhou Dynasty's King Mu

The Zhou Dynasty, which succeeded the Shang Dynasty, was founded by a new nationality originating in Shaanxi of North China. Calling themselves Xitu (Westland), they enjoyed favourable contacts with the Qiang and Se tribes in the northwest.

Zhou's ancestral ruler, the Grand Duke Gugong Danfu, was known to have sent his favourite vassal Jichuo to set up a duchy of his own on the east side of the Congling range in western Xinjiang. Thus, Jichuo became the chief of Zhou emigrants in the first major migration of the Hua Xia (Chinese) nation in history. Such a development drew Xinjiang closer to Central China. In the Persian epic *Shahnameh*, written by Firdusi (935-1025), there was a story saying Zohak had sent his men to chase Jamshid to the border between India and China, and found that Jamshid had married the daughter of Mahang, the King of Machin. Here, Mahang was none other than Gugong Danfu, and Jamshid was apparently Jichuo. It was also since then that the Hua Xia nation began to have contacts with other nationalities, who travelled on horseback, and learned from them the skills of raising and riding horses.[1] This was revealed in a poem of "Mian" in the *Book of Songs*, which said that the Zhou ancestral ruler Gugong Danfu

---

[1] According to results of archaeological research, North China was one of the ancient horse breeding centres (Equus Caballus). Relics of Asian horses (Equus Przewalskii) had been found in the paleolithic ruins of Dayao in Inner Mongolia and the ruins in Banpo Village near Xi'an of Shaanxi.

went to his court on horseback.

During the reign of King Mu (1001-947 B.C.) of the Zhou Dynasty, Zhou troops defeated the invading nomadic Quanrong tribe and drove them away from the eastern Hexi Corridor, reopening the route to the Congling range. Since then, the Hua Xia inhabitants in the Yellow River valley began to turn their attention from the northern steppe and the Siberian Minoshinsk Basin to the oases south of the Tianshan Mountains, and in the distant region of the Caspian Sea.

Later, a beautiful legend emerged from this development. According to the legend, King Mu of the Zhou Dynasty and his entourage travelled in carriages—each drawn by eight horses —from Central China to the West. Having overcome many foes and obstacles on their way, they crossed the oases in the south of the Tarim Basin and loaded three of their carriages with some ten thousand jade discs collected there. King Mu and his aides then travelled westward, across the Congling range, to arrive at the site of Xiwangmu tribe near the Syr-Darya River. In the end, King Mu and his entourage were given a warm reception by Xiwangmu —before they returned in triumph along the grassland route north of the Tianshan Mountains to Central China.

The legend, written in a style similar to the Greek epic *Odyssey*, described the colourful exchange between Hua Xia and their western neighbours—who lived in wealth and happiness —through the symbolic narration of a years-long royal expedition to the West.

The book, containing this legend, was called *Biography of King Mu, the Son of Heaven*. It was unearthed in 279 in Jixian County of Henan Province from the tomb of Prince Xiang of Wei Kingdom, who died in 296 B.C. The book was written in the 4th century B.C.—some 30 years before the eastward expedition of Alexander the Great of Macedonia. At that time, the tribe of Xiwangmu, inhabiting the Ferghana Basin near the Pamirs, became the converging point of the eastern and western cultures on the Asian continent. In the legend, the author described the westward expedition of King Mu and his visit to the Pamirs tribe, with vivid details based, at least partly, on the historic events of

20   CULTURAL FLOW BETWEEN CHINA AND THE OUTSIDE WORLD

that period. According to the ancient Chinese book *Zhushu Jinian* (*The Bamboo Annals*), King Mu's expedition took place in the 17th year after his enthronement (985 B.C.).

In the book *Biography of King Mu, the Son of Heaven*, King Mu was said to have ascended the suspended garden, arriving at the domain of Xiwangmu (Western Queen Mother), and presented her with brocade, black and white jade, then, entertained her at a banquet held on the lake of Yaochi.[1] At the banquet, Xiwangmu sang an ode to the nomadic folks for King Mu and asked him, "Would you come again in your lifetime?" King Mu replied "In three years, I shall see thee again." According to the book, Xiwangmu was then no more like the "barbarian" as described in *Shanhaijing* (*Classic of Mountains and Rivers*), but was a very civilized "daughter of the heavenly emperor" instead. The lake of Yaochi was presumably the ice-free Lake Issyk Kul in the Altay Mountains, while Xiwangmu or "the daughter of the heavenly emperor" was probably a ruler of the Scythians. In *The Bamboo Annals*—which was unearthed at the same time as the *Biography of King Mu, the Son of Heaven*—there was yet another story that tells of Xiwangmu's visit to Central China as an honourable guest of the Zhou court. The cultural exchange between the East and the West, during that period, was reflected in the story of King Mu's bringing such presents as silk, bronze and shell coins to all the tribes visited on his tour to the West. From these tribes he received such gifts as horses, sheep, oxen and wine.

The legendary westward tour of King Mu was, possibly, a symbolic description of the ancient East-West exchange, which took place after the continental route was opened—following the expedition of Alexander the Great to the East. In the legend, historical events throughout the 700 years, beginning from the 10th century B.C., were condensed by the author into one dramatic expedition of the Zhou Dynasty's King Mu, in the form of an exotic romance. An important historic revelation of the *Biog-*

---

[1] Brocade was first made in China in the 8th century B.C., near the end of the Western Zhou Dynasty and in the early Spring and Autumn Period. This fact indicates that the *Biography of King Mu, the Son of Heaven* was actually written, or at least largely revised, by authors of a later period.

raphy of King Mu, the Son of Heaven was that during the early years of the Western Zhou Dynasty—when a marked development was taking place in the social economy of Central Asia—the Hua Xia nation in China had sought to open an expedient short cut to the West through the oases south of the Tianshan Mountains, bypassing the Altay Mountains and the Pamirs.

IV   Nomadic Travellers and the Silk Trade

1. Silk—the Earliest Link Between China and Greece

During the reign of King Mu of the Zhou Dynasty, sophisticated Chinese commodities such as silk and bronze were greatly admired by the Se tribal people living in the west of Congling range. The Se tribe then occupied a vast area, extending from Dunhuang of Gansu in the east all the way to the Syr-Darya and Amu-Darya rivers in the west. They spoke an eastern Iranian language, which was closely related to the language of the Scythian people, living in areas north of Caucasia and near the Aral Sea. These people were in the course of moving from a mixed economy to the pastoral economy, focusing on horse-rearing. In the 8th century B.C., a part of the Se people migrated from northern Central Asia to the northwestern coast of the Black Sea, where they began trading with the Greek Colony in the Black Sea region. And these Se tribesmen, who travelled on horseback across the Eurasian Steppe, became the earliest silk traders, shuttling between China and the Greek Colony.

The Greek historian Heraclitus had early noticed the existence of an Eurasian trade route, which started from the Don on the north shore of the Black Sea to reach the northern coast of the Aral Sea, then turned towards Syr-Darya and Ili rivers to go eastward to the Eurasian Steppe to the north of the Tianshan Mountains. He even listed the nations along this route, such as the Cimerians in south Russia; the Scythians, Sauromathae, Budini and Tyssagetae in areas farther east; the Turkai, Massagetae and Argippaei in areas between the Caspian Sea and the Tianshan Mountains; the Issedon, Arimaspea, Hyperborean and the Yuezhi living east of the Tianshan Mountains.[1] The Yuezhi was, then, a part of the Xirong nationality mentioned in ancient Chinese history.

During the 7th century B.C., as a result of a southward invasion by the Rong and Di tribes in China's northwest, a campaign was launched by the Chinese feudal princes to oust invaders and defend the kingdom, which continued through the Spring and Autumn Period (770-476 B.C.). It was then that the princedom of Qin in western China became powerful under its ruler Prince Qin Mugong (659-621 B.C.), which began trading silk and metal-ware for livestock, fur and jade from the nomadic tribes. Since then, Chinese silk had found its way to the West not only directly from Central China, but also in a continuous flow from the Hexi Corridor of Gansu to the Asian Steppe across the Congling range. This was evidenced in the discovery of a batch of Chinese silk in the excavation of a 5th century B.C. Se tomb in the Altay region, including a silk saddle-cover finished with phoenix-and-peacock-pattern embroidery, found in No. 5 Bazarik Tomb. Another excavation in 1977 at Alakou of Xinjiang also found some lacquer ware and rhombic patterned thin silk, which was believed to be fashionable new product from Central China during such ancient period. All these were apparently brought to the area by Se traders.

During the period from the emigration of Jichuo to the West until the unification of China under the First Emperor of the Qin Dynasty (Qinshihuang), cultural exchange between China and the West had seen at least two climaxes. The first took place during the reign of the Persian King Darius the Great (521-481 B.C.), when the Persian Empire sprawled across the vast area from Egypt to India. And the second climax occurred during the reign of the Greek conqueror Alexander the Great (336-323 B.C.), when Macedonia conquered Greece and established an empire as vast as that of the preceding Persian King Darius.

---

[1] W. Tomaschek: Kritik d. ältesten Nachrichten ü.d. Skythischen Norden I. ü.d. Arimaspische Gedicht des Aristeas, *Sitzungsberichte d. Akademic d. Wissenschaften, Wien* (Phil.-hist. Klasse), 1888, No. 116, 715. E.H. Minns, Scythians and Greeks, Camb. 113.

Cultural exchange flourished during these two periods, as Persian culture, Greek culture, and the more profound Mesopotamian and Egyptian cultures were introduced to the other end of Tianshan and Kulun mountains. In return, Chinese silk arrived at Greece across the continental steppe.

As a result, a marble statue of Greek Goddess Kore of Acropolis engraved during the period between 530 and 510 B.C. was seen to wear a thin silk piece over her chest. And the transparent chiton worn by the Goddess Athena in Parthenon, built during the period between 438 and 431 B.C. appeared to be also made of soft silk. Since the 5th century B.C., the red floral-patterned pottery batch-produced in Athens also bore such designs. The most remarkable example, however, was the painting of *The Trial of Boris* on a Greek ivory plaque dateable to the 3rd century B.C., which, unearthed in Kul Oba of Crimea Peninsula, showed the breasts and navels of three Greek goddesses half covered by transparent silk gauze gowns.[1]

2. Silk Fabrics Make China Known Throughout the World

What was primarily responsible in making China world famous? To this question, there was only one answer: The whole world was fascinated by Chinese silk. For as long as 3,000 years before the 6th century B.C., China was the only country in the world engaging in silkworm (Bombyx mori) breeding and silk-weaving. The excavation of Neolithic ruins at Wuxing's Qianshanyang of Zhejiang Province in 1958 found silk patches, ribbon and thread woven with silkyarns drawn from home-bred silkworm dateable to 2700 B.C., which were marked by a count of 40 yarns both ways per square centimetre. Later in the Shang Dynasty, there emerged for the first time a kind of woven silk fabric (damask) with simple embossed patterns. In the Malmö Museum of Sweden was a Yin (the Shang Dynasty) bronze, which had on it a patch of ancient silk fabric showing embossed rhombic pattern. Similar rhombic-patterned silk fabrics were also seen among the unearthed relics from a Chu tomb in Changsha in

---

[1] E.H. Minns, *Scythians and Greeks*, Camb. 1913, P. 204, Fig. 101.

1956, and from another Chu tomb of Henan's Xinyang in 1957. In the 8th century B.C., China began to produce coloured silk fabric (brocade), which soon gained worldwide fame. Damask was known for its fine, smooth and soft texture and shiny colours, and became a coveted commodity in both Asia and Europe. China had first become known to the West because of its silk which excelled other fabrics—cotton, linen and wool—in texture and beauty.

China, as a nation, was mentioned in foreign literature—even before the expedition of Darius the Great to the East—because of its silk. In a 5th century B.C. Greek ode, China was called Saini. In the ancient Persian book of *Genesis*, Sini was used to describe China. China was referred to as Čīn, Činistān and Činastān, which were close to Čyn in Sutra language. It was probably introduced from the East Iranian language. While Westerners later assumed that the title sounded close to the name of the Qin Dynasty, the Greek word for China "Seres" was really derived from "Ser" or Chinese silk. During the period from 416 to 398 B.C., Ktesias, a Greek doctor in the Persian court, was the earliest to have mentioned China. Since the Greeks had very early begun to buy silk from China, it was only natural for a Greek to know China as a nation. It should be noted, however, the Chinese as mentioned in earliest Western history was not the Qins of Hua Xia nation. According to Apollodorus of Damascus of the 1st century, the Kingdom of Bactria expanded its territory in 201 B.C. to Seres, where the people of Seres were "green-eyed and red-haired"—referring obviously to the Se people living in the south and north of the Tianshan Mountains. A book written by a Greek ship's captain in the 1st century B.C. entitled *The Periplus of the Erythraean Sea* told that it was possible to reach China from the south by way of the South China Sea, which was called "Thin" in the book. The book also referred to China's inland capital as "Thinae," a word derived obviously from either Persian or Sanskrit.

In Sanskrit, the Indians also called China Cīna. In the book *Arthasastra* written by Kautilya, an aide of the Indian Emperor Chandragupta Maurya (320-286 B.C.), the word Cīnapaṭṭa was used to describe Chinese silk, meaning "bound silk rolls imported from China"—here "Cīna" was connected with "silk" from very beginning.

Both ancient Persia and India used Ci (Chinese word silk) to refer to China—the country of silk. Therefore, in ancient Persian language, brocade is called "dīb" or "dép," tough silk is called "balas," silk fabric called "parnikān," and satin is called "barnū" or "barnūn"—without mentioning Cina." It was the same with Sanskrit, which called brocade "citra," tough silk "paṭṭa, netram," satin "pringa," embroidery "sūcikarma," and silk thread "paṭṭa."

The word Cina in both languages, which originated from the Chinese word "silk," was later used solely to define China as a nation. Silk had been the symbol of the Chinese nation long before the Han Dynasty, and was responsible for making China famous throughout the world.

3. The Route of Glass and Gem Trade

Jade and gem were used as ornaments coveted by civilized people throughout the ancient world. The jade of Hotan and Junggar were the best found in China, and had long since been exported to the West. Jade weapons and tools unearthed from European Neolithic ruins were once believed to have come from nephrite resources to the east of the Congling range. This became doubtful later when an ancient jade mine was discovered in the Harz Mountains of Central Europe. Nonetheless, the introduction of ancient jade from Asia to European culture during that period was still not to be completely ruled out, when viewed from historical records. In ancient China, jade was used to make weapons, which was also known to the West. In the unearthed tomb of the Egyptian King Tutankhamen of the 18th Dynasty (1580-1314 B.C.), nephrite rings were found. During that period, ancient jade production was believed to take place in areas of the Kaxgar River to the east of the Congling range or on the west bank of Lake Baikal. Although scattered jade ores were also produced in Seleucia and Liguria of West Asia, and Harz Mountains of Europe, it was doubtful whether they had been explored as early as 4,000 years ago.[1]

The various gems produced in Central Asia, India and areas farther to the west were highly attractive goods in the ancient world; and especially valuable among them were the green gems. In "Yugong" from the ancient Chinese book *Shangshu* (*Book of History*), Yongzhou was said to be the production centre of *qiulin*, a general name for green gems. And many of such products were made of stones brought over from places to the west of the Congling range. The word *qiu* had probably come from the Iranian word Kŭk, which could include all kinds of precious stones, ranging from turquoise, epidote, olivine, and serpentine to malachite. These stones were produced in Central Asia, Afghanistan, Syria, Amenia and Egypt. The one most used was turquoise, which was found to have been used in Qijia culture of Gansu (1800 B.C.). Gems made of turquoise were later unearthed from Shandong's Dawenkou culture as well as in ruins dateable to periods after the Shang and Zhou dyansties. Ancient mines of turquoise were found in Nishapur's Maden Village of Central Asia, Kara-tjube Mountains of southern Samarkand, and Serabit el Khadim and Wadi maghara of Egyptian Sinai Peninsula. The Egyptian mines were said to be the oldest in ancient history, whose products began coming to China during the early period of ancient Egyptian Kingdom.[2] An imported gem called "rose" was known in China during the Warring States Period, and "rose" was probably the translation of mafkat—turquoise in Egyptian language.

Langgan, another kind of precious stones next to *qiulin* popular among the ancient Chinese, was also imported from the West. The name applied to both beryl and emerald gems. India had long since been the main producer of beryl, and was a principal exporter of *langgan* to China. Emerald, however, was largely produced in Egypt, where it was mined in Sikait Zubara on the west bank of the Red Sea since the reign of Amenhotep III (reigned 1417-1379 B.C.), and was introduced to China following the years of the Persian Empire under Darius I. And that

---

[1] L.J. Spencer, *A Key to Precious Stones*, London, 1936, P. 211.

[2] J.H. Breasted, *Ancient Records of Egypt*, Vol. 5, Appendix, PP. 95, 102.

was why the gem was first known in China in its Persian name "Zumurrud." By the Warring States Period of Qin Zhaowang's reign (306-251 B.C.), emerald gems were separated from the general term of *langgan* and called Zumurrud, because, in fact, the gem was different from common beryl in having a crystal-clear texture and a bright green colour.

Apart from valuable stones and their products, ancient China also imported from the West glass products, which were considered precious substitutes for natural gems. In the ancient Chinese novel of *The Tour of Ten Continents*, a story tells how King Mu of the Zhou Dynasty accepted the offering of white-jade cups from the Xihu tribe, in which the cups were described as made of "essence of white jade." The description gave the impression that they were made of alabaster produced in Egypt.[1] Relics of dragonfly-eye-shaped glass beads, produced in Egypt around 2000 B.C., were discovered in a tomb of the late Spring and Autumn Period (6th century B.C.) unearthed in Hougudui's No. 1 Excavation of Gushi in Henan Province.[2] The glass beads were found by chemical analysis to contain sodium-calcium used in the West for glass-making.[3] Similar glass beads were later found during tomb excavations in Shandong, Shanxi, Henan, Hubei, Hunan, Guangdong and Sichuan. The State of Chu in the south, during that period, was where such glass beads had been most popular, and became a centre for glass-making industry with technique introduced probably from West Asia and India. This was related to the presence of Indian immigrants in western Yunnan at that time. Archaeologists, excavating a tomb of the late Spring and Autumn Period in Jiangchuan's Lijiashan of Yunnan Province, discovered a pink glass bead bearing etched pattern and circular lines, which was identified as an early

---

[1] P. Pelliot thought that the cups were made of serpentine produced in Suzhou of Gansu. (P. Pelliot, Les prétendus Jades de Sou-Tcheou, T'oung Pao, 1913, 14, 258.) However, since both the Shang and Zhou dynasties were known for their expertise in appraising jade, it was unlikely that a product of serpentine would be taken as the "essence of white jade."

[2] S.M. Goldstein, *Pre-Rome and Early Roman Glass*, 1979, P. 78.

[3] Zhang Fukang and Cheng Zhuhai, "A Study on Chinese Ancient Glass," *Silicate Society Journal*, No. 1 Issue, Vol. 11, 1983.

product of Iraq and the Indus valley cultures existed before the 4th century B.C.

Discoveries of glass beads after 1972 from ancient tombs in Henan's Luoyang, Shaanxi's Baoji and Fufeng pushed back China's own glass-making industry to the 9th or 10th century B.C. These glass beads resembled the Iranian and Egyptian Faience in shape, but contained the same aluminium isotope as the glassware made in the Han Dynasty. Besides, the Zhou Dynasty glass beads differed from the Egyptian Faience in their content of uneven quartz particles glued by glass paste, in contrast with the Egyptian products' crystal content under their glass surfaces. China's glass-making industry originated approximately from the bronze-casting industry of the Shang Dynasty, since glassy quartz powder was found in the ruins of an early bronze-casting site of the Shang Dynasty in Zhengzhou of Henan. The chemical content of ancient Chinese glass was different from that of Western glass in its aluminium-barium properties. However, the prescription of aluminium glaze was seen in Babylonian literature of 17th century B.C.; and another prescription of aluminium glass was found in a 7th century B.C. script unearthed in Nineveh.[1] It should be noted that India had also begun producing glass in 1000 B.C. According to *Biography of King Mu—the Son of Heaven*, King Mu followed up his westward expedition with another expedition to the East, where he had weapons cast with coloured stones as beautiful as those seen in the West. Therefore, the information on casting stone was possibly obtained from the West. Despite the fact that China already had its own primitive glassware, its knowledge of glass-making was likely introduced from forerunners in the industry to the west of the Congling range, namely, Babylon or India, since China did not have its own glass products until the Warring States Period.

4. The Animal Style in the Northern Chinese Art Designs

Apart from exchanges in materials, culture and technical

---

[1] R.J. Forbes, *Studies in Ancient Technology*, Vol. 5, Leiden, 1957, PP. 131-135.

information, there were also extensive exchanges between the Eurasian Steppe nations and the ancient inhabitants of northern China in horsemanship, archery and daily lifestyle.

During the Spring and Autumn Period, military operations depended mainly on chariots, which were suitable for actions on the flatland only. But in the 7th century B.C., both Qin and Jin, the two leading powers of the period, had formed their cavalry units to fight on horseback against the invading nomadic tribes. The flexibility and efficiency of cavalry soldiers became more evident in actions across woodland and desert in the north during the Warring States Period. It was then that King Wuling (325-299 B.C.) of the Zhao State launched a reform to switch his men from wearing long robes to short jackets and train them to fight on horseback.

The influence of the northern neighbouring nationalities was also seen in the introduction of the Scythian-Siberian animal designs in sculptures and decorative art design in China's northern grassland culture, following the surge of the Xiongnu nationality during the late Spring and Autumn Period and the Warring States Period. The new style enriched the original artistic genre of ancient China's decorative designs such as the animal-head patterned knives and swords of the Shang and Zhou dynasties and the animal-flock pattern on rectangular plaques of the Spring and Autumn Period and the Warring States Period. As a result, zoomorphic designs of Scythian style were widely used in areas, extending from north of the Black Sea to Central Asia and Altay. Patterns like crouching deer, twisting beasts, dueling animals and imaginary beasts with eagle-heads had appeared in the art designs of northern China.

Recent archaeological discoveries in China showed an example of how the ancient Chinese art designers had absorbed the style of a continuously-spiralling animal pattern—the most exquisite of Scythian zoomorphic design—in their work. This sculpture, unearthed from an ancient tomb in Shenmu County of Shaanxi Province, was of a circular-shaped animal with eight eagle heads sticking out from deer horns set on a lion's body. The whole sculpture was covered with cloud patterns, a design very common during the Shang and Zhou dynasties. It was a unique adaptation of Scythian art by ancient designers of northern China.

It is now clear that past assumptions that the zoomorphic designs, *taotie* (ogre-mask) designs and dragon patterns often used in ancient China had originated either in the Near East or some other cultural transit centre between China and Mesopotamia were unfounded.[1] Many archaeological discoveries have now shown that ogre-mask design originated from Longshan culture, while the dragon design could be traced back to some 2,000 years B.C.[2] All these were indeed China's own unique traditional animal style in art design.

---

[1] M. Rostovtzeff, *The Animal Style in South Russia and China*, Princeton, 1929, PP. 70-73.

[2] A coloured dragon-shaped pottery basin was among the ritual vessels recently unearthed from the earliest Xia ruins found in Guchongshan (now Ta'ershan) in Taosi of Xiangfen, Shanxi Province. See "Report on Excavation of Taosi Tomb in Xiangfen of Shanxi" in *Chinese Archaeology*, No.1 Issue, 1983.

Chapter Two

Opening of the Sino-Western
Communications During the Han Dynasty

I   An Open Society and Smooth Traffic

By the time Darius the Great expanded the territory of the
Persian Empire to the vicinity of the Congling range, promoting
a gradual increase in exchanges between the West and China via
routes in both the north and south of the Tianshan Mountains,
China had already entered the Warring States Period (475-221
B.C.). Then, after the Qin Dynasty conquered the other six states
and began its reign over a unified China in 221 B.C., the nomadic
nationality Xiongnu had grown into a powerful invading force in
the north and started an expansion to both the east and the west.
As a result, the Yuezhi tribe living along the Hexi Corridor region
of Gansu was forced to migrate, en masse, farther to the west.
During the two years after 177 B.C., the Yuezhi tribe came to
settle in the north of Tianshan Mountains, and the Se tribes,
pastors on both the south and north sides of the Tianshan Mountains, were forced to move southwards in two separate groups.
One group, led by the Se King, crossed the Mingteke Pass and
entered Kashmir from the east side of the Congling range; the
other group, comprising the bulk of the Se tribes, moved in the
direction of Bactria in Central Asia and gradually infiltrated the
Indus Valley. This historic relocation of the Yuezhi and Se tribes
brought new impetus to the East-West communications in that
period.
    During the decades that followed, the Yuezhi tribe moved
westward on the heel of the Se, while the Xiongnu people contin-

ued to expand their influence to the Tianshan Mountains, domi-
nating all the tribal nations in Xinjiang's Xiyu (Western Regions), not only blocking trade between the Han Dynasty (206
B.C.-A.D. 220) and the Central Asian nations but also threatening
its northwestern border. The threat by Xiongnu became the top
concern of the ruling Han Emperor Wudi, Liu Che, (140-87 B.C.),
who had already stabilized his reign over the country and was
ready to repulse any external foe. As the first step of his strategy
to deal with the threatening Xiongnu, the Han emperor sent
Zhang Qian in 138 B.C. as his envoy to the Great Yuezhi in the
west in a bid to persuade the western tribe to enter an alliance
with the Han Dynasty, so that the two nations could launch an
attack against the Xiongnu from both east and west at the same
time. Zhang Qian and his entourage of more than 100 departed
from Chang'an, but when they arrived at Longxi (western Gansu)
on their way to Xinjiang, they were detained by Xiongnu troops,
who held them in custody for 11 years. Later Zhang managed to
get away, fled to Dayuan, and eventually found his way to the
Great Yuezhi via Kangju. But the Great Yuezhi had already
conquered Bactria and become the ruling power of Central Asia,
no longer thinking of returning to their homeland. Since the
Great Yuezhi rulers were not interested in the Han Dynasty
suggestion of a military alliance against the Xiongnu, Zhang Qian
started his journey home after having stayed for over a year in
the Bactrian capital of Bark (now Waziristan). But on his way
back from Xinjiang to Chang'an, Zhang was again seized by
Xiongnu troops at Qiangzhong (now Qinghai), which was under
the Xiongnu's control. He was held for more than a year there
until the outbreak of an internal strife within the ranks of the
Xiongnu tribe, which gave him the opportunity to escape in the
company of his servant Tangyijiao, who was possibly a native of
the Se tribe. Zhang was back in Chang'an in the year 126 B.C,
and there he won respect for his geographic and political knowledge about the western nations, which he had visited during his
14-year-expedition. His reports on the conditions of the nations in
Central Asia were later recorded by the Han Dynasty historian
Sima Qian in the first three volumes of his famous *Shiji* (*Records*

of the Historian), in a chapter entitled "Stories from Dayuan."
This chapter became a reliable historical record of the geographic
conditions of regions beyond China's western border.

As China's first envoy to travel abroad and study international affairs, Zhang Qian furnished the Han Dynasty with first-hand
materials on the Xiongnu and Central Asia. He also pointed out
in his report that nations in Central Asia were invariably attracted by Chinese goods, particularly by China's silk products. Zhang
also played a key role in planning the Han Dynasty's military
strategy against the Xiongnu, resulting in the Han's successful
campaign to drive the Xiongnu from the Hexi (west of the Yellow
River) region. By 121 B.C., Han troops had completely wiped out
Xiongnu forces from an area extending from west of the Yellow
River to the east of Lop Nur. Having occupied the entire Hexi
Corridor, the Han Dynasty set up four prefectures to control the
area, severing the link between the Xiongnu and the Qiang, in
addition to building up two border garrison posts at Yumen and
Yangguan to serve as gateways to the Western Regions.

In the year 119 B.C., Zhang Qian departed on his second
mission to the Western Regions, intending to form friendly ties
with the Wusun nation to the west of the Tianshan Mountains
and further expanding the Han Dynasty's influence in Central
Asia. With an entourage of more than 300 aides, and taking with
them thousands of sheep and oxen as well as a large quantity of
silk and gold coins, Zhang and his delegation toured several
nations west of the Congling range in separate groups, travelling
to Dayuan, Kangju, Great Yuezhi, Bactria, Parthia and India.
His tour paved the way for a series of journeys to the west by
other Han Dynasty envoys in the years that followed, resulting in
a flourishing exchange of gifts, commodites and other activities.
The Han envoys reached as far as Yancai near the Caspian Sea
in the north, Iran and Syria in the west and the Indus Valley in
the south. As official trade delegations, they traded silk goods for
their supplies on the journey. The size of such delegations ranged
from one hundred to several hundred men, who travelled by
camel or donkey caravans across deserts, steppe and gullies as far
as Antioch on the east coast of the Mediterranean Sea and then

back to China. During the trade activities of that period, a dozen or more such delegations were sent out each year from China to the West, and each return trip would take eight to nine years.[1]

Since the year 60 B.C., when southern Xinjiang was annexed to the Han Dynasty, its rule reached as far as Dayuan and Wusun to the north of the Pamirs as well as the Ferghana Basin in Central Asia. As a result, the two routes leading to the west of the Congling range through Xinjiang were completely open to traffic during that period. The northern route, which started from Yumen, proceeded on to Lop Nur, then, turned northward to Turpan and along the northern edge of the Tarim Basin to Shule; from there it went across the Congling range and reached as far as the Caspian Sea across the land of Dayuan, Kangju and Yancai. Along the northern route there was once also a shortcut, which turned from Lop Nur to Lolan, then proceeded on to Korla, bypassing Turpan. The southern route went from Yang-guan to Qiemo, then proceeded along the southern edge of the Tarim Basin to Pishan, Shache and the Mingteke Pass by way of Taxkorgan, finally reaching Balkh of Great Yuezhi and Hecatom-pylos of Parthia along the Pyandzh River. The western section of the southern route, which proceeded westward along the south of the Caspian Sea, was called the northern Iran route. There was another southern Iran route, which started from Pishan in Xin-jiang to run across Kashmir and reached its destination at the Persian Gulf through the south of Afghanistan. This route, which passed through Wuyishanli nation, a nation split from Parthia, was not open until the Eastern Han Dynasty.

The main route linking China with its great neighbour India passed through the snow-capped Hindu Kush Mountains to reach Charsadda in the Indus Valley, and was called the Sino-Indo Snow Mountain Route. Farther south, there was another route, which ran across the Ganges Valley to reach Yunnan and Sichuan

---

[1] During the Western (or Former) Han Dynasty, the Han envoys travelled to Antioch, which was the capital of Kingdom of Antiochia in Western Asia, before Syria was conquered by the Romans in 30 B.C.; and it was not at the same destination of the west-bound envoys of the Eastern (or Later) Han Dynasty, who travelled to Spasinu-Charax on the Persian Gulf.

in southern China through Assam or Bangladesh, and was called the Sino-Indo-Burma Route. Liu Che, Han Emperor Wudi of the Han Dynasty, upon the suggestion of Zhang Qian, planned to conquer the ethnic tribes in China's southwest by military force in order to open the Sino-Indo-Burma Route and trade with the southern neighbours. However, the advance of the Han troops was checked by the local tribes at Yunnan's Erhai Lake, frustrating the plan. However, trade between the local people of both countries continued along the route.

II   Parthia and the Monopoly of Silk Trade

With the intent of opening the silk trade route Alexander the Great, King of Macedonia, launched expedition to as far east as the Ferghana Basin. And two centuries later, Liu Che, the Han Emperor Wudi, sent his army westward to conquer Dayuan. He was seeking a direct link with another major nation called Parthia. The Chinese called Parthia Anxi, which sounds similar to the name Arsak, who founded Parthia in 248 B.C. It was Zhang Qian, who had heard that Anxi was the biggest country in the west, during his first trip to Central Asia. He also learned that the country was noted for its well-developed communications and commerce. Later, Zhang Qian sent his aide to Parthia, who was warmly received by the ruling King of Parthia and escorted to and from the Parthian capital by a cavalry of 20,000 and all the way to the border town of Mulu (now Mary). A Parthian emissary followed the Han envoy all the way back to the Han capital of Chang'an, where he offered such gifts as ostrich eggs and an Oxus magician to the Han Emperor.[1] After that, the two countries commenced regular exchange of official envoys and traders, whereby Chinese silk, ironware and lacquerware flowed onto the

---

[1] The magician in question was from Lixuan, which, according to the *History of the Han Dynasty*, was located to the north of Anxi (Parthia). The place was not Alexandria of Egypt as usually claimed, but was Traxiane by the Oxus River (Amu-Darya). Therefore, the man was not an Egyptian but a migrant from Central Asia.

markets in West Asia and Mediterranean countries through Parthia, while such products as jewelry, perfume, ivory, fur and woolens began pouring back to China by the same route. In the Western Han Dynasty Parthia became China's major customer of silk goods and also its principal business broker. The extensive use of silk banners of various colours in the Parthian army was also introduced from China.

The rise of the Roman Empire brought sudden changes to the political map of the Mediterranean region, one of which was the further extension of the Silk Road finally to Port Alexandria of Egypt since the first century. By then, Egypt had become a province of the Roman Empire, and re-named Alexandria. The routing of the Han Dynasty's silk trade was altered to accommodate political changes in the region. The trade route with Alexandria was divided into three different sections. The east section connected Chang'an with Yumen, from there extending farther westward in two lines—one to Waziristan to the south of Amu-Darya and another to Mary, north of Amu-Darya. The middle section of the route went on from Mary westward to Ktesiphon-Seleucia in Mesopotamia, which was the centre of the Silk Road in West Asia and the starting point of the west section of the route, by land or by sea, leading to Port Alexandria.

The east section of the Silk Road was basically under Chinese control, as the Han Dynasty had, since 60 B.C., set up a Xiyu Garrison Command in Wulei of Xinjiang and extended its rule over the entire region to the east of the Ferghana Basin. In the year of 36 B.C., Han Dynasty generals Gan Yanshou and Chen Tang allied with the Wusun tribe to launch an attack on the Xiongnu in Kangju, annihilating the westbound army of the Xiongnu's chieftain, Zhizhi chanyu. This action prevented the Xiongnu from invading the south of Syr-Darya and strengthened China's ties with the nations in the region, thereby ensuring the safe passage of traders between the Han Dynasty and Parthia. The boom of silk trade along this route during this period of the Han Dynasty went down in history as a monumental chapter of the fabulous Silk Road known to one and all today.[1]

The middle section of the Silk Road was, for a long time, controlled by the Persians, first the Parthians and then the Sassanids. This section extended from Mary in the east to Hecatompylos and Ktesiphon-Seleucia in Persia, then, went on to Spasinu-Charax on the Persian Gulf by way of the Euphrates, reaching the western border of Parthia at Gerrha in the end. From Gerrha, the west section led to Egyptian ports along the Red Sea.

However, political instability in the region of the Tigris and Euphrates had caused problems for travellers along the west section of the Silk Road. The situation worsened in the first century B.C., when the expanding Roman Empire became the top rival of Persia in West Asia, and armed clashes continued between the two powers in the region until the middle of the fourth century. One reason for their conflict was the Romans' desire to break Persia's monopoly of the East-West trade, which had not only put the Romans at a disadvantage, but also hampered their economic development. The Roman opposition to the Persian monopoly of trade was understandable to the Chinese. In Volume 88 of the *History of the Later Han Dynasty*, there was an analysis of the economic disadvantage imposed upon Rome by the Persian monopoly of the East-West trade, explaining that despite the Roman Emperor's wish to trade with the Han Dynasty directly, the trade was monopolized by Persians who re-sold Han'a silk goods to the Romans while blocking direct trade between the Han Dynasty and Rome.

The west section of the Silk Road had two lines, one to the north and another to the south. The northern line proceeded along the Euphrates River from Al Hillah and Al Fallujah to Raqqa, then, reaching Antioch or other Roman ports in Levant region across the Aleppo Plateau. The southern line turned from Raqqa down to Palmyra and, then, went on to

---

[1] The name Silk Road was first proposed by F. von Richthofen in his book *China* (5 vols., Berlin, 1877-1912). It was established in 1910 by A. Hermann in his Die alten Seidenstrassen zw. China und Syrien, Beitrage zur alten Geographie Asiens, I, Berlin.

Levant or Alexandria. The region had seen intense clashes between Rome and Persia, whose interests were in sharp conflict in this area. During the reign of Emperor Antoninus Pius (138-161), the Romans were in control of all the crossroads along the Euphrates. Earlier, Roman Empror Trajan (98-117) had led his army to overrun the region on the Persian Gulf, which was the farthermost point the Romans had ever reached in their eastward expedition. However, despite their efforts, the Romans were unable to hold on to their positions in the occupied area, and failed to seize control of the traffic routes in the Persian Gulf or along the Euphrates River.

III   China and the Oriental Trade of the Roman Empire

1. The Biggest Customer of Chinese Silk

The silk products of the Han Dynasty were very desirable internationally. These products, generally called *zeng* or *bo* in Chinese, including such goods as brocade, embroidery, damask, satin, silk yarn and gauze. The success in the planting of mulberry trees during the Han Dynasty further improved the quality of the silk. This was proven by ancient silk gauze unearthed from a Han Dynasty tomb in Mozuizi of Wuwei, Gansu Province, in 1972. It was woven with silk filaments measuring only 0.0055-0.006 millimetre in diameter—finer than the filament of artificially-bred silkworm cocoon in any country today. The Han silk producers during those years kept upgrading their breeding and weaving skills and developed more and more sophisticated silk goods. As a result, such silk goods became the most popular "hard currency" and expensive gifts in Central and West Asia in those days. An increasing number of foreign merchants flocked to China to buy silk, and the volume of their purchases from China exceeded the volume of China's own sales abroad. According to the Roman historian Pliny the Elder (23-79), "Seres (Chinese) did not have to wait for buyers, all the silk trade was done with foreign customers who came to get the goods." The booming silk trade during the Han Dynasty was substantiated by the successive discoveries of such relics all along the Silk Road, beginning from Chang'an (now Xi'an) in Shaanxi to Dunhuang in Gansu, and Baicheng, Bachu and Minfeng in Xinjiang. They were also found in Samarkand and other places in Central Asia. The shipments of such silk goods were traced as far west as the territory of the Roman Empire.

During the Han Dynasty, Rome was called Daqin, meaning "Great West" in Chinese to symbolize its important position in the West. In the first three centuries, Rome had replaced Parthia as the biggest customer of Chinese silk goods. After the Roman occupation of Syria in 64 B.C., its demand for Chinese silk quickly mounted; and silk industry was established in such cities as Beirut and Tyre of Levant and other towns in the Nile Delta to process plain or patterned silk imported from China. As was told in the ancient Chinese history book *Tong Dian*, the Romans had "profited through processing Chinese silk yarns into their own patterned silk fabrics and damask."[1] The Chinese plain silk yarns or rolls were cheaper and could be used as raw material for processing more expensive silk fabrics. According to Roman historian Procobius (500-562), Chinese silk, after arriving in Beirut or Tyre, were disjoined into threads, then reprocessed or interwoven with linen by the local industry into satin, damask or gauze, which were later dyed or embroidered into more expensive silk products.[2] In fact, the silk industry of Levant and Egypt depended on imported Chinese silk to produce the fabulous golden-threaded embroideries and clourful satin, which were the fashion of the Roman Empire at that time. The Roman aristocrats coveted extravagant styles and took pride in dressing themselves in silk. The luxurious gown, worn by the Egyptian Queen Kleopatra (51-30 B.C.) at her banquet, was a dress of Chinese silk made specially for her by the workers of Tyre. Caesar, the Roman dictator, had attended a theatrical performance also in an exquisitely-tailored silk gown, made by the best silk workers at that time. He was also said to have used a silk sun-shading

---

[1] *Tong Dian*, Vol. 193, "Bianfang" 9, "Xirong" 5, "Daqin."

[2] Procobius, *De Bello Gothico*, Loeb Library, 297.

umbrella. Evidences of such relics have been discovered, including a blouse with blue and red silk trimming une⁀ ⁓thed from a Roman ruin, which was woven with Chinese silk instead of the local tussore silk.[1] Silk fabrics were especially popular on the Italian Peninsula during the early centuries. This was evidenced by the opening of a Chinese silk market in Rome's Tuscan District. In the fourth century, Roman historian Ammianus Marcellinus had to admit that silk clothes were worn even by loaders and messengers.[2]

Archaeological excavations of an ancient tomb in Palmyra dateable to A.D. 83-273, produced several Han damask clothes showing patterns of lion-pairs and twin-horned animals with eagle heads. The discoveries showed that the aristocrats of Palmyra wore Chinese silk gowns even when they were entombed. Relics of Chinese silk goods had also been unearthed from fourth century ruins in Egypt and former Roman border pass in the middle reaches of the Euphrates River. History indicated that the Roman Empire strengthened its control of the smaller states in Syria in the early second century in a bid to ensure the safety of silk trade with the East. After the Roman occupation of Petra in A.D. 106, trade began to flourish between Damascus and Alexandria. The city of Petra remained an important trading centre in North Arabia during the Roman era, when it, along with the southern Eudaimon Arabia of Aden, became the eastern gateway of the Roman Oriental trading stronghold in Egypt.

The Roman merchants, engaging in silk trade, had to traverse rugged plateaus and mountains in their journey to and from the East. According to ancient records in the *Geographia* (A.D. 150), a business agent sent by a Macedonian merchant Maes Titianus from Syria to China, told of his experience travelling from Zagma across the Euphrates to Ktesiphon, and farther north to the Caspian on his way to Waziristan via Antioch Margina (now Mary) from there he climbed to Kumidh on the plateau to travel across the Congling range by way of Lithinos Pyrgos in Afghanistan and finally arrive in the country of Serres (China). The silk

---

[1] G. Brunton, *Qau and Badari*, III, 26.
[2] H. Yule, *Cathay and the Way Thither*, Vol. I, P. 203, 1915.

traders from both the East and the West all had to traverse the similar arduous course during that period, while the caravan traders from both Levant and Syria faced heavy taxation and extortion by the Persians, before they could cross the Congling range to do business with China.

✦ Silk trade with China had an immense impact on the finance of the Roman Empire. According to an estimate by Pliny the Elder, Rome had to pay about 100 million sesterces per year for its imports from the Arabian Peninsula, India and China —amounting to some 100,000 ounces of gold. As a result, a large quantity of Roman gold coins flowed into India and China. In Shanxi Province, Roman coins dateable to A.D. 14-275 had been unearthed. According to an estimate by a twentieth century European historian, Rome had sustained a deficit of about 100 million pounds (assessed at the exchange rate of 1930) from its unfavourable balance of trade with the East during the 220 years from 31 B.C. to A.D. 192.

2. The Proposed Diplomatic Relations Between China and Rome

The silk trade boom led to clashes between Rome and Persia over the control of the Silk Road. The Persian monopoly of the East-West trade overland prompted Rome to seek another trade route via the Red Sea and India to reach China. Meanwhile, the Romans reopened the "Fur Road" leading to the Black Sea and southern Siberia, in order to get Chinese silk goods from the nomadic tribes in the north of the Tianshan Mountains.

China, for its part, was trying to drive away the Xiongnu invaders from the south of Tianshan Mountains, in a bid to keep the trade route open across the oases on both sides of the Congling range. In A.D. 97, Ban Chao, the Han Dynasty garrison commander of the Western Regions, sent his aide Gan Ying as his personal envoy to Rome, seeking to establish ties with Egypt. Since Ban Chao had been engaged in armed conflict with Yuezhi, he trusted Persia as an ally and let his envoy Gan Ying proceed to Persia, along the same path pursued by Chinese envoys since the days of Zhang Qian. However, Persia was then involved in conflict with Rome and troubled with internal strife after A.D. 77. As a result, after Gan Ying arrived in Persia, the Persians did not let him go on to the Mediterranean. Instead, they led him to the Persian Gulf coast. Finally, when Gan Ying reached Gerrha, planning to cross the Red Sea, the Persians persuaded him to abandon the trip by exaggerating the difficulties and dangers involved in such a voyage. Persians, who were still unable to control trade in southern Arabia, were obviously unwilling to see China develop ties with Rome and open a trade route by sea.

To open a sea route was the most effective way for Rome to develop its trade relations with the East. In 24 B.C., Roman Emperor Augustus Caesar (27 B.C.-A.D. 14) dispatched his army to attack Aden and seize the key port essential to its trade with India. Since then, the Romans, taking advantage of the southwesterly monsoon known to the Arabs, set sail every July from Myos Hormos on the west coast of the Red Sea to reach Ocelis (now Sella) on the southern tip of the Arabian Peninsula, a voyage that took 30 days. From there they could cross the Indian Ocean in another 40 days and moor at port Musiri (now Cranganore) on the west coast of south India. There, they could obtain not only such Indian goods as pepper, gems, ivory carvings and cotton yarn, but also Chinese silks brought there by the Tamils. In the second century, the frequent wars in the Euphrates region and the resultant profiteering by the middle-men of Palmyra and other small nations in the region prompted the Romans to further develop the overseas trade route. As a result, the Romans opened several seabound trade routes to China, one by way of the Greek transit port of Harmozia-Omana on the northern coast of the Strait of Hormuz to reach the east section of the Silk Road on land through south Iran. The Romans could also go from Harmozia-Omana to such eastern ports as Demetrias-Patala at the mouth of the Indus River, or Barygaza farther south, where they could conduct trade with China's Xinjiang through the Yuezhi businessmen in India. Also in the second century, the Romans had reached Yongchang Prefecture of China's Yunnan Province, by way of the Irrawaddy River in Burma, after travelling by sea from the Arabian Peninsula. At the same time, the Roman traders had also tried to establish direct contact with China's

Jiaozhou and Guangzhou through the maritime route via the Red Sea and Indian Ocean. Greek ships had then sailed to Sopadma (now Makana) on the Coromandel Coast of the Indian Peninsula, nearer Chinese ports.

Despite the Han envoy Gan Ying's failure to reach his destination of Egypt, he had travelled to many parts of West Asia, never before visited by other Chinese. And his visits to these countries sparked the dispatch of envoys by such remote states as Mocha and Adulis to Luoyang, capital of the Later Han Dynasty, to seek friendly ties with China. Both located by the Red Sea, Mocha was a commercial centre in south Arabia, while Adulis was the principal port of the ancient Ethiopian nation Axum. Envoys of these two remote states arrived in Luoyang in A.D. 100, marking an increase in East-West trade spurred by the Roman effort to develop economic ties to the Orient. Axum's desire to promote trade relations with China was readily accepted by the Han Dynasty rulers. As a token of the newly-established friendship, the Han Emperor granted the kings of the two states gold seals wrapped with purple ribbons to be delivered by their envoys on their return. Axum thus became the first African country to establish ties with China.

Trade relations continued to develop in subsequent years, as a Roman envoy sent by Emperor Marcus Aurelius Antoninus (161-180) arrived at Luoyang by way of Ri'nan, the Han Dynasty's southernmost port on the coast of the Vietnam Peninsula, where he landed after a voyage across the Indian Ocean. The Roman envoy offered ivory, rhino-horn and hawksbill turtle to the Han emperor as gifts from the Roman ruler. While the Han court rated the gifts as ordinary, it agreed to establish formal ties with the Roman Empire, because this marked the first official communication between the two great powers in the East and the West, according to the *History of the Later Han Dynasty*. The two countries then reached an agreement on the need to develop overseas trade, exchange cultural information and other views.

3. The Voyage of Chinese Sailing Ships to Port Adulis

Until the second century, the overseas trade between China

and Rome had been carried out through south India as its midway transit. The first leg of the trade route began at south China's Jiaozhou and ended at India's Coromandel Coast. Destination of the second leg was Myos Hormoz in Egypt. In practice, a Han Dynasty sailing ship would set out from China's southern port of Hepu or Ri'nan and, with help of trade winds, sail along the coast of the Indo-China Peninsula southward until the Malacca Strait, turn northward, then southward again along the Burma and India coastline to arrive at Conjeveram of the ancient Indian nation of Kanci. From Kanci a Roman or other foreign vessel would take over the cargo and sail around Cape Comorin to the Musiri port on the other side of the Indian Peninsula, then along the route of the ancient Greek voyager to reach Aden and other ports of the south Red Sea.

The first leg of the sea trade route had been used by Chinese traders since the end of the second century B.C., when the Han envoys brought such popular items as gold and silk there and traded them for pearls, veruliya (sapphire), gems and rhino-horns with the Indian merchants. However, no Chinese vessel had ever sailed around the western tip of Cape Comorin at Takola until the end of the second century. But the arrival of a Roman envoy spurred the Chinese to make fresh attempts. Several decades later, in the beginning of the third century, Chinese sailing ships finally extended their voyage to Port Adulis by the Red Sea. In 226, south China's ruling Wu Kingdom (222-280) dispatched Zhu Yin and Kang Tai as envoys to the South Asian nation of Fu-nan. On their arrival in Cambodia, they sent their aides on to other parts of Southeast Asia and India and gathered information on the possibility of developing direct trade with the Roman Empire. Their reports, which appeared in historical literature, told of a Chinese merchant ship which set sail from Conjeveram of India and arrived at Kusa of the Roman Empire after a voyage of over one month. Kusa was the Kushite nation living in Ethiopia and Nubia in Africa at that time.[1] The Chinese merchant ship sailing

---

[1] D.C. Sircar, *Cosmography and Geography in Early India Literature*, P. 51, Calcutta, 1967.

on this line was a big vessel with seven sails.[1] In the same year of the Chinese envoy Kang Tai's visit to South Asia, a foreign merchant from as far as Cyrene in Libya arrived in Jianye (now Nanjing), the capital of Wu Kingdom. Since then, the Chinese people had come to know more about the geography, products and trade of North Africa, which helped enrich their own vacabulary with such foreign words as *poli* (Bahri), a general name for gems imported by Bejas from Nubia, and *wuwenmu* (Diospyrus ebenum) based on the Egyptian Coptic word "heben."

4. The Acclaimed "Land of Treasures"

Kang Tai, the Chinese envoy sent in 226 by Wu Kingdom to visit South Asia, wrote in the report of his travel, entitled "An Introduction to Foreign Nations During the Reign of Wu," that it was recognized by foreigners that China was rich in population, Yuezhi was rich in horses and Rome was rich in treasures. Prosperity of the Roman Empire was then widely acclaimed throughout the world, including China. Roman civilization was described as superior to any other country, according to the book *Wei Lie* (*Memorable Things of the Wei Kingdom*), written between 240 and 253. The book gave a vivid illustration of the products in Daqin (the Roman Empire). The book listed a total of 65 items, including 12 kinds of aromatic drugs and many other goods which were divided into six major categories as follows:

9 kinds of minerals, including gold, silver, copper, iron, lead, tin, realgar and orpiment.

10 kinds of animals, including tortoise, white horse, rhinoceros, hawksbill turtle and ivory.

15 kinds of gems, including large conches, cornelian stones, pearls, ambers, corals, blue gems, beryl, crystal, emerald and semi-precious stones of nine colours.

18 kinds of fabrics, including ghashiyat or rugs of ten different colours, takhtdar or pelts of five colours, golden-thread embroideries, asbestos cloth, byssus, tadmor cloth, habasat cloth, and

---

[1] Shen Fuwei, *Development of Shipping on the Indian Ocean During the Two Han Dynasties and the Three Kingdoms, Cultural History*, Vol. 26, Beijing, 1986.

Egyptian woollens.

12 kinds of aromatics, including ebony, storax, myrrha, frank incense, gum olibanum etc.

10 kinds of glass, including red, white, black, green, yellow, blue, orange, pink, maroon and purple.

This rare list of ancient cargo covered both the popular products of the Roman Empire and its colonies and also exported goods from countries on the banks the Red Sea or on the Arabian Peninsula along the sea route to China. Many of these products came from West Asia and North Africa. For instance, the white horse was an animal from Arabia, while rhino, ivory and hawksbill turtle were from the Red Sea or Africa. Pearls were products of the Dahlak Archipelago in the Red Sea or from the Persian Gulf, semi-precious stones came from Syria and emeralds were produced in Egypt. The rugs and pelts were Arabian products, while golden-thread embroideries were widely known as a product of Levant. Asbestos cloth came from Ethiopia,[1] and tadmor cloth and other five kinds of linens were produced in Asian or African countries along the Mediterranean coast. The cotton fabric Habasat was an African product; Egyptian woollens were dyed in Heliopolis of Egypt, a town praised by Strabo for its water which was best suited for dyeing woollens. Egypt began producing such dyed woollen fabric after the Roman occupation, but the Chinese soon heard of it and included it on their import list.

Of the other goods, most of the aromatic drugs were produced in Arabian and African countries, while coloured glass was a special product of the Mediterranean countries, known as unique in the world. It is noteworthy that the Roman glass-makers had produced a special kind of dazzling glass for export to China, in accordance with Chinese customers' orders. The glass was used by Chinese aristocrats as an ornament on their dress.

The trade relations between China and Rome were an East-West exchange of immense scale and significance in the ancient

---

[1] Pliny, *Naturalia Historia*, XXXVII, PP. 54, 156; in the original script, "India" was given for "Ethiopia," because the Horn of Africa was often referred to as "India" in Greek classics.

world. The booming oriental trade which continued for three
centuries during the prosperity of the Roman Empire—when
such close ties existed between China and Alexandria (of Egypt)
—was a miracle that had become nearly forgotten by the world
centuries later. Chinese ships had sailed as far as the Red Sea in
those years, while Roman merchants returned the visits to China
as later as 281 and 284 to exchange goods and information. In the
fourth century, following the decline in the oriental trade based
in Alexandria, the Roman Empire's new capital Constantinople
re-established diplomatic relations with China. The first instance
of such exchange occurred in A.D. 313, when Zhang Gui, a
garrison commander of the Western Jin Dynasty (265-316) in
Xinjiang, sent back two man-size golden vases made in Constantinople to the Western Jin Emperor in Chang'an. Decades later,
an envoy from Constantinople arrived for the first time at Nanjing, the capital of the Eastern Jin Dynasty, during the reign of
the Eastern Jin Emperor Mudi (345-361). He travelled the route
connecting the Hexi Corridor of Gansu and the mountain path in
north Sichuan. In 363, a Chinese envoy was dispatched by the
Eastern Jin's Emperor Aidi to pay a return visit to Constantinople. Before long, however, such visits were discontinued when
China was split into the Northern and Southern Dynasties and
the Eastern Jin Dynasty was forced to retreat to the southern
provinces.

IV   Earliest Cultural Exchanges Between China and India

1. The Origin of Buddhism and Its Introduction to the East

Buddhism first originated in India in the sixth century B.C.
During the reign of Maurya Emperor Asoka (273-232 B.C.), it
was adopted as the state religion of India. Asoka, who became a
Buddhist himself, sent monks to proselytize throughout India and
the neighbouring countries, including China. During the Eastern
(Later) Han Dynasty (A.D. 25-220), Indian monk Kayamudan

came to the Han capital of Luoyang to preach Buddhism, where he was said to have told his Chinese followers that the late Indian Emperor Asoka had left 84,000 Buddhist relics, of which 19 were located in China. The 19 Buddhist relics were said to be scattered over areas in the south of Xinjiang and the west of Yunnan, both of which were China's gateways to India, then the two countries began their exchanges.

Asoka was also involved in the founding of the ancient state of Yutian. Legend had it that Prince Kustana first led 10,000 Chinese emigrants to the lower reaches of the Keriya (Yutian) River. Shortly afterwards the vizier of Emperor Asoka brought another 7,000 people there. Together they founded the Yutian State around the year of A.D. 250. The story was later repeated by the well-known Chinese monk Xuanzang of the Tang Dynasty (618-907), who said the ancestor of the Yutian King had come from Taxila in ancient India.

The Chinese classic *Stories from Ancient Yunnan* tells of troops led by the three sons of Emperor Asoka once chased their father's runaway stallion all the way to the valley between Mount Jingma and Mount Biji in west Yunnan, crossing Dali region near the Erhai Lake; but when the Indian princes finally turned to go back to India, they were stopped by the local tribe, who asked them to stay. The princes settled down in the western Yunnan region. And this was said to be the origin of the Indian emigrants in west Yunnan's Yongchang Prefecture during the Han Dynasty. Another legend has it that Zhuang Qiao, a native of Chu State, led his men to Yunnan and became the King of Dian (Yunnan) during the period between 328 and 263 B.C. Zhuang became a Buddhist himself in his later years when he moved to live in Baiya (now Midu) of western Yunnan. The ethnic Bai nationality in the region were said to be descendants of Zhuang Qiao. There was, nonetheless, no doubt that the region was the gateway to India in ancient China. Some Indian classic fables came out of the area.

It was believed that among the early Indian emigrants in China were a number of Buddhists, who were responsible for the spread of Buddhism. In the year 242 B.C., 18 Buddhist monks from the Western Regions brought Sanskrit scripture to the city of Xianyang in Shaanxi; however, their attempt to gain a foothold for the religion in the heartland of China failed. The earliest success of Buddhism as a religion in China was seen in Yutian of western Xinjiang, which was a close neighbour to the birthplace of the religion. In 80 B.C., Kashmir monk Vairotchana won the approval of the Yutian ruler to build a Buddhist shrine at a place several kilometres to the south of the city of Yutian, which became the first Buddhist temple in Chinese history. The worshippers at that time, however, were mainly Indian emigrants. In inland China, Buddhism was not accepted by the rulers of the Han Dynasty until the middle of the first century. In A.D. 65, the Han Prince Chu became a Buddhist convert and followed the Buddhist doctrine of Cramana and Upasaka in his daily lifestyle. This caused a stir in the Han imperial court, and even the Han Emperor Mingdi was said to have seen a golden image of Buddha in his dream. As a result, an 18-man delegation, led by Cai Yin and Qin Jing, was dispatched by the Han court to study Buddhist religion in the Great Yuezhi. In A.D. 68, the delegation returned to China, bringing with them Buddhist portraits, scripture and two Indian monks Kasyapa Matanga and Dharmaratna. Soon after, a Buddhist temple called Baimasi (White Horse Temple) was built in Luoyang, where the monks began their translation of the scripture, symbolizing the first instance of an official approval of the religion. During the reign of Han Emperor Huandi (147-167) and Empror Lingdi (168-189), Buddhism became so popular in China that statues of Buddha were even erected and worshipped in the palace, while equal respect was paid to Buddhism as to Huang Di (Yellow Emperor) and Lao Zi—the traditional Chinese saints. In the years that followed, Buddhist monks were invited from India, Yuezhi, Kangju and Parthia to Luoyang, where they joined in the translation of Buddhist scripture along with their Chinese colleagues, marking the beginning of the most magnificent translation venture seen in the history of cultural exchange between China and other countries.

Thanks to the successive visits to China by many learned Buddhist monks from India, Yuezhi, Parthia and Kangju, including Zhufoshuo, Vizinan, Lokaksena, Zhiqian, Anqing, Anxuan, Kangju and Kangmengxiang[1], the theories of Buddhism began to be introduced more extensively in China, while Chinese scholars also began their study of Buddhism. This led to the first Chinese Buddhist book written by a Confucianist writer Mou Rong, entitled *Li Huo Lun* (*On Truth and Doubts*) in the third century.

2. The Bridge Between China and Egypt

In the year of 60 B.C., when the Romans occupied Syria, the Great Yuezhi troops also crossed Amu Darya and annexed Bactria, seizing control of the route linking the East and West across the Congling range. Then, in the beginning of the first century, the Guiba Dynasty of Yuezhi Kingdom expanded its territory to Kashmir and Gandhara. Later it was extended to cover the Ganges River region and the Gulf of Khambhat of India, during the reign of King Kanishka (78-120), when the Yuezhi troops once invaded Shule across the Congling range in Xinjiang. Speaking the Se language, the Yuezhi used the Brahmanic script, which was popular in the northwest Indian sub-continent and somewhat similar to that used in the region south of Tarim Basin. Thus, during the period from the first to the fourth century, all trades going through either the Iran Plateau or the Indus Valley and Khambhat Gulf had to pass through Yuezhi territory. Here, businessmen and scholars from India, Greece and elsewhere could freely exchange goods or views at Antioch near the Mediterranean or Alexandria of Egypt.

The book *The Periplus of the Erythraean Sea*, written by a Greek captain in 20s, tells of seeing cargoes of raw silk, silk yarn and silk textiles from north China being shipped by land via Bactria to Barygaza (now Broach) in the Khambhat Gulf of India, or by way of the Ganges River to Tamil Nadu. Such a shift of shipments, from the expensive overland route across the Iran Plateau to the less costly maritime route leading to the Red Sea ports, resulted in a lowering of the cost of imported Chinese silks and satin for the Roman aristocratic consumers. In return, such

---

[1] The names of the foreign monks were mostly in their Chinese version.

Roman goods as glassware, sculpture and Arabian aromatic plants found their way to China along the same sea route.

During this period of the East-West trade boom, Taxila in the Indus Valley and Begram in the north of the Kabul River were the two major entrepots, playing a monumental role in this period of history. In the ancient town of Taxila near Sirkap, Indian archaeologists launched a major excavation during the years from 1913 to 1934, and unearthed a large quantity of Graeco-Roman sculpture, utensils and jewelries, which verified the town's overwhelming importance as the key link in the oversea trade route to Alexandria, and its superiority over the overland trade route across West Asia. It was from Taxila that many Roman goods had been shipped across the mountains into China's Xinjiang region. The ancient town of Begram, similarly, was a Roman cultural post nearest China. Located 70 kilometres to the south of Kabul in Afghanistan, Begram was the site of the ancient Kapica Nation, first built in the second century B.C. and destroyed by the Yada invaders in the fifth century. During the years from 1936 to 1942, French archaeologists discovered the ancient ruins and unearthed a substantial amount of Roman sculpture and glassware, which were dateable to the 300-year-long period of the oriental trade boom of Alexandria. Among the finds of the Kapica ruins were numerous Chinese relics, including various kinds of exquisite Chinese lacquerware, which filled two chambers in the unearthed ancient palace. The rich store of the ancient palace of Kapica was considered the best-preserved underground museum of a combination of Chinese-Roman culture.

Ever since the visit to China by a Roman envoy in A.D. 166, trade between the two countries had ceased to use the overland route across the Iran Plateau, but was shifted to the oversea route by way of India. The new trade link with India had resulted in many of the Roman products getting Indian names. For example, rhinoceros were called "haiji" in China after the Sanskrit name "khadga." Also, Egyptian emeralds were renamed "merukuta" in India, according to Buddhist scripture. They were called *munan* gem by the famous Chinese poet Cao Zhi of the Three Kingdoms (A.D. 220-280) in his poem *Beauties*. Another popular imported item, the aromatic "Suhe Incense" produced in Shihr in the southern Arabian Peninsula, was listed by China as a product from Da Qin (Rome). The same incense was again described as a product of Yuezhi by Ban Gu in his *History of the Han Dynasty*, because it was shipped to China from Yuezhi. Ban Gu also mentioned, in a letter to his brother Ban Chao, that Yuezhi was famous for its fine rugs, which were actually not all produced in that country. Anyhow, all this indicated that the Indian subcontinent—whether it was the Indus Valley in the northwest or Tamil Nadu in the south—had been an essential link in the trade ties between China and Rome, and played an important role in that relationship between the great powers of East and West in that era.

Chapter Three

The Introduction of Culture and Art from the Western Regions During the Han and Tang Dynasties

I   The Steppe Empire and East-West Cultural Exchange

Since the disintegration of the Xiongnu Steppe Empire in Mongolia, and following the westward migration of the northern Xiongnu tribes from the Altay Mountain region in A.D. 91, other ethnic nations, including Xianbei, Rouran, Yada and Tujue (Turk), began to come to the fore in the area. Of these, the Rouran, Yada and Tujue played a far more important role than the Xiongnu in the East-West cultural exchange.

In the year of 402, Rouran Chieftain Shelun entitled himself Qiudoufa Khan and expanded his territory to the vast steppe, extending from the north of Yanqi in western Xinjiang to the south of Lake Baikal, setting up his tribal centre of ruling just north of Dunhuang and Zhangye in Gansu. After that, for nearly a century Rouran continued to dominate the area and posed as the strongest rival in the north of the Northern Wei Dynasty, which was founded by the Xianbei people in northern China. Until the year of 552, when Rouran was finally conquered by Tujue, it had served as a bridge in the cultural exchange between northern China and the Western World. From 411 to 414, Khan Hulü of Rouran formed friendly ties with King Feng Ba of the North Yan State in northern China, even became in-laws. Later, when internal strife within the Rouran tribe erupted, Hulü fled to seek shelter from Feng Ba in North Yan State. Then, 15 centuries later, the tomb of Feng Sufu (died in 415) was unearthed in Beipiao of Liaoning Province in 1972. Among the relics found in the grave of this brother of the North Yan King Feng Ba were five rare transparent glass vessels of light and dark green colour. Four of the five pieces, including a concave-bottom cup, a round pot, a fractured goblet and a duck-shaped water container, were markedly different from traditional Chinese products in both their design and structure. This ancient glassware, bearing distinct Roman style—particularly the 21-centimetre-long duck-shaped water jar made of ornate blown glass—were not only discovered for the first time in China, but also rarely seen abroad. The jar looked similar to the two Roman fish-shaped glass bottles unearthed earlier from a Guiba ruin in Begram of Afghanistan, which were perfume containers originating in Egypt and popular in the Roman world. Glassware of similar design was also produced in the Rhine region during the Roman reign, which had probably been imported to North China from Byzantine by way of Rouran.

Meanwhile, the Yada tribe had, for about 100 years since the mid-fifth century, seized control of the East-West trade route in the Congling range area, to the west of the Rouran territory. The Yada, first originating in the Altay Mountains, had been called the Xiongnu or the Bai-Xiongnu after they moved westward into Central Asia. By the end of the fourth century, the tribe had set up its political centre at Warwaliz (now Kunduz) of Tukhara and greatly expanded its territory, wiping out the Great Yuezhi and forcing its remnant into exile southward. Then, it defeated Persia, whereby Theophanus, the Byzantine historian, took note of the name Ephthalanus of the Yada King, and Yada was thus called Hephthalites. Yada rose to its peak in the early sixth century, when it controlled a large part of Central Asia to the west of Ferghana and farther crossed the Congling range to seize Yanqi, Qiuci and Yutian in Xinjiang. In the year of 511, it conquered Gandhara, forcing Kangju and even Persia to offer tribute to the Yada Kingdom. Then, in alliance with the Tukuhun tribe in Qinghai, Yada seized control of the southern trade route between China and the West. The southern trade route had, since late fifth century, largely passed through the Altun Mountain dividing

Qinghai and Xinjiang, and was called the Henan (South of the River) route because it turned southward from the traditional Hexi Corridor along the upper reach of the Yellow River. In the year of 518, when the two Chinese envoys Song Yun and Hui Sheng departed from Luoyang to go to India, they travelled by this route from the Tukuhun-controlled Qinghai to Wakhan and the Yada capital of Kunduz, then, from there to Gandhara. The Tukuhun tribe used the route to trade with Yada and Persia, and obtained Persian horses, which were later bred into a new steed noted for its speed and endurance. Yada was known to use the same Sassanian silver coins as Persia. Such coins had been unearthed in an extensive area from north to south China, including the 76 silver coins of Persian King Cyrus the Great unearthed in 1956 at the old city of Xining in Qinghai and another silver coin found in the bottom of a tower at Dingxian County of Hebei, which bore a line of Yada script on its edge. The discoveries were evidence of the close ties between China, Yada and Persia during this historic period.[1]

The Tukuhuns were known also to serve as interpreters for Yata merchants. In the year of 516, a Yada envoy with his Tukuhun interpreter travelled from Qinghai to Nanjing to offer his friendly tribute to Emperor Wudi, Xiao Yan, of the Liang Dynasty. During the decades of the Southern Dynasties (420-589), many Chinese traders from Sichuan travelled to Central Asia by the southern trade route to sell their silk products, because, for them, it was shorter than the old trade route through the Hexi Corridor. The famous Sichuan silk thus found its way to markets in Central and West Asia.

In the sixth century, the rising Tujue tribe occupied Rouran and, then in 568 annihilated Yada, dividing the former territory of Yada with Persia, along the Buzgala Pass of Baysum Tau Mountain in the north of the Amu Darya. During the successive reigns of Mugan Khan (553-572) and his brother Tabo Khan (572-581), the powerful Tujue Khanate dominated the vast area, extending from North China's Liaoning Peninsula in the east to

---

[1] Xia Nai: "On the Persian Sassanian Silver Coins Unearthed in China," *Archaeology Journal*, No. 1 Issue, 1974, Beijing.

Caspian Sea in the west, across North Asia, and controlled all the trade routes passing over the Congling range. Facing such a formidable neighbour in the north, both the Northern Qi and Northern Zhou dynasties of China vied to woo the Tujue rulers by marrying their daughters to the Tujue rulers and offering large quantities of silk goods as tribute to them.

The Tujue rulers, in turn, sold Chinese silk to Persia and Byzantine, earning huge profits each time. The rapid growth in trade and exchange, following the rise and fall of the nations in North Asia, brought about a new art and cultural boom in the south of the Tianshan Mountains, featuring an interwoven style of Indian, Persian, Tujue and Tukhara characteristics, with variety in both form and fashion.

II   The Influx of Art from the Western Regions

1. The Buddhist Art in Inland China

Buddhist art, as an important arm of the religion, was introduced to Yutian in Xinjiang from Kashmir, soon after the founding of the Yutian State. The gypsum inset statue of Buddha and the red pottery sitting Buddha—unearthed from a ruin dated to the first century B.C. in Malikewati south of Yutian in 1979 —were the oldest Buddhist art symbols found in China. Apart from these, the earliest Buddhist painting known in China was a portrait of Sakyamuni drawn on cotton fabric, which was brought to Luoyang from the Great Yuezhi (India) by Cai Yin in the Eastern (Later) Han Dynasty. Upon the order of Han Emperor Mingdi, the portrait was reproduced by Chinese painters and preserved in a shrine of the Han palace. After the Temple of Baima (White Horse) Temple was built in Luoyang in A.D. 68, a mural called "Thousands on Horseback Pay Tribute to the Stupa" base on an original sample from India, was painted on the temple wall. This was also the first known mural in a Chinese Buddhist temple. However, earliest Buddhist paintings or sculptures during the Han Dynasty were drawn by artists from their own imagination, thus resembling super-natural images in Chinese fables or fairy tales. Such examples were seen in the wall painting of an "Immortal on White Elephant" discovered in a late Eastern Han tomb unearthed in Horinger of Inner Mongolia in 1971; also in the portrait of a boy dressed in skirt, discovered in a tomb of ancient stone paintings in Yinan of Shandong, unearthed in 1953.

Following the arrival of more and more Buddhist monks from India since the third century, Buddhist paintings were introduced across China. In 247, the India-born monk Kansenghui brought an Indian Buddhist painting to the Wu Kingdom's capital of Jianye (now Nanjing), which attracted the attention of Cao Buxing, a renown painter serving in the Wu court. Cao became the first famous Chinese artist to engage in copying Buddhist portraits, and his works created quite a stir in the country. Thus, Buddhist paintings were gradually introduced to inland China, through either the visiting Indian monks or Chinese pilgrims returning from abroad. As Buddhism grew more popular during the Jin Dynasty (265-420), many Chinese artists who engaged in Buddhist painting were themselves Buddhists. They included the noted painter Gu Kaizhi whose work of a Buddhist portrait "Weimojie" was chosen to be enshrined, along with a Buddhist sculpture carved by another contemporary artist Dai Kui, in Waguan Temple of Nanjing. The third Buddhist relic, celebrated in the Waguan Temple alongside the two other artworks at that time, was a 1.4-metre-high jade Buddha statue given to China by Sri Lanka, which was shipped to Nanjing after a journey of ten years across sea and land. At the time, most famous Chinese Buddhist painter was Wei Xie. Wei, a student of Cao Buxing, won the reputation of Master Artist for his Buddhist paintings, which topped all other artworks throughout six dynasties (222-589) in their fame and value. His paintings had such vividness that the Buddha in them looked real "If only they opened their eyes"—so the saying went. Wei was believed to have acquired his skill of "shadow rendering" from artworks introduced from India, which gave his pictures a three-dimensional image. Later, another famous painter Zhang Sengyao of the Liang Dynasty (502-557) used the Indian art style to paint the gates of Nanjing's Yicheng Temple with convexo-concave pattern in vermilion, bluish green colours. This caused a sensation in the Liang capital, earning the temple a new name of the Convexo-Concave Temple. Zhang, who was also known for his skills of mural painting and Buddhist portraits, was the most celebrated Buddhist artist in southern China.

While Zhang Sengyao became the leading Buddhist artist in the south, another artist from Central Asia held the spotlight in the Northern Qi Dynasty of northern China also for his outstanding skill of convexo-concave paintings. The artist, Cao Zhongda, was best known for his vivid portrayal of Buddha images in angelic dresses, which appeared "real and well-matched." His Buddhist artworks, which were comparable to the masterpieces of the celebrated Tang Dynasty (618-907) painter Wu Daozi (700-760) in the art of "perspective presentation," included more than 300 delicate mural paintings preserved in the temples and shrines of Chang'an and Luoyang. He was not only one of the most talented artists but also one of the most prolific painters of his time.

In the early seventh century, the art circle of Chang'an in north China was stirred by the exotic talents of two emigrant artists from Yutian of Xinjiang. Yuchi Bazhina and his son Yuchi Yiseng impressed the Chinese artists with their bold style in depicting the Buddha in a straightforward but more lively way. The rugged but sharp strokes of their artworks differed markedly from the traditionally even and moderate lines of Chinese paintings, known since the early Qin Dynasty. They gave their Buddhist paintings, particularly the semi-nude portraits, a more lively and physical image. The unique "steel-like" line drawings by Yuchi Yiseng were examples of an integration of Chinese traditional painting skills with Indian Buddhist art. Such an art style was often seen in the Qiuci art, which emerged after the Jin Dynasty (265-420) in China and was called "the bold style."

The Buddhist art of mural painting became even more popular during the Tang Dynasty, when examples from India and Qiuci were widely imitated. The contents of such murals were no longer confined to the life or teachings of the Buddha, but focused on stories from Buddhist scriptures. The best and richest collection of such Tang Buddhist mural paintings—once seen in all China's major temples—is now preserved only in the Mogao Grottoes of Dunhuang in Gansu Province. Then, in the late Tang Dynasty, it became more fashionable to paint Buddha portraits on tough silk and hang them on walls. This kind of "fanhua" (banner paintings) first emerged during the Northern and Southern Dynasties (420-589), when they were used as portable Buddhist portraits to be hung on walls for believers to worship, anytime and anywhere they wished. Then, during the late years of the Tang Dynasty, the silk-based "fanhua" were mounted on paper back and rolled into a scroll around a wooden cylinder, so that they could be better preserved and easily carried around. This has since become the conventional practice in handling Chinese paintings.

2. Popularity of the Xiyu Theme in Art Style

The introduction of arts from the Xiyu (Western Regions) first resulted in the breakthrough of the traditional limits in themes and forms of Chinese arts, greatly expanding their variety and genre. These were shown in zoomorphic designs which first appeared since the Warring States Period (475-221 B.C.) and further developed during the Han Dynasty. Additionally, there emerged such sculptures as the stone beasts guarding entrance to a tomb, and stone statues carved in similar Egyptian style in relief of incised lines. The themes of these carvings included winged beasts, lions, camels and also other themes introduced from the Western Regions.

The earliest example of such winged beast pattern was a pair of silver inlaid bronze biwinged-animal with upturned head and spread wings, unearthed in 1974 at Pingshan County of Hebei Province from the tomb of the Prince of Zhongshan State during the Warring States Period. The relic resembled the style of winged animals in the Persian artwork at that time. Similar artworks had been imported from Persia as auspicious symbols called *tianlu* (heavenly gift) and *bixie* (guardian against evils) during the Eastern Han Dynasty. Another example of imported art style was the stone lion erected in 209 to guard the tomb of Gao Yi in Ya'an of

Sichuan, which had obviously originated from the ancient Persian sculpture of a multi-winged stone lion guarding the Artaxerxds Palace, but had its spread wings changed into folded wings resting on its chest. Similar winged-animal was also seen in the stone relief on the tomb gate of Zen Jiabao's grave in Chengdu of Sichuan, which had short wings on a Scythian-style crouching deer.

The use of stone winged-animals as tomb guards was discontinued in north China in the third century. Then, 200 years later in the fifth century, it was revived during the construction of the imperial tombs of the Southern Dynasties in Nanjing and Danyang, but in a more refined Chinese style. The most outstanding examples of these vivid stone sculptures included the stone lions guarding the Liang tomb of Xiao Yan's brother Xiao Xiu in Nanjing, the stone unicorns at the entrance to the tomb of the Song Dynasty's Emperor Wudi (Liu Yu) of the Southern Dynasties as well as the unicorns before the tomb of the Liang Dynasty's Emperor Wudi (Xiao Yan) in Danyang near Nanjing. These sculptures had completely changed the wings' original Persian fish-scale pattern into Chinese-style wave or cloud patterns. In addition to stone sculptures before tombs, winged-animal designs were also found in the stone reliefs of the Eastern Han Dynasty, which could be seen throughout China—from the Pengshan Cliff in Sichuan to the Wu Family Shrine of Jiaxiang and the ancient tomb of Yinan in Shandong. In these stone reliefs, the Western art style of winged ox, tiger and unicorn had merged completely into the traditional Chinese art style.

Griffin, the fabulous creature with the head and wings of an eagle and the body of a lion, was the symbol of the imaginative art of the Eurasian Steppe nations and a further development of the art style of winged animals, which became very popular in West Asia. The earliest example of such art style was the gilded bronze griffin of seventh century B.C., which was unearthed in Toprake Kale and now preserved in the Berlin Staatliche Museum. This art symbol was first introduced to China through the Se people. In 1925, the Russian archaeologist Kozlov discovered an embroidered curtain from an excavation in Mongolia, which bore the symbol of a griffin, decorated with Greek pattern and

with a horn on its head. Relics unearthed in Bamiyan of Afghanistan included plaques engraved with pairs of griffins.[1] Similar
sculptures had also been found by S. Harding near Yutian.
Another instance was the Sino-Graeco-style woollen fabric found
by Mark Aurel Stein (1862-1943) from a tomb in Loulan, Xinjiang, which was said to bear patterns of winged-horses. These
symbols, which were actually the Chinese version of griffins,
resembling the image of Chinese phoenix in the shape of both
their heads and wings. After the second century, more symbols of
winged animals were used in the stone reliefs of Liangcheng
Mountain and Yinan of Shandong, but these already represented
the last phase of such art style in China.

The lion pattern was first introduced into north China before
the Han Dynasty, as a winged-animal called *tianlu* (heavenly gift)
or *bixie* (guardian against evils). At that time, lion was idolized
in both Persia and northern India as the symbol of power.
The memorial monument of Indian King Asoka in Lauryia-
Nandangarh had lion symbols on the pillar capitals while the
stone pillars of Sanchi had capitals bearing four lions. In A.D. 87,
live lions were first offered to China by envoys from the Great
Yuezhi (India) and Persia; and since then, the Chinese sculptors
had live models for their artworks. Later, following the flourishing of Buddhism, stone lions were adopted as decor for Buddhist
temples, but designed in a genre which was more Chinese than
Indian or Persian. A typical example of the Chinese-style animal
design was the recumbent lion beside the Buddha statue in
Lashao Temple of Wushui, Gansu, dateable to 559 during the
Northern Zhou Dynasty, which had a head resembling a wild
boar. There was also a recumbent deer beside the recumbent lion
in the temple, which was also a remodeled design of the crouching
deer popular in the earlier art style of north China but showed
no more trace of the Scythian art.

Another decorative art introduced from the Western Regions,
which became popular during the Han Dynasty, was the grape
and honeysuckle pattern. Grape pattern was widely used in the

---

[1] J. Hackin, J. Carl, *Nouvelles Recherches Archeologiques à Bamiyān*, Paris,
1933, Fig. 93, 94.

design of both silk textiles and polished bronze mirrors, and grape and animal pattern was then the fashion of mirror designs. The honeysuckle pattern was introduced from the Graeco-Roman art style, which was also a principal decorative pattern of the Gandhara art. The earliest honeysuckle pattern in China was seen in the mural paintings in the Western Han Dynasty tomb of Bu Qianqiu, unearthed in Luoyang. The best collection of honeysuckle pattern was found in the early mural paintings of Dunhuang Grottoes in Gansu. Such art pattern became less popular in cave murals in the early Tang Dynasty.

The image of winged-immortals appeared widely in stone murals of the Han Dynasty, primarily under the auspices of Qin and Han rulers who favoured Taoist philosophy. It became popular as the symbol of paradise advocated by Buddhists and as winged angels introduced from Graeco-Roman fables. Samples of such Graeco-Roman angels were found in the painted plaques unearthed by Stein from the Loulan ruins in Xinjiang, which were believed to be fashionable patterns in China during the second and third centuries. Many brick reliefs found in the Wu Family Shrine of Jiaxiang in Shandong, built in 147, bore images of winged-immortals, winged-humans and such winged-animals as dragons, tigers and horses. The winged image of Xiwangmu (Western Queen Mother) in stone relief dateable to the Han Dynasty could be viewed as the earliest imaginary reproduction of the Graeco-Roman culture. Among the stone reliefs unearthed from an Eastern Han Dynasty tomb in Qishan of Peixian County, Jiangsu Province, were, in addition to Xiwangmu, such strange images as snake and horse with a human head and man with a head of bird—reflecting the personification of the supernatural beings as told in the ancient book of *Shanhaijing* (*Classic of Mountains and Rivers*). When Chinese legends merged with the images of winged animals with human heads, as introduced from West Asia, there emerged in China such fairy tales as the ancient king Hou Yi obtaining the herb of longevity from Xiwangmu only to be eaten by his wife Chang'e, who flew to the moon. The fairy tale was again linked with the Indian fable of the moon and white rabbit and became an even more interesting legend, widely circulated in China.

The art of nude image which was found in the West as early as the Stone Age, had not been a part of the traditional Chinese culture. In contrast to the discovery of numerous nude goddess statues in Europe, dateable to the late Palaeolithic period, and similar discovery in the Neolithic ruins of West Asia, the only ancient nude female sculpture was found in China from the Hongshan culture ruins at Dongshanzui of Kezuo, Liaoning Province, in 1982, which was dateable to 3000 B.C. While there had been a few nude human images seen on the exterior pattern of some Shang Dynasty jade or bronze vessels, they were invariably coarsely finished. However, nude images were seen in China during the Han Dynasty, mostly on the pedestal of pottery jars, in stone reliefs or cliff carvings. Such art style had been seen on pottery of that period, which were unearthed in Shaanxi, Henan, Guangdong, Shandong, Sichuan, Yunnan, and particularly, in Xinjiang. These included a pottery piece, showing a nude human figure carrying a pot on the shoulder. The piece unearthed in Hotan, Xinjiang, pottery nude images unearthed from the late Western Han tombs in Jiyuan of Henan and the pottery nude figurine carrying a lamp unearthed from a Han Dynasty tomb in Guangzhou in 1969. But the most accomplished ancient nude art was seen only in the Xinjiang grottoes, whereas in heartland China, it had existed very briefly during the Han Dynasty, then completely vanished, probably under the increasing pressure of Confucianism which advocated strict ethical principles. However, it was a different story in Xinjiang, where, spurred by the introduction of Buddhist culture and the nude art of Brahman fables, the art style of nude images flourished throughout the period from the third to the seventh century.

The nude art boom of Xinjiang was the result of the strong influence of Indian culture. Nude bronze statues wearing only bracelets dating back to 3000 B.C. were unearthed in Mohenjo-Daro. Many semi-nude idols were found in the Gandhara and Mathura cultures. Another typical example was the Graeco-style mother and daughter goddesses found among the terracotta unearthed in Taxila. Magnificent art of nude sculpture was found in the Ellora and Ajanta grottoes built during the period from the fourth to the seventh century. Discovery of the Buddhist art of nude in Xinjiang, especially the large number of nude paintings found in the Qiuci's Kzir grottoes, was evidence of the intense reflection of the Indian art at that time in north China.

3. Paintings and Sculptures of the Graeco-Roman Genre

The first example of Greek culture introduced to China was the decorative art brought to this country by the Graecized Se people. Examples of such Graecized art were seen in the Chinese silk fabrics unearthed by Kozlov from the ruins in Noyinula of Mongolia. Then, after the Se people migrated southward to the Indus Valley, as a result of the occupation of Bactria by the Great Yuezhi, Greek-Roman culture began flowing through the Indus Valley and Kabul river region into China across the Congling range.

A number of Greek sculptures had been unearthed in Xinjiang. The earliest relic was a Medusa head unearthed near Yutian in 1892 by the Asian Plateau Exploration Team led by Dutreil de Rhins. This was believed to be one of the many Roman bronze, gold and silver sculptures unearthed in Taxila and shipped over by traders from Egypt during the first century. Other Greek relics of a later date, discovered in Xinjiang, included similar sculptures found in the One-Thousand-Buddha Cave in Kuqa and portrait carvings of Athene, Eros and Hercules dateable to the first century, which were unearthed by Stein from the Lavak and Niya ruins near Yutian. Also unearthed there were some scriptures of Hotan-Se language written in the Tocharian script of northwest India. These artifacts had obviously come into Xinjiang from India, and were later reproduced in the cultural centre of Kuqa.

According to the Chinese book *Han Shu* (*History of the Han Dynasty*), the Han Dynasty expeditionary army, led by two Han generals Gan Yanshou and Chen Tang, annihilated the Xiongnu chieftain Zhizhi Chanyu and his forces at Kangju, and captured some 150 Roman soldiers serving with Xiongnu troops during the campaign. After the Han generals returned to the capital in 35 B.C. they submitted the captured Roman literature to the Han court, which was then given by the Han Emperor Yuandi to his lady consorts for "perusal." Scholars believed this "literature" was not maps but war drawings.[1] However, some of them could be a Roman album of secular drawings not directly related to war, and that was why they attracted the interest of the Han consorts. This event marked an important occasion in the introduction of Roman paintings to China, whereby some Roman nude artwork might have found their way into the Chinese imperial court, too.

The most astonishing discovery of the Graeco-Roman fine art in Xinjiang was the Roman angelic paintings found in the ruins of a Buddhist temple in Miran west of Lop Nur. In 1907, Mark Aurel Stein discovered exquisite water-colour paintings of winged angels on the wallpanels of this ruined temple, dateable to the second or third century. There were seven such classic images of angels (cherubim) in the wall paintings, drawn after the style of Taxila temples. According to *The Buddhist Art of Gandhara* by John Marshall, the explorer of Taxila, the images were the Indian god Deva, which were painted after the model of Roman angel Eros. The painter, who used bluish pink chroma as the base, and by means of skillful perspective rendering, produced a bright colourful picture with distinct Roman genre comparable to the Roman paintings unearthed in Egypt. It was noteworthy that the carriage driven by Prince Vicvantara and his consort was painted in the shape of a Roman chariot in the picture. The nuns were also painted in Roman style. All the subjects in this wooden wall painting featured Greek facial characteristics with Levant or Circassian opulence. And from the caption written in Tocharian script on the picture, it could be seen that the painter of this temple wall art was a Greek, using the Indian-Graeco name Tita. Since early painters of the fledging Gandhara art had been trained in Greek culture, the theme of their works often betrayed a Roman genre while their style and skill were mostly Graeco-

---

[1] J.J.L. Duyvendak, *An Illustrated Battle-Account in the History of the Former Han Dynasty*, T'oung Pao, 1938, Vol. 34, P. 249; H.H. Dubs, *A Roman Influence in Chinese Painting, Classical Philosophy*, 1943, Vol. 38, P. 13.

Roman.

In architectural designs, Greek style capitals were also found on the pillars of Indian Buddhist temples built in China. The colonnade of the Buddhist temple in Miran was composed of stone pillars of Greek Doric order. Other Greek-style columns were also found in north China, including the Yicihui stone pillars of Yixian County, Hebei Province, built in A.D. 562; these pillars, having octagonal shafts and Sassanian-Persian style crowns on their capitals, were erected upon Chinese-style pedestals. Greek-style columns with concave patterns were also found in Shandong and Jiangsu. The stone pillars of the tomb of Xiao Shun, father of the Liang Dynasty Emperor Wudi, located in Danyang, and pilliars in front of the emperor's nephew Xiao Jing's tomb in Nanjing, were built resembling the Greek Ionic style—but with the Chinese traditional dew receptacles on their capitals. While the Greek-style pillars found in both north and south China had become somewhat Sinicized, the introduction of Greek and Persian architectural design to China through India resulted in their superseding the traditional Chinese ornamental columns in many parts of China.

4. The Gandhara Buddhist Art of North China

During the Han and Jin dynasties, the Buddhist fine art, which absorbed the art style of Graeco-Roman paintings to form its own ethnic culture with Gandhara as its geographical centre, gradually spread into the Xinjiang region. It followed the Buddhist religious influence and flourished in a new cultural boom first in areas inhabited by Indian emigrants and people speaking the Tukhara language. The birth of the Gandhara fine art marked the beginning of a new epoch in the Asian history of art, glorifying the vast Central and East Asia region with its brilliant feats through the centuries. In the south of the Tianshan Mountains, the boom of the Buddhist art spread along both the south and north edges of the Tarim Basin, with Yutian and Qiuci as its centre. While the art relics unearthed at Yutian were fragmentary, many magnificent grottoes had been discovered in Qiuci, retaining the best examples of Gandhara Buddhist art.

Of the 14 better-preserved Buddhist grottoes in Xinjiang today, the "Sanxiandong" (Three-Imortal Caves) on the cliff overlooking the Bashklim River north of Kashi, were built in the early third century. In the area of Qiuci, there were the Kizir Grotto in Baicheng, Kumtura Grotto and Semsam Grotto in Kuqa. In the ancient Gaocang area were the Burklik Grotto and Tuyugou Grotto in Mutougou of Turpan. Most sculptures and some mural paintings in these grottoes—removed by a German exploring team in the early twentieth century—are now kept in the Indian Art Museum in Berlin; the remaining mural paintings in the grottoes were largely dilapidated.

A few oldest caves in the Kizir and Kumtura grottoes had existed since the third century and remained open to worshippers during the eighth and ninth centuries, when Xinjiang was under the reign of the Tang Dynasty. Located 57 kilometres southeast of Baicheng, Kizir Grottoes became the treasure house of the Gandhara art in Xinjiang, which now includes 236 caves. Mural paintings have been found in more than 160 caves. In the Kumtura Grottoes, 25 kilometres southwest of Kuqa, half of the existing 100 caves contain mural paintings. The Kizir Grottoes were built over several centuries, with each phase of the construction showing a marked difference in the skill and style of the artists. Caves of the first phase were built during the third and fourth centuries in a shape similar to the Bamiyan Grottoes of Afghanistan, and their murals were crude in form. Caves of the second phase, built in the fourth century, had two kinds of murals, namely, paintings telling about stories of Buddha's *birth* on the coffer ceilings in the caves and the seated Buddhist portraits painted at the bottom of the vault ceilings. Caves of the third phase, built in the fifth and sixth centuries, had three types of murals—the coffer painting on the ceilings, the Buddhist *birth* stories painted in the lowest row of the coffers and the paintings telling about stories of preaching Buddha on the east, west and north walls in the caves. The third phase mural paintings, which were remarkable in their sophisticated skill and attractive style, represented the best of the Gandhara art in its prime. These mural paintings displayed an outstanding combination of the

Qiuci art with Chinese drawing skills in the clean yet gentle contours of the Buddhist images, seen as typical of the Gandhara art. The Buddhist portraiture in Gandhara art featured a Greek realistic style, as shown in the Greek mythological art, in presenting broad-shouldered, trim Buddhist images clad in neat floral garments. The Buddhas in the paintings were often seen as symbols of solemnity, courage and wisdom in their Greek style attire and crowns. Such a trend of Gandhara art continued in China from the fourth through the seventh century, but became obsolete in the eleventh century, when it was finally merged into the mainstream Chinese art.

An attractive part of the Qiuci art was its nude paintings —which were influenced by the Brahman ideology of indulgence —reflected the social life of the Qiuci community during the period from the fourth to the seventh century. Such Indian art scene as the Buddha Mahaisvara enjoying an erotic pleasure with his wife had also been seen in the Qiuci art. Some of the Qiuci nude art, such as the headless and armless girl shown in the mural on the right-side wall of Cave 193 and the nude female dancers painted on the inner wall of the right-side tunnel in Cave 175, were remarkably presented for their beautiful images and well-coordinated motions, as had been noted in the Greek classic nude art. As a trait of the Indian nude art, female dancers would often be presented in a swinging posture, jerking their hips sideways to stress their feminine charm; such a feature was also found in the mural paintings of the Qianfodong (Thousand-Buddha Cave) of Kizir and the Dandanulik Temple of Yutian.

The Kizir mural paintings were outstanding in their creative application of the Greek and Indian skills depicting human bodies as well as in the use of a convexo-concave presentation of images. The paintings stressed the muscular undulation in their illustration of human body by means of localized rendering, like the picture of the prince's birth shown in the inner chamber of Cave 175, which was remarkable for its creative application of the Greek classic presentation of human physical beauty. These paintings, which focused on illustrative effect, achieved a balance of traditional Qiuci art style with the realistic theme of the Indian

Buddhist art. Their drawing skills were, however, different from the Indian convexo-concave paintings which resembled the Roman Pompeii wall paintings. Qiuci paintings, futhermore, featured the traditional water-colour mixing process used in Chinese paintings which were different from either the Chinese or the Greek and Indian art. The most spectacular artworks among the Kizir wall paintings were seen as the Sleeping Buddha in Cave 110, the reclining nude girls in Caves 8, 38 and 98, in addition to the grand painting on the main wall of Cave 18.

According to a plan of the Kizir grottoes as given by Grünwedel in his book of *Alt-Kutscha* (*Ancient Kuqa*), while most of the mural paintings in the grottoes were by local Buddhist artists, some of them were the works of artists from Syria, Byzantine and India. This explained why Graeco-Roman genre was featured in many of the figures in the paintings, which showed a trace of Greek god in the image of Gandhara Brahman and also such naked youths like those on the Greek vase or males like the Pompeii Romans. In short, their art style was directly linked with that of Alexandria; it also related with that of Asia Minor. The Graeco-Roman themes of sea horse and mermaid were found in the banquet scene in many of the grotto paintings.[1] The Roman influence was still seen in such mural paintings of Turpan grottoes, built as late as the sixth century. It was seen in the Roman Byzantine attire and posture of the images in the wall paintings of Burklik Caves and the similarity between the images of flying angels in the paintings of Turpan's temple ruins and in the murals of Baicheng's Kizir grottoes. The style of the Gandhara art was also detectable in the Buddhist garments as shown in the mural paintings in Dunhuang grottoes, which was built after the seventh century. During the eighth century, Buddhist paintings of the Tang Dynasty style had become popular in religious art in Turpan and Yutian. The Roman genre was still preserved in western Xinjiang, as shown in the striking likeness between the nude dragon-maid in a wall painting unearthed in 1907 from the Dandanulik ruins near Yutian and the traditional Greek image

---

[1] Grünwedel, Altbuddhistische Kutstatten in Chinesisch-Turkistan, Berlin, 1912, PP. 125, 126, 128.

of Venus.

There were not as many sculptures among the Gandhara artwork unearthed in Xinjiang as paintings, and most of them were made of stucco, gypsum or clay. The stucco sculptures discovered in Xinjiang were the same as those unearthed in Taxila or Bègram in material, motif or design. Their roots are traceable to the ancient Egyptian bas-relief and gypsum clay moulds. Replicas of Taxila clay moulds were found in Xinjiang at Tumbshuk and Karashar west and east of Kuqa, even at places near Turpan. Such relics had been unearthed in both Karashar and Yanqi.

The popular introduction of Gandhara Buddhist sculptures in Xinjiang began after the fourth century. The Gandhara stone carvings there were often engraved upon green schist and finished with stucco and clay, many of which had a coloured appearance like the original Buddha statues in Bamian Temple of Turpan, which had coloured clay finish over stone base. Another example was the coloured clay Buddha statue sitting on a pedestal in the Kulchuk Unicorn Cave near Karashar. The statue was a masterpiece of realistic art style, remarkable in its solemn image, gentle contours and harmonial proportion. Like other sculptures found in the Qiuci grottoes it had been removed from its original site and carried away to Berlin by the German explorers. Only the following ancient sculptures still remain in the Qiuci grottoes of Xinjiang:

Six Buddhist sculptures in Kizir New Cave 1, including five standing statues and one nirvana, all in dilapidated condition;

One Buddha statue in Kizir Cave 196, eroded;

One sitting Buddha statue in Kumtura New Cave 1;

One stone core of a sitting Buddha statue in Kumtura Cave 70; and

One stone core of a sitting Buddha statue in Kumtura Cave 71.

In heartland China, meanwhile, the introduction of Gandhara art was seen far more in sculpture than in paintings. Most of the Gandhara style engraving art was shown in the grotto artworks of the Later Qin (384-417), the Western Qin (385-431)

and the early Northern Wei (452-493) dynasties. Noteworthy were the Caves 70,71,74, and 78 of Maijishan in Gansu's Tianshui and the five Tanyao caves (Cave 16—Cave 20) of Yungang in Shanxi's Datong. These Buddha sculptures, while retaining the Gandhara features, had already acquired Chinese art style with their upturning brows and decorative refinements. The last trace of the Gandhara sculptural art influence in heartland China could be found in the Northern Qi Dynasty's Xiangtangshan grottoes in Hebei's Cixian County, built in the sixth century.

During the Gandhara art boom in Xinjiang, a new art style had emerged by adapting the Buddhist art of Central India such as the bathing Buddha and some images of the Brahman art. Such an art style, as soon as it was introduced to the Hexi Corridor region, was absorbed by the traditional Chinese art and ceased to exist as an independent style of its own. However, its introduction helped to enrich the aesthetic expression of Chinese art, enhancing its decorative art style.

The art trend in Xinjiang, particularly, the Buddhist art of Yanqi and Qiuci, was influenced more by the West in its early phase, then by Chinese traditional culture in its later phase as it drew closer to the heartland of China. After the eighth century, when the Tang Dynasty restored its control over the Western Regions, the local culture became more Chinese in its art style. Then, following the migration of the Huihu tribe from the north of the Tianshan Mountains to Turpan, localization of traditional Chinese culture was enhanced by the Huihu people, who further developed it into their own ethnic culture. This was shown in the coloring of Buddha's forehead and depicting of such images in the Tang Dynasty style attire.

5. Fine Arts of Sassanian-Persian Style

The introduction of Greek and Indian paintings to China was coupled with the arrival of painters from eastern Iran and Central Asia. Their Sassanian-Persian art style was shown in the lines and style of the images in Miran mural paintings of Xinjiang. Artworks in the grottoes of Kizir and Kumtura, from the sixth through the eighth centuries, Sassanian style dominated the Qiuci paintings, as could be seen in the Painters Cave, Sea Horse Cave, 16-Sword-Belt Cave and Moya Cave among the Kizir grottoes, and in the Cave of Knights of the Kumtura grottoes. The mural painting of Eight Nations Sharing Buddhist Relics in the Sea Horse Cave in Kizir presented an all-Sassanian image of the knights, featuring a strong decorative effect. Another example was the Drawing of Rustan, discovered near Yutian by Stein, in which the image of Buddhist prince was portrayed in a Sassanian-Persian style popular in Qiuci during the sixth and seventh centuries.

The Sassanian-Persian type diamond-scale form mural paintings were the principal patterns used on the vault ceilings of Kizir grottoes during the period from the fifth to the seventh century. These patterns were first drawn in diamond-shaped squares, then overlapped one upon the other like fish-scales to produce images of human figures, animals and flora. Such a coffer-ceiling mural system differed from the Gandhara-type diamond-and-square mixed ceiling mural system, which was also found in the caves of Kizir grottoes.

Another art style of stringed pearls with birds and animals patterns became popular in Xinjiang after the fifth century, and was introduced and absorbed into the art of inland China since the seventh century. This style featured a design of linked circles formed by double lines, on top of which were pictures of confronting birds and animals, ranging from wild geese to pigs and lions, often with additional patterns of stringed pearls of the same size in circles. Such patterns were often used in the design of Persian brocade or paintings seen in Central Asia, as in the case of the design of pig-head patterned brocade found in the Balarik-Jebi ruins of Ozbekstan, dateable to the fifth and sixth centuries. Similar patterns were also seen in mural paintings of Bamian in Afghanistan and the relics unearthed from the Astana Tomb in Turpan. Brocade with neck-standing birds patterns, as unearthed in the Astana Tomb, had also been found in mural paintings in Baicheng's Kizir grottoes and on the surfaces of the unearthed Sassanian silverware. Qiuci brocade, using the Sassanian pattern since it was first produced in the fifth century, soon became the typical design of Gaochang textile produced by emigrant weavers from inland China. However, the Chinese still used their traditional plain-weaving style guided by warp, in contrast to the weft-knitted twill style of the Persian brocade. Gaochang textiles were produced with a Sassanian pattern to attract foreign buyers. During the 100 years since the mid-seventh century, brocade with patterns of stringed pearls was also produced in west China, resembling Persian brocade in both design and method of production.

During the Tang Dynasty, Sassanian-Persian gold-and-silverware was popular in China, giving rise to the emergence of many imitation products. Sassanian relics discovered in China included sea-animal-patterned curved silver bowl and high-stemmed gold and silver cups, unearthed from kilns of the Northern Wei and Northern Zhou dynasties. Another valuable Sassanian relic was a silver pot with a foreign portrait upon the joint between its top and handle. It was unearthed in 1957 along with other silverware from an early Liao Dynasty tomb in north Aohan Banner of Inner Mongolia. In 1983, a gilded silver pot was unearthed in Guyuan of Ningxia from Li Xian's tomb of the Northern Zhou Dynasty. It was believed to be a Sassanian silver relic. Chinese imitation of Sassanian relics began to appear in the middle of the eighth century. Examples included the three octagonal gilded silver cups unearthed in Hejia Village in Xi'an, marked for their Chinese style portrait engravings. The fancy designs of Sassanian gold-and-silverware were also found on some Chinese porcelain products sold abroad.

Glassware, widely produced in Persia after the fourth century, soon found its way into China. Among the Sassanian-Persian glassware unearthed in China were frosted glass bowls, convex-line patterned glass bowls and thin-necked perfume bottles. The frosted glass bowl unearthed from a Western Jin Dynasty (265-316) tomb in Wulidun of Hubei's Echeng featured three rows of oval patterns around the middle of its body. Persian glassware continued to flow into China during the Islamic era, as shown in the colourless transparent cut-glass bottle unearthed from the base of Pagoda No. 5 of the Northern Song Dynasty in Hebei's Dingxian County. Another cut-glass bottle was found under the Huiguang Pagoda of Zhejiang's Rui'an County. Both were products fashionable during the Islamic period, and similar to the glass bottles of tenth century, unearthed from Shahpur. These are preserved in Tehran's archaeological museum. Such Persian glassware had flowed from China into Korea and Japan. Some of them are now kept in Japan's Shosoin Museum.

III Music of the Western Regions

The traditional music of heartland China began to decline after the beginning of the Han Dynasty. Much of the ethnic music and dance was absorbed by the Chinese, following in expansion of the Han Dynasty and the opening of the trade route linking China with Xiyu (the Western Regions). The introduction of Xiyu music and dance greatly enriched the Chinese traditional art. The Eastern Han Emperor Lingdi (168-188) openly advocated foreign (Hu) music, sparking a boom in Xiyu music. During the reign of the Northern Qi Dynasty (550-577) and the Northern Zhou Dynasty (557-581), integration of Chinese and Hu music was further encouraged. Even greater enthusiasm for Xiyu music came during the reign of the Tang Emperor Xuanzong (712-756), when Xiyu music was officially designated as the principal music of the imperial court. As a result, the whole nation was swept by the popular Xiyu tunes, marking the complete assimilation of Xiyu music into the Chinese music.

1. The Introduction of Persian Musical Instruments and Songs During the Han Dynasty

The introduction of Western musical instruments to China first began with those from the Mesopotamia region ruled by Persia. The most popular were *konghou*, *pipa*, *bili* and other string, wind or percussion instruments. These imported instruments soon became predominant in China and played a leading role in the development of Chinese music. Then, having been fully absorbed by Chinese culture, they were remodelled by Chinese musicians into typical Chinese instruments.

(A) *Konghou*

Konghou, an ancient stringed instrument, originated in Mesopotamia. In China, *konghou* was first produced in the Western Han Dynasty in the form of a bow-shaped instrument after an ancient Chinese model. According to both *Shi Ji* (*Records of the Historian*) and *Han Shu* (*History of the Han Dynasty*), the Han Emperor Wudi ordered Hou Diao, a musician, to make *konghou* as an instrument to be used at a ceremony marking the conquest of Nanyue (Viet Nam). The instrument made by Hou Diao was named *konghou*, because such an instrument had been used by the aristocracy of the Kong State (Cambodia). It was believed that this instrument was first introduced to China via India probably deriving its horizontal bow-shaped structure from a Mesopotamian model.

The ancient Sumerians were the first to use harp to make music, and had produced bow-shaped harps as early as 3000 B.C. Archaeologists found that the earliest such instrument was a three-stringed vertical *konghou*, which appeared on the clay slab of Uruk IV (2800 B.C.). It was followed by the 11-15 stringed horizontal bow-shaped *konghou* that emerged during the reign of Ur I (2600-2350 B.C.). Horizontal multi-stringed *konghou* had been seen in Indian carvings dateable to the second century. It was later introduced to Burma (today Myanmar) where it has remained to this day. The *konghou* in China was a small stringed instrument resembling the 25-stringed *se*, designed by Hou Diao after the original type introduced from abroad. It ranked as a principal ancient Chinese musical instrument along with bell and chiming stone *qing* in the first century B.C.

Sometime later the vertical triangular *konghou* (harp) was introduced to heartland China and became one of the major large instruments there. It was favoured by the Se and Yuezhi people, evidenced by the discovery of a clay figurine playing *konghou* dateable to the third century B.C. near Hotan, and also the wooden figurine playing *konghou* in the One-Thousand-Buddha Cave in Kizir. Both had originated from the same source of the ancient harp of Assyria dateable to the seventh century B.C.[1] Their history was early noted in the stone carvings of Elamite Orchestra of Qul-i Firáun. Such vertical *konghou* was shaped like an outward-protrucing bow on its upper part and horizontal on the bottom—forming a triangular frame—with 18 to 20 taut wires strung vertically in it. During performance, it was held vertically by the player, plucking the wires with both hands. The most popular musical instrument in Persia at the time, it was called Hu (foreign) *konghou* after being introduced to the Chinese capital Luoyang. It was adopted by the Han court as one of its palace instruments, thanks to the Han Emperor Lingdi, who admired Western music. When the Han Dynasty was succeeded by the Northern Wei Dynasty, people began to call it vertical *konghou* or *baikonghou*, which, by then, had 22 wires. The word "bai" originated from the Sanskrit "Bharbhu," meaning plucking strings instead of tapping the board in performing. The bow-shaped triangular harp had been a favourite instrument of such northern tribes as the Ostyaks of Siberia. The vertical type of harps were seen in the murals and carvings in both the Yungang Grottoes of Datong and the One-Thousand-Buddha Cave of the Dunhuang Grottoes in Gansu.

Since the Northern Wei Dynasty, the vertical *konghou* was used in playing such ethnic music as the songs of Anguo, Shule, Qiuci, Xiliang, Gaochang and Korea. During the period from 589 to 618 in the Sui Dynasty, the imperial court set up its own song and dance troupes, adopting the vertical *konghou* and four-stringed lute (*pipa*), introduced from the West, as their principal music instruments. After the Tang Dynasty succeeded the Sui Dynasty, the name *konghou* was adopted regardless of shape and size, and it became a major musical instrument for palatial banquet or entertainment in A.D. 640. The size of *konghou* varied, corresponding to the features of the Gaochang music. The large *konghou* was a variation of the vertical harp, which had as many as 71 wires on both sides and was played by a musician

---

[1] J. Rimmer, *Ancient Musical Instruments of Western Asia in the British Museum*, London, 1969.

sitting on the floor. It was considered the biggest triangular harp in the world. The small *konghou* was 2.8 *chi* (96 centimetres) high with 8 brass wires, and could be carried by a musician on a belt tied to the waist. The musician plucked it with both hands in a manner similar to the way the Babylonian triangular harp was played. Both vertical and horizontal harps were the principal Sassanian-Persian musical instruments, where they were called Chang and Vin. However, they were known as the large and small *konghou* after being first introduced to China's Gaochang region. Evidence showed that the vertical triangular harp first became popular in China as early as 100 years before the founding of Sassanian-Persia; therefore, it was incorrect to say that China acquired its *konghou* from the Persian "Chang."

The *konghou* used by the Tang Dynasty folk musicians was generally fitted with 13 wires, as were those seen in the mural paintings of the Mogao Cave in Dunhuang and the bas-relief on the pedestal of the Twin Pagodas in the Lingquan Temple of Anyang. Imported types of *konghou*, both vertical and horizontal, had also been found in Sichuan and Yunnan. Near the end of the eighth century, Hu music (foreign music) was listed as a regular programme in the imperial music book *Nanshao Fengsheng Yue* (*Holy Music of Nanshao*), which recommended the use of such instruments as the large and small *konghou*, five-stringed *pipa*, large and small *bili*. The large *konghou* was used by Chinese musicians, continuously, until the Ming and Qing dynasties.

Another type of the instrument called Fengshou *konghou* had also been used in north China during the Northern Dynasties. This instrument was introduced to China from India, following the widespread use of horizontal triangular *konghou* in Indian. The Fengshou (phoenix-headed) *konghou* had a bird-shaped head at the end of its curved neck, and could produce notes of a wide range. It was used in both Indian and Gaochang music in the beginning, later employed in the performance of Funan and Biaoguo music during the Tang Dynasty. The instrument was also seen in ancient Indian terracotta figures, as a bow-shaped harp called Vipanci Vina in Sanskrit. It was later introduced to Burma, where it was called Saung-Gauk and has remained popular to this day. The Burmese instrument, which was believed to originate in Indian Buddhist culture, did not seem to have any linguistic connection with India in its name. On the contrary, the name Saung-Gauk appeared to be related to the Chinese words "Shen-gyue" out of *Nanshao Fengshengyue.*

The variety of *konghou*, which were introduced through different channels to China, developed in different forms and then found their way to Japan. The horizontal *konghou* was called kudara-koto, and vertical *konghou* was called kuko in Japan. The Fengshou *konghou* was also seen in the Buddhist painting, "Amitabha Buddha Greeted by the Holy Community," by the Japanese monk Huixin during the Heian Era.

(B) *Pipa*

Pipa (lute) orginated in Mesopotamia, and later became one of the popular musical instruments in Persia, where the short-necked *pipa* was called barbat and the long-necked one was called tanbur (tunbur). Both were seen in the Taq-i Bustan stone carvings of Sassanian-Persia. An instrument of this kind was first used in Syria. It was possibly a borrowed Greek Barbiton or lyre, but not the Greek lute called pandura. The Persian barbat was also believed to have got its name from the Sanskrit term Bharbu, meaning string-plucking. During the reign of the Sassanian-Persian King Shahpur I (241-271), *pipa* became the rage in Persia. It was known to have a wide range of musical notes and loud sound, but it had only two strings. The *pipa* introduced to China during the Han Dynasty, was an instrument which played by tribesmen of the Central Asia Steppe on horseback. Such curve-necked Persian *pipa* with four strings differed from the Chinese traditional long-necked Qin *pipa*.

The origin of the Chinese Qin *pipa* was a subject of controversy. In volume 144 of his book *Tong Dian (Encyclopaedia)*, the Tang Dynasty writer Du You suggested that it was developed from a small stringed instrument with a handle called *xiangu*, which was once popular in north China. His view was questionable, insomuch as the Qin *pipa* was a long-necked instrument from the north, probably resembling the Persian tanbur. Regrettably, a real tanbur has not been found. However, it is presumed to have had a form similar to the Chinese Qin *pipa* or its sister instrument *ruanxian*. As for the *xiangu* mentioned by Du You, it sounded more like the Arabian instrument Mizhar, which had been popular in ancient Mesopotamia. Mizhar was a kind of *pipa*, which had a leather top covering a resonance box, and looked like the leather-topped drum. A Han Dynasty story is told that when Princess Wusun set out to marry Kunmi, she carried a dowry that included a Qin *pipa* featuring a wooden surface with 4 strings and 12 columns, and that the name "*pipa*" was used widely in Central Asia to describe the instrument.[1] Obviously it was believed to originate from the so-called "Hu" or Iranian language. In fact, both the Qin *pipa* and the similar *ruanxian* of the Six Dynasties (third—sixth century) were the long-necked lute or tanbur which had been improved by the Han people; therefore, they had originated also in West Asia, but were not traditional Chinese instruments. Another Song Dynasty (960-1279) musical instrument called *jiqin* was also a variety of *ruanxian*, which, according to Volume I of Shen Kuo's book *Meng Qi Bu Bi Tan* (*A Supplement to Dream Stream Essays*), was two-stringed and more like the two-stringed lute of the early Sassanian-Persia. Since Qin *pipa* was also an instrument introduced from abroad, it was seen being used together with *konghou*, *pipa*, *yaogu* (waist drum) and other Hu instruments in musical scenes portrayed in the mural paintings of Dunhuang and Yungang grottoes. In short, there was more literature in China about *pipa* lute than in its homeland Persia.

The earliest plucking musical instrument like *pipa* was seen in ancient Persia, India and Central Asia. In India, arched harp and short-necked oval-shaped *pipa* had been popular for a long time from the second century B.C. until the eighth century, which showed that the short-necked *pipa* could have come to the Indus Valley from West Asia at a very early age.[2] The terracotta figurines, unearthed in Hotan, Xinjiang, in the early part of this

---

[1] Fu Xuan, "Preface to *Pipa Lute*" from *Song Shu* (*History of the Song Dynasty*), Vol. 19, the Jin Dynasty.

[2] J. Becker, *The Migration of the Arched Harp from India to Burma*, *The Galpin Society Journal*, XX, 1967, P. 17; L. Picken, *The Origin of the Short Lute*, *The Galpin Society Journal*, VIII, 1955, P. 32.

century, which were dateable to the third century or earlier, showed through their images that such musical instruments as Chinese bamboo-flute, drum, reed pipe and four-stringed oval-shaped *pipa* were being played by musicians. It was another evidence that such *pipa* had long since been introduced from the West to the Indus Valley. Also in the earlier paintings of the Qiuci arts, in Kizir grottoes, such long-necked *pipa* like *ruanxian* could be seen. Among later artworks there were found straight-necked stick-shaped *pipa*, five-stringed *pipa* and one four-stringed curve-necked *pipa*, in addition to the long-necked ones. More images of the four-stringed *pipa* were seen in the archaeological findings from Hotan and Dunhuang. They showed five-stringed *pipa* and long-necked *pipa* as well as the curve-necked oval-shaped *pipa*—an instrument developed by integrating *pipa* with Mizhar—a new instrument based on the combination of the Indian *pipa* (four to six-stringed) and the Persian *pipa* in the east of the Congling range.

The four-stringed curve-necked *pipa* was the principal instrument of Qiuci music. It was called Qiuci *pipa* or just *pipa*. During performance, the musician would hold it horizontally with the left arm, plucking the strings with the right hand. Both the five-stringed *pipa* and the straight-necked stick-shaped *pipa* were Indian instruments, which were seen in the third century carvings of Amravati and the fourth to eighth century mural paintings of Ajanta. The Ajanta paintings also showed *pipa* with three, four or six strings. Such Indian *pipa* was called *huqin* (foreign instrument) during the Tang Dynasty. The dragon-head *pipa* listed in *Nanshao Fengshengyue* was three-stringed Indian *pipa*. In the early Tang Dynasty, Chinese musicians were known to have plucked five-stringed instruments to make music, which marked the beginning of a boom of the performing art of plucked-string music instruments.

(C) *Bili*

Originally, a Qiuci musical instrument, *bili* had been translated into Chinese in several different versions of similar pronunciation. It was essentially a vertical wind pipe of short bamboo, fretted with reed. A double-reed wind instrument was noted in the historical records of the nineteenth Egyptian Dynasty of Turin (C. 1320-1200 B.C.), which indicated that it had long since been widely used in the Near East. Later, it was introduced to China from Central Asia and was given the name *bili*. A *bili* player was found in the stone-carving on the cliff of Xiaotangshan in Shandong Province. In Sassanian-Persia, *bili* was called Surnay, which had been translated into *sona* in Chinese. During the Southern and Northern Dynasties, there were several kinds of *bili*, including large *bili*, small *bili* and *tiaopi bili*. In Japan, there was double-*bili*. *Bili*, in the Tang Dynasty, was made of a bamboo pipe with nine holes and fretted with reed. A man from Central Asia, named Anwanshan, was a very famous *bili*-player at that time. In the Song Dynasty, *bili* was also called *touguan* (head-pipe). Reed instruments like *bili* were widely used in the performance of the Xiyu music.

(D) Drum and Cymbal Music and Songs

The Xiyu music introduced to heartland China during the Han Dynasty consisted of two parts, drum music and cymbal songs. The Han Dynasty envoy Zhang Qian, on his return from Xiyu (the Western Regions), brought back some Hu wind instruments to Chang'an, the Han capital. He also introduced two Indian songs called "Mokedole" by the Han musicians there, who described these as "horizontal pipe music." The well-known Chinese composer Li Yannian was thus enabled to write his masterpiece of "28 New Sounds," on the basis of the Xiongnu and Xiyu music introduced by Zhang Qian, to create a new generation of Chinese military music. This marked the beginning of a reform of traditional Chinese music during the reign of the Western Han Emperor Wudi. Then, Emperor Mingdi of the Eastern (Later) Han Dynasty formally issued a decree classifying music into four categories—traditional music of imperial rituals, Zhou ceremonial odes, new military music of palace drum music, and short pipe and cymbal songs—the latter originating from the Xiyu music and performed with imported instruments. Palace drum music consisted of 20 songs, the short pipe and cymbol songs numbered 22, thus foreign music dominated half of the imperial court music. When the

Han Dynasty was succeeded by the Wei and Jin dynasties, the drum music and cymbal songs merged into one and were called drum music in general. Its performance relied mostly on Hu (foreign) musical instruments, including leather drums, metal cymbals, wind and string organs and *bili*. Such music passed on to the end of the sixth century, when it was again re-modelled and absorbed partly into the new imperial ceremonial music and partly into the Chinese folk music.

2. The Collation and Promotion of Xiyu Music During the Northern Zhou, Sui and Tang Dynasties

During the Southern and Northern Dynasties, when north China was separated from the south and ruled by the ethnic nations, Xiyu culture was promoted by the imperial court. This contributed to the Xiyu music and dance boom in heartland China—in the court and in public. Towards the end of the fourth century, General Lu Guang took Liangzhou (Gansu), and in the year of 389 he conquered Qiuci, introducing into Gansu the Qiuci music, from which adapted a complete new set of songs called "Qin-Han Songs and Dances." Then, after the Hexi Corridor region—covering Gansu and part of Xinjiang—was annexed by the Northern Wei Emperor Taiwudi (424-451), more of the Xiyu music, including those from Anguo in Central Asia and Shule in western Xinjiang, were introduced to inland China. The Persian-style Anguo music and the Indian-style Shule music were added to the "Qin-Han Songs and Dances" and renamed "Xiliang Music." Since this music was mainly adapted from the Qiuci music, which in turn had originated from the northern school of Indian music, this gave rise to the predominance of Indian-style music in north China and China's capital of Luoyang. As a result, such Qiuci music instruments as Qiuci *pipa*, five-stringed lute, *konghou*, Hu reed pipe, Hu drum, brass cymbal and gong became popular in the Chinese heartland, along with Xiyu dances.

The Xiyu music boom in north China continued through the Northern Qi (550-577) and Northern Zhou (557-581) dynasties, when *pipa*, five-stringed lute and Xiyu songs and dances were further promoted. In the year of 568, following the Northern Zhou Emperor Wudi's marriage with Tujue princess, more Xiyu musicians, dancers and their repertoire came to Chang'an as part of the new queen's dowry. Under the tutelage of Qiuci musician Bai Zhitong, these Xiyu migrants soon mastered the songs and dances of Qiuci, Shule, Angou and Kanguo, in addition to many new songs of their own. New Qiuci music compositions continued to emerge after that. Among them were the "Western State of Qiuci," "All Present at Qiuci Court" and "Qiuci Land," which became popular during the Sui Dynasty. In the early years of the reign of Kaihuang (581-600), Qiuci music was the fashion across the country, and the Sui court appointed Qiuci musician Bai Mingda as the emperor's music superintendent, top position of imperial musicians. The performing skill of Qiuci's principal musical instrument—*pipa*—was further improved during this period by such noted musicians as Cao Miaoda, Wang Changtong, Li Shiheng, Guo Jinle and An Jingui with many new tunes and new songs. Several of these musicians were foreign immigrants, among whom Cao Miaoda's grandfather Cao Brahman was an Indian immigrant born in Uratupe of Central Asia. Both Cao Miaoda and his father Cao Sengnu were known for their superb *pipa* performance, winning the patronage of high officials and aristocrats. Gao Yang, the first emperor of the Northern Qi Dynasty was so impressed by Cao Miaoda's performance that he personally beat the drum to accompany Cao's *pipa* solo. Following Cao Miaoda's example, other Western musicians like An Weiruo and An Maju from Bokhara ascended to aristocracy thanks to their musical talents. The tireless promotion of musical composition by the imperial elite resulted in the creation of a variety of songs and lyrics, giving rise to another music boom in China, marked by a flowering of the Xiyu musical art. The cultural boom was, however, accompanied by a worsening indulgence in pleasure and favouritism of the imperial rulers, whose abuse of power and neglect of government inevitably led to the downfall of the ruling dynasties, leaving a bitter historical lesson for their successors.

During the reign of the Northern Zhou Emperor Wudi,

among the Qiuci musicians who accompanied the Tujue bridal queen to her wedding in Chang'an in the year of 568 with the emperor was Sujiva. He was the man who introduced the famous "seven tones" of Qiuci *pipa* to heartland China. His *pipa* music, originating from the northern music school of India, carried seven consecutive notes in each separate tune. Later, in the early Sui Dynasty, Sujiva's seven-tune scale was further adapted by Zheng Yi with the help of musician Wan Baochang. He sought to improve the traditional Chinese musical scale of five tones, and he succeeded in developing a new music structure of 84 melodies based on seven tones with a Qiuci four-stringed lute. By combining Chinese music tunes with the Qiuci tunes, he changed the Chinese tradition of setting tune by wind instrument to using stringed instrument for tune-setting, thereby revolutionizing the tradition of Chinese music and leading to the birth of the Yanyue tone of the Sui and Tang dynasties. Sujiva's seven tones, which were tantamount to China's seven sounds, could be traced to the literature of seven tunes discovered in 1904 at Kudimiyamalai of south India's Pudukkottai State. The Indian seven tunes were called madhyama-grama, Sadja-grama, Sadava, Sadharita, Pancama, Kaisika-madhyama, and Kaisika. While not entirely identical in names, they had doubtlessly shared the same Sanskrit origin, and were used to correspond to the seven Indian musical notes of Sa, Ki, Ga, Ma, Pa, Dha and Ni. According to the Indian music structure, there were five Dans ("that" in Sanskrit) in addition to the seven tunes, whereby a total of 84 new melodies were derived to form the new Chinese music structure. The temperaments of Qiuci music were higher than the Indian but closer to that of Iranian music.[1] It was, therefore, believed that the temperament of Qiuci music was formed on the basis of the Indian music temperament, but absorbing the Iranian music theory.

When China was unified under the Sui Dynasty, the govern-

---

[1] Kenzo Hayashi, *A Study on the Yanyue Music of the Sui and Tang Dynasties*, translated by Guo Moruo.

ment took steps to regulate the music system by combining all the traditional, foreign, old and new music in the country into seven categories, which, in 610 were further expanded to nine categories. They included "Qingyue," "Xiliang," "Qiuci," "Indian," "Kangguo," "Shule," "Anguo," "Korean" and "Libi." Included in the nine categories were also parts of the music and songs of Baiji, Xinluo, Tujue and Japan. Of the nine categories, six, including the Xiliang and Qiuci music, belonging to the Indian and Iranian music system. Hundreds of Sui Dynasty wind and stringed music compositions were in the Xiliang category, while an equal number of drum and dance music themes fell in the Qiuci category. Qiuci music temperament also dominated the entire nine categories, giving it a strong Iranian style. Even the traditional Chinese "Qingyue" and the ceremonial "Libi" had absorbed part of Xiyu music, using newly-introduced foreign instruments in their performance.

When the Tang Dynasty succeeded the Sui Dynasty, it kept the Sui music system and added "Gaochang," expanding it further to ten categories in 642. The ten categories were: "Yanyue," "Qingguo," "Xiliang," "Indian," "Korean," "Qiuci," "Anguo," "Shule," "Gaochang," and "Kangguo." All ten categories were listed as the regular programme of the imperial orchestra, drawing musical talents from all parts of Asia to the Chinese capital of Chang'an. In addition to the listed categories, the imperial musicians also played music like "Biaoguo" of Burma and "Funan" of Cambodia. The Tang Dynasty Emperor Xuanzong, Li Longji, himself an expert in music, re-organized imperial musicians into two departments of "standing performers" and "sitting performers." The standing performers consisted of eight parts, while the sitting ones had six. During a presentation, all the standing performers beat drums and played Qiuci music in accompaniment, while the sitting performers played solely Qiuci music. Of the 15 instruments used in Playing Qiuci music, eight were Indian and the rest were Iranian or Chinese traditional ones. The Tang Dynasty's Qiuci music band was a typical East-West combined orchestra.

IV   The Xiyu Dances and Acrobatics

1. The Xiyu Music and Dance Boom During the Sui and Tang Dynasties

The Xiyu music and dance had become increasingly popular in China since the early Northern Qi Dynasty (550-577). During the Sui and Tang dynasties, they were absorbed into nine and later ten categories of imperial music programmes of which the "Indian," "Qiuci," "Anguo," "Shule," "Kangguo" and "Gaochang" categories were entirely composed of Xiyu songs and dances. They dominated the stage in both the imperial court and in the capital of Chang'an.

In the Tang imperial court, even the ceremonial "Yanyue" music contained mainly dance music, which accounted for all its 46 principal songs and most of its 278 miscellaneous songs.[1] The names of these songs clearly indicated that they were Xiyu music, such as the principal themes like "Zhezhi" (Chaj), "Tujue Three Tunes," "Qiuci Dance," "Drunk Huntuo," and miscellaneous songs like "Moon-gazing Brahman," "Sumuzhe," "Suhexiang," "Zhezhi (Chaj) Overture," and "Western Nation's Tribute to Heaven."

Apart from the numerous songs within the ten categories, there was yet another "Faqu" music which were developed from the traditional "Qinggao Music." These songs carried Indian tunes, but were not related to Buddhist music. The famous "Nishang Yuyi Qu" (Song of Rainbow Dress and Plume Gown), which was composed by the Tang Emperor Xuanzong himself and praised widely as the outstanding work of that time, was then also categorized as "Faqu" music. The song was based on the music of Xiliang's "Brahman Song" and Emperor Xuanzong revised the words of the song in 754 under the new name, with 12 versions of stanzas (and 12 varied tunes). In 838, the Tang Emperor Wenzong renamed "Faqu" as "Xianshaoqu" and listed the "Nishang Yuyi Qu" as one of them. This song was especially remark-

---

[1] "The Notes of Jiaofangji" with remarks by Ren Bantang, published by the Zhong Hua Book Company.

able for its integration of the traditional music of the Southern Dynasties with the northern Hu (foreign) music. It symbolized the creation of a new Chinese dance music during the full bloom of the Tang Dynasty culture by successfully absorbing the Xiyu music art. The "Song of Rainbow Dress and Plume Gown" was time and again quoted by Chinese poets, as the most beautiful of all dances.

In the Tang Dynasty, music and dance became almost inseparable and were both received by aristocrats and high officials with great enthusiasm. As a result, dance flourished as a performing art and continued to develop in style and variety. Among the new dances were "Jian" (Power) Dance, Soft Dance, Character Dance, Flower Dance and Horse Dance. Some of the dances were named after their symbolic style, such as Character, Flowers and Horse dances; while others were named after the dancers' movements, such as the power dance and soft dance. The Tang Dynasty dances differed from ancient Chinese dances in both name and style. For instance, the Power Dance got its name from an Indian dance. This was evidenced by the stone carvings of Tandava Laksanam (Power Dance) in 108 forms, based on the Natya sastra of Bharata of the fifth century, which were found in the Shiva Nataraja Temple built in 1014 in Cidambaram of south India. The Indian temple dance carvings, resembling the Chinese martial arts in many ways, served as a good example of the cultural interchange between China and India. The Indian Power Dance was introduced to China either directly or via Central Asia. One of the dance music in this group called "Damozhi," described how the Indian Monk Damo taught martial arts to his pupils in Henan's Shaolin Temple. It showed that the Chinese martial arts of self-defence also belonged to "Power Dance." There were two other foreign-style dances introduced during that period, namely, the Aliao (Alai Rha) and Folin (Byzantine). Rha was the Volga River, where the Cossack-Turk residents understood the Chinese language and observed Chinese court ceremonies. They played an important role in introducing Chinese culture to the region. It was only natural that their dances of the nomadic style would be introduced to China along with Byzantine dances.

Of the various Power Dance themes, the three Iranian-style dances of Hu Teng (Jumping Dance), Hu Xuan (Whirling Dance) and Zhezhi (Chaj) Dance were most popular in both Chang'an and many other places in northwest China during the Tang Dynasty's Kaiyuan and Tianbao era (713-755).

The Hu Teng dancers were natives of Tashkand whose superb performance won the admiration of many Chinese writers. One of them, the Tang Dynasty poet Li Duan described in his poem that the "fair-skinned and pointed-nosed" dancers, wearing Iranian-style pearl-laced tall-hats and tight-fitting shirts, swayed and rolled in such dazzling movements that they "caught the hearts of all watchers." Another poet Liu Yanshi noted in his poem entitled "Watching Hu Teng Dances at Night" that the dancers "flew like birds before the wine glasses." Similar dance style is still retained in today's ethnic dances in Xinjiang.

Hu Xuan dancers came from Samarkand. They were mostly sent to the Tang court by the ethnic nations of Samarkand, Maimargh, Kesh and Kumidh during the reign of the Tang Dynasty Emperor Xuanzong. The emperor enjoyed it so much that he encouraged his favourite consort Yang Yuhuan to learn the Hu Xuan dance and perform it before him. This led to Yang's secret affair with An Lushan, a garrison commander, who was a good Hu Xuan dancer and a trusted vassal of the emperor. An Lushan later rose in rebellion against the Tang emperor and almost overthrew the Tang Dynasty. Historians say one of his motives was to seize the beautiful Yang Yuhuan to make her his own consort. The charm of Hu Xuan dance was mainly in its graceful whirling movements that dominated the dance from beginning to end. Throughout the performance, the dancer kept turning about with both feet never leaving a small round rug. In his poem entitled "The Hu Xuan Dance Girl," the Tang poet Bai Juyi described her as "whirling about tirelessly until the end of time, with such a grace as unparalleled in the human world." Today, similar style can still be seen in Uygur dances of the Xinjinag region.

The Zhezhi Dance originated in Tashkand, which was also called Chaj, hence, the dance was also named Chaj Dance. In the dance, two young girls performed face to face while stirring the golden bells sewed to their caps. The show began with the dancers hidden within a large lotus blossom, which gradually opened to expose the girls, who then danced following the beat of drums, while turning their heads from side to side and their eyes moving with their heads, and finally showing their bare shoulders as the dance came to an end. The performance was acclaimed as wonderful by the Tang Dynasty admirers.

One of the "Soft Dance" numbers was the Arabian-style "Suhexiang," which was also introduced to China from Xiyu.

2. The Hu Drama of the Tang Dynasty

Some of the Xiyu dances, after their adaptation in China, gradually developed into dance drama with their own stories, becoming one of the earliest form of dramatic performance in this country. Such a development, attributable to the introduction of ancient Indian song dramas, opened a new arena in the history of the Chinese drama in addition to its traditional form of acting-and-talk only.

Sanskrit dramas from India were first introduced to Xinjiang. This was shown in the discovery in Turpan of the remnants of three Sanskrit plays written by Ma Ming of the second century, which had already been stolen by a German exploratory team in the beginning of the twentieth century. The most important one of the three unearthed plays was the nine-act drama of *Saradvatiputra-Prakarana*, which told the story of Saradva's deeds following his conversion to Buddhism. The Tang Dynasty dance drama of Saradva had originated, presumably, from the above-mentioned Sanskrit drama which was then popular in Gaochang of Xinjiang. Buddhism-preaching dramas found in Xinjiang were not limited to Ma Ming's works. Earlier, remains of different copies of the drama *Meeting with Maitreya* in both Tukhara and Uighur versions, had been discovered in Turpan. In 1959, another copy of the *Meeting with Maitreya* containing 293 pages in Uighur version was found in Hami, which was followed by the discovery of another Tocharian version of the same drama in the One-Thousand-Buddha Cave of Yanqi's Qikexing in 1974.

The Tocharian copy was believed to have been written during the period between the sixth and eighth century, which told the story of Badhari sending his disciple Maitreya to see Sakyamuni and ask him a series of questions on Buddhist myths and doctrines, in a bid to test his faith in the religion. The story had been circulated in India for a long time before that, and was also translated into Chinese.

The dance drama "Brahman" which was also a simple drama story popular in the Tang Dynasty. Connected with the drama were two other Tang "miscellaneous songs" called *Moon-gazing Brahman* and *Monk Su's Hu Song* (later renamed *Nostalgia*), which were probably used as musical accompaniment to the dance drama "Brahman."

To link song and dance with acting was a major characteristic in Qiuci culture before its introduction to heartland China, where it was again separated into two categories. The most famous Hu play was the "Sumozhe," which meant "grassland warrior" in Qiuci. In China, it was renamed "Pohuqihan." It was the fashion to wear masks and top hats in dramatic dances called "Huntuo," "Damian" and "Potou." The Chinese envoy Wang Yande, who visited Gaochang in 981, described "Sumozhe" as a dance of actors wearing "oiled caps." "Huntuo" was a Turkish term for bags made of calf-skin, which were worn by actors in the dance. During their performance, the actors all wore animal- or ghost-shaped caps but no clothes. They danced bare-footed, while pouring water over passers-by or catching them with rope or hooks for fun. The open performance was on for a period of seven days at the beginning of the seventh month of each year as an annual traditional rite to ward off disasters and devils.

The dramatic performance originated in Byzantine and later was introduced to Smarkand as a festive performance held every eleventh month, featuring drum dance and pouring water over one another to greet the coming of winter. Such performance was first seen in heartland China in the year of 579, when the Northern Zhou Emperor Jingdi held a sumptuous dance party in his palace, allowing the Hu actors to perform a "winter-greeting dance" with water-pouring features. During that period, the Xiyu immigrants in the Chinese capital were believed to have such festive performance each year. The Tang Dynasty Empress Wu Zetian was known for particularly favouring such Xiyu festive dance, and sponsored a Huntuo dance troupe to perform regularly during her later reign. All Huntuo actors in the troupe wore Hu garments and on horsebacks. In a performance they lined up in two military formations and clashed with each other making a scene for fun and it grew in scale each time.

In the year of 705, the Tang Dynasty Emperor Zhongzong travelled to the Nanmenlou (South Gate-Tower) of Luoyang to watch the performance. In 709 he encouraged his officials to go and watch such performances. Sometimes visiting Xiyu aristocrats were said to have taken part in these performances. The event was unprecedented, winning praise from both Chinese and foreign visitors in Chang'an. Such carnival-style dance drama had, for a period, become a rage in heartland China in spite of traditional constraints until December of 713, when the Tang Emperor Xuanzong banned it in a decree soon after he had come to the enthrone. The dance drama as a performing art was also introduced to Japan, where it was called "Sumozhe" and was completely different in content from the dance drama of the Tang Dynasty.

3. Introduction of Xiyu's Acrobatics and Magic Arts

Acrobatics, which had been a traditional art in China, became very popular during the reign of the Han Dynasty Emperor Wudi. The Han ruler made a practice of entertaining foreign envoys with lavish banquets and performances, featuring a rich variety of acrobatics and magic arts. One such performance was "dulu" which was performed by Indian immigrants from Talaing in Southeast Asia, featuring somersaults atop a pole. The performances also included magic arts, such as "fish and dragon transformation," which were called "illusionary art." After this, more and more magicians and acrobats arrived in the Chinese capital from Xiyu, including those who imitated animals and legendary monsters in their performances. According to the description given by the famous Han Dynasty writer Zhang Heng in his article "Ode to the Western Capital," almost every fantastic creature or scene—from ocean monsters to land demons—appeared on the stage in the Chinese capital of Chang'an during the performance boom. These programmes, introduced from India and Persia, were added to the jugglers and magicians from Xiyu to present an increasing variety of acrobatic and magical entertainment in heartland China.

During the Eastern (Later) Han Dynasty, court entertainment also included Indian acrobatics and magic, which was described by historians as "Sheli from the West." Sheli was the legendary sacred bird cuckoo of India, where it was also used as a family name. The Indian magicians, who came to perform in the Han Dynasty palace in Luoyang, were said to turn into halibuts or yellow dragons as soon as their performance was finished. They also presented such programmes as letting two actresses dance face to face on two tight silk ropes or such magic as hiding a man in a jar and finally changing him into a fish or dragon. In the year of 120, it was said that a Roman magician from Egypt came to Luoyang from Yunnan, following an envoy to Burma. The man performed such acts as swallowing fire, dissecting his own body, changing the head of a bull to that of a horse, in addition to juggling with 10 balls. The man could juggle with as many as 12 balls at the same time, as compared with Chinese jugglers who could handle only 7 at one time.

After the fall of the Han Dynasty, the Persian Zoroastrianism and Indian Brahmanism were introduced to China. This further prompted the spread of the mystic art characterized by Xiyu magic, known as the art of "Swallowing Knife and Chewing Fire" in interior China. In the year of 448, a Persian magician was sent by the Ruiban tribe in the north of Tianshan Mountains to Luoyang. The magician told the Chinese ruler that some of his countrymen could wield such magic power as to summon wind, rain or snow at will. It was said that the visiting Zoroastrian sorcerer could perform such magic as to stab his belly and turn the knife inside his body before making a sermon. The wound would automatically heal when his sermon was finished. Visiting Sanskrit monks were said to be also well-versed in magic. In fact, most of Chinese magic arts had come from India, during and after the Han Dynasty. According to the book *Fayuan Zhulin*, Volume 61, an Indian magician visited south of the Yangtze River during the reign of the Western Jin Dynasty's Yongjia period (307-312). The man was said to perform such feats as cutting off his tongue, extending tendons and spitting fire. The book, *Notes Recollected*, by Wang Zinian told of an Indian magician from Manipur named Shilo who could produce "blue dragon and white tiger" out of his ears. Another Indian sorcerer from Pallava could transform himself into a bird or animal and throw out a man from his mouth. Still another fantastic story was told about how the Tang Dynasty Prime Minister Zhang Yan-shang met a Sanskrit monk in Chengdu, who could walk freely through fire, high water or rocks.

Throughout the Tang Dynasty, magic art was very popular in the country, and most of the noted magicians had come from India. All visiting Indian Mizong (Esoteric Sect) monks were said to know the magic of summoning wind and rain, rock and sandstorm. Some of them even took part in military scheming in battles. In the early seventh century, Mizong Buddhism was introduced to the Dali region of Yunnan. Then, during the Nanzhao period, the whole country was affected by the influence of Mizong, which was especially popular in Yunnan and Burma.

During both the Sui and Tang dynasties, acrobatics were performed along with music and dance and considered part of popular entertainment. In 606, the reigning Sui Emperor Yangdi organized a magnificent performance of music, dance and acro-batics to entertain the visiting Turk tribe chief Rangan Chanyu at the royal garden of Fanghuayuan in Luoyang, where the programme began with a hilarious Sheli dance. The masked dancers poured water all over the place. After that, it became a regular event held the first month of each year for as long as 15 days to entertain the foreign envoys who came to pay tribute to the Chinese emperor in Luoyang. The programmes were per-formed by as many as 30,000 dancers and actresses along the 4-kilometre-long avenue-stage, which extended from the Top Gate to the Jianguomen Gate in the capital. In 610, when Turk tribe chief Qimin Chanyu and other foreign leaders arrived in Luoyang to pay their respect to the Sui court, Emperor Yangdi staged another lavish show to entertain them, in which 18,000 perform- ers took part in an unprecedented variety of music, dance and acrobatic performance on Luoyang's Tianjin Street, according to the book *History of the Sui Dynasty*. At night, the street was illuminated like the day by hundreds of torches for the colourful gala.

The performances underwent some reforms under the Tang Dynasty. Tang Emperor Taizong, who was an admirer of Xiyu acrobatics, ordered nearly a hundred of his royal orderlies to dress themselves like the Hu acrobats, and learn the art from them day and night. Meanwhile, Xiyu skills were also introduced into China's martial arts. By the eighth century, even the tradi- tional "Sword Dance" of famous swordswoman Aunty Gongsun had absorbed the style of Xiyu's acrobat, instead of following its original style all through. The Xiyu-style acrobatic dance, which was first introduced to inland China during the Northern Dynas- ties, became more sophisticated in the reign of Tang Emperor Ruizong (710-712), when the Brahman dance was performed by acrobats who walked on their hands and danced bare-footed on knife blades. Some acrobat was said to lie on knife blades, while another performer stood on his belly playing a *bili*. The man underneath emerged unscathed after the show. Such acrobatic art was obviously developed by combining the Indian yoga with the Chinese *qigong* and Xiyu acrobatics.

V   The Introduction of Foreign Folk Arts and Games

1. Puppet Shows and India

Puppet shows had a long history in both China and India. In China the performance with wooden idols was used, at its begin- ning, as part of a funeral service. It was gradually included as entertainment for parties towards the end of the Han Dynasty. In the book of *Notes Recollected* by Wang Zinian published in the mid-fifth century, a story is told about an Indian puppet show, in which a magician from Pallava of south India performed a variety of shows with little actors and actresses that moved at the manipulation of his fingers. The miniature acting figures were only a few inches tall, but could perform various fantastic scenes, attracting an uproarious crowd of watchers. The Indian puppet art was soon adopted by artists of the Chinese imperial court and passed on to succeeding generations in the form of "pohou show," based on the Pallava puppet shows. The Indian puppet shows were also performed in southern China, probably in the name of "tuohou show," which was still remembered during the Qing Dynasty (1644-1911).

During the Tang Dynasty, puppet show was described as "wooden sculpture with strings attached." When Tang Emperor Xuanzong was forced, in his later years, to abdicate and live in an inner palace, he wrote a poem entitled "The Sighs of a Puppet," saying "I am like an old wooden sculpture attached to strings." In the Indian epic *Mokopolodo* (III, 30, 21), the puppet string was called "Sutraprata." Later, the puppet manipulators were called Sutra-dhara in India or "string-pullers." As a possible result of the Indian influence, string-pulled puppets became popular in the Tang Dynasty as a part of the funeral procession. After the mid-eighth century, puppet shows were performed on very high sacrificial platforms which followed the funeral procession of celebrities. When a sumptuous funeral was held for Taiyuan Military Governor Xin Yunjing, who died during the reign of Dali (766-779) of the Tang Dynasty, other military governors across the country sent delegates and symbols of condolence to the funeral. The largest sacrificial platform was sent by Fan Yang. A series of popular puppet shows were staged on an elevated movable-platform following the procession to the tomb site. After the ceremony, Fan Yang's delegates were awarded two horses by Xin's son, for their impressive performance at the funeral.

Another form of puppet show was the *panling* (ringing cymbal) show, which was also introduced from the Western Regions. Its name came from the musical accompaniment of a ringing cymbal during the show. *Panling*, sometimes also called

Lingpan, was made of brass, as was mentioned in a poem written by the Southern Dynasties' Liang Emperor Yuandi. The ringing cymbal, originated in Central Asia or India, was a musical instrument used by a northern tribe during the Tang Dynasty. The *panling* puppet show was most popular in Yangzhou of Jiangsu and known to young or old common folks in the city. As a result, high officials shunned it, for fear they should lose their dignity. A young intellectual called Du You resented the snobbish behaviour of officials, and decided to mix with the crowd of puppet-show-watchers if he became an important official himself. Not long afterwards, Du realized his ambition and did what he planned to do, bringing criticism from bureaucrats in the court. The *panling* puppet show was strongly influenced by Indian puppet art in both name and style. As a principal metropolis of the Tang Dynasty, Yangzhou had attracted numerous foreign merchants, and was naturally an ideal site for the Indian-style puppet shows.

Puppet shows were the rage in Fujian's port city of Quanzhou during the Song Dynasty (960-1279). They featured mainly two types of performances, stringed puppets and *budai* puppets, the latter resembling the Indian Sanskrit "Puttali" meaning puppet. There were, at that time, Indian merchants and Brahmans in Quanzhou, so Indian puppet shows could have found their way into the region. Also during the Song Dynasty, there was another type of the show called "water puppet," which attracted watchers for its tragic stories and its combining of Indian magic art of transformation from one creature to another with Chinese puppet shows.

2. Indian Chess

Indian chess, with a long history, was called "Four-Ranked Chess" (Charturanga Dipika) in ancient times. Its chessboard was divided into 64 little sqaures shared by two sides, each holding 16 chessmen of either black or white colour. On each side, the 16 chessmen were arranged in two rows with eight foot soldiers on the front row, while the king and raja—each sitting on an elephant—were at the centre of the back row and flanked by advisers, horsemen and warships. The game 'was played by two sides with a total of 32 chessmen. The Four-Ranked Chess, dating back to the years before the Christian era, was said to have been invented by the wife of King Ravan of Lanka in Sri Lanka. It was later called "Chantrang" in Persian, "Shatranj" in Arabic, and "chess" in Europe. The word chess was borrowed from "Shah" in Persian.

Chess was introduced to China from India during the third century. According to the book of *Lei Yao* (*Summary of Books*) by Yan Zhu, chess was described as "a game originating in the Nirvana Scripture of India," and was introduced to China during the early Wei State era (220-226) of the Three Kingdoms. Yan Zhu was wrong when he said in his book that chess was a game called Prasaka in Sanskrit, actually Prasaka referred to the game of dice-throwing, not chess. Nevertheless, chess had been introduced to China at an early age, since it was said that the Tang Dynasty Empress Wu Zetian once dreamed that she had played chess with an Indian heavenly angel and lost the game. Again it was said that in 762, the Tang Dynasty official Cen Shun dreamed that he saw a game of "elephant performance" in which the two sides each had a general surrounded by horsemen, war-carriages and foot soldiers. He remembered the moves of the horsemen, the generals, the carriages and the foot soldiers must follow precisely the same rules of chess. The Tang Dynasty chess was soon introduced to Japan, where it was called chess of the general.

Modern Indian chess was first developed in the eighth century. It was offered by Harun er Rashid to Emperor Charlemagne of Frank as a gift; and one of the original chessmen is now preserved in the Louvre Museum of Paris. European chess first emerged in the mid-11th century, and differed from Indian chess in having the "gun" as a chessman. Gun, as a Chinese invention, first appeared in Chinese chess in the 11th century when two guns were listed in the chess games described in the book *Art of Chess* written by Chao Wujiu. The chess of the Southern Song Dynasty (1127-1279) had a new chessboard marked by a river in the middle dividing the two sides, with 16 chessmen on each side, including carriages, horses, ministers, aides, guns and foot soldiers. This type of chess was already very similar to the Chinese chess today. Chinese chess was later also introduced to India, Persia and Europe. Modern European chess followed Chinese chess in including "guns" in its chessmen, since the 12th century. China and India experienced cultural exchange in their development of chess. But Chinese chess had prospered greatly in its content, following centuries of research by its experts; and it was then introduced again as part of Chinese culture to the whole world.

3. The Arabian *Shuanglu* Game

The *shuanglu* game, which originated in Arabia, became popular across Central Asia in the Middle Ages. The game was played by two sides, each holding 15 chess-horses to move along a total of 12 lines, with the white horses going from right to left and the black horses from left to right. Every move was preceded by dice-throwing to determine which side should take the first move. Each move could involve either one or two horses. The game was first introduced to the Tang Empire from Central Asia, and became a favourite pastime in the court of Empress Wu Zetian, who had often played it with her top aides, including Prime Minister Di Renjie. *Shuanglu* (game), like chess, was also introduced from China to Japan, where two sets of Tang Dynasty *shuanglu* of red sandalwood have been preserved in the Shosoin Museum. In 1973, another set of wooden *shuanglu* with metal inset was unearthed from a Tang Dynasty tomb in Astana of Turpan. Then, during the Song Dynasty, the game further developed into two different types called the north *shuanglu* and the south *shuanglu*, each having its own playing pattern. The *huihui shuanglu* of the northern type followed the Uygur pattern, while the southern type used the Guangzhou playing pattern. Additionally, there was the Nanfan *shuanglu*, Dashi *shuanglu* and finally the Japanese *shuanglu*. In his book *A Review of Shuanglu*, written in 1151, Hong Zun elaborated on the various playing patterns of the game. The rich contents of the book proved that *shuanglu* was a very popular game and had numerous patterns in China.

4. The Polo Game

The polo game, which originated in Persia, became a popular sport in heartland China during the Tang Dynasty. This Persian game had been introduced first to the Byzantine Empire and Central Asia before coming to China, and then via China to Korea and Japan. It was also adopted by India and Tibet from Central Asia. The game differed from the ancient Chinese game which was played by kicking a ball up and down a field. Polo was played by two teams on horseback, who hit the ball with long clubs and whoever knocked the ball into a bag-net would be the winner. The game was called *polo qiu* in Chinese, and the word *qiu* originated from the Persian word "gui."

In the early years of the Tang Dynasty, polo was played by Persian and other Central Asian immigrants on the street of Chang'an, where it attracted the attention of the Tang Emperor Taizong. Under the emperor's auspices, the game was introduced to the imperial court and ball teams were organized. When the young Prince Linzi (future Emperor Xuánzong) grew up, he became such a polo expert that he and three other players teamed up to play against ten Tufan (Tibetan) players and won the game. After Xuánzong (685-762), other young emperors like Xuànzong (817-858) and Xizong (873-888) were all polo fans. Emperor Xuànzong was the most remarkable in his polo skills, beating even the best polo players among his imperial guards. The successive emperors of the Tang Dynasty, including Muzong (821-824) and Jingzong (825), were also fascinated with the game. Emperor Jingzong indulged himself in the game and often played late into the night with his favourite playmates. In the end he was assassinated at the age of 18 by Shi Dingkuan, one of his polo players.

The aristocrats and high officials in the Tang court followed the examples of their emperors to enjoy polo. During the reign of Emperor Xuánzong, celebrities had polo courts built in their own estates, some of which were paved with oil to provide a smooth surface. While the aristocrats played the game on their own courts, others played polo on the street.

Polo was first adopted as a military sport in the Tang Dynasty. Many excellent players were seen in the Imperial Guards Corps. In the reign of Emperor Jianzhong (780-783), a northern general was said to have scattered more than a thousand coins over a polo court, then hit them one after another into thin air with a club from horseback, never missing a stroke. Polo was not only a healthy sport, but also the most fashionable activity for the upper class youths of Chang'an, the capital of the Tang Dynasty, during those decades. It became their major pastime, along with music, dance, hunting and cock-fighting. Even scholars made it a practice to hold a game of polo at the court of the Moon Lantern Pavilion near the palace following the annual imperial examination. Some of these academics were said to be as good as the veteran players in the Imperial Guards Corps.

Polo games in the Tang Dynasty were played by not only male teams, but also teams organized among female court attendants. Such games in the court were often played with musical accompaniment, one of which was the "polo song" played on horseback. Court polo games were played both on horseback and on foot by the royal women attendants, who even played a game called "donkey polo" in the Tang court of Chang'an.

Polo games continued to be popular during the Song Dynasty, particularly, in the Southern Song Dynasty, when the imperial court polo teams would play in the capital of Hangzhou on the third day of the third month each year. As a popular sport, polo remained a favourite until the end of the Ming Dynasty.

VI   The Translation of Buddhist Scripture and Its Influence on Chinese Literature

1. The Inception of Buddhist Scripture in China

The earliest Buddhist scripture introduced to China was in its Sanskrit version. This fact was corroborated by paragraphs of ancient Buddhist scripture written upon wooden boards in Sanskrit, dateable to the beginnig of the first century, which was unearthed in the Niya Ruins near Yutian of Xinjiang in 1906.

The discovery was believed to be the oldest Buddhist scripture ever found. Since the land of Great Yuezhi had then become the holy site of early Buddhism, the Buddhist scripture introduced to China in that period was all translated from Prakrit, the vernacular used in northwest India, called *Futu* (Buddha) in Chinese. In the year of 65, the first Chinese religious delegation was dispatched from Luoyang to Great Yuezhi where they copied 42 chapters of Buddhist scripture and brought them back to China. After they returned to Luoyang in the year of 68, they started to translate it into the Chinese "Forty-two Chapters of Scripture." While this translation itself was no longer in existence, it was quoted in an introductory article written by Xiang Kai of the Han Dynasty, which said the translation had come from *Futu*, thereby indicating it was based on a vernacular Indian version. Later, during the period from the second to third century, many Xiyu monks came to China from such Western nations as Kangju, Anxi and Great Yuezhi, bringing with them a number of rare copies of Buddhist scriptures that had already been translated into their respective languages. Furthermore, the translation was, mainly conducted through oral recital instead of writing. This was also the case with such famous early Buddhist translators as An Shigao and Zhiloujiachen who were known for relating the scripture through oral recital. There were few written scriptures available even in the Buddhist religious centre of Great Yuezhi, before the fourth century. And in the beginning of the fourth century, when Chinese monk Fa Xian visited north India, he found that there was no book to read, and the monks there depended on oral preaching to keep the Buddhist lineage to continue through the generations. However, while the doctrines were conveyed orally, their understanding differed from one to another, and the variety in language causing further divergence. As a result, there were marked differences in the Buddhist scripture introduced from different sources, giving rise to many problems in their assessment.

The Chinese Buddhists, anxious to seek the truth of Buddhism, resorted to going on a pilgrimage to the West by themselves, in a bid to obtain more and better copies of scripture on the spot. Earliest pioneer of the pilgrimage was Zhu Shixing, a Chinese Buddhist who had been preaching the *Dao Xing Jing* scripture in Luoyang during the Northern Wei Dynasty. Zhu arrived in Yutian in 260, where he collected an authenic copy of the Buddhist "Banruo" scripture in 90 chapters and more than 600,000 words of Sanskrit. After bringing it back to Luoyang, Zhu gave the original copy to an Indian immigrant named Zhushulan and a Yutian native called Mokshala, for them to translate it into Chinese. At that time, Yutian was the first port of entry for Buddhist Mahayana scripture to China. The venture of Zhu was followed by Dharmaraksha—a Yuezhi descendant whose family had lived in Dunhuang for generations. In 265, he travelled deep into northwest India and obtained 156 volumes of Buddhist scripture in various Indian and Xiyu languages. Having learned a variety of languages while in India, Dharmaraksha translated the scriptures into Chinese during his journey home from India to Dunhuang and then to Chang'an, the capital. After that, copies of Buddhist scripture were available in both Luoyang and Chang'an.

During the 400 years from the second half of the fourth to the mid-eighth century, the search for and collection of Sanskrit Buddhist scripture by Chinese Buddhists continued with growing enthusiasm. Such noted monks as Kumarajiva, Fa Xian, Dao Tai, Zhi Meng, Bao Xian, Xuan Zhuang, Yi Jing, and Bu Kong travelled one after another to north and central India, in quest of original Buddhist scriptures. Xuan Zhuang was most successful, collecting 657 volumes of Sanskrit scripture, including Mahayana scripture, Mahayana theories, and Fami lectures. As a result of the efforts of these pilgrims, the city of Chang'an became virtually the centre of Buddhist literature in China. During the years when the famous translator Kumarajiva (334-409) from Qiuci was engaged in the translation of Buddhist scripture in Chang'an, some of the Sanskrit originals were actually copies written from oral chant by visiting monks. Zankabaqin from India chanted the Abhidharma Sutra to Dharmanandi from Yuezhi, then wrote it down in Sanskrit to be translated orally by another monk Fudrosha, and finally copied in writing by Han monk Min Zhi. It is likely that many of the Sanskrit scriptures brought back to China by the pilgrims were also written copies of oral chants. After the sixth century, Sanskrit scriptures, written on dried foliage and bound in wooden folders, began coming into China in large numbers. Buddhist monks from both India and Funan brought them to proselytize in China. Chang'an and Luoyang had since become the centres of Sanskrit Buddhist literature. The centre for scripture research then began to shift from India to China.

The Sanskrit folders brought a reform to the Chinese traditional binding style of scrolls. At first it was used in popular publications by glueing the pages, in an order of sequence, upon a lengthy sheet of paper, while keeping religious literature and scripture in the folded book of a continuous long sheet of paper. This style is still used in Chinese calligraphic copybooks.

2. The Endeavours of Masters Fa Xian and Xuan Zhuang

The two most prominent figures in the history of Chinese Buddhism were Fa Xian (338-423) and Xuan Zhuang (596-664). Their selfless dedication to the religion contributed significantly to the brilliant achievements of Buddhist culture in China. As the two outstanding examples of the hundreds of pilgrims, who braved all sacrifices and hardships to seek truth in unknown lands thousands of miles from home, their deeds have lived in history long after their demise.

Fa Xian, born in Pingyang of Shanxi towards the end of the Eastern Jin Dynasty, had been a Buddhist monk since his early years. Concerned that the lack of scruples in the local Buddhist schools had disrupted the religious life of many Buddhist followers, he decided to make a pilgrimage to the holy land of Buddhism to seek the truth of Buddhist moral principles. He was 62 at the time. In the company of ten other prominent monks, including Bao Yun and Zi Yan, he departed from Chang'an in March of 399 to travel westward. Their first stop was Yutian in western Xinjiang. From there they crossed the precipitous mountain pass to reach Kashmir and then the Indus Valley. Fa Xian toured central India and arrived in the renown Buddhist centre of Patna, where he stayed for three years to study. He travelled far and wide to seek Sanskrit books of Buddhist ethics in many parts of India, while studying the religious rules and local language. Some of his companions chose to stay in India, but he was determined to return home to publicize the Buddhist ethics among the Chinese Buddhist followers. In 410, Fa Xian travelled by boat from the mouth of the Ganges to Sri Lanka, where he stayed for another two years before boarding a ship in September of 411 for his journey home. The ship, lost its way twice in the sea and drifted for a long time in Southeast Asian waters. Fa Xian, being the only Buddhist on board, almost lost his life at the hands of Brahman passengers, who blamed the "heretic" in the ship as the cause of disaster. However, he managed to save himself and the valuable Buddhist scriptures he had brought with him from India. In July of 412, he finally arrived at Qingzhou port of Shandong—thirteen years and four months after he left his home country—having travelled across 34 countries. He spent his later years in Nanjing, translating his Buddhist collections into Chinese. Fa Xian died at the age of 85 in Jiangling of Hubei.

Sino-Indian cultural exchange prospered during the Tang Dynasty, particularly, through the increasing religious ties between the Buddhists in both countries. Chinese Buddhists emerged as the guiding force of Buddhism. Fifty-two Chinese pilgrims travelled all the way to India to seek the religious truth at its original site, while only 16 Indian monks came to proselytize in China. The centre of Buddhist research had also shifted from India to China during the period, with Xuan Zhuang as the hero of the pilgrimage and study drive, marking the peak of a Buddhist cultural boom.

Xuan Zhuang, whose original name was Chen Yi, was born in 596 as a native of Yanshi in Henan. Known as a talented student in his youth, he became interested in Buddhism and travelled to Chang'an and Chengdu to visit leading monks and study both Hinayana and Mahayana doctrines. However, the more he studied, the more he became concerned with the lack of authenticity in the scriptures which were translated mostly by foreigners. He was troubled by the endless dispute among the domestic Buddhist factions and the factional strife over the religion's "leadership right." One faction asserted that such right was innate, because the Buddha was born as such; the other faction claimed such right was acquired through devoted study because the Buddha was the result of enlightenment. These concerns led Xuan Zhuang's decision to seek the fundamental truth of Buddhism by travelling to India, thereby bringing about a unity in the Buddhist schools of China. In August of 627, he left the western border post of the Yumen Pass without official permission, to begin a long pilgrimage to Nalanda Temple in central India, known as the top academy of Indian Buddhism. He travelled by way of Gaochang and Samarkand to enter Gandhara (Peshawar) through the Khyber Pass. He left Kanauj to visit more than 30 Buddhist nations in central India and paid tribute to the six holy relics connected with the life of Sakyamuni, including his birthplace, his residence, places of his first sermon and his enlightenment, his preaching site and his nirvana place. Afterwards, he stayed for five years in Nalanda Temple to study Buddhism under the tutelage of the temple's head-monk Jiexian.

During his stay in India, Xuan Zhuang engaged in an extensive study of both Buddhist and Brahman scriptures, seeking to grasp the fundamental truth in religion and philosophy through exploring all knowledge available. Not satisfied with what he could learn in Nalanda, he set out again to travel across the entire Indian subcontinent from Assam in the east to Conjeveram in the south, and from Ajanta Grottoes in the west to Punjab in the north. In 641, he returned to Nalanda Temple where he preached Mahayana scripture in the Indian language to an Buddhist audience, winning widespread praise.

Xuan Zhuang's wisdom was highly respected by Rajaputra siladitya (Prince Jieri) (590-647) of central India, to whom the Chinese pilgrim gave an introduction of Chinese politics and culture and especially the Tang Dynasty music of "The Song of Prince Qin's March," which later became a favourite Chinese song among the Indian people. Upon the invitation of Prince Jieri, Xuan Zhuang presided over the sixth Buddhist congress, held in December of 642 at the Indian city of Kanauj, which was attended by 18 Indian princes and more than 6,000 Buddhist and Brahman monks and priests. Xuan Zhuang gave a sermon of Mahayana at the congress and prevailed over his opponents in an open debate that ensued. Soon afterwards, he declined the Indian friends who asked him to stay on and preach Buddhism in India, and decided resolutely to return home for the unfinished task of restructuring the religion in China. He finally arrived in the Chinese capital of Chang'an in January of 645 to an enthusiastic welcome by both the emperor and the local people. Soon after, he gave an open exhibition of his collection of Buddhist scriptures, Buddhist statues and foreign flower and plant seeds at the capital.

After his return, Xuan Zhuang devoted most of his time and energy to translating and preaching the Buddhist scriptures he brought home from India. The work continued throughout the remaining 20 years of his life. The many volumes of Sanskrit Buddhist literature he wrote and the large number of Buddhist scriptures he translated played an unparalleled role in upgrading Chinese Buddhism to international prominence. His achievements were outstanding also in developing the idealist philosophy of Vijnanamatrasiddhisastra and Yoga, thereby sparking a resurgence of Mahayana Buddhism that had already seen a declining trend in the Buddhist homeland of India.

The twelve volumes of *Da Tang Xi Yu Ji* (*Records of the Western Regions in the Tang Dynasty*), written by Xuan Zhuang and finished in 646, were of lasting significance. The book gave a categorized account of the 110 countries which he visited and another 28 nations which he heard about, during the 17 years of his travel abroad. In India alone, he had visited 75 out of a total of 80 states across the subcontinent. In his encyclopaedic book concerning countries in Central Asia and India during the seventh century, Xuan Zhuang elaborated on the history, geography, nationality, customs, religion, language and legends of each country, giving particular prominence to the influence of Chinese culture on these countries and their peoples.

In his book, Xuan Zhuang told the story of a former hostage prince from Shule who preserved a Chinese style mural in his summer resort at Jiabishi where there was also a Hinayana

Buddhist temple; the same hostage prince named his winter resort Cinabhukti, meaning "land granted by China" to stress his respect for the Chinese nation. Xuan Zhuang noted that the Shule immigrants there respected him, because they thought he had come from the homeland of their late monarch, the former hostage prince. Xuan Zhuang pointed out in his book that peach was called "Cinani" in Sanskrit, meaning that it had come from China, while pear was called "Cinarajaputra" which stood for "Chinese prince." For a period, when there was not an authentic historical record over the Indian and Central Asian regions, the *Records of the Western Regions in the Tang Dynasty* written by Xuan Zhuang stood out not only as a remarkable geographic lexicon but also as a valuable contribution to Chinese literature, related to its neighbouring countries.

Xuan Zhuang continued his effort in promoting cultural exchange between China and India after his return. He kept a regular correspondence with his Indian friends such as Zhiguang and Huitian to exchange gifts or views and information on religious research. He also found time to re-translate a Mahayana scripture, which was out of print in India, back into Sanskrit for the Indian Buddhists. A prince of a central Indian state, who had heard about China from Xuan Zhuang, twice sent his envoy to pay tribute to the Tang court. In response, the Tang emperor had dispatched his envoy Wang Xuance to visit central India in 643. Wang, on his return, brought a message to the Tang ruler from Prince Kumara of the east Indian State of Kamarupa, requesting a Sanskrit translation of China's Taoist scripture. As a result, Tang Emperor Taizong asked Xuan Zhuang and Taoist monk Cai Huang to organize a translating team of more than 30 people to translate Lao Zi's *Dao De Jing* (*Canon of the Dao and Its Virtue*) into Sanskrit. In 647, the finished translation was delivered to the Indian Prince Kumara by the Chinese envoy Wang Xuance, who had visited India three times since 643. Prince Kumara was also known to have offered the map of his country to the Tang emperor and asked for a portrait of Lao Zi in return. The Indian prince was an ardent admirer of Taoism.

Xuan Zhuang was remembered as a great envoy in the

historic development of Sino-Indian cultural relations. He was also a great master in promoting Mahayana Buddhism in both China and India, and in seeking the religion's survival under new historic circumstances. As was aptly described by the famous Indian scholar Dr. Radakrisinan in his book *India and China*, Xuan Zhuang's name was "the symbol of Sino-Indian cultural cooperation."

3. A 700-Year-Long History of Translation Work

The translation of Buddhist scripture in China, which began in the year of 68 when Zhufalan and Zhumoteng first started the work in Luoyang, and ended at 789—when the book *Records on Translated Scripture of the Zhenyuan Era* was completed—lasted seven centuries. The lengthy course progressed from crudity to perfection and from brevity to comprehensiveness. During all that time, the dedicated efforts of some 186 Chinese and foreign translators had produced 1,095 sets of scriptures in 4,749 volumes. This did not include another 240 Buddhist scriptures in 447 volumes, which were translated during the period from 789 to 1285. Most of the translated works were Mahayana scriptures, totalling some 897 sets in 2,980 volumes; and the rest included 291 sets of Hinayama scriptures in 710 volumes and 118 sets of Mahayana treatises in 628 volumes.[1]

The massive translation of Buddhist scriptures from Sanskrit to Chinese had made it possible to preserve a major portion of Sanskrit Buddhist scriptures, which were no longer in existence in India, the religion's homeland. Thanks to the continuous efforts of translators, Buddhist literature which originally had been conveyed orally within the Indian Buddhist circles was also finally preserved in written form. All these Buddhist relics had, in a religious form, retained valuable treasures of Indian ancient science, literature, philosophy, logic and other branch of learning, providing rich materials for research on classic Indian culture.

---

[1] *Da Zang Jing* (*Tripitaka*) and *Xu Zang Jing* (*Continuation of Tripitaka*), as were published in Japan, comprises 3,673 texts in 15,682 volumes of Buddhist literature.

The 700-year-history of translation roughly consisted of three phases—the first phase of 200 years spanning the Eastern Han Dynasty, Three Kingdoms and the Western Jin and Eastern Jin dynasties; the second phase of 300 years extending from the Eastern Jin Dynasty to Southern and Northern Dynasties; and, finally, the last phase of 200 years, covering the Sui and the early Tang dynasties.

During the first phase most of the translators were of foreign origin, of whom the two most famous were An Qing from Anxi (Parthia) and Zhiloujiachen from Yuezhi. An Qing, a Buddhist scholar who had given up his Parthia princehood to become a monk, arrived in Luoyang in 148, where he learned the Chinese language and finished translating more than 34 sets of Buddhist scriptures, emerging as the most prolific translator of that time. However, his translation, while simple and readable, contained many errors. There were very few Chinese monks at that time who could translate directly from the Sanskrit, with the exception of Zhufahu (Dharmaraksa), who himself was a Yuezhi descendant. The translations were mainly handled by foreign monks, who knew little or no Chinese and had to depend on their Chinese assistants who were ignorant in both the Sanskrit and the Buddhist doctrines. The foreign and Chinese monks relied much on assumption to determine the meaning of script, and to communicate with each other. As a result, many mistakes were made in the unsystematic translations during this period.

During the second phase, extending for some 300 years from the Eastern Jin Dynasty to the Southern and Northern Dynasties, the quality of the translation work had improved through the cooperation between the Chinese and foreign monks. Their linguistic skills improved following their progress in the study of Buddhist doctrines. Representatives of this era included such personages as Kumarajiva, Buddhabhadra of India and Konarodo of west India, but Kuramajiva was outstanding among all the translators during this period. An accomplished Buddhist scholar who had studied in India, Kumarajiva arrived in the Northern Wei Dynasty's capital of Chang'an in 401 to undertake the gigantic task of translating Buddhist scriptures into Chinese under the auspices of the leading Chinese monk Dao An and with the support of the imperial court. With the help of some 800 assistants, he had finished translating as many as 94 sets of scriptures in 425 volumes during the 11 years from 402 to 413, surpassing the later works of Xuan Zhuang of the Tang Dynasty in both size and variety. The tremendous impact created by the massive translation of Buddhist scriputres by Kumarajiva was responsible for the emergence of the first group of Chinese Buddhist schools, including the San Lun Zong (Three Treatises School) and the Cheng Shi Zong (Satyasiddhisastra School). The man, who was known for his perfect knowledge of the Chinese language, emphasized the expression of true idea but not formality in his translation. He had his works polished by his Chinese disciples. Sometimes, he even used his own Qiuci vernacular in order to retain the true meaning of the original script. Kuramajiva helped his contemporaries acquire a firm grasp of basic Buddhist ideas by lecturing on his translations before large assemblies of Chinese monks. Because of his efforts, the Mahayana Buddhism was eventually established in China. His enormous contribution to popularizing Buddhism through his high quality translations was comparable to that of Xuan Zhuang of the Tang Dynasty.

The last phase of the translation history saw Chinese Buddhists as the protagonists, who were helped by foreign monks in their work. Representatives of this period, stretching over some 200 years from the Sui Dynasty to the Tang Dynasty, included Yan Zong, Xuan Zhuang and Yi Jing. All the principal translators were Buddhist masters well-conversant with both religious doctrines and linguistic skills in Chinese and Sanskrit. They stressed both truthfulness and colloquialism in their translations, resulting in a perfect interpretation of the original scripture in the best possible form. Xuan Zhuang, who devoted all his wisdom, knowledge and energy to the translation work after returning to Chang'an, distinguished himself as the most respected translator in the world. Having brought back a total of 520 folders or 657 sets of Buddhist scriptures and treatises from India, Xuan Zhuang organized a joint group of Chinese and foreign Buddhists

CHAPTER THREE 111

to engage in another massive task of translating Sanskrit scriptures into Chinese, with the support of the Tang Dynasty Emperor Taizong. From March of 645 through January of 664, his team finished translation of 75 sets of Buddhist scriptures, totalling 13 million words in 1,335 volumes. His works, such as the 100-volume *Yogacara Treatise* by Maitreya, set a new standard of quality and accuracy reflecting the achievements of Indian Buddhism before and after the fifth century. Xuan Zhuang's cause was succeeded by Yi Jing, who returned from India many years later and organized another translation drive of the Buddhist scriptures; his achievements were only next to those of his predecessor.

At the conclusion of the 700-year-long translation campaign, China had acquired comprehensive collections of Buddhist literature through the translations, needed for the compilation of a complete volume of Buddhist doctrines called *Tripitaka,* which was later introduced to and reproduced in other Asian countries, including Xinluo, Korea and Japan.

4. The Indian Touch in Chinese Literary Styles

Buddhist scripture was itself a literary creation, especially, when it used beautiful poems to enhance Buddhist doctrines and illucidate the life and deeds of a Buddha before his nirvana, as such, it had provided much food for thought to Chinese literature, whether in vocabulary, theme, style or genre. The introduction of Sanskrit language to China led to the use of Chinese phonetic spelling called *fanqie* by chanting two different characters to pronounce a third word. The Indian-style of script-chanting prompted the Chinese scholars to intensify their research into the rhyme of lyrics. In the matter of vocabulary, the introduction of translated Sanskrit expressions had enriched the Chinese language, by turning them into conventional Chinese words and phrases, such as *niepan* (nirvana), *banruo, yujia* (yoga), *shana* (instant), *heshang* (monk) and *mo* (demon). These borrowed words and phrases totalled some 30,000, all of which were connected with Buddhist concepts.

The use of metaphor was another outstanding feature of the

Buddhist script, which often sought to explain a complex philosophical idea by attributing it to various phenomena in ordinary life. In fact, quite a number of Buddhist scriptures were, essentially metaphorical Buddhist literature. Some Buddhist works such as *Zhuan Ji Bai Yu Jing* (*A Hundred Metaphors in Buddhist Scriptures*) and *Wei Mo Ji Jing* (*Vimalakirtinirdesasutra*) had been translated into Chinese, since the second and third centuries. Chinese upper class personages were the first to adopt the style of Buddhist metaphoric literature. One of these was the famous strategist Cao Cao of the Three Kingdoms. In one of his best-remembered poems, Cao Cao characterized his feeling in this metaphoric expression: "Life of man has days but so few; for it glitters—only to vanish like the morning dew!..."

The direct translation of Sanskrit Buddhist scriptures into Chinese had created a new literary style, which differed markedly from the traditional style of Chinese writing in such aspects as the former's frequent use of inversions and noun modifiers, listing a variety of sentences of the same case for contrast and mixing poems with commentaries in the same piece of writing. In short, Buddhist writings stress on proselytizing through simple and readable script which led to the emergence of a colloquial writing style, different from the traditional Chinese way of writing. Such a new literary style was first introduced to China through the Buddhist translations by Kumarajiva. Early Chinese colloquial literature was confined to folklore, but a new tide of such folk literature appeared during the Tang Dynasty, when many monks composed colloquial writings based on scriptures for preaching to their audiences. This new style of Chinese folk literature—*bianwen*—whose earliest examples are found in the *Xiang Mo Bian Wen* (*Colloquial Scripts Based on Subduing of Demon*) and *Vimalakirtinirdesasutra* preserved in the Dunhuang Grottoes of Gansu. The latter was written in 947. *Bianwen*, as a new literary style, first emerged in dramatic scripts used by lyric-singers in their performances. The best-known of such performers was Seng Wenxu who became popular in the reign of Emperor Wenzong (826-840) of the Tang Dynasty. Seng's singing was said to be so moving that Emperor Wenzong, himself a lover of wind-instrument, composed a song after the singer's tune called "Wenxu's Song." A *bianwen* was, in essence, a Buddhist story adapted into a readable lyric piece by using the Indian-style; a 30-word script in the original could be extended to a 3,000 to 5,000-word story. In order to appeal to a wider audience, the writer of a *bianwen* could sometimes overstep religious bounds to add secular anecdotes into the Buddhist story. Examples of this kind of mixed *bianwen* included the *Wu Zixu Bianwen*, focusing on a romance of the Spring and Autumn period, and the *Wang Zhaojun Bianwen*, telling the story of a Han Dynasty court maid, who was married to a foreign khan by order of the Han emperor. *Bianwen* was officially banned at the end of the tenth century, but reappeared in an altered form in the Yuan and Ming dynasties as musical stories, which further developed into the modern lyrics to be told by performers with music accompaniment.

Ghost stories became popular in China after the Jin Dynasty and during the Southern and Northern Dynasties. Many of them were taken from the Buddhist legends but rewritten into narratives by the writers. However, most of these stories retained their themes and writing-style as Buddhist stories. For instance, the story of "Yang Xian and His Goose-Cage" from the book *A Continuation of Qi Xie Records* written by Wu Jun (469-520) of the Liang Dynasty was quoted from the Jin Dynasty's *Book of Spirits and Ghosts* by Gou Shi, who had originally rewritten the story out of a Sanskrit legend told in *Old Metaphors in Buddhist Scriptures* as translated by Kang Senghui. The original story was an old Indian fable. There was also Chinese fiction written to substantiate the Buddhist idea of cause-and-effect pattern of human life. Included were the *Story of an Innocent Soul* by Yan Zhitui and *Posthumous Fortune* by Wang Yan. It was in the Tang Dynasty that the Chinese legendary literature finally freed itself from the Buddhist influence and developed a style and artistic conception of its own. Nevertheless, the growth of Chinese legendary literature had certainly been affected by the Indian literary trend.

VII   The Introduction of Science and Technology from Egypt, Persia and Arabia

1. Persian Armour Widely Adopted Across China

Persia was among the earliest nations to use interlocking metal rings and plates to protect its soldiers and horses in battles. And such Persian-style mail was introduced to China as early as the second or third century. During the third century, the mail was brought to the Chinese heartland from Xinjiang and used by the military leaders to armour their cavalry. Cao Cao, the founder of Wei Kingdom, one of the Three Kingdoms, was known to have given a set of the interlocking-ring mail to his son Cao Zhi. Mail was, at that time, already widely used in Qiuci and other northern nations in the Xinjiang area. When the Jin Dynasty general Lü Guang led an expeditionary army to conquer Qiuci in 382, he found that the arrows of his archers could not penetrate the mail worn by the Qiuci cavalry. Mail was produced in heartland China during the Tang Dynasty, but was not widely used by the military and ranked the 12th in its ordnance system. However, the troops of the northern nations in Xinjiang began adopting the Persian-Sassanian style mail since the sixth century, which featured an openable chest and a fan-shape knee-covering skirt. Such Central Asian cavalry mail was seen in use in the Xinjiang area until the 20th century.

Cavalry was widely used in China since the Qin Dynasty. And in the early third century, the Later Han warlord Yuan Shao equipped 300 of his fighting horsemen with Persian-style mail to boost their combat strength. Then, during the war period involving 16 tribal states (304-439), tens of thousands of northern cavalry troops fought with armoured men and horses. Evidences of such developments were found in the murals and figurines of armoured cavalry and horse mail, unearthed from a mid-fourth century Eastern Jin Dynasty tomb located in Yuantaizi of Liaoning Province's Chaoyang. The murals, believed to be the earliest of its kind, showed a horse clad with interlocking mail made of diamond-shaped metal rings. Other similar relics unearthed included a mural in the tomb of Huo Chengci dateable from the reign of Taiyuan (376-398) in the Eastern Jin Dynasty and also the horsemen figurines in No. 1 Tomb of Xi'an's Caochangpo, dateable from the Eastern Jin Dynasty. More figurines of such type had also been found in the tomb of the Northern Wei, Eastern Wei, Northern Qi and Northern Zhou dynasties, Similar images were found in the brick carvings in the tomb of Chen Chaoda located in Danyang of Jiangsu, which was dateable from the mid-sixth century, when horse mail was believed to be widely used across China to as far south as Yunnan. In fact, the Nanzhao State of Yunnan was a country using mail cavalry during the late eighth century, according to Volume 10 of *Man Shu* (*Book of the Barbarians*). History also showed that horse mail in the Tang Dynasty was also introduced partly from Sassanian Persia, which were called "die xie" (plate mail) or "xin ye" (apricot leaf).

China and its northern nomadic neighbours had been in constant exchange on the use and development of harness, leading to the emergence of the complete set of harness during the period from the third to the fifth century. Such development, particularly, the invention and improvement of saddle and stirrups had played a significant role in upgrading the riding skills of horsemen. The earliest leather strap stirrups were seen in a late second century B.C. sculpture in the Great Tope at Sanchi of India, as well as in the engraved image upon a large Scythian silver vase unearthed from the Chertomrik Tomb in the lower reach of the Dnieper River, which was dateable from the fourth century B.C. However, the earliest single stirrup was the one seen in the terra cotta figurine of a horseman, unearthed from a tomb dating back to the second year of Yongning reign (302) during the Western Jin Dynasty, located in Changsha of Hunan. It was believed that the usefulness of stirrups was then widely recognized by the Chinese, who quickly put them into practical use across the country. In 1974, a metal stirrup, believed to be the earliest of its kind dateable to the Jin Dynasty, was unearthed in a Jin tomb at Anyang's Xiaomintun in Henan. Another metal stirrup linked with a saddle, found in a painting on a cliff in Yinshan of Inner Mongolia, could possibly date from an even earlier period. In

1982, another pair of painted leather stirrups with wooden cores were found in an Eastern Jin Dynasty tomb located in Chaoyang's Yuantaizi of Liaoning. The loops were probably made of rattan.[1]

The invention of the stirrup was an advantage, especially, to the heavily-clad cavalrymen and their horses clad in saddles and mail; hence, it was rapidly introduced across the continents. Hungary was the first country to have the stirrup in Europe, which was possibly introduced from China through the ethnic Rouran tribesmen, who began emigrating to the west since the fifth century.

2. Glass-Making Based on Egyptian Prescription

Levant on the eastern Mediterranean coast and Alexandria of Egypt were the two industrial centres of glass-making during the reign of the Roman Empire. From the beginning of the first century, when the cost of glass-making dropped, as a result of the introduction of glassblowing device, new glass products flooded the market and the Roman glassware predominated the trade because of their rich variety and clourful designs. The Roman glassware found its way to China through India during the Han Dynasty, giving the Chinese buyers the impression that the imported glass products had come from India. A story was told in the book *Xi Jing Za Ji* (*Misce llaneous Records of the West Capital*) that Emperor Wudi of the Han Dynasty had once received a gift from India in the form of a white transparent saddle, which lit a dark room with its light to a distance of 30 metres. Another story in the book said that India also gave the emperor a crystal jade platter, which looked pure as ice but broke when dropped on the floor. In fact, such glass objects were, then, produced in Egypt only.

Following the opening of a maritime trade route to the East, Roman glassware shipments tended to come directly to China's southeast coast by way of south India. That was why a large

---

[1] Lynn White, *Medieval Technology*, (D. L. Mongant, Archaeology in the CCCP), Moscow, 1955.

number of Roman glass relics had been unearthed in south China by archaeologists. The earliest of such glassware, thus far confirmed, included the three mould-cast blue-purple polished glass bowls found in a middle Western Han Dynasty tomb located in Guangzhou's Hengzhigang. Another sodium-calcium glass bowl was found in an Eastern Han Dynasty tomb located in Guixian County in Guangxi. Also unearthed from another Eastern Dynasty tomb in Hanjiang County of Jiangsu was the remnant of a Roman stir-cast glass pot with vertically-lined exterior finish, which was known as a popular pattern in the Mediterranean area at the turn of the first century. And from the Eastern Jin Dynasty tombs, located in Nanjing, polished Roman cylinder-shaped glass cups had been discovered several times. These skillfully-polished glassware corroborated the classic records about the use of transparent glassware by local noble and wealthy families during that period in southeast China. But of all such imported glassware, the most popular was the white transparent glass products from Egypt, which had been described as "jade crystal" or "water crystal" since the Han Dynasty.

Egypt's Alexandria, as the centre of Roman glass-making industry, had played a pivotal role in the oriental trade. It became the terminus of the maritime "Glass Route" leading from the Red Sea to Jiaozhou (northern Viet Nam) which was, then, the southernmost territory of the Jin Dynasty. According to the third century Chinese book *Guang Zhi*, the glass trade route then linked the four countries of Rome (the glass producer), Sri Lanka, Conjeveram of India and Cambodia, before ending in China. Its first stop was at Adulis of Axum or Kane of Yemen, which was then a port of Eleazos Kingdom, located some 3.5 kilometres to the southwest of today's Bir Ali Village. It was in this village that the British archaeologist Jervase Mathew unearthed many glass shards in 1961, the oldest of them dateable from the second century B.C. Farther east, it stopped at Sri Lanka and Conjeveram State in India's Coromendel, where a systematic excavation, beginning from 1937 and through 1948, had unearthed many pieces of Roman pottery and glassware at a location called Poudouke by the Greeks. The trade route's third stop was at Oc-Eco in Longsam of Cambodia, where Roman glassware and sculptures had also been unearthed. After Cambodia, the trade route finally reached its destination—China.

The imported Roman glassware was highly attractive to the Chinese for their sophisticated manufacturing skills, such as polishing, cutting, moulding or raised design and pattern impression—at a time when China was beginning to develop its glass-making industry. The Chinese started making glass during the Han Dynasty, producing some glassware with a silica content of more than 10 percent; but such products were not transparent despite their fine quality. Therefore, they were anxious to learn the glass-making skill from the Romans, especially the technique in making transparent "crystal bowls." In the third century, some Chinese people in the southern coastal area had succeeded in imitating the Roman technique to produce such transparent glass bowls. Many people in south China's Jiaozhou and Guangzhou had learned how to produce transparent crystal bowls "by using a mixture of five kinds of powders." The prescription of five elements for making glass was, first introduced to the coastal areas of Jiaozhou and Guangzhou, which had direct link with Rome through the oversea trade route. The five elements were the five components of the Egyptian glass, namely, silica, soda, lime, magnesium and aluminum oxide.[1] Such a prescription indicated that glass-making had turned from using the lead-and-barium composition to adopting the sodium-and-calcium composition. Similar imitation of the Roman was also made in the design and finish of the glassware. The variety of glass products produced in Guangdong and Guangxi—as shown by the many relics unearthed—had gradually shifted from such traditional Chinese articles as plaque, ring, seal and ornament to household utensils as bowls and trays since the first century B.C.

Another important feature in the development of glass-making in south China was that some raw materials used in producing the sodium-calcium glassware might have been imported from Rome. The classic book *The Periplus of the Erythraean*

---

[1] B. Neumann, G. Kotyga, Antike Gläser, 1925. Earle R. Caley, *Analysis of Ancient Glasses* 1790-1957, Corning, 1962.

Sea, New York, 1912, p. 45, had mentioned that unprocessed "crude glass" had been shipped to the Orient. An evidence of this was found in the discovery of a glass plate from the tomb of Prince Nanyue located in Guangdong. In the making of sodium-calcium glass, it was necessary to use soda ash (Na_2CO_3) or plant ash (K_2CO_3) as the solvent; and the soda ash had to be imported. In fact, the glass-making process, which was introduced to south China during the period from 220 to 420, had depended on imported raw materials. Therefore, the industry could not survive in the long run; and even the technique was lost in the end.

Despite its failure in south China, renovation of China's glass-making industry had registered new success in the north, thanks to its reliance on indigenous materials. This success was regarded as a historic evidence showing the introduction to China of India glass-making technique in the fifth century. It is described in *Wei Shu* (*History of the Wei Dynasty*). A merchant from Great Yuezhi in India came to China during the reign of Wei Emperor Shizu (424-452) and taught the people of Pingcheng (now Datong) to make coloured glass with local minerals. Their products were said to be better than the glittering glassware imported from the West. The people of Pingcheng eventually built a shiny "glass palace" in the city with their own products.

The continued production of glassware in north China led to a drop in the price of glass in the area, according to the book. As a result, these transparent glass products were no longer viewed as valuable rarity in heartland China. Recent archaeological discoveries showed that such glassware was produced with the mouldless glass-blowing technique introduced from Great Yuezhi, as was told in the book. Typical examples included seven glass bowls and bottles unearthed from the stone base of a Northern Wei Dynasty pagoda in Dingxian County of Hebei.[1]

The glass bottle was remarkable for its Western-style ornate circular trimming at the bottom, which was considered a new skill unseen in previous discoveries. Archaeologists believed that these

---

[1] Hebei Provincial Cultural Bureau Working Team, "The Northern Wei Dynasty Stone Case Unearthed in Dingxian County of Hebei," *Archaeology Journal*, 1966, Issue No. 5, PP. 252-259.

glassware were products of a royal glass-making shop and given to the Buddhist pagoda as offerings by the Northern Wei's imperial court.[1]

Archaeologists have verified through chemical analysis that three out of the eight indigenous glass pieces unearthed from Li Jingxun's tomb of the Sui Dynasty were made of sodium-calcium glass; and so were two out of the four indigenous pieces found in Li Tai's tomb of the Tang Dynasty. These proved that there had been production of such glassware in China since the Sui Dynasty. It was presumed that such production in north China had used local plant ash as solvent in the glass-making process. Unfortunately such technique also got lost in ensuing era, leading to the emergence of "green porcelain," which was a kind of high-aluminum glass—with an aluminum oxide content of over 60 percent—invented by He Chou to fit in with the blowing process. Such a development was apparently a result of the convergence of domestic and Western glass-making techniques.

3. The Introduction of Medicine from Arabia and Persia

Arabian medicine made its entry into China in large quantities during the Tang Dynasty. Opening of a maritime trade route further bolstered the influx of drugs to China from both the Arabian and Southeastern Asian regions. The drug and herb traders consisted mainly of Persian merchants. One of them was a naturalized Chinese merchant of Persian origin called Li Susha, who was known for his wealth and his offering of the valuable aromatic drug *chen xiang ting zi* to Emperor Jingzong of the Tang Dynasty in 824. Later, in the turbulent era of the Five Dynasties, more people became known for their dealings in drugs or aromatics and the study in alchemy. They included Wang Shu and the brothers Li Xuan and Li Xian, who were of Persian parentage. The Tang Dynasty official pharmacopoeia, *Xin Xiu Ben Cao* (*Revised Materia Medica*) and *Ben Cao Shi Yi* (*Materia Medica Addenda*), both listed many foreign drugs in their contents. Then

[1] Xia Nai, "Persian-Sassanian Silver Coins from the *Sarira* Case in the Pagoda Base of Dingxian County, Hebei," *Archaeology*, 1966, Issue No. 5, P. 269.

a special book of foreign drugs came out during the reign of Emperor Xuanzong of the Tang Dynasty, namely, the *Hu Ben Cao (Hu Materia Medica)* in seven volumes by Zheng Qian. And in the final years of the Tang Dynasty, Li Xun's book *Hai Yao Ben Cao (Overseas Materia Medica)* in six volumes also emerged, which contained only imported medicinal items, indicating there were a great many foreign drugs available in China at that time.

Li Xun's book, though its original version could not be found, was widely quoted in other classic writings, indicating it has listed at least 124 kinds of foreign drugs. Li was believed to have studied the Arabian pharmacopoeia before writing his own book. A classic story had it that the famous Islamic physician Razi (865-925) had helped a visiting Chinese scholar in Bagdad study the works of ancient Roman medical master Claudius Galen (129-199); the Chinese scholar finished reading the Arabic translation of the Roman master's works in three months, then returned to his homeland with the book. Judging from the historic background of this story, the Chinese scholar could very well be the bilingual Chinese pharmaceutical expert Li Xun.

Despite the rich resources of Chinese traditional medicine, the Chinese appreciated the medical knowledge of the Arabs and Persians and tried to obtain as many prescriptions from them as possible. A number of foreign prescriptions were found in such leading medical literature of the fourth and fifth centuries in China as the *Wai Tai Mi Yao (Medical Secrets Held by an Official)*, the *Qian Jin Yao Fang (The Thousand Golden Formulae)* and the *Qian Jin Yi Fang (Supplement to the Thousand Golden Formulae)*. A prescription given in Volumes 30 and 37 of *Wai Tai Mi Yao* said that drinking a dose of one litre of boiled aniseed juice three times a day could cure such severe disease as malignant tumour, diarrhoea or subcutaneous ulcer on the back, while applying the dry leftover of the juice upon the swelling on the body. The book also said this prescription had been used with "miraculous effect" on many such patients since the Yongjia era (307-312). Listed in Volume 12 of *Qian Jin Yi Fang* was a Persian prescription of *Bosantang* or Milk Tonic which was made by putting half a Chinese ounce of the ground powder of *bibo* herb into a cotton packet, and boil it in three litres of milk; the finished dosage should be drunk by the patient once or twice a day, before meals. A cure or healing could be expected in seven days. This prescription was popular in both Persia and Byzantine.

The drugs and prescriptions introduced from abroad were widely accepted by the Chinese people and became part of the Chinese medicine, thereby forming a closer tie between the development of Chinese traditional medicine and the supply of imported resources.

VIII   Science and Technology Introduced from India

1. The Nine-Volume Calendar and Gautama

The rulers of China's Sui and Tang dynasties were very interested in the Indian experience in astronomical research and calendar system. In India astronomy was called "jyotisha vidya" and closely related with astrology. The book *History of the Sui Dynasty* listed Chinese translations of Indian astronomical and calendar literature totalling 60 volumes in seven categories, 21 volumes of Brahmasiddhanta and 30 volumes of Gargi-sanhita. After the Sui Dynasty proclaimed the official calendar of "Kai Huang Li" in 584, progressive Chinese astronomers Liu Xiaosun and Liu Zhuo tried to correct its errors by introducing the lunar system and annual intercalation. However, it was in 665 that the lunar calendar was formally adopted, when the "Lin De" calendar designed by another astronomer Li Chunfeng was promulgated. Li's calendar still had many shortcomings in its computation of the lunar cycle, and also in his ignorance of the error of annual intercalation. The inadequacy of the Chinese ancient calendars led to the introduction of the Indian system in the late seventh century. Since then, Indian astronomer Gautama and four generations of his descendants had served in the Tang Dynasty's "Sitiantai" (Astronomical Observatory) as the general astronomer, continuously for over 110 years. The post had, therefore, won the title of Gautama General.

Gautama, as a Tang Dynasty official, offered a copy of the

nine-volume Indian calendar to the Tang emperor, who agreed to use it as a supplement to the Chinese "Lin De" calendar, marking the first instance of an Indian calendar being introduced to China. In 698, when the imperial court wanted to reset the title of the reign, the young Gautama was asked to compile a new calendar called "Guang Zhai Li," but it proved to be a failure and was abolished after only three years and replaced again by the old "Lin De" calendar. However, the Tang court still wanted to learn more about the Indian calendar system and ordered Gautama to translate the Indian nine-volume calendar into Chinese. The finished translation was then included in the book *Kai Yuan Zan Jing (Kai Yuan Classic on Astrology)* edited by him. During this period, the errors of the official "Lin De" calendar had become more apparent, and the Tang imperial court decided in 712 to let the celebrated astronomer Monk Yixing (originally named Zhang Sui) compile a new calendar "Da Yan Li," based on the lunar-solar cycle. The new calendar was completed in 727, but Monk Yixing died in the same year. Next year, the "Da Yan" calendar was officially promulgated to be the national standard, and so it remained for many centuries.

In his compilation of the "Da Yan" calendar, Monk Yixing had adapted a part of the Indian calendar, quoting them in two of the 52 volumes in his new calendar. This had, nevertheless, created a misconception among some Indian astronomers, including Gautama who was said to have jeered at the "Da Yan" calendar, saying that it was a poor imitation of the Indian calendar. The truth was, however, Monk Yixing had absorbed only the useful part of the Indian system and given up its erroneous or useless parts, while adhering to the basic principles of the "Lin De Li" in following the calculated rules of the lunar-solar cycle. As a result, the new calendar—while still containing many shortcomings in its annual intercalation and its estimation of the celestial movement—was, nonetheless, far superior to either the "Lin De" calendar or the Indian calendar. According to an astronomical observation recorded in 733, the accuracy rate of the "Da Yan" calendar was close to 80 percent, while it was only some 40 percent for the "Lin De" calendar and less than 20 percent for the Indian nine-volume calendar. This was evidence showing that the Chinese astronomers had succeeded in achieving continued advancement in their country's calendar system by integrating their own creation with technical skills introduced from abroad.

2. Indian Medicine and Longevity Drugs

China had long since been respected for its well-developed medicine. Early in the third century, the famous doctor Hua Tuo invented the anaesthetic called "Mafeisan," which, when inhaled by the patient, would make him lose consciousness, enabling the surgeon to operate on him. Although the prescription was later lost, it might be presumed that the drug was derived from the herb *da ma* (hemp) or Cannabis sativa seeds. Hemp was a native plant in China and was called bhanga in Sanskrit. According to B. Laufer, the plant was later introduced to Persia, where it was called bang, meaning an anaesthetic made of hemp seeds. There was another Persian word "sabili" which meant intoxicating hemp seeds. All of these were related with the Chinese ancient prescription.

During the Tang Dynasty, Chinese medicine continued to enjoy a favourable reputation abroad. When the Chinese monk Yi Jing visited India, he was gratified to hear the Indians praise the excellence of Chinese medicine. Nevertheless, the Chinese doctors had always been interested in learning from the skills of Indian doctors and absorbing their best prescriptions. They translated seven books of Indian prescriptions into Chinese in the Sui Dynasty, among which was the medical literature written by the famous Indian physician Charaka. The fame of the Indian ophthalmology had early been known to the Chinese in the Tang Dynasty. In a poem dedicated to the Indian ophthalmologist Brahman, the Tang Dynasty poet Liu Yuxi tells how he became blind in middle age but regained his eyesight, thanks to the treatment by the Indian doctor. Another Indian medicine known in China was a tonic prescription called Vakuci in Sanskrit, based on a herb of the same name grew in both India and Sri Lanka. According to the prescription, mixing ten ounces of Vakuci and

20 ounces of walnut meat with wine and taking it regularly could make one stronger, live longer and help prevent rheumatism. The prescription, introduced to Guangzhou by a Javanese merchant-ship captain called Li Moco in 812, was believed very useful to the local residents of southern China's humid region.

But what interested the Tang Dynasty rulers most was the Indian medicine of "longevity" (Rasayanatantra) which consti-tuted one of the eight components of the Indian medical struc-ture. Rasayana was described as a drug that could make a person live forever, a blessing which had been craved by all the Tang emperors. Having tried in vain to realize their dream through the help of Taoist alchemy, these monarchs now turned to Indian drug for longevity. In 648, the Tang envoy Wang Xuance returned from his second visit to India, bringing back with him the Indian alchemist Narayanasvamin to Chang'an. Upon the order of Emperor Taizong of the Tang Dynasty, a Sino-Indian pharmaceutical team headed by Narayanasvamin was organized to prepare the longevity drug under the super-vision of the minister of war Cui Dunli. Their effort failed and the Indian alchemist later died from old age in the Chinese capital. After Emperor Taizong died, his son Gaozong came to the throne. The new emperor again sent a visiting Indian monk back to India to find the drug of "long life" for him. Decades afterwards, when Emperor Xuanzong was enthroned, the young monarch, a believer of Taoist immortality, tried by every means to find the drug of longevity. In 716, a Tang envoy was sent by Xuanzong to Sri Lanka to search for the longevity drug. When the news spread to the neighbouring countries, rulers of Kapica, Kashmir, Tukhara and other nations began to send their special envoys, offering all kinds of rare drugs or pres-criptions to the Tang Dynasty court. In 729, a north Indian monk even brought with him an aphrodisiac (vajikarana) called *zhi han* in Chinese to the Tang imperial palace. Most of the longevity drugs had originated from either the Indian subcon-tinent or Afghanistan, a country which was known for the long life of their people.

3. The New Creative Buddhist Architecture

In the history of architecture, the design of religious structure had seen the most ambitious development in China. Most of the new structures belonged to religions of foreign origin, especially Buddhism. Ever since Buddhism was introduced to China, the construction of grottoes became the rage in Xinjiang as well as in northern China. These cave structures, which could last for a long time in dry desert or hilly regions, comprised mainly two kinds: the shrine (chaitya) and the monastery (vihara). The design of temple buildings had also followed the Indian pattern in the beginning. However, the structure of pagodas, which had originated from the Indian stupa, had seen remarkable developments. The Indian stupa (thupa in Sanskrit) was originally built to preserve Buddhist relics. The first of these was said to have been erected in the third century B.C. at Sanchi, in the shape of an overturned bowl resembling a Chinese mud-grave. Then in the first century B.C. a huge stupa was built at the site of Sakyamuni's enlightenment in Budagaya, in a radically new shape. The five pagodas built upon a square platform in Beijing's Wutasi Temple (Temple of Five Pagodas) were basically an imitation of the ancient Budagaya stupa in India. But since their introduction into China, the design of such stupa structure had undergone a major evolution to assume a characteristic Chinese style. With exception of a small number of Buddhist relic pagodas, which still retained the original Indian style, most of the new structures had departed completely from the square-based or semi-circular Indian design to become typical Chinese highrise towers. And these attractively-designed religious structures soon mushroomed all over China, as evidences of the inherent ingenuity of Chinese architects.

The earliest type of Chinese-style tower structures was the multi-storied wooden pagoda, represented by the Baimasi (White Horse Temple) Pagoda in Loyang built in the Eastern Han Dynasty, the Yongning Temple's seven-storied pagoda in Datong built in 467 during the Northern Wei Dynasty and the Yongning Temple's nine-storied pagoda in Loyang built also during the

Northern Wei Dynasty in 516. The Yongning Temple Pagoda in Loyang, which totalled 1,000 Chinese *chi* (330 metres) high. Brick pagodas began to appear in China during the sixth century. The oldest and most spectacular structure was the Songyu Temple Pagoda built at Mount Songshan of Henan in 524. The 15-storied, multi-eaved and polygonal brick pagoda was built in the form of a curvaceous skyscraping spire. It stood as a typical symbol of the beautiful Chinese-style "stupa" structure. It should be noted, however, that the design of Chinese multi-eaved structure had been influenced by the style of Gandhara stupa, which attracted the attention of a visiting Chinese pilgrim named Dao Rong in 451, who was said to have made a sketch of the design and introduced it to his countrymen upon his return.

The Buddhist pagodas built in the Tang Dynasty included both the stupa-type and the multi-storied pavilion-type or multi-eaved brick structures. Existing examples of the stupa-type Buddhist structures included the Tang Dynasty tomb pagoda located on the hill behind the Foguang Temple of Mount Wutai in Shanxi; also existing in the same temple was the country's oldest wooden pagoda. Examples of Tang Dynasty pavilion-type brick pagodas were the Dayan (Big Goose) Pagoda in the Daci'en Temple in Xi'an and the Xuanzhuang Pagoda in the Xingjiao Temple in Xi'an. The multi-eaved brick pagodas were represented by such examples as the Xiaoyan (Small Goose) Pagoda in the Jianfu Temple in Xi'an, the Qianxun Pagoda of Dali's Chongsheng Temple in Yunnan, and the Chongxing Temple Pagoda in Shandong's Zouxian County. In later development, Buddhist pagodas of the octagonal shape began to appear in the ninth century, as were represented by the several pagodas built during the Liao Dynasty in north China, and by the tilted-eaved twin pagodas found in Quanzhou of Fujian.

4. The Improvement of Sugar-Refining Skills

India, as a producer of sugar cane, had long since engaged in sugar refinning. The sugar industry flourished in the State of Bengal, where the product was called "guda," meaning squeezed ball, which was a kind of crude sugar. The refined sugar product was called "sarkara," which was translated as "shimi" (stone honey) in the classic *Tang-Sanskrit Dictionary* of the Tang Dynasty. Actually it was white crystal sugar. By the fifth century, sugar was being produced from cane juice in south China under the reign of the Southern Qi and Liang dynasties. Sugar cane was grown in Jiangdong, Luling and Guangdong regions. Guangdong was probably the first province in China to grow sugar cane. The plant was offered to China by Funan (an ancient country located in today's Cambodia) in 285. Sugar-refining was also introduced to south China, but in north China, sugar was being imported from as far as Persia at that time.

In 647, an Indian envoy arrived in Chang'an, where he boasted of Indian superiority in sugar production. This prompted Emperor Taizong of the Tang Dynasty to send his envoy Wang Xuance again to India to gather information on the technique of sugar refining. Upon his arrival in India, Wang managed to recruit two sugar technicians and eight monks, (through the help of the monastery of Bodhi Temple) and brought them back to Chang'an. They started the process of sugar refining, using sugar cane produced in Yangzhou and following Indian refining techniques. The result was an immediate success, as the sugar they produced proved to be far better than those imported from the West—in both colour and taste. The Indian refining method, which required the use of milk as an ingredient, yielded a solid form of refined sugar of "stone honey" that could be easily handled and stored. In 659, pharmacist Su Jing explained in his book *Revised Materia Medica* that the "stone honey" was made by boiling sugar with milk and rice powder in water until the mixture became a solid cake. The raw materials came from both western and southern regions, but those from Sichuan were said to be low in quality. The sugar-refining technique was first introduced in the Yangtze River valley, where there were abundant sugar cane. By the eighth century, when Meng Shen's book *Materia Medica et Dieta* was published, Sichuan's sugar product was ranking with Persian sugar in quality, surpassing that of the Yangtze River region. In the literary relics of Dunhuang grottoes, milk was not mentioned as an ingredient in processing sugar;

therefore, its information was believed to have come from sources in the Western Regions years before the Indian envoy's visit to China in 647.

However, the fact that the information on sugar refining did appear in the historic literature kept in Dunhuang was enough to assume that Dunhuang was once a translation centre, where bilingual and multi-lingual Buddhist monks engaged in translating wide-ranging subjects covering both religion and technology. That was why the technical information on such a sub-tropical plant as sugar cane would be listed in the literature of a desert relic house like the Dunhuang grottoes. This also demonstrated the unique role played by Dunhuang as both a national "gate" and international "window" in the history of religious and cultural exchange between China and the West.

Chapter Four

Cultural Exchange During the Course of Founding a Unified Empire

I   The Famous Conqueror Gürkhan

A major event, which occurred in 840 on the Mongolian Steppe, was the sudden collapse of the Khanate Uygur (Huihu or Huihe). About 100,000 Xiajiasi cavalry troops seized the khanate's headquarters on Mount Yudujin. The remnants of the beaten Uygurs retreated in three separate groups to the south-west, and moved into areas south of the Tianshan Mountains. The biggest of the three groups settled down in the territory of the Turkic Karahakan Khanate, located between the Ili River and the Chu River. The group's leader, Pangle, became a member of the ruling family of the Karahakan Khanate. The khanate had two tribal chiefs; one was the Grand Khan Arslan Karahakan stationed at Gus Ordo in Central Asia, the other was the Deputy Khan Bugra Karahakan stationed first at Talas, and then at Káxgar. It was believed that the later Bugra Karahakan was a descendant of the Uygur Pangle. The brave Uygur warriors then became the main force in Karahakan's military structure.

The Bugra Karahakan of Kashi was an Islamic follower. In the eyes of the Sarman rulers in Bukhara, the Bugra Karahakan was the "Chinese King." It was said that in the eleventh century, a man called Abur Hasan Muhammad Kalimadi was arrested by the Bukhara ruler for being a heretic; however, he managed to escape from jail and fled to China, where he urged Chinese rulers to attack and conquer the Sarman Dynasty. According to the story, a Chinese envoy arrived in Bukhara in 939 to impose

tribute obligation on the Sarman ruler, but he was so impressed
with the prosperity and power of the Sarman Dynasty that he did
not insist on imposing those ureasonable demands upon the
Bukhara kingdom. Instead the Chinese King himself converted to
Islam, as a result of Kalimadi's preaching. This "Chinese King"
was none other than Satuk Bugra Khan Abud Klim of Karahakan, who was enthroned in 955. In 1097, the ruler of Karahakan
sent a message, through an envoy of Yutian, to the Song Dynasty
court in Bianliang (now Kaifeng), saying that the khanate was
ready to attack the Buddhist-dominated Western Xia Kingdom
located in the Hexi Corridor region. The proposal was readily
accepted by the Song Dynasty, which considered Western Xia a
menace to its safety. However, the proposed joint attack never
materialized.

It was at this time that the Qidan tribe in north China thrived
and founded a state of its own (916-1125), changing its name to
Liao, whose domain reached the upper reach of Yenisei River in
the west, joining borders with Gaochang Uygur and Karahakan
khanate. Trade began flourishing between them, as caravans
travelled back and forth across the northern steppe. The Uygur
traders were regular visitors in Liao's Shangjing (Upper Capital)
Linhuangfu, bringing with them "Sanskrit monks and prestigious
physicians." They also introduced the famous Uygur medicine,
which was known to have absorbed the best of Arabian and
Indian medical achievements, to the Liao Dynasty. The cultural
exchange between the Liao Dynasty and the western nations was
further evidenced by the recent discovery of an ornamental cross
from the ruins of the Upper Capital of the Liao Dynasty, indicating that the place had been visited by Nestorian Christian from
Central Asia. The Islamic and Nestorian missionaries had both
been very active in north and west China during the eleventh
century, and their activities were closely related with the political
situation in West Asia.

When the Liao Dynasty fell in 1124, a member of its imperial
family named Yelü Dashi assumed the rule in July of that year,
and escaped with 200 cavalry men to Jimsar in the north of
Tianshan Mountains. After consolidating his forces at Jimsar, he

launched a westward expedition in 1130 and occupied Balasagum of Central Asia and Kashi of Xinjiang, causing the Uygurs and Qidans, who had migrated to the Karahakan Khanate from China, to rally around him. Yelü Dashi's army then went on to defeat the Khwarezm ruler in Central Asia and finally established an empire in February 1132, at Kalmynik. Yelü Dashi, the ruler of this new empire, was called Gürkhan in Qidan language, meaning "khan of the whole world." He also had a Chinese title: "*Tian You Huang Di*," meaning "heaven-blessed emperor." His empire was called West Liao in Chinese history, but described as "Kara Kitai" by Arab historians, which meant "magnificent Qidans." A Buddhist follower hismelf, Yelü Dashi, however, adopted a liberal religious policy in his Central Asian state and gave protection to all other religions, including the Christians, in order to ensure a stable political situation. Having consolidated his empire, Gürkhan led his West Liao army to march eastward in an attempt to recover the old Liao Dynasty's lost territory, but his expedition was disrupted by disastrous weather, forcing him to give up his ambitious plan. In 1142, Gürkhan's troops defeated the massive Muslim army under the command of Turkic Sultan Sanzal, thereby establishing his undisputed rule in Central Asia and making himself a well-known and well-respected ruler of the region.

The defeat of the Muslim army by Gürkhan's West Liao troops was a major boost to the enthusiasm of the many Nestorian Christians living in West Liao, prompting them to spread rumours to their friends in Syria, claiming that Gürkhan was himself a Christian and preparing to help them take back Jerusalem from the Muslims. Such rumours came at a time when the city of Edessa again fell to the Turks—in the wake of the First Crusade—in 1144. The Christian countries of Europe earnestly hoped to see the emergence of an Eastern ally. In 1145, when the Bishop of Gabala in Syria was sent by the Armenian King to pay a tribute to Pope Eugenius III (1145-1153) in Rome, he told the Pope that there was a Nestorian King John in the East, who had earlier overrun Medes, Persian Samiard and Ecbatana (Hamadan), and was ready to march on Jerusalem, but was blocked by the Tigris River and had to withdraw his army. This so-called "King John" referred actually to Gürkhan of West Liao in the twelfth century, and the King of Kleb in the thirteenth century. According to a thirteenth century book written by the Syrian scientist Abu Falaj, King John was originally the title assumed by the Nestorian King of Kleb in the Mongolian Steppe, since he converted to Christianity in the eleventh century. Then, in the fourteenth century, the Wanggu tribe of Inner Mongolia was called by Ordolik as the Kingdom of Prester John, because they followed the Christianity. Anyway, the rise of West Liao was enthusiastically acclaimed by the Nestorian population of Asia. They came to view the westward migration of the Turkic tribe as related to the Gürkhan's conquest of Central Asia and that the West Liao army was compatible to serving as an ally of the European crusaders in the West.

In 1253 when William Rubruck went to Mongolia as an envoy, he heard that King John was the Gürkhan of Kara Kitai. He was also quoted as saying that after the death of Gürkhan, a Nestorian chieftain of the Naiman tribe succeeded him as the ruler and was named King John by his followers. He was referred to as the Naiman chieftain Quchulü, who usurped the throne of West Liao towards the end of the dynasty. Quchulü had at first fled to West Liao, after his tribal army was defeated by Genghis Khan. After winning the trust of reigning Gürkhan who married his daughter to the Naiman warrior, Quchulü organized his tribesmen to overthrow his father-in-law and seized control of the West Liao. In 1218 when Genghis Khan launched his westward expedition, his army again defeated Quchulü at Kashi and chased the retreating Naiman chieftain to Saliheikun, where he was killed. The death of Quchulü at the hands of the Mongolian cavalry marked the end of the West Liao Dynasty. Nevertheless, the story of King John continued to circulate in the West, even after Quchulü's death. Later, when Marco Polo returned from his tour of China, he related the story that Prester John was the Khan King of the Kleb tribe. And based on the information given by Nestorian Christians in Asia, the Europeans continued to believe there was a powerful Christian nation in the East, and cherished the hope that someday the Eastern Christians would join force with the Western Christians to stem the spread of Islamic influence. The existence of a Nestorian tribe in the steppe of north China was the root cause of their illusions.

II   The Westward Advance of Chinese Culture During the Mongolian Rule

1. The Three Mongolian Expeditions to the West and the Tide of National Amalgamation

The Mongolian Steppe was unified under Genghis Khan (1162-1227) in 1206, when he became the Great Khan. In his later years (1218-1223), Genghis Khan launched his first westward expedition, during which his cavalry, using new fire-powder and weapons obtained from China and West Liao, annihilated Khwarezm, conquered Kankly and overran the Kipchak steppe and Russian plains. Then, the Mongols followed up with their second westward expedition, under the command of Batu—a grandson of Genghis Khan. During this war (1235-1244), a quarter of a million Mongolian troops swept across East Europe, occupying Russia and Kipchak before conquering Poland and Hungary, and then, after defeating the heavily-armoured Teutonic Order of Knights at Varstadt plains, reached as far as the Adriatic coast, threatening the heart of the Holy Roman Empire. In fact, Frederick II, the Holy Roman Emperor had already received a message from Batu, the Mongolian army commander, urging him to come immediately to Helin, where he would be given an official appointment by the Great Mongolian Khan. Frederick II gave the Mongolian messenger his positive reply, and was preparing to go and meet the Mongolian conqueror—in the capacity of an "eagle-breeder" which was his gifted specialty —when the news suddenly came that the Great Khan of Mogolia Ogdai had passed away. The issue of succession became more important for the Mongolian conqueror, who called off the westward expedition and returned home.

The Mongols launched yet another expedition to the west ten years later in the reign of Mangu Khan, who despatched an army led by his brother Hulagu, to conquer West Asia in a campaign lasting from 1253 to 1260. During the eight-year campaign, the Mongolian army completed their task of wiping out the resistance of the Arab warriors, overthrowing the Caliphate of Bagdad and occupying Syria. The renewed Mongolian invasion shattered the Frank occupation of Sidon and shocked the crusader knights in Levant, causing as much panic in Europe as the previous Mongolian expedition launched by Batu. As a result, Roman Pope Alexander IV sent his envoys to the European countries, urging mobilization of new crusaders to resist the advancing Mongolians from Hungary and Syria. Meanwhile, the Mongolian army was setting its next target on the Muslim Dynasty of Mameluke; however, its advance was repulsed by the Muslim army under the command of Mameluke Sultan Guduz, in the decisive battle of Ayn Jalut north of Jerusalem on September 3, 1260. Since then, the confrontation between the Muslims and the Mongolians reached a deadlock in Syria.

The westward expeditions of the Mongolian army caused great destruction in many parts of Europe, razing a number of cities there. However, following the advance of the Mongolian military force to the West, the communication and exchange between the cultures of the East and the West also developed quickly as they began infiltrating and assimilating each other with unprecedented force and intensity. This development was propelled by the massive migration of population within the new large empire, which assimilated a rich variety of ethnic cultures simultaneously.

In the wake of his conquest of Khwarezm, Genghis Khan forced many local craftsmen to move from Samarkand to Mongolia, where they were ordered to work alongside the Han Chinese, Qidans and other emigrants from the Hexi Corridor, at farming, horticulture and handicrafts. Samarkand had been known for its well-developed silk, paper-making and pottery industry, whose workers were mostly Han craftsmen.

When the Mongolian conquerors entered Bagdad, they found

the ruling caliph had kept many Chinese Han and Qidan women in their harems. Among the Mongolian troops, there were also many Han Chinese, serving as sorcerers, astronomers or surgeons. As the Mongolians moved into their new settlements in the occupied territories, these people brought along with them the Chinese culture and technology, which soon began to flourish in the areas.

And while the Mongolian expeditions caused a westward expansion of Mongolian colonies, they also resulted in the eastward migration of many Europeans, Kipchaks, Russians, Persians, Arabs, Syrians and Armenians. The multi-ethnic Muslims accounted for the largest number. These immigrants settled down in China to engage in handicraft, agriculture, trade, commerce or serve as soldiers or government officials under the Mongolian regime. The continued co-existence of such a large number of ethnic nationalities, who kept up a free cultural exchange and free interracial marriages, inevitably led to an amalgamation of nationalities in the Chinese society. The Mongolian rulers, themselves, favoured having marital ties with the ruling families of neighbouring states or the conquered nations. After their conquest of Hungary, the Mongolian aristocrats married members of the Hungarian court; and when Hulagu occupied Iran, his Mongolian successor married a member of the Byzantine ruling family. Hezan, another Mongolian conqueror, also chose his bride from among the royal community of Armenia.

After Genghis Khan died in 1229, his successor Ogdai Khan established his capital at Haraholin (in the vicinity of the current Ulan Bator), where new palaces were built and people came from all parts of Asia and Europe to pay tribute to the Mongolian emperor or serve in his court. They included Uygurs, Arabs, Persians, Armenians, Hungarians, Russians, British and French. Among the foreign servants in the Mongolian court were the Hungary-born Englishman Basil, who served as an interpreter, and a French woman, Paquette de Metz from Lorraine, who was a maid servant of the Mongolian court ladies. Particularly remarkable was the French jeweler Guillaume Buchier from Paris, who was known for making a marvelous "silver tree" to decorate

Mangu Khan's palace. The silver tree was built upon a base supported by four silver lions, each of which could produce a different drink—horse milk, honey, rice wine or grape wine from its month. Moreover, there was a little angel sitting on top of the silver tree with a trumpet in her hand, who blew the trumpet to signal for the servants to pour in more drinks when necessary.

The Great Khan Kublai, having founded his capital at Dadu (now Beijing), launched a major construction project to build it into the largest city in the world, attracting visitors from abroad. The Mongolian ruler in Dadu maintained close relations with the Kipchak Khanate and the Il-Khanate, and their envoys travelled to and from Dadu frequently. The ties were especially favourable between Dadu and Il-Khanate in Persia, which still looked to the Great Khan in Dadu for the appointment of its Khans. Facing stiff resistance of the Muslim Egypt, the Il-Khanate's rulers sought allies from among Europe's Christian countries; and their friendly gestures led to a flourishing trade between the Il-Khanate and the Western countries, further prompting the Austrian, Venetian, Genoan and Jewish traders to travel by sea all the way to the coastal ports in southeast China. In return, large numbers of Mongolians, Uygurs, Hans, and Turks migrated into areas in India and the Arabian countries. Such a major inter-movement of ethnic nationalities greatly increased the cultural contacts between the East and the West, paving the way for their amalgamation.

2. The Khanate Golden Horde and the Northern Passage of Chinese Culture to the West

The vast territory of the Mongolian Golden Horde Khanate (Kipchak Khanate) sprawled across the continent from China to Europe during the thirteenth century. It took as long as 200 days to travel from the first stop at Harahelin, north of Dadu, to Batu Khan's residence of Sarai in Seletren, located in the lower reach of the Volga River. Sarai meant "palace" in Mongolian, and the name was used to mark the site of Batu's gleaming golden-topped tent camp, which suggested the Russian title, "Golden Horde" for Batu's Khanate. The caravan traders from China or Central Asia usually exchanged their goods with the traders from Europe's Hanseatic League towns and Nikini Novgorod to the west of Moscow, turning the Russian city into an East-West trading centre. There remains today a "Qidan District" in Novgorod, where the Chinese traders lived during that era. In the Kipchak Steppe of south Russia, most of the Cuman natives there were descendants of emigrants during the twelfth century from north China and Inner Mongolia, sharing the culture and language of the Qidans. They were also partly responsible for bringing Chinese culture to this part of Russia. The feudal rulers of Russia wore oriental boots (Bashmak), gowns (Kaftan) and round caps (Kolpak). All derived their names from Qidan or Mongolian sources. The Russian warriors, like their Mongolian counterparts, used bows made of birch-bark—in addition to sabres—as weapons. They also learned from the Mongols how to use such new weapons as metal powder-cans.

Chinese golden brocade, tea and the abacus were among the goods that had found their way into Europe through the Golden Horde trade route. Garments woven with gold thread were popular during the Song (960-1279) and Kin (1115-1234) dynasties; and, during the Yuan Dynasty (1279-1368), such garments were made with a variety of golden fabrics, including golden satin, golden gauze and golden tough silk. The golden satin was made by weaving raised patterns with gold thread upon a pelt base with large width. The design of golden brocade garments originated from an Arab style called "nasij," hence the name nasij brocade. The Yuan Dynasty court set up special workshops in Dadu and other nearby towns to make such luxury garments for the Mongolian aristocrats. These workshops utilized several departments to engage in making different kinds of silk fabrics. The golden brocade, patterned satin and purple gauze produced at these workshops were distributed to the three northeastern khanates of Ogdai, Golden Horde and Il-Khanate. The nasij brocade was called "nac" in Cumanian, "nax" in Persian, "nasicius" in Latin and "nachiz" in Italian. The nasij brocade trade was mainly conducted by Venetian merchants at the Sudak Port of Crimea and the Hanseatic League businessmen in the Volga River valley.

The Chinese craftsmen, who came to settle down in Golden Horde (Kipchak) Khanate, brought with them the skills of making bronze mirrors. This explained the discovery of Chinese Yuan Dynasty bronze mirrors in the area of Berke Sarai and other towns in Kipchak. The one locally-made had Arabian letters engraved on its back, but bronze mirrors made in China, unearthed in Berke Sarai, had Chinese characters carved on the back.

The habit of drinking tea was another Chinese tradition, learned by the Mongols from Western Xia and Uygurs of Gaochang, then introduced by them to West Asia. Afterwards, the habit was taken up by the Russians. Tea was called "Cai" in Mongolian, Persian, Turkish, Russian and Hindi languages, which showed the drink originated from the same source.

Abacus was generally believed to have first become widely used during the Yuan Dynasty. Although it was claimed that a 13-centimetre-long miniature abacus had been unearthed from a first century tomb in Italy, there was no confirmation whether the discovery was a genuine relic or an input of the later generation. The Yuan Dynasty abacus was also called *ding pan zhu* (Beads Fixed on Board) or *zou pan zhu* (Moving Beads on Board). A poem written by Liu Yin (1248-1292) in Volume 11 of the book *Collected Literary Works of Master Jingxiu* dwelled on the features of abacus, calling it *deda bing* in Zhejiang dialect, indicating the calculating gadget was first developed in the Southern Song Dynasty's capital of Lin'an (now Hangzhou). *Deda bing* meant stacks of pancakes, obviously referring to the flat wooden beads that looked like pancakes stacked one upon the other. The abacus was a major improvement over the former "calculating sticks" in efficiency and portability. It was introduced to Russia and Poland in the fourteenth century and continued to be used in the twentieth century.

It is believed that the technique of wooden-block printing was introduced to the West via the Golden Horde Khanate. Paul Jowett in his book *Secular History*, published in 1550, says books were being printed at that time in China. While serving as a diplomatic envoy in Moscow he had seen books printed in China, which were given by the King of Portugal to Pope Leo X (1513-1521). He records in his book: We may therefore easily conclude that the people of Se or Moscow had already introduced to us an example of how to promote human knowledge unlimitedly—long before the Portuguese arrived in India. The people of Se refers to the Uygur people who had used movable wooden type in printing since the thirteenth century. The Uygurs enjoyed very high civilization, and it was on the basis of the Uygur script that the Mongolians developed their own alphabets. And when the papal envoy, John of Plano Carpini, arrived in Helin in 1245, he received a written response from the Mongolian Guyuk Khan, which bore an imperial seal in Mongolian letters. John of Plano Carpini recognized the seal as an engraving by the Russian sculptor Kosmos. It is assumed that the Russians learned seal-engraving from the Uygurs, and possibly, the printing technique from them. Later, such technique was probably introduced to Gutenberg, who once lived in Prague. The next step was movable-type printing, adopted by Gutenberg. This enabled Europe to enter in 1454 the era of movable-type printing.

3. Il-Khanate and the Southern Passage of Chinese Culture to the West

Ever since the reign of Hulagu Khan, Sino-Iranian cultural cooperation had made great headway. Iranian authorities adopted many established Chinese laws and systems. They took positive steps to absorb Chinese science and culture, which were introduced to other parts of the world by their Muslim subjects, European guests and travellers in the country. The Il-Khanate's capital of Tabriz was linked directly with the Chinese capital of Dadu by an official mail route, which also served as the passage of regular caravan traders every year. Turpan and Kabnam—the east and west ends of the mail route—had been the front posts of trade and cultural exchange between China and the Arab world. Tabriz, since it became the capital of Il-Khanate, had replaced Bagdad as the busiest city between the Mediterranean and the Black Sea. It also had many Chinese residents. In his book the

Arab historian Ras Dedin lavished praised on this cosmopolitan city, saying: "Under the grace of the Islamic Monarch (then, the Hezan Khan of Il-Khanate being an Islamic follower), this city has become converging centre of philosophers, astronomers, scholars and historians of all religions and schools." These people came from north China, south China, India, Kashmir, Uygur, other Turkic nations. They also included Arabs and Franks.[1] Cultures from all over the world had come together at the Il-Khanate capital.

In 1259, under the order of Hulagu, the Persian scientist Nasir al-Din al Tusi (1201-1274) undertook the job of founding the Malag Astronomical Observatory. He recruited a number of Chinese astronomers to work with him. Together, they compiled the "Il-Khanate Astronomical Table" (al-Zij al-ilkhani). This spurred Chinese astronomers on to compile their new calendar system, the "Shou Shi" (Time-Regulating) Calendar.

Under the reign of Gaikhatu Khan (1292-1295), the Il-Khanate faced a financial crisis, resulting from continued internal and external conflicts. Someone suggested to the Khan that he should copy the example of the Yuan Dynasty in publishing paper money, because "when gold was replaced by paper notes, there would be no poor people in the world, and food would be very cheap too." Gaikhatu Khan turned for advice to the veteran Yuan Dynasty official Boro, who had come to settle down in Iran. Boro told him how the Yuan Dynasty had adopted its paper money system, and said it was practicable in Iran.

So, on July 23, 1294, Gaikhatu Khan issued a decree to publish paper money for circulation across the country. On September 12 Yuan-Dynasty-Style paper notes were printed in Tabriz. Like the Yuan Dynasty money, it was made of mulberry tree bark and used engraved wood type. It bore the Han character "cau" (money) and an Arab denomination from half a dinar to ten dinars. The Il-Khanate ruler ordered circulation of paper money, outlawed the use of gold or silver and imposed the death penalty on anyone refusing to accept the paper currency. Howev-

[1] Henry Yule: *The Book of Sir Marco Polo, the Venetian*, London, 1930 (rep. 1921), Vol. I, P. 76.

er, only eight days after the paper money went into circulation, the market was in chaos and there was a shortage of goods everywhere. In less than two months, all commercial activities stopped, and people began to flee the cities. This forced Gaikhatu Khan to revoke the paper money and reinstate hard currency. Despite the fact that the publishing of paper currency in Iran became a laughing stock in history, it was, nevertheless, an occasion for the Chinese printing technique to demonstrate itself in West Asia.

Following the enthronement of Hezan Khan (1295-1304), the Il-Khanate proclaimed Islam as its national religion, thereby accelerating the amalgation of the Mongolian regime with the Shiite Persian culture. Hezan Khan also launched a series of social reforms, which included the introduction of the Mongolian mail station system, allowing the free passage throughout the country of any official traveller—who held government-issued identification (paizah). However, as the number of such "official travellers" grew, the mail stations had no means of providing all the necessary travelling subsidies. Inhabitants along the mail routes began complaining of the outrageous burden imposed upon them by these free travellers. As a result, Hezan Khan followed the example of Kublai Khan to further reform the mail station system. Special hostels were built along the mail route to provide free boarding and horses for those officials holding gold or silver identification pieces. All other travellers were required to pay for lodging and horses.

Both Hezan Khan and his successors Helbanda Khan (1304-1316) and Busain (1317-1335) were interested in developing trade and political ties with China, and took positive steps to learn from China's achievements in science, medicine, art and history. The first wide-ranging book of world history *Historical Literature* (*Jami at-Tawarikh*) compiled by Ras Dedin (1247-1318), contained chapters on Mongolia and China, which were written with the assistance of the veteran Mongolian official Boro. During this period, China's porcelain, metalwork, textile, paintings and garments were popular in Iran; Chinese brocade became the fashion in West Asia. The Persian words "Kimxaw" and "Kamxa" for brocade were derived from the Chinese expression "jinhua" (golden flower). It is believed production of golden satin in Tabriz was taught by Chinese craftsmen. The names of many plants in the Persian language were topped with the word "China," indicating that they were probably introduced from China to that country during the Mongolian reigns. These plants included Chinese rose (ward sini) or (gul-cini) and Chinese sarsaparilla (cubi cini). Other Chinese expressions absorbed by the Mongols, such as "wan" (king), "dai wan" (great king), "kao wan" (king of the state), "tai hu" (queen mother), "fu cin" (madam), "kun cu" (princess) and "jinksanak" (prime minister) were all used in their original sense in Il-Khanate. Chinese tea was probably introduced to Iran at that time, although coffee had long been a popular drink in Persia. The Italians first learned about tea from the Persians. Needless to say the Arab expressions of "Sahm ratai" (Chinese arrow) and "talj al-Sini" (Chinese snow), which referred to the Chinese archery and saltpetre, were closely connected with the westward expeditions of the Mongols.

III   The Mongolians and the Roman Catholic Church

1. The Vatican Envoy's Trip to the Orient

The second westward expedition of the Mongols threw Europe into panic, which, coupled with the split between the Roman Empire and the Roman Pope, caused the Western Christian world to break in two. Despite discord between the three Mongolian Expeditionary Army commanders Batu, Guyuk and Buri, following the death of the Great Khan Ogdai in December 1241—which caused the Mongols to halt their advance in Europe—Batu was still stationed at his tent camp by the Volga River, imposing his rule over some European Christian states. Pope Innocent IV (1243-1254), after his ascension to the throne, tried to stop the continued westward advance of the Mongols by exerting his influence through Christian followers among the Mongolian high officials. Hence, a number of papal or Christian state envoys were dispatched by Vatican, after 1245, to the Mongolian capital of

Helin for this purpose. These special envoys included John of Plano Carpini, Ascelin, Andrew of Longjumeau and William Rubruck.

John of Plano Carpini was originally a Catholic Franciscan clergyman of Carpini near Perugia in Italy. In 1245, he was dispatched together with the Portuguese priest Laurence to Mongolia by Pope Innocent IV. John of Plano Carpini departed from the papal capital of Lyon on April 6, carrying two decrees of the Roman Pope addressed to the Tatar Emperor. After arriving at Batu Khan's headquarters, by way of Poland and Galicia, he was provided with an escort by Batu Khan to accompany him for his trip to Helin in China. Having travelled three and a half months on horseback, he finally arrived in Helin on July 22—a month before the enthronement ceremony of Guyuk Khan was held on August 24. Later, when Guyuk Khan received them, they were told by the Khan that the Mongols had never mistreated Christians as accused by the Pope, and that the Pope should send a high-ranking envoy to negotiate with him if he desired peace. On November 13, 1245, they obtained a letter of response from Guyuk Khan and left the Mongolian capital for home, arriving in the Roman Catholic capital in the autumn of 1247. Despite his failure in the papal mission, John of Plano Carpini wrote a book about his experience during the trip to the Mongolia Empire, *Historia Mongolorum quos nos Tartaros appellamus*. His book, along with the *Trip to the Orient*, written by William Rubruck who visited Mongolia after him, had been acclaimed as the two outstanding books of the Eastern World written by Europeans before Marco Polo.

In 1247, the Pope sent another Dominican clergyman, Ascelin, to take his message to the Mongolian troops stationed near the Caspian Sea. He got only a curt letter of response from the Mongolian commander Baiju. Nevertheless, the Mongols also sent two of their envoys with the papal envoy back to Europe. The two—a Turk called Aybeg and a Christian called Sargis —were the first envoys ever sent by the Mongols to the Roman

Catholic Church[1]. In the meantime, two other Christians, Moriffat David and Marcus, were sent by the Mongolian Minister Eljigidei to see the French King Louis IX, who was then stationed with his troops in Cyprus[2]. They proposed to the king that the Mongols would agree to help him attack the Saracens and recapture Jerusalem. So, in 1248, Louis IX sent a delegation, headed by Dominican clergyman Andrew of Longjumeau, to travel from Antioch to the headquarters of Mongolian Regent Guyuk Khan's Queen Ogul Gamish near River Imil for negotiation. But, to the disappointment of Louis IX, the Mongolain answer was that the King of France should pay tribute in gold and silver to the Mongols in exchange for peace.

However, Louis IX, having then learned that there were many Christians among the Mongolians, including Batu's son Sartak, decided to send another delegation, headed by Franciscan clergyman William Rubruck, to persuade the Mongols for the second time. Rubruck, a native of northern France, left the French King's headquarters at Acre in 1253 to travel to the Mongolian camp by way of Constantinople and the Black Sea. Upon his arrival at Sartak's headquarters, he learned the Mongolian commander was not a Christian. The Mongols, nevertheless, sent Rubruck to Batu's camp, then again to the capital of the Mongolian Empire, where he was granted an audience by the Great Khan Mangu and received by the Prime Minister Bolgay. Rubruck explained to the Mongolian court that he came as a Christian missionary to China to pray for the health of the Great Khan, but had no political intent or mission. After he was given a letter from the Mangu Khan to the King of France, he travelled back to Antioch and from there to his home in France, where he wrote a long report of his travel and his suggestions to the French King on how to deal with the Mongols.

The Christian mission to the East, pioneered by Rubruck, began to make headway by the time John de monte Corvino (1247-1328) came to China. Missionaries from both the Domini-

---

[1] Matthaei Paris, Monachi Albanensis, Angli, Historia Major, 1571, P. 985; the envoys were under strong suspicion.

[2] *Ibid*, P. 1023.

can and Franciscan orders had already started preaching in Tabriz with the approval of the Il-Khanate rulers, who were interested in allying with the Western Christian nations to combat the Islamic powers in West Asia. In 1289, a Franciscan missionary, was sent by Aluhun Khan of Il-Khanate to the Roman Pope to inform him that the Christian church was well established in the East. In the same year, Roman Pope Nicholas IV again sent the missionary to China, taking a letter to the Mongolian Great Khan Kublai. Corvino travelled by way of Tauris and India to arrive at Khanbalik (Beijing) in 1293, where he stayed on to preach Christian doctrines until he died in 1328. By the year of 1305, there were more than 6,000 Christians in Beijing, prompting the Roman Pope Clement V to establish the Khanbalik Archbishopric in the area. After that, the Chinese Christian church had a direct link with the Roman Catholics in addition to the Nestorian missions.

2. An Mongolian Envoys' Visit to Europe

Since Guyuk Khan became the Mongolian Great Khan in 1246, his disagreement with Batu Khan caused him to shift the westward expansion of the Mongolian Empire from Europe to the Islamic nations in West Asia. That was the reason the Mongolian official Eljigidei, a close aide of Guyuk Khan, received the papal envoy Ascelin during the latter's visit to the camp of Mongolian commander Baiju in 1247. It was said that the Mongolian official gave the papal envoy a written reply from the Mongolian Great Khan, in addition to sending two Mongolian envoys, Aybeg and Sargis, to go with Ascelin to Europe as the first Mongolian envoys to visit the Roman Pope. It was also Eljigidei, who sent Moriffat David and Marcus to see French King Louis IX in his camp at Cyprus to discuss possible cooperation between the Mongols and the crusaders. Their mission was disrupted by the sudden death of Guyuk Khan, which occurred a month before their departure. The proposal of the two Mongolian enovoys, who arrived in Cyprus in December of 1248, prompted the enthusiastic French King to send Andrew of Longjumeau to go with Moriffat David back to Mongolia for negotiation with the Mongolian Great

Khan. The French envoy's mission failed, as a result of the death of Guyuk Khan.

Following the death of Guyuk Khan, the throne of the Mongolian Great Khan was left empty for two years, until Mangu Khan was enthroned in June 1251. The new Mongolian Great Khan in his written reply to the French King, delivered by William Rubruck, accused the former Mongolian envoy Moriffat David of being a "dishonourable plagiarist," while denying that the Mongols wished to ally with the Franks. In 1252, when the Mongols began their expedition against the Islamic world, the Mongolian commander Hulagu Khan still refrained from seeking support from the Franks in the Middle East, even giving orders to drive away the Franks from Syria. But not long afterwards, the discord widened between the Mongolian princes. The Il-Khanate ruler had, since 1262, been compelled to use a sizable part of his force to cope with the provocations of his powerful northern neighbour the Golden Horde Sarai Berke and their successors. Sarai Berke (1257-1266), an Islamic follower, allied himself with the Mamelukes of Egypt, who had become the common enemy of both the crusaders and the Il-Khanate Mongols in Middle East conflicts. After Hulagu died, his successor Abaha (1265-1282) dispatched his envoy to visit the Roman Pope[1]. In response, Pope Clement IV (1265-1268) sent his envoy James Alaric of Perpignan to visit Il-Khanate in 1267. Next year, the eastern Mediterranean stronghold of Antioch fell to the attacking forces of the Egyptian Sultan Beybars. This happened when King Louis IX of France had turned his last Crusade towards Tunis, leaving only King Edward I of England to seek help from the Il-Khanate Mongols in fighting against the Muslims. When the English king arrived at Acre in May of 1271, he sent his envoys Reginald Russel and John Parker to see Abaha Khan, with whom they reached an agreement on joining their forces to fight the Egyptians. Unfortunately, another war broke out between Abaha Khan and the separatist Haitu's forces of the Chagatai Khanate,

---

[1] Antoine Mostaert, *Francis Woodman Cleaves, Trois Documents Mongols des Archives Secretes Vaticanes, Harvard Journal of Asiatic Studies*, XV, 1952, PP. 419-506, see PP. 430-445.

so Abaha could only dispatch a cavalry unit to Syria in helping the crusaders led by Edward I to fight the Egyptians. However, the Egyptian Muslim Army led by Beybars and Qala'un overpowered the outnumbered crusaders, then defeated the Il-Khanate Mongols first in 1277 at Abalas and later in 1281 at Himse.

In 1287, Abaha Khan's son Aluhun Khan (1284-1291) sent an important delegation to Rome and Paris. This delegation, described as the most significant in the history of Mongolian-European relations, was headed by the Khanbalik (Beijing)-born Uygur Nestorian Rabban mar Sauma (1245-1294); and its mission was to consolidate the alliance between Il-Khanate and Europe in their fight against the Muslims of Syria and Palestine.

Earlier, Sauma had been on a pilgrimage with Marco, a Nestorian from Wangu tribe, in 1278; and Marco had become Yaballaha III, the Archbishop of Bagdad in 1281. It was Yaballaha III who recommended Rabban mar Sauma, known for his fluent Latin, to serve as Il-Khanate's envoy to Europe. The Il-Khanate delegation left a Black Sea port in March of 1287 for Constantinople, from there they went by way of Naples to arrive in Rome on June 23. Since Pope Honorius IV had died two months before their arrival, they were received by a Cardinal who was later elected to be Pope Nicholas IV (1288-1292). Having met the Roman Cardinal, Rabban mar Sauma left Rome for Paris via Tuscany and Genoa; in Paris, he stayed for more than a month and met the French King Philippe IV (1285-1314), who agreed to send his troops to join with Aluhun's forces in an expedition against their common enemy in West Asia. From Paris, Sauma and his delegation went on to Kasonia (Bordeaux) to visit the English King Edward I (1272-1307), with whom they also had a very amicable conference. Sauma, then, went back again to Rome, where he formally delivered Aluhun Khan's letter to the new Pope, who was enthroned on February 20, 1288. In April 1288, Sauma returned to Il-Khanate, in the company of Gobert of Helleville, the ambassador of the English King to Il-Khanate. The journey of Rabban mar Sauma to Europe marked a very successful diplomatic activity conducted by a Chinese, in his capacity as a Mongolian envoy.

After the death of John de monte Corvino, there was no one to succeed him as the Archbishop of Khanbalik and be responsible for leading the Christian Church in China. In 1336, a group of Christians in China and Kipchak Khanate wrote an appeal to the Pope, urging him to appoint a new archbishop for Khanbalik. Their appeal was seconded by the Yuan Dynasty's Emperor Shundi, who dispatched a 16-man delegation, headed by Bishop Andrew of Quanzhou, a Frank, and several others, to travel by land to deliver Emperor Shundi's personal message to the Pope in Italy. In 1388, the delegation arrived at the papacy of Avignon, where they delivered the Yuan Emperor's message to the Pope. Then, having toured the Italian cities of Venice and Florence, they joined the Papal Envoys Nicholas Bonet, Giovanni de Marignolli and two others in Naples, before heading for home by way of Constantinople, the Black Sea and Sarai. With the exception of Nicholas Bonet, who returned to Europe halfway on the journey, the rest of the delegation, now 32 strong, finally arrived in Dadu (Beijing) in August of 1342 to a solemn welcome by the Yuan court. Giovanni de Marignolli, after staying four years in the Chinese capital to preach Christian doctrines, departed for home in 1346 and arrived in Avignon in 1353 to deliver a formal letter from the Yuan Emperor Shundi to Pope Clement VI (1342-1352) to the papacy. In his letter, the Yuan emperor reiterated the Great Mongolian Khan's respect for the Christian Church and the Christians' loyalty to the will of the Pope. Diplomatic ties continued between the Yuan court and the Roman Pope throughout the reign of the Yuan Dynasty, while the Christian community had become a part of the Christian world with its centre in Europe.

IV   The Arabian Culture During the Yuan Dynasty

The domain of the Yuan Dynasty comprised three large khanates, whose subjects included large numbers of Muslims. Therefore, the Arabian culture represented by these people formed a major portion of the international culture assimilated within the Dynasty.

During the Yuan Dynasty, marked developments were seen in the Arabian calendar system and astronomical observation, which then became models for Chinese astronomers in their study. Particularly noteworthy was the compilation of the "Hui Hui" (Muslim) Calendar, to which such astronomers as Yelü Chucai and Jamal al-Din ibn Mahammad al-Najjari contributed significantly. In 1220, Yelü Chucai joined Genghis Khan's expedition to the west and arrived at Samarkand, where he made astronomical study at the local observatory in order to re-compile the "Hui Hui" Calendar. In 1236, his revised calendar—called "Ma Ta Ba" or Muhummed Calendar—began to circulate among the Muslims in north China. Later, the Persian astronomer Jamal al-Din ibn Mahammad al-Najjari came to China in 1267, and offered a "Ten Thousand Year Calendar" (al-Zij al-Shamila) to the Yuan Emperor Kublai Khan. This became another version of "Hui Hui" Calendar which was also circulated among the Muslims as an official calendar.

These "Hui Hui" Calendar while somewhat better than the Chinese traditional calendar in its application of spherical astronomy and its calculation of planetary orbits—still contained almost as many errors as the then popular Da Ming Calendar. Hence, the Yuan Dynasty ruler decided on the compilation of a new and more accurate calendar. It would be based on thorough investigation and with reference to the Il-Khanate Astronomical Table (al-Zij al-Ilkhani) finished by the Malag Astronomical Observatory in 1272. The job was given to two Chinese astronomers Wang Xun and Guo Shoujing. The Il-Khanate Astronomical Table, which was then kept in the Beijing Imperial Archives, was originally written in Persian and called "Zij Assorted Calendar" in China. This was because the "al-Zij" (astronomical table) was compiled on the basis of assorting the astronomical achievements of Greece, Arabia, Persia and China. Wang and Guo adopted the spherical trigonometric formula of "Hui Hui" Calendar in their astronomical computation, while making thorough calculation of the daily motion of the solar system. The completion of their work marked the fourth major reform in the history of Chinese calendar system. The formal introduction of their "Shou Shi" (Time-Telling) Calendar in 1281 was the greatest success seen in the Chinese calendar research until the introduction of Western calendar system in the last years of the Ming Dynasty. Their achievement was due partly to the scientific ties then existing between the astronomical observatories in Beijing and Malag.

The spectacular progress in geographical studies, during the Yuan Dynasty, was attributable also to the availability of important Arabian maps and navigation manuals—in addition to information from Chinese and Mongolian sources. In fact, China's first terrestrial globe came from the Persian astronomer Jamal al-Din ibn Mahammad al-Najjari. This was probably a replica of the globe kept in the Malag Astronomical Observatory. The surface of the globe was divided into small squares, 70 per cent of which was painted in green to stand for water and the rest was in white to represent land areas. The introduction of this globe marked the first time in China that the concept of a globe-shaped earth was demonstrated by means of an instrument.

Later Mahammad al-Najjari participated in the compiling of the national atlas of the Yuan Dynasty *Da Yuan Yi Tong Zhi* (*Unified Map of the Great Yuan Dynasty*)—which covered the territory of the Mongolian empire. The major project, which depended much on information from maps of the Arab world, was edited by Mahammad al-Najjari himself. In 1287, the Yuan court issued an order to collect navigation manuals from Arab countries, through the port authorities at Quanzhou in Fujian. The collected materials were also assimilated into the national atlas, which eventually emerged as a huge book consisting of 500 volumes. It was unfortunate that the voluminous *Da Yuan Yi Tong Zhi* was no longer available, and that the world atlas attached to it was also lost—excepting for the replica drawn in 1402 by a Korean cartographer, after the world map first made by Yuan Dynasty draftsmen, which is now kept in the library of Japan's Kyoto University. The existing map showed the southern tip of Africa, very accurately, in the shape of an inverted triangle, which far surpassed its contemporary Islamic maps in precision.

In its maritime definition, the Yuan cartographer followed

the Roman and Arab tradition in dividing global waters into the east and west oceans. But in the Yuan map, the east ocean, which ended at Malaysia and Java, was smaller than the west ocean, which included the vast area extending from Malaysia to the Mediterranean. Such a geographic concept had been observed by the Chinese navigators through the Ming and Qing dynasties (1368-1644 and 1644-1911).

The use of Arab medical expertise was given particular attention during the Yuan Dynasty, which set up in 1263 a Xiyu (Western Regions) Medical Bureau in charge of the Arab medical service. In 1270, the bureau changed its name to Guang Hui (Public Service) Bureau to specially provide medical service for foreign soldiers and Muslims living in north China. An Arab-style hospital, which was set up by a Syrian doctor called Aixue in Kaiping near Beijing, later became Guang Hui Bureau's affiliated institute. Many of the more than 20 Muslim surgeons, working under the bureau, were known for excellent surgical skills, with which they had cured some cases of seemingly incurable diseases. In one case, Prince Kanharaze, nephew of the Yuan Emperor Shundi, was suddenly caught with a seizure and fell from his horse, with his eyes turning upwards and his tongue stretching out all the way down his chest. When other doctors were at a loss to treat the patient, Arab surgeon Nizir from the Guang Hui Bureau was able to cure his disease by cutting off his outstretched tongue. Also well-known to the Chinese was the Arab pharmacopoeia "al-Qanun fi al-Tibb," written by the famous physician ibn Sina (980-1037), which was then widely used by Chinese Muslim doctors. Chinese physicians had, since the twelfth century, adapted from the Arab pharmacopoeia the method of packaging medicine with gold or silver foil. During the last years of the Yuan Dynasty, the Arab book was translated into a Chinese book called "Hui Hui Prescriptions" and published and distributed across the country.

Arab music and dances were very popular during both the Yuan and Ming dynasties; Arab wind and stringed instruments were used in the Yuan court to perform at royal concerts. The well-known Chinese two-stringed instrument *er hu* was also introduced to China from the Arab world during the Yuan Dynasty. Another instrument called *hu bu si*—a four-stringed pluck instrument—was also introduced to inland China during the same period, and is now still used by the Uygur musicians as one of their principal musical instruments.

Chapter Five

Cultural Communication Across the Maritime "Silk Road" During the Period from the Ninth to the Fifteenth Century

I Developments of Ocean Shipping in the Tang, Song and Yuan Dynasties

1. Maritime "Silk Road" to the Indian Ocean

As a result of the remarkable development in ocean shipping following the Tang Dynasty, distance between China and the rest of the world was greatly shortened by the easy access to any part of the globe via sea route. This not only accelerated the circulation of trade but also enhanced the exchange of information between China and other countries. Regular sea routes were soon established between China and Japan, China and Southeast Asia, China and the Indian subcontinent as well as the Persian Gulf and Arabian Peninsula. Maritime traders were active during this period, some even travelling across the ocean between China and East Africa. Economic exchange flourished along this Maritime "Silk Road", which connected the coastal areas of southeast China with Asia and Africa.

The eastern section of the Maritime "Silk Road" linked east China's port of Ningbo with Japan. A total of 37 voyages were registered on this route during the period from 839 to 907, after Japan had ceased sending its envoys to the Tang Dynasty. Ships used on the voyages were all built by Chinese workmen either in Chinese or Japanese shipyards, and were said to be much safer than the earlier boats used by Japanese envoys for their trips to

China. Shipping trade also made headway between China and areas around the Indian Ocean, according to a record made by Jia Dan, during the reign of Zhenyuan (785-805) of the Tang Dynasty. The record showed that there were sea routes between south China's Guangzhou port and the Persian Gulf—through the Malacca Strait and south India—and also Sufala in East Africa, by way of the Arabian Peninsula and African coast. The African state of Sufala, rich in gold and ivory, was located in Unguja Kun near Zanzibar of Tanzania. Chinese merchant ships, sailing from Guangzhou through the Persian Gulf and the Arabian port of Shihr, called regularly at Sufala to trade with Africans, so as to minimize the cost of brokerage paid to Arab middlemen. The route they followed was the historic path of migration from Sumatra of Indonesia to Sufala—from east to west along the equator. Chinese ships, which arrived at East Africa from south India, were able to take advantage of the southwest trade winds to sail northward to Oman or the Persian Gulf, then turn southward again to India in the next trade wind season, there to wait for the following southwest winds to send them back to Guangzhou. As a rule, the ships used to leave Guangzhou port in November, and return in May or June. China thus became an active trading partner in the flourishing commerce of the Indian Ocean, during this period.

From the twelfth century on, Chinese merchant ships opened a new trade route from Guangzhou through Sumatra to Mahrah in the Arabian Peninsula, which was called the Mahrah al-Arabi route. By this route, Chinese ships would leave Guangzhou or Quanzhou in late November aided by the northeast trade winds, and arrive at Sumatra in about 40 days. They had to wait there for another northeast wind to come next year, which would bring them straight to the Arabian Peninsula in a voyage of 60 days without having to stop over in Sri Lanka or south India. Once in Mahrah, they would load their ships with goods from the Persian Gulf, Aden, Red Sea, North and East Africa, then prepare to return home in the coming southwest wind season. There was another maritime trade route to the Arabian Peninsula ports from China. In its first lap, it was the same as the other, as the ships would leave the Chinese ports in November for Sumatra, there to stay through the winter until the northeast wind came next spring. But, then, they would sail from Sumatra straight to the port of Quilon in south India. From Quilon, the ships—if they could not cross the Arabian Sea before the northeast trade winds were over—would set sail northward to Mirbat or Sohar in the Arabian Peninsula after the southeast winds set in, and return to Malabar with Persian and Oman spices and other goods. However, they had to stay for the winter in Malabar, before returning home with the southwest winds in the next year—a voyage of more than 18 months. Both Quilon in India and Dhufar in the Arabian Peninsula were principal ports of destination for the Chinese merchant ships from the mid-twelfth century on.

The Chinese merchant ships, built during the Song Dynasty, were large ocean-going vessels with watertight partitioned hulls and mariner's navigation compass. They were capable of sailing more than 5,000 nautical miles continuously within a comparatively short duration—a performance superior to their Muslim counterparts. China's overseas traders had, since the late eleventh century, set up their business bases in Sumatra, Maldives, Zanzibar and Madagasgar islands. By the thirteenth century, the Maritime "Silk Road" had reached as far as Kilwa in Tanzania in the south, and along the Mediterranean all the way to Morocco's Atlantic coast in the north. The shipping route linking Guangzhou and Quanzhou with the south Indian port of Quilon was dominated by Chinese merchant ships beginning in the twelfth century. Few Arab ships sailed farther than Sumatra on their voyage to the East. This dominance continued for about three centuries, along the Maritime "Silk Road."

During the Yuan Dynasty, Quanzhou became China's largest port and also one of the few world-famous harbours acclaimed by international travellers. Ibn Battutah (1304-1377), the great Islamic traveller, noted that he had found three different types of Chinese ships at the port of Quilon: the large-sized "junk," the medium-sized "zao," and the small "kakam." This description fit the Yuan Dynasty's specification, which provided that a large ship might be accompanied by a medium-sized *chaisui* (fuel and water) boat and an eight-oared boat. Such a specification was indeed well-considered for ocean-going Chinese merchant ships, including a great variety—ranging from 3 to 12 sails capable of carrying 1,000 passengers each. Some such ships were said to have as many as four decks.

During the thirteenth and fourteenth centuries, these Chinese merchant ships, serving as maritime envoys, helped maintain a close link between China and the Islamic world and provide a bridge of cultural and economic information between the East and West.

2. Delegations Sent Overseas by China During the Song and Yuan Dynasties

The Song Dynasty court had been interested in developing overseas trade, attaching much importance to improving its ties with other countries from the very beginning. As a result, it had received envoys from Sumatra, south India and Arabian Peninsula through maritime routes. The Srivijaya Kingdom of Sumatra, which was called Sambhoja (after the neighbouring Java Island) by the Chinese during the Song Dynasty, occupied a strategic position in the bottleneck of the sea route linking the South China Sea with the Arabian Peninsula. Taking advantage of its favourable location, Sambhoja, whose capital had moved to P. Weh from Palembang during the period between 1079 and 1082, blocked the sea lane with iron chains to force the passing ships to moor at its port. As a result, both the Chinese and Arab ships often called at P. Weh port and exchanged cargoes there. In 971, the first shipment of Arab petroleum was delivered to China by a Sumatra emissary. Cola in south India's Coromandel Coast also formed friendly ties with China in the eleventh century, hoping China could persuade Sambhoja to ease its blockade and allow Cola to develope maritime trade with Chinese ports. Since the tenth century, China had also made progress in developing its relations with both the Caliphate of Bagdad and Egypt, thereby enhancing its trade ties with the Red Sea ports. A number of Arab mariners visited China during this period, and one of them was Captain Abu Himyarite of the Yemeni merchant ship *Himyarite*, who toured Guangzhou port in 993 during one of his many trade voyages to China. Another was Captain Domiyat of Egypt, who visited China many times during the same period. He took part in the imperial pilgrimage to the Buddhist holy site of Mount Taishan in Shandong in October of 1008, when he was received by the Song Emperor Zhenzong. The Egyptian captain offered the Chinese emperor a gift from the Egyptian King and received, in return, a present given by the Chinese monarch to the Egyptian ruler. This event marked the establishment of formal ties between the Song Emperor (Zhao Heng) Zhenzong (998-1022) and the Egyptian King Fatima Caliph Hakim (996-1021). That was also the beginning of diplomatic relations between medieval China and Egypt.

Soon after the Yuan Dynasty was founded in China, the Mongolian Prince Khaidu staged a rebellion in 1268 in Central Asia against the rule of Great Kublai Khan, making it vital to keep the sea route open between China proper and the Il-Khanate in West Asia. It was under these circumstances that the Uygur emissary Ihemish visited Malabar in 1272, and again in 1275, to seek continued economic ties with these countries. After the Yuan Dynasty troops took Quanzhou, the Yuan emperor dispatched envoys ten times to visit overseas states. In 1280 and 1282, the Yuan Dynasty envoy Yang Tingbi made two trips to Quilon in Malabar, where he was given a ceremonious reception by the local ruler, receiving promises of support from both the Egyptian traders and the Muslim chieftains. From Malabar, Yang went to Kenya in East Africa, before returing home. By 1286, ten states in Malaya, Sumatra, India and East Africa had established diplomatic relations with the Yuan Dynasty, sending their envoys to open trade relations with China. The Yuan Dynasty had solidified its relations with the Indian Ocean countries.

In 1283, the Yuan emperor dispatched his vice prime minister Boro (1246-1313) to Il-Khanate by sea. Boro had since stayed in Il-Khanate and served as a trusted aide to the successive Il-Khanate rulers—Aluhun, Gegatu, Betu, Hezan, and Helbanda khans. He was appointed commander of the 10,000-strong Imperial Guards by Hezan Khan, and was also responsible for furnishing information about the Mongolian tribes and the Yuan Dynasty to the Il-Khanate historian Ras Dedin. Ras Dedin was so impressed with his great knowledge that he praised the Mongolian high official as "the Great Emir Commander of Iranian Army and the International Leader—our Prime Minister Boro." The *History of Mongolia*, which was completed by Ras Dedin in 1307, as the first volume of his *Book of History*, was based on the dictated narration by Boro. Their close cooperation was the indispensable condition to the completion Ras Dedin's celebrated works on the history of Mongolia and the Yuan Dynasty.

II The Maritime "Silk Road" and the Communication in Materials and Culture

1. Overseas Markets Opening to Chinese Silk

According to *Song Shi* (*History of the Song Dynasty*), Chinese exports had, since the tenth century, been composed mainly of coloured silk goods, porcelain, tea, lead, tin and copper. Chinese copper coins were very popular in Southeast Asia and Sri Lanka, where the local traders favoured the Chinese merchant ships who paid for their purchased goods in copper coins. In fact, Chinese coppers were in circulation as currency in all the seaports frequented by Chinese ships in these areas. Archaeological discoveries from areas in Southeast Asia and the Indian Ocean have listed a variety of Chinese copper coins, ranging from the Tang Dynasty's Kaiyuan (621) coins to the Ming Dynasty mints. Chinese copper coins dating back to the reign of Emperor Taizong (976-997) of the Northern Song Dynasty had been unearthed even in Kilwa of Tanzania.

The medieval Arab geographer Idrisi (1099-1166), in his book of *Geography*, stated that Chinese merchant ships had frequented Bharuch in India's Khambhat Gulf, mouth of the Indus, Aden, mouth of River Euphrates and other ports—bringing such Chinese goods as iron, swords, leather, silk, velvet and other textiles. At the improtant trading centre of Sumatra, which lay between Southeast Asia and the Indian Ocean, Chinese merchants traded in gold, silver, porcelain, silk and satin, brocade, sugar, iron, wine, rice, *gaoliang* ginger, medicinal herb and camphor. Their exports covered a wide range of marketable goods from grain to textiles and metals. But the prized Chinese goods on the foreign market were silk and porcelain.

The Song Dynasty rulers encouraged silk exports in order to boost the national income. At the same time, they also used such silk products as brocade, gauze, satin and tough silk as gifts to foreign envoys. Since the twelfth century, there was a marked growth of silk industry in the coastal region of southeast China. Silk products increased rapidly in cities like Suzhou, Hangzhou and Quanzhou, and exports kept pace. The Song Dynasty court became more generous in giving out silk as gifts to foreigners. When an envoy from a subordinate state of Cambodia arrived in the Song capital in 1200 to offer tribute to the Song emperor, the Song court gave him a remarkable return-gift of 1,000 rolls of red silk gauze in additon to 200 rolls of pink patterned satin.

While Chinese silk continued to enjoy an extensive market abroad for its unique style and excellent quality, it was facing growing competition from the more and more attractive Persian and Iraqi silk products—especially, in the Mediterranean and the Red Sea areas. During twelfth century, a variety of new silk products emerged in West Asia and soon became popular in Europe. They included the silk baldacco of Bagdad, fashionable striped attabi (called tabi in Europe), golden silk scarf (kufiyah) of Cufa, silk curtain and mantle of Kurdistan, brocade and gauze of Shiraz, sophisticated embroidered gowns (tiraz) and brocade of Fasa and other places, taftah (called taffeta in Europe) of Persia, Persian multi-coloured "atlas," the damask of Damascus, and camlet. All these new silk products were coveted by the Italian and Frank merchants, who rushed to buy them in Palestine and Aleppo and then sold them on the European market. Nevertheless, Chinese silk, brocade and satin continued to sell well in Japan, Korea, Southeast Asia, and in India, Sri Lanka, Persia, Mecca, Egypt, Somali, Kenya and Tanzania.

The Arab geographer Idrisi, a resident of Sicily, stated in

1154 that, to his knowledge, the silk goods produced in Quanzhou (Susah) were unparalled in their excellent quality and luxuriant beauty, and that Hangzhou (Janku) was known as a producer of both glassware and silk goods. Chinese poet Su Song wrote a poem in the late eleventh century to praise Quanzhou for its wonderful silk products, which were just as good as the Sichuan or Suzhou silk to match the beauty of springtime. The silk industry of Quanzhou had grown to such magnitude as to be comparable to the famous silk-producing centres in Sichuan or east China. Relics of Quanzhou silk were seen in the 334 pieces of various gauze, satin and tough silk garments, unearthed in 1975 from the tomb of Huang Sheng (died in 1243) at Mount Fuchang in suburban Fuzhou. The silk products of Sichuan were well-known to the Persians, who called the Sichuan brocade "parniyan" or "parnikan" in classic Persian language. Beginning in the twelfth century, Quanzhou silk became a very popular item on the international market. It was called zeituni in Persia after the name of its producer Quanzhou, which was known as the city of Zeitun (thorny paulownia) to foreign merchants. Later, Quanzhou silk was called zetani by Italian buyers, and satin by the French, and seide by the Germans. But the Chinese "satin" bought by the Europeans actually included both the Quanzhou silk and the multi-coloured silk of Suzhou and Hangzhou, which were also exported through Quanzhou port.

During the Yuan Dynasty, high-quality Chinese silk, such as brocade and coloured satin and floral thin silk, like Persian dibaj and atlas or Arab thin silk and tabi, sold well on the markets of Middle East and Mediterranean region. The silk producers of China and Arab states continued to exchange their skills in making brocade and satin. They even adopted the names they each had used for their products. For isntance, the Persian word "nasij" was used for brocade in the Yuan Dynasty, while the Persians called the golden satin "kimxaw" or "kamxab" after the Chinese name *jin hua* (golden floral pattern). The Persian name of "kimxaw" was also used by the Arabs, and "kamxab" was used by the Indians. Chinese coloured satin was sold on distant markets of Egypt and Morocco of North Africa and Kilwa in Tanzania of East Africa. Trade link also existed between Kilwa and Guangzhou, as indicated in the classic Chinese book of geography *Nan Hai Zhi* in which the port of Kilwa was listed.

Marco Polo, the Venetian traveller, noted in his book that China's excellent silk and brocade were produced in such cities as Kaifeng, Zhenjiang, Suzhou and Hangzhou. Ibn Battutah, the famous Muslim traveller, had also lavished praise on the silk products produced in China, saying that China produced so much silk that even poor people could afford it, because it would cost almost nothing but for the transportation fares. He pointed out that Quanzhou satin was even more attractive than those produced in Hangzhou or Beijing. He had seen 500 rolls of Chinese brocade—presented to the Sultan Mohammed of Dehli, India, by a Yuan Dynasty envoy on behalf of the Great Khan of the Yuan Dynasty—which included 100 rolls of Quanzhou silk and 100 rolls of Hangzhou silk. During this period, following the expansion of Chinese merchant shipping in the India Ocean, Chinese silk, as well as Chinese porcelain came onto the overseas market in an unprecedented quantity.

2. The Chinese Porcelain Boom Across Three Continents

As early as the first century, China had—following its invention of silk—become the world's first porcelain producer, when the kilns in Shangyu area to the south of Hangzhou began turning out the earliest batch of blue chinaware, which was soon followed by the successful production of white porcelain in north China. During the many centuries that followed, the kilns in the coastal area of south China specialized in producing blue porcelain, while white chinaware were widely produced in the north. In the Tang Dynasty, porcelain products had become the most popular household utensils used for eating, drinking, cooking or storing water and other items. When these smooth-finished, light and durable vessels began to appear on the international market, they won the immediate admiration from around the world.

Exports of Chinese porcelain began on a major scale at the end of the eighth century. The Arab geographer Ibn Faqih stated in his Book of *Geography* (903) that China was reputed for its three major export products, namely, silk, porcelain and lamps. And for Arab and Jewish merchants, Chinese porcelain as well as Chinese silk were seen as the major source of wealth in their trade. Chinese porcelain first created a sensation in the court of the Caliph of Bagdad Harun al Rashid (786-809), when 20 pieces of exquisite Chinese imperial chinaware were offered, in tribute to the Caliph, by Ali ibn'isa, one of his provincial governors. The governor, then, followed by presenting another 2,000 pieces of Chinese porcelain utensils to the Bagdad court. The Bagdad Caliphate was excited to see such finely-finished chinaware. Their surprise was comparable to what the Chinese felt when they first set eyes on Roman glassware. This event marked the beginning of large-scale exports of Chinese porcelain to the Islamic world —a development facilitated by the burgeoning maritime shipping. While shipping transport ensured the safe delivery of the fragile cargo, the relative density of the porcelain freight provided the merchant ships with ideal ballast.

The first foreigner, who personally witnessed the making of porcelain in China, was Sulaiman al Tajir, an Arab merchant. He stated in his book of travel in 851 that Chinese used a fine-grade clay to make various kinds of vessels as transparent as glass, "which, when filled with wine, could be seen through."[1] That was when Chinese porcelain had begun to attract the attention of foreign traders. The Muslim historian Ibn Khordadhbah said in his book *Sheng Dao Zhi*, China had four major seaports, of which Port al-Wakin in Indo-China Peninsula was the first to export porcelain. However, during the Tang Dynasty, Mingzhou (now Ningbo) and Guangzhou were best known for their large volume of porcelain exports. Mingzhou was, then, the biggest exporter of blue porcelain, which was shipped to Japan, Korea and indirectly to other Asian and African countries, by way of Guangzhou and al-Wakin. Products of Changsha's Tongguan Kiln, which was the first to develop porcelain with colourful paintings under a glazed finish on the surface, were also exported via Mingzhou port. Evidence of this was found in relics unearthed from ruins of the

[1] E. Renaudot, *Ancient Accounts of India and China by Two Mohamedan Travellers*, London, 1733, P. 21.

ancient Ningbo docks. Even the Ghazni Muslim scholar al-Biruni (973-1049), who was a long-time resident in India, knew that Chinese porcelain had come from the port (Ningbo) at the mouth of the Yongjiang River. According to the appraisal prevailing in the Islamic world, Chinese porcelain was then rated at three different grades. Top grade was given to the apricot-yellow china-ware, characterized by its thin base, clear colour and crisp sound (at percussion). Next came the creamy-white porcelain; the various light-coloured products fell into the lowest grade. When they were arranged according to source of production, porcelain produced by Changsha's Tongguan Kiln was rated as the top grade; white porcelain from the Xingyao kilns in north China was next, and the Zhejiang-based kilns' blue porcelain took the third grade. Nonetheless, such an appraisal also suggested that the various household utensils produced by the Zhejiang kilns accounted for the bulk of the Chinese porcelain exports sold on the international market.

Chinese porcelain utensils, including bowls, trays, cups, plates, bottles and jars became popular in the households of foreign countries, following the large-scale export of such products. Blue porcelain was particularly favoured by the Ghaznavid Dynasty of Afghanistan, who named the product "Ghuri" after its monarch. In the twelfth century, Egyptian Sultan Saladin (1138-1193) of the Ayyubid Dynasty emerged as a famous collector of Chinese blue porcelain. This legendary rival of the crusaders was known to have presented many attractive articles as personal gifts to the monarchs in Europe. Thus Europe got its first blue porcelain vase from the Egyptian Sultan, and the Europeans began to call the blue porcelain "Saladon."

The blue porcelain products of Zhejiang kilns were sold to a vast overseas market, extending from Japan in the east, to Iran, Iraq and Egypt in the west, and Kilwa of Tanzania in the south. Such a relic, dateable to the tenth century, has been unearthed in Kilwa. Exports of Chinese porcelain continued through the centuries to these regions. The popular Longquan porcelain included such Song-style items as double-layer bowls, lotus-petal pattern plates, plates with folded rims, basins with straight or fan-shaped sides, vases with fish-shaped or ring-shaped ears; also Yuan-style lotus-patterned bowls, bowls with spread round stem and cone-shaped bowls. All were sold to an extensive region around the Indian Ocean. Comparable to Longquan blue porcelain in popularity on the overseas market, was the various blue and white chinaware produced by the Jingdezhen kilns of Jiangxi. Known for its thin base and clear glaze, Jingdezhen porcelain attracted much attention both at home and abroad, resulting in the widespread imitation of the product not only in Jiangxi but also in other provinces such as Fujian, Guangdong and Guangxi. Such similar blue and white porcelain produced by kilns in Dehua, Tong'an, Quanzhou, Jianyang of Fujian and in Guangzhou and Chaozhou of Guangdong were also sold extensively in Southeast Asia. Archaeological discoveries of the Song, Yuan and Ming dynasties' porcelain in the Philippines ranked first in Southeast Asia in both quality and quantity. They included—apart from a sizable amount of chinaware produced by Zhejiang and Longquan kilns as well as the blue and white porcelain of Jing-dezhen and Dehua kilns—a good variety of the porcelain products of the Xicun Kiln of Guangzhou. Relics of Chinese porcelain unearthed in Malaysia were mainly products of Guangdong and Fujian, while more than one million unearthed porcelain samples have so far been collected by the Museum of Sarawak.

During the Yuan Dynasty Chinese kilns began to produce —in addition to the blue and white porcelain—a newly-designed blue-floral porcelain, which soon attracted the attention of overseas users in Japan, Thailand, the Philippines, India, Iran and Egypt. They liked its bright colour and delicate pattern.

Like other Chinese major inventions as paper, printing, compass and gun powder, Chinese porcelain was introduced to Europe through Egypt. In fact, Chinese porcelain was still not widely seen in Europe in as late as the fifteenth century, when the famous Chinese navigator Zheng He made his expeditions to the Indian Ocean. In the mid-fifteenth century, the ruling Egyptian Sultan, seeking better trade ties with Europe, sent Chinese blue-floral porcelain to the Dome of Venice as gifts. Then he gave more such gifts to the "Magnificent" Lorenzo de Medici

(1449-1492) of Florence. In the early sixteenth century, before the Portuguese had come to India and China, shipments of Chinese porcelain to Europe were mostly handled by the traders of Genoa or Venice. Florimond Robertet, who had served as minister of finance under the French Kings Charles VIII, Louis XII, and Francis I, was the owner of the earliest collection of porcelain in Europe in the early part of the sixteenth century. He wrote for his collection the following caption: Exquisite porcelain, the first batch brought back to Europe from the Orient by the Eastern Europeans, in white colour and elegant style and having miniature paintings on their surfaces.[1] The porcelain in his collection was probably white porcelain exported from Quanzhou.

Since the fourteenth century, Chinese porcelain utensils had been widely used by the people of East Africa in their daily life, almost by every household there. Both the Muslim immigrants and the Black residents in this area preferred to use the reasonably-princed chinaware as their dinner sets or containers, although they still bought a lot of Aden pottery. Yuan Dynasty porcelain had been unearthed in such African sites as the old Gedi port of Kenya, Chwaka of Zanzibar, the ancient tomb of Kaole in the south of Pangani, even in the African heartland of Mapungubwe. During the Yuan Dynasty, a wide range of Chinese porcelain products became the rage on markets across the three continents of Asia, Africa and Europe. Particularly popular on the Mediterranean market were the black and brown-glazed porcelain produced in the Jianyang's Shuiji Kiln of Fujian (called Jian Kiln), which were noted for their unique finish. The famous Arab geographer Idrisi had, after praising the exquisiteness of Susah (Quanzhou) porcelain, pointed out that China's Jian porcelain (Ghazar-Sini) was simply "unique," whose fame had travelled far and wide. Insofar as the Mediterranean region had, since the eleventh century, become a booming market of all kinds of Chinese porcelain, the maritime route leading from China to the Mediterranean was called "the Porcelain Route" by Japanese

---

[1] M. Beurdeley, *Porcelain of East India Companies*, London, 1962, P. 103.

scholars.

3. The Influx of Spice, Rhinoceros Horns and Ivory into China

After the ninth century, coupled with the export boom of Chinese porcelain, imports of all kinds of spice began to pour into Chinese ports. The variety of imported goods continued to grow during the Song and Yuan dynasties, covering approximately the following ten categories: spice, rhinoceros horns and ivory, jewelry, fur and pelt, textile, glass, food, bamboo and wood, metals and minerals. However, spice topped all other goods not only in variety but in quantity of all imports into China. Even the *Song Shi* (*History of the Song Dynasty*) admitted that the Song court's tax revenue depended mainly on four commodities—tea, salt, alum and spice. The fifteen varieties of spice imported during the Song and Yuan dynasties included: frankincense, borneol, Persian spice, agalloch eaglewood, sandalwood, clove, sweet osmanthus, nutmeg, pepper, aloe and ambergris. They were imported from places in Viet Nam, Cambodia, Thailand, Malaysia, Indonesia, south India, south Yemen, Oman, Ethiopia, Somali, Kenya and Tanzania.

Next to spice, two other popular imported goods were rhinoceros horns and ivory, which were consumed in large quantities in medieval China. Ivory, for instance, was used to make imperial carriage, emperor's bed, high officials' tablets, belts, sculptures, boxes and dinner sets. Emperors of the Tang and Song dynasties travelled in ivory carriages, and the Great Khan of the Yuan Dynasty used ivory sedan-chairs, which were made with ivory imported from Arab nations. At the time, Somalia was the leading ivory exporter of Africa. East Africa then exported elephant tusks 2.5 metres in length weighing 75 kilogrammes, which were desired for their fine texture, colour and configuration, as well as their reasonable price. Ivory was chosen by the Chinese for high-grade sculptures. Since the ninth century, Arab and Persian traders shipped ivory from the heartland of Africa to India and China. In the fourteenth century, China began importing high-grade rhinoceros horns from Kenya.

China began to import cotton fabric from abroad during the Song Dynasty. In the Yuan Dynasty, though the country made much headway in cotton production and even began exporting cotton goods to Southeast Asia, import from India and Java of high-quality cotton fabric continued in large quantities. Chinese historian Wang Dayuan listed some forty kinds of imported cotton fabrics, including Bandjarmasin cloth, Tunisian Mehdiye cloth, Indian Masuli-patnam cloth, and Java cloth. Java cloth and Bandjarmasin printed cloth were known for their fast colour, while Indian masuli was known for its fine texture. Among the most popular imported cotton goods were also the finely-woven cotton sheeting of Sambhoja and Jangala (now Surabaya) of Java, and the thin cotton cloth of Bombay measuring 2.1 metres wide and over 3 metres long. This Bombay cloth had also been taken by Chinese traders and sailing boats for sale to other regions. The continued increase in domestic consumption of cotton goods during the Yuan Dynasty was responsible for the brisk trading and large-scale imports of cotton products in this period.

III   The Three Famous Travellers of the Yuan Dynasty

The Yuan Dynasty was most remarkable as an era of unprecedented brisk exchange of cultural information across the continents, owing partly to the frequent visits to China by overseas tourists and the interesting reports they wrote about their travels in this historic period. Three major books were left by three great travellers during the Yuan Dynasty. They were *Travels* by the Venetian traveller Marco Polo, the memoir of the African Muslim Ibn Battutah on his travels to Asia, Africa and Europe, and the book written by the Chinese traveller Wang Dayuan on his experiences in the Asian and African regions. All three books were written during the decades between the late thirteenth and the mid-fourteenth centuries. Each had its own distinct character, playing its unique role in history and leaving an unforgettable imprint upon the course of world culture.

1. Marco Polo and His Trip to China

Marco Polo (1254-1324), the greatest traveller in medieval history, was also a legendary politician and essayist who had accomplished an immortal feat in his lifetime. His book *Travels* stirred Europe in the fourteenth century and served as a bridge of information that linked the West with the East, through a protracted period of time.

Born of a prestigious Venetian family in Italy, Marco's father Nicholas was a prosperous businessman. In 1260, when Nicholas and his brother Matthew travelled from Crimea to Buhara on a business trip, they came across a Mongolian envoy, who was on his way to deliver a message sent by the Il-Khanate conqueror Hulagu to the Great Khan Kublai Khan in China. The Mongolian envoy took pains to persuade the two Italian merchants to follow him to the Chinese capital, because he thought the Great Khan would be delighted to see two Latins for the first time in his life. Nicholas and his brother finally agreed and went along with the envoy to China.

Arriving at the capital in 1266, the two Italians were warmly received by the Great Khan, who asked them about the government and people in the European countries and was greatly pleased with their answers in fluent Mongolian language. So the Great Khan appointed the two Italians as his envoys to bring a letter from him to the Roman Pope, requesting the Pope to send a Christian with extensive knowledge in science and arts to work in China, and also asking the Pope to let this Christian bring some oil from the lamp in the Holy Tomb of Jerusalem with him to China. The two Italians, then, departed from the Yuan Dynasty capital for Europe, in the company of an envoy of the Yuan court named Ohatai. But the Mongolian envoy fell ill halfway on the journey, and had to let the Italians proceed by themselves on to Rome. On their arrival in Rome, Nicholas and his brother found the Roman Church was waiting for the election of a new Pope, so they returned to their home in Venice. Marco Polo, son of Nicholas, who was fifteen years old, was fascinated by his father's stories of the Orient, and insisted on joining Nicholas and Matthew on their journey back to China. On September 1, 1271, the new Pope Gregory X was elected and he gave Nicholas and his brother a message of reply to the Mongolian Great Khan. On their return trip to China, they travelled overland by way of Bagdad, across the Congling range and the Xinjiang desert to Dunhuang, and then turned eastward, arriving at Yuan Dynasty's capital of Shangdu (now Duolun of Inner Mongolia) in May of 1275—at the end of a three-and-a-half-year long journey. At the Yuan capital, they were received by the Kublai Khan himself.

According to his *Travels*, upon his arrival in China, he took pains to study the Mongolian language and customs, thus winning the favour of Kublai Khan, who then sent him to Yunnan for inspection. Knowing that the Great Khan wanted to find out the condition and customs of different regions through his envoys or inspectors, Marco Polo paid attention to collecting information from every region he visited, and reported them to the Yuan court on his return. As a result, he won the confidence from both the Great Khan and the Mongolian high officials, whereby the people around him began addressing him as "Your Excellency Marco Polo." During his seventeen years' service in the Yuan court, Marco Polo had been sent as an imperial envoy to many regions in and outside the empire, and even filled a local official post in Yangzhou for several years. He said he could write in four languages—Uygur, Persian, Han or Tangut and Mongolian.

In his book Marco Polo tells of travelling through much of China and visiting Viet Nam and Java after 1280 as an official envoy of the Yuan court. In Volume III of his book, he tells of his experiences abroad, including his final mission to the Il-Khanate, which led to his eventual return to his hometown of Venice.

In 1286, the beloved Queen Consort Buluhan of Il-Khanate's Aluhun Khan left a will before she died, asking the khan to choose a girl from her own tribe of Boyawutai in Mongolia to succeed herself as the new queen consort. The Khan of Il-Khanate, who respected the will of his late queen, dispatched three officials—Oulatai, Apousca and Coja—to Beijing to seek the Great Khan's approval in finding a new queen. In response to Aluhun Khan's request, Kublai Khan decided to let his 17-year-old daughter, Princess Gogojen, go to the Il-Khanate and marry Aluhun as his queen consort. With the consent of the Il-Khanate officials, Marco Polo went along with them, as a member of the Mongolian princess' entourage, on an oversea journey to the Persian Gulf.

The princess and her entourage set sail from Quanzhou in early 1291 in a fleet of 13 large vessels, each of which had four masts to carry a total of 12 sails; and they brought with them letters from the Kublai Khan to the kings of France, England, Spain and other Christian states. After a voyage of three months, their fleet arrived in Sumatra, where they waited for five months, then sailed again westward for another eighteen months, before reaching the Hormuz Strait; from Hormuz, they continued the journey overland to the north. But by the time they arrived at the Il-Khanate's capital in 1294, they discovered Aluhun Khan had died three years earlier, on March 12, 1291. Princess Gogojen had no choice but to marry the new Il-Khanate ruler Hezan Khan. She died soon after their marriage.

It was already 1295, when Marco Polo finally returned to Venice, and found himself facing an unbelieving family, who could hardly recognize that this stranger—speaking and looking like a Mongolian—was their own kinsman. But when the Venetians saw the countless jewels and valuables which he had brought home from China, they began calling Marco Polo's house "the Millionaire's Mansion." And Marco Polo, himself, became the "Marchus Paulo Millioni" and a senator of Venice.

Four years later in 1298, Marco Polo fought for Venice in a sea battle with Genoa, which resulted in the defeat of the Venetian Fleet. Seven thousand Venetians, including Marco Polo, were captured by Genoan forces. While in jail, Marco Polo attracted attention of his fellow inmates with his colourful adventures in the Orient. There he dictated the stories of his adventure to prison-mate Rusticiano of Pisa, who recorded it all in classic French. It was the earliest manuscript of the book *Travels* of Marco Polo. In August, 1299, Marco Polo was released from prison in Genoa and returned to Venice, where he lived until his death in 1324. The great Venetian traveller treasured his memory of China and all those Chinese souvenirs he brought home. Of the many valuable Chinese porcelain he took back with him from the Chinese port of Quanzhou, at least one small blue and white glazed vase produced by Dehua's Chunling Kiln is now kept in the Italian Museum.

The earliest version of the book of Marco Polo, written in classical French well understood in Europe, was soon widely circulated and reproduced across Europe. The four-volume book was prefaced by an eighteen-chapter introduction by the recorder, Rusticiano, summarizing the travels of Marco Polo and his family to the Orient. Volume One covered Marco Polo's experiences during his early journey from the Mediterranean to Kublai Khan's capital of Shangdu. Volume Two, which comprised three parts, gave a description of Kublai Khan and his palace, capital, court, government, festivities and hunting trips. It also furnished an account of the hero's travel from Shangdu to the southern state of Burma. Finally, it detailed his tour to the coastal cities of Hangzhou, Fuzhou, Quanzhou and other towns in southeast China. Volume Three covered stories about Japan, Viet Nam, east India, south India, the coastal region of the Indian Ocean and east Africa. Volume Four was devoted to a description of the conflict and wars among the Tatar princes within the Mongolian ruling family of Genghis Khan and also between the other tribes in North Asia.

In his book of memoir, Marco Polo produced a vivid image of the brilliant, powerful and benevolent Great Khan of a vast Oriental Empire, of his magnificent palaces, his prosperous capital, his cities, his people and the unparalled culture and strength of his country. He described Japan as a country full of gold, where gold bricks were used to pave the floor and build roofs and windows in the palace, because the country was seldom visited by overseas traders and had no konwledge of the value of gold. Such a colourful Orient as described in his book created widespread illusions among the people of the medieval Europe, who became fascinated by the "book of world wonders." While Marco Polo's memoir of his travels had won many admirers, it had also given rise to derision and scorn among those who believed the book contained preposterous lies designed to fool the public. That was why, during his final hours, relatives and friends gathered around his death bed and urged Marco Polo to confess that he had lied in his memoir, so that God might forgive him and allow him to ascend to heaven after he died. The dying Marco Polo rejected such suggestion, insisting that what he told in the book was not only truthful, but contained "less than half of what I had seen with my own eyes."

After the mid-nineteenth century, people began to pay more attention to the study of Marco Polo, as information available from Oriental literature proved that most of his memoirs were factual. There was also evidence in Chinese historical records to show that Marco Polo had returned home in the company of Persian (Il-Khanate) envoys. This was found in the Ming Dynasty's book of *Yong Le Da Dian* (*Great Encyclopaedia of the Yongle Reign*), which quoted a Yuan Dynasty official document—dated the 17th day of the 8th month in the 27th Year of Zhiyuan (1290) —saying the Yuan Dynasty's governor of Jianghuai Province had received a decree authorizing the three Persian envoys Oulatai, Apousca and Coja to return to Il-Khanate. That was when Marco Polo and the envoys were on their way to Quanzhou port. The names of the Persian envoys as given by Marco Polo in his memoir were identical with the names in the Yuan Dynasty document, which served as another verification of his book of *Travels*.

Marco Polo's book provided valuable information on his route of travel from West to East in its first volume, and the fourth volume gave an account of the conditions in the three Mongolian prince khanates of Il-Khanate, Kipchak (Golden Horde) and Chagatai Khanate—which covered a vast area from East Europe to Central Asia. Both contained important data for research into history of the Mongol Empire and West Asia. The second volume, which gave details on events in China, such as the quelling of rebellions, the execution of traitor Ahuma, the battle of Yongchang, the seige of Xiangyang and the massacre of Changzhou, was a useful supplement to the book *Yuan Shi* (*History of the Yuan*

Dynasty); so was the third volume's description of the ill-fated Mongolian expedition against Japan. All such historical data could not possibly have been created through the imagination of a Venetian merchant. The allegation which has since recently re-surfaced in Britain—claiming Marco Polo had never been to China—was apparently based on nothing but prejudice.

The most remarkable part of Marco Polo's memoirs was his description of China as contained in the second volume, which accounted for 40 percent of his entire book and comprised 82 chapters. In this volume, Marco Polo expressed admiration for the Great Khan's capital of Khanbali (Beijing), describing it as a "metropolis of immense population and prosperity" that enjoyed trade ties with some 200 cities around it, and received as many as 1,000 cartloads of silk per day. The scenic beauty of the Beihai Lake and Qiongdao (Jade Island) was emphasized in his description of the Chinese capital. He went on to depict the booming southern cities of Suzhou and Hangzhou, calling Suzhou a bustling town of colourful silk and numerous bridges known as "City of the Earth,"[1] whereas Hangzhou was "City of the Heaven," which boasted a population of two million engaging in 12 major trades and transacting deals, involving "tremendous sums of money." He added that even he would not have believed that the Great Khan was able to collect such a huge amount of tax revenue, until he had actually seen it with his own eyes. Marco Polo was also deeply impressed with the magnificent Song Dynasty palace in Hangzhou, which he said was the largest palace in the world with a perimeter of ten miles. He lavished praise on the neat stone-paved streets, urban amenity of Hangzhou and, particularly, the beautiful West Lake and the luxurious villas around it, not forgetting to mention the regular festivities staged on the island pavilion in the West Lake. And when he came to introducing the Yuan Dynasty's largest seaport of Quanzhou, Marco Polo called it the "City of Thorny Paulownia" and said that he

---

[1] Marco Polo said in his book that there were as many as 6,000 bridges in Suzhou. This was an exaggeration, because Matteo Ricci, the Jesuit who had come to work in China since 1580 and described Suzhou as the "Oriental Venice," noted there were some 400 bridges in that city.

was "stunned by the huge volume of trade" going through the port.

Marco Polo devoted a chapter to introduce to his readers such items as the Yuan Dynasty's paper currency, the Chinese use of coal and the sugar-refining process in Fujian's Yongchun. Marco Polo's book reflects his deep love for China, indicating he was a true friend of the Chinese people as well as a valuable envoy of the Italian people.

Within a few months after its publication, copies of the Marco Polo's *Travels* were widely circulated across Italy and read by almost every household. In 1477, the German translation was published, marking the first printed edition. The circulation of the book was further enhanced by the introduction of movable-type printing. The book attracted an increasing number of researchers since the mid-nineteenth century, leading to the publication of a revised edition in 1938, which was by far the most comprehensive version of the book. By the end of 1970s, there had emerged more than 120 translated versions in different languages in the world.

The book *Travels* of Marco Polo was first introduced to China in 1874, when the "*Zhong Xi Wen Jian Lu*" (*Sino-Western Information Review*), published by Tongwen Institute in Beijing, carried in its 21st issue an article by Yingtang Jushi, which told the story of Marco Polo's travel to China during the Yuan Dynasty. The book was also quoted by the writer Hong Jun in his *Supplements to the Translated History of the Yuan Dynasty*. However, the Chinese translation of the book of Marco Polo was first conducted by the late Qing Dynasty writer Wei Yi, and published in installments on the Beijing-based *Jing Bao* newspaper, owned by Wang Kangnian. Then, in 1913, the translation was formally published in a book form entitled *Travels of Marco Polo, A Visiting Official of the Yuan Dynasty*. This was followed by two more Chinese translations: one by Li Ji and the other was a translation of excerpts, based on Henry Yule's English version of the original book, by Zhang Xinglang. However, the 1935 Chinese edition translated by Feng Chengjun from Charignon's French version of the original was by then the most complete edition. It was considered better than all previous translations. The most recent Chinese translation of the book was published in 1980 in Fujian Province; it differed from all previous editions in its use of the colloquial instead of the classical Chinese.

Despite the fact that Marco Polo's book had once been viewed by many as fictitious or even full of lies, it had, nevertheless, stirred the hearts of many adventurers in Europe. In 1428, the Portuguese traveller, Pedro got a copy of *Travels* in Venice, and gave it to his brother Henry, the Navigator (1394-1460), prince of Portugal, prompting the latter to pursue a series of explorations overseas. Even Christopher Columbus (1451-1506) was said to have read the book, before he set sail on his expedition to discover the "New World"; this was proven by the copy of Latin translation of *Travels*, found among the Columbus relics now preserved in the Columbus Museum in Seville, which contained Columbus' handwritten notes on as many as 45 pages. And when the great Spanish navigator's ship arrived in Haiti in the Caribbean Sea, he at first thought it was Chipangu (Japan) mentioned in the book of Marco Polo. When he reached Mexico, he was almost certain that he had arrived in Hangzhou of China.

The book of Marco Polo played an unprecedented role in broadening the vision of the medieval Europeans. The publicized wealth of the Orient spurred the burgeoning maritime powers on to exploring the "new world" overseas, thereby opening a fresh chapter in global history.

2. Ibn Battutah's Tour of the Orient

Not long after the legendary adventure of Marco Polo, another great traveller emerged in the Islamic country of Tangier in Morocco. He was Ibn Battutah (Shaykh Abu 'Abdallah Muhammad Ibn Battutah, 1304-1377).

Ibn Battutah, called Shaykh for his reputation as a Muslim scholar, went as a pilgrim to Mecca at the age of 21. During the 30 years that followed, he had travelled continuously across a large part of Asia and Africa, and to Granada in Spain, spending most of his active life plodding across the vast steppe or sailing over the turbulent seas.

In the course of his career, Ibn Battutah had travelled 120,000 kilometres across three continents. He had served as an emissary for India—during the years while staying in Delhi of India and in Maldives—to visit China, travelling extensively in its coastal area. He visited Byzantine in the company of the envoy dispatched to Constantinople by the Kipchak Khanate. And as an Islamic traveller, he paid tribute to Mecca in four separate pilgrimages, and toured Cairo four times. He was appointed Grand Judge by the Sultan Toclak of Delhi and received by Yuzub Khan of Kipchak (1312-1342) and by Tarmasli Khan of Chagatia. Having made such firsthand observation of the countries and cultures under the rule of Islamic, Byzantine, Indian and Mongolian empires, Ibn Battutah, surpassed Marco Polo in exprience and konwledge of the world.

While serving as Grand Judge, Ibn Battatuh enjoyed free access to the court. In 1341, an envoy sent by the Yuan Dynasty's Emperor Shundi arrived in Delhi from Dadu (Beijing), requesting the Sultan to rebuild the Buddhist Temple in Sahar at the foot of Mount Harajir for the benefit of pilgrims from China. In response the Sultan of Delhi sent a delegation led by Battutah to China. Ibn Battutah and his delegation set out from Delhi in July of 1342 for Khambhat; from there they took a boat to Calicut to wait for a Chinese sailing ship to pick them up. However, by the time they reached Calicut, they found the city in political turmoil. Ibn Battutah and his delegation had to change their itinerary and sailed instead from Quilon to Maldives. Having stayed for two years in Maldives, they set out again to Sri Lanka, then to Bengal and Assam, and finally boarded a ship sailing to China at the Bengalese port of Souargaon. The ship took them first to Java, where Battutah again stayed for some months before embarking for a 17-day voyage to the Chinese port of Quanzhou. His date of arrival in Quanzhou (according to the author's study of historical data) was June 1, 1345 (the 29th day in the first month of 746 by the Islamic calendar).

Ibn Battutah stayed in China for less than one year, and left Quanzhou for India approximately on May 18, 1346 (the 25th day in the first month of the Islamic year of 747). During his stay in China, he travelled first from Quanzhou to Guangzhou, and then back to Quanzhou again before going north along the coast from Fujian to neighbouring Zhejiang—across the Xianxialing Mountains and the Fuchun River—finally arriving at the metropolis of Hangzhou, the former Song Dynasty capital, whose thriving prosperity deeply impressed him. From Hangzhou, the Muslim traveller went along the Grand Canal to the Yuan Dynasty capital of Dadu (Beijing). However, he hadn't had an opportunity to meet the Yuan Emperor Shundi, because he had earlier lost all the gifts intended for the emperor during his stopover in Malabar; so he did not have anything to prove his identity as an envoy from India. All he had, to identify himself in China, was the introduction by the captain of a Chinese ship to the local official on his behalf, when he first arrived in Quanzhou. While in Beijing, he had heard about a dispute in the Yuan court on the issue of succession to the imperial throne. Such an issue, in fact, had already been solved, after the Yuan Emperor Shundi was enthroned. This indicated that the Islamic mullah, from whom Battutah heard the story, was not well-informed.

The Christians were enjoying a more favourable social status in the Yuan capital compared with the Muslims during those years. The Muslim traveller stayed in Beijing for nearly two months, during this time, he said he had heard that the throne of Great Khan was usurped by the late Khan's cousin Feluz; this Feluz was none other than Emperor Shundi, for "Feluz" in Persian meant "success" or "auspice"—the same as the Chinese character "shun" used for the reign title of Emperor Shundi.

In November of 1349, Ibn Battutah completed his tour of Asia and returned to his home country. However, the elderly Muslim traveller continued his tour by visiting Granada on the other side of the Gibraltar Strait, then, the upper reaches of the Niger River in West Africa.

Ibn Battutah, in his late fifties, was brought to the attention of Moroccan Sultan Feli Abu Ina, who ordered his secretary Mohammed Ibn Yosse to put Battutah's dictated travelling memoirs in writing. Then in 1355, the world-famous *Rihla* (*Travel Stories*) was worked out after a three-month effort by these two men. Its original manuscript was discovered, centuries later, in Constantine of Algeria and sent to the French National Museum in Paris for preservation. The book was as voluminous as the legendary *Travels* of Marco Polo.

In his book Ibn Battutah recalled his travel in China, starting from the Yellow River, which he had, however, mistaken as a river joining the sea at "Sin Kalan" (Guangzhou) of "Sin ul-Sin" (Guangdong). Guangzhou as well as Quanzhou were the two places in China best known to Ibn Battutah. During his extensive travel in south China, he was impressed with the thriving agriculture and well-developed irrigation system, the sugar which was "as plentiful as in Egypt but more refined than the Egyptian produce," and also the ubiquitous grapes, plums and watermelons. He concluded that "China had everything I could find in my homeland." Moreover, Ibn Battutah praised China as the largest producer of wheat in the world, and that Chinese porcelain was "the best on earth." He paid special attention to China's porcelain, silk and coal. He pointed out that China was exporting porcelain to various ports of India for transhipment to Morocco and other parts of the world. He noted that silk garments were worn even by the poor in China. And like Marco Polo, he was surprised at the extensive use of coal as fuel by the inhabitants in both north and south China. He described it as a special clay cake that burned better than charcoal and could be reused by mixing its ash in water and then drying it to hardness.

In his book, Ibn Battutah expressed great admiration for the talented skills of the Chinese people, describing them as "the most skillful and most talented in arts and crafts among all the nations." And he went on to say that "the Chinese were so unique in their painting art that no other nation—no matter whether they were Christians or non-Christians—could match them."

Ibn Battutah used the best possible phrases to depict the prosperity of Chinese cities. He rated Khanbali (Beijing) as the equal of Cairo, and said Hangzhou was "the largest city I have ever seen in the world, for it took me three days to walk across the whole town." According to the Muslim traveller, the south China port of Quanzhou was, then, undisputably, "one of the five leading seaports in the world" along with Calicut and Quilon of India, Sudak of Crimea and Alexandria of Egypt.

Ibn Battutah also stated that China was a country with exemplary law and order, well-developed post road system and transportation network, guaranteeing the safety of travellers. In short, the great Muslim traveller was deeply impressed with China's well-established political system and prosperous economic and social environment.

In 1985, a Chinese edition of *Travels of Ibn Battutah* was published in Yinchuan of China's Ningxia Hui Autonomous Region. This edition, based on the popular Arabic edition published in Cairo, was a complete translation of the original, enabling Chinese readers to appreciate the adventures of the great medieval Muslim traveller.

3. Wang Dayuan's Two Voyages Across the Indian Ocean

During the era when two great travellers from Europe and Africa came to visit China during the Yuan Dynasty, Wang Dayuan—a Chinese maritime trader—had also set sail twice to visit places in Southeast Asia, the Indian Ocean and Mediterranean. He was known to have toured more than 100 foreign places, which had maritime links with China at that time.

Wang Dayuan alias Wang Huanzhang, of whom little was known besides his overseas adventures, was born in 1309 in Nanchang of Jiangxi Province. Since the age of 20, he had been going abroad on ships from the port of Quanzhou; and in less than 20 years, he had twice visited many parts of Asia and Africa for trade or for travels, surpassing all his domestic predecessors in both navigational practice and geographical experience. His enthusiastic dedication to the overseas venture made him the greatest and most experienced traveller in the Chinese history.

Wang's two overseas tours, both originating from Quanzhou port, covered nearly 10 years. His first trip began in 1328 when he was 20, and his second trip ended at 1339 when he was 31. During both journeys, he travelled along similar routes from the

South China Sea to the Indian Ocean, then going to as far as the Red Sea, Mediterranean and East Africa.

It took Wang some years—from 1328 to 1333—to conclude his first maritime journey around the South China Sea and the Indian Ocean. The places he visited during this trip included Luzon and Mindanao of the Philippines; Maluku and Bandar of Indonesia; Pekalongan and Cirebon of Java; Begawan of Brunei; Chon Buri and Prachuap of Thailand; Pahang and Kelantan of Malaysia; Singapore; Palembang, Jambi and Aceh of Sumatra and Colombo of Sri Lanka. From there he sailed on to Malabar Coast in 1331, then westward to Dhufar and Aden, before returning to Quanzhou in the summer of 1332. This journey marked the first overseas touring voyage by a Chinese sailing ship.

Wang's second voyage, which closely followed the first, lasted six years, from late 1334 to 1339. During this time, he conducted an in-depth commercial survey in Africa—the region that formed an essential part of the Islamic world of that era. Wang's journey, this time, was prompted by the fact that an entrepot trade between India and the Mediterranean was then prospering under management of merchants from Karami of Egypt. Other Islamic traders flocked to the East African coastal region to trade in gold, ivory and slaves. During the period from the winter of 1334 to the summer of 1335, he travelled along the Indochinese Peninsula coast from Viet Nam to Burma, then, sailing northward from Tavoy of Burma to Bengal. In the winter of 1335, he travelled along the Indochinese Peninsula coast from Viet Nam to Burma, then, sailing northward from Tavoy of Burma to Bengal. When they arrived in Aden from Quilon of India, he changed to an Arab ship to continue his journey along the African coast. Wang started the second leg of his second voyage by making a pilrimage to Mecca, then travelled on to the Mameluke's capital of Cairo by way of the Halaib port of today's Sudan. From Cairo, he went on to Tangier of Morocco, recording what he had seen of the four ports and cities in Northeast and North Africa.

He sailed around the Cape of Guardafui to arrive at Mogadishu of Somali; from there he went on to the Kenyan coast, finally, reaching the port of Kilwa Kisiwani in Tanzania. Later he sailed from Kilwa to a nearby island called Sango Mnara, which was almost the extreme limit where the trade winds could reach at Cabo Delgado along the East African coast. That was also the farthermost place visited by Wang Dayuan in the South Hemisphere. In July 1339, Wang finally returned to Quanzhou from his second journey abroad. By then, he had visited every continental coast that a sailing ship could reach from China during that era—excepting Japan, Korea and European countries.

Many palces Wang Dayuan had visited during his two journeys abroad were unknown to both Chinese and foreigners. This prompted him to record his experiences in a brief memoir called *Dao Yi Zhi Lüe* which was first published as a supplemen: to the book *Qing Yuan Xu Zhi* in Quanzhou in 1349. The next year, when Wang Dayuan returned to his hometown in Nanchang, he had the revised edition of the memoir published in an independent volume under the name *Dao Yi Zhi Lüe*, which contained a total of 100 anecdotes, each focusing on a different geographic location. As Wang noted in the book, all but one of the anecdotes were written from his personal experience.

Wang Dayuan's book of travels, which played a monumental role in allowing the outstanding achievements of this great Chinese traveller to go down in history, has occupied a significant position in Chinese and international records of navigation and in the Yuan Dynasty's developments of relations with foreign countries.

In the navigational history of the Indian Ocean, Wang, as a Chinese navigator, had left a reliable record of conditions along the coastal area of both the Indian Ocean and the Mediterranean, based on an on-the-spot survey. It is now clear that he had visited an extensive area, covering the Philippines and Maluku in the east, Egypt and Morocco in the west, and Kilwa Kisiwani of Tanzania as well as Sango Mnara in the south. He was the first Chinese to visit the Atlantic coast of Morocco, which was described in an anecdote entitled "Dajina," meaning "the ancient Xiyu (Western Regions)"—a translated version of the Arab "Magreb" (Occident). He said the place was inhabited for generations by Dali people, which meant it was the homeland of Darisa, a major Berber tribe. Wang Dayuan was also the first identified Chinese traveller to have visited Kilwa in Tanzania. In his experience, the only other large country which could be compared with China had been the Mameluke Dynasty of Egypt—"an empire ruling many states across a distance of 18,000 *li* (9,000 kilometres) along the Indian Ocean coast prospering with brisk trade." The rich resources of Bengal, and the Chinese sailing ship's familiar calling port of Quilon all reappeared vividly in his book. The vital geographic information contained in his book enabled the cartographer of the Yuan Dynasty to draw a correct map of Asia, Africa and Europe. The "Atlas of the Unified Territory of Dynasties and Capitals," as drawn by the two Korean cartographers Li Hui and Quan Jin in 1402 to cover Europe and Africa, had depicted Africa in the shape of an inverted triangle with its tip pointing to the south. This marked amazing progress from the previous Arab maps, which had, invariably, described the south end of Africa as bending eastward in the direction of Sumatra. In fact, the map drawn as late as 1456 in Cairo, based on the information provided by Idrisi, still showed Africa as stretching eastward all the way to a continental region in the Pacific Ocean. The above-mentioned Korean map was made on the basis of two preceding Yuan Dynasty maps, the "Sheng Jiao Guang Bei Tu" by Li Zemin and "Hun Yi Jiang Li Tu" by Qing Jun, which were finished in the 1330s and 1360s, respectively, after Wang Dayuan's maritime trips abroad. The geographic success of the Yuan Dynasty was obviously connected with the correct information provided by Chinese navigators and tradesmen, who had been very active during that period. Wang Dayuan was undoubtedly one of these important contributors.

On top of being a great traveller, Wang Dayuan was also a shrewd maritime businessman, who was keen in observing trade developments as well as the life and custom of the local residents abroad. Everywhere he went during his overseas journeys, he had made careful observation of living conditions and habits of the native people, local products, their need for imports and also the local geographic environment. During the fourteenth century, trade activities around the Indian Ocean centred on textiles and household utensils, while the Indian cotton fabrics, such as Batula cloth, Bengal cloth, Muslin and Batan cloth were the popular goods sold in both Southeast Asia and East Africa. China's four major export items—silk, porcelain, coloured beads and ironware—were also highly favoured on the markets of Southeast Asia and regions around the Indian Ocean. For example, Wang Dayuan had noticed that Chinese sailing ships were bringing to the Indian port of Quilon such cargoes as gold, silver, blue-white patterned porcelain, Batan cloth, coloured satin and ironware. To the Arab port of Aden, they were bringing blue satin, red beads, coloured silk from Suzhou and Hangzhou, blue-white patterned porcelain, and china-vases. They were also bringing such goods as coloured satin, blue-white patterned porcelain, ironware and coloured beads to the African port of Mogadishu. Chinese merchant ships were then engaged also in entrepot trade in such goods as sapanwood, rice, cotton fabrics, clove, round cardamom and ironware, etc. Wang Dayuan was very careful in observing the outstanding features of local products, such as the excellent quality of Sumatra kapok, low price of Malabar rice, high-grade aloes-wood of Kelantan, famous horses of Aceh, pungent pepper of Calicut, red sandalwood, ambergris and gold ore of Malindi and the cobalt ore of Mogadishu, which were all listed in his book among the best native products.

Many geographic characteristics of the Asian and African continents as seen in the Yuan Dynasty were preserved in historical data, thanks to Wang Dayuan's memoirs. In his book, Wang described the outer appearance, ethnic race, and customs of local natives as well as climate and geography of their country. He pointed out in his book that what he had seen in Cambodia verified the popular proverb "Prosperity comes from Cambodia." In Sumatra, he noticed that the bumper rice harvests had enriched Palembang to the extent of "reaping a harvests of gold every three years." In Dumyat, he noticed that the Nile valley of

Egypt had become the "land of abundance," thanks to irrigation projects. From the port of Ad Dab'ah, he noted, it could lead southwestward to reach a country called "Guoli"—the Chinese name for ancient Ghana—which was connected by a caravan trail through Darfur and Aswan with the Mediterranean port. Ghana, then, known the "country of gold" was under the reign of Mansa Musa (1312-1337) of the Mali Empire. Wang was obviously acquainted with the trade route running across the African continent.

The book *Dao Yi Zhi Lüe* was not only a geographic directory and traders' handbook, but also a navigation manual. Well acquainted with the maritime route in the Indian Ocean, Wang Dayuan took special care to outline the navigation lanes in the South China Sea and the Indian Ocean in his book. He made particular mention of such key seamarks as "Kunlun-shan" (Paulo Condore), Colombo and Male Isle. The "Kunlun-shan" or "Kunlun Island," which is located not far from the mouth of the Mekong River, stretches a few hundred kilometres in a towering ridge over the South China Sea, forming a natural seamark for shipping in the area. The currently-used name of "Kunlun Island" (Con Son) was based on Wang's original designation. The island overlooks the rapid current in a rock-infested area, called "Kunlun Yang" (Kunlun Ocean) in the old days, where ships sailed with great caution often taking seven days and seven nights to pass safely. The danger of the voyage in the area was compared by old navigators as "sailing in a devilish torrent without rudder or compass." After the ship crossed the waters of Kunlun Island (Con Son) and reached the northwestern tip of Sumatra, other dangers lay ahead, in the turbulent Indian Ocean, on the way to Sri Lanka. This part of the ocean, called Lamuri Sea in ancient days, was constantly threatened by equatorial currents and would take the sailing ship two weeks through rolling high waves to reach Colombo. Then there were hidden rocks in the waters south of Colombo, which could be fatal to ships sailing in a storm. Farther on, unpredictable currents in the waters around Male Isle of Maldives posed yet another treat to navigators. Most ships sailing directly from Aceh of Sumatra to Maldives would moor at Male Isle, which lay on the curved maritime route observed by prudent navigators sailing from Sri Lanka to Aden in the west. This route was discovered by earlier west-bound navigators seeking to bypass the equatorial currents in the sea south of Sri Lanka. In maneuvering around the currents they found themselves blown by the shifting trade winds to Male Isle, where they had to wait for the next trade wind to continue their voyage. Veteran navigators before Wang Dayuan had, in as early as the twelfth century, discovered during their voyage off Maldives a shorter sea route to lead direct to the East African coast of Somalia. Wang Dayuan gave a brief introduction of this route in his book, leading the way for the maritime expedition of the great fleet led by the next famous Chinese navigator Zheng He, which opened the direct route from Sumatra to Mogadishu.

The book *Dao Yi Zhi Lüe*, which recorded the maritime accomplishments of Wang Dayuan through his journeys across the Indian Ocean, was considered the most valuable navigation manual of that region in the fourteenth century, comparable to *The Periplus of the Erythraean Sea* written by an unknown Greek captain in the first century. The Greek captain's book, which described his voyage, starting from the Red Sea to reach Tanganyika in the south, Persian Gulf in the north and Sri Lanka in the east, had been a historically reliable navigation manual of the Indian Ocean for centuries. His achievement was succeeded, some 1,300 years later, by Wang Dayuan, whose more extensive navigational experiences enabled him to compile an unprecedented sailing record, covering more than 100 overseas places. His experiences surpassed many of his contemporary Arab counterparts. It was interesting to note that Wang and his Muslim counterpart had visited each other's home country almost in the same decade. In 1336, Wang toured Battutah's hometown of Tangier near the Atlantic and appreciated the pleasant winter in the southern coast of Mediterranean. Then, nine years later in 1345, Ibn Battutah arrived in Quanzhou from India and enjoyed the busy scenes of this second hometown of Wang Dayuan, who had many friends and relatives in Quanzhou and kept travelling between this port city and his home in Nanchang. Wang and Ibn Battutah had, indeed, through their historic voyages, helped to link the whole world into one unity. The medieval navigation boom enabled people to communicate with each other from both ends of the world. Wang Dayuan, as the most experienced and respected navigator and traveller of ancient China, had set a brilliant example for his follower Zheng He.

IV   Zheng He's Voyages to the West and China's New Ties with the Asian and African Countries

1. The Itinerary of Zheng He's Seven Voyages

The Ming Dynasty, since its founding in 1368, had for the first thirty years adopted a policy of maritime embargo preventing private merchant shipping from leaving the country. As a result, the traditionally flourishing foreign trade along the country's southeastern coast was virtually strangled. Many tradesmen and political exiles organized their own contraband market to counter the limited official trade operated by the government in the name of exchange of tribute or gifts. Eventually, the Ming Dynasty had practically lost its normal links with the countries of Southeast Asia.

But the government's closed-door policy was reversed in 1402, after Zhu Di, Emperor Chengzu of the Ming Dynasty, seized the throne by military force. Immediately following his enthronement, the new emperor took steps to develop overseas relations and trade by sending envoys to such regions as Calicut of India, Java, Thailand and Malacca, indicating his determination to revive the country's lost ties with the outside world. His intent was to gain control of the international trade in the Indian Ocean, through a powerful maritime campaign initiated by his government with the cooperation of the neighbouring countries. He sought to eradicate the overseas remnants of the anti-Ming Dynasty military or political force and create a new international climate of peaceful cooperation between China and countries abroad. This was accomplished by repeated westbound maritime expeditions, launched by the massive Chinese fleet led by Zheng He (1371-1435) during a period of 28 years. The unprecedented maritime expeditions had resulted in linking the destinies of China and many other countries in Asia and Africa. The result was renewed activity in economic and cultural exchange. They had developed China's shipping to new heights throughout the world.

During the period from 1405 to 1433, China's *Baochuan* (Treasure Boat) Fleet launched seven voyages, each time passing the *Xi Yang Guo* (West Ocean State) located in the area of Calicut and Fandarina in Malabar of India. Throughout the seven voyages, Zheng He as supreme commander of the fleet, distinguished himself as a maritime leader, competent military commander and talented diplomat. Born as the sixth generation descendant of the well-known Yuan Dynasty governor of Yunnan, Seyyid Edjell—a Muslim native of Bukhara—Zheng converted to Buddhism in 1403 and served as eunuch in the Ming imperial court, thereby earning the title of San Bao Tai Jian in historic legends. San Bao was his child name, and Tai Jian meant eunuch.

According to Ming Dynasty annals, *Guo Que*, the first maritime expedition of Zheng He's fleet, which lasted from December of 1405 until September of 1407, reached an extensive area across Southeast Asia and the Indian Ocean. These ports including Java, Palembang, Malacca, Calicut, Hormuz, Dhufar, Aden and Jidda. This showed that from the beginning of the expeditions, Zheng He had planned to visit all these Southeast Asian, Indian and Arab ports, which had been the traditional terminals of Chinese merchant ships. This brought the entire Indian Ocean and the Islamic holy region of Mecca into the range of his expeditionary voyages. Earlier, some foreign scholars such as Paul Pelliot and J.J. Duyvendak claimed that Zheng He had not sailed beyond Calicut during his first three voyages; but facts show otherwise. Historic data left from the Ming Dynasty indicate that, except for his second voyage which ended at Calicut owing to the limited time scheduled, Zheng He sailed straight from Malacca to Hormuz. The three ports of Malacca, Hormuz and Aden, which commanded the strategic channels along the East-West shipping route accross the Indian Ocean, had thus become the destinations of regular Chinese merchant sailing ships, thus establishing the Chinese as a leading power in international trade across the Indian Ocean.

The second voyage of Zheng He's fleet, (December 1407 to August 1409), chose Calicut as its destination, with stopovers at Thailand, Java and Sri Lanka. In its third voyage, (December 1409 to June 1411), the fleet not only stopped at Calicut as usual, but sailed on to call at Mecca. According to the memoir, *Shu Yuan Za Ji*, written by Zheng He's learned secretary Lu Rong (1436-1494), this voyage extended to reach Ryukyu Islands and the Philippines in the east, and Hormuz and Jidda in the west. For the first time, Zheng He paid visits to the three African ports of Mogadishu, Brava and Juba in southern Somalia, thereby defining the routes of the successive voyages in the years ahead. The opening of the East African navigation course was conducted by a special task flotilla, which sailed via Bengal and Quilon direct to Mogadishu, under the command of Hou Xian, one of Zheng He's deputies. The flotilla set sail near the end of the northeast trade wind in February of 1413, from China to Bengal, where it stayed for some time before sailing on to the East Africa via Quilon. Since the fleet of the fourth voyage was then just being organized, this flotilla designated as a special contingent of the third voyage. Hou Xian and Wang Jinghong were both deputy commanders of the third voyage fleet. Also taking part in this special expedition to East Africa was Fei Xin, who was sailing with the Zheng He's fleet for the first of his four consecutive voyages.

The fourth voyage (December 1413 to July 1415) of Zheng He's fleet surpassed the previous three. It sailed straight to Hormuz, then on to Aden, Jidda and the Egyptian port of Ad Dab'ah in the Red Sea. From there, it turned southward to visit Mogadishu and Brava, then proceeded down the East African coast to Kilwa in Tanganyika, finally reaching the ports of

Mozambique and Sofala which were already beyond the trade wind's navigation range. The port of Kilwa was called "Malin" in the Ming Dynasty files which listed the port as "Malindi." The name originated from the Mahdali (Mahadila) Dynasty founded in Kilwa by immigrants from the defunct Shirazi Dynasty of Aden. Also in the Ming Dynasty files, the ports of Mozambique and Sofala in Mozambique State were called "Bi-que" and "Sun-la," and were described as places "extremely remote from China" visited by an official Chinese delegation.

As a direct result of the effort of Zheng He and the fleet under his command throughout their four successive expeditionary voyages to the Southeast Asia and the Indian Ocean, the Ming Dynasty had achieved great success in realizing its strategic objective of restoring peace in the Southeast Asian region and improving the international status of the Ming Dynasty in both the South China Sea and the Bengal Bay areas. During these maritime campaigns, Zheng He and his soldiers were able to put down the anti-Ming Dynasty revolt of Chinese emigrants in Palembang, capturing their leader Chen Zuyi. They also succeeded in deposing the intransigent king of Sri Lanka and enthroning a new king. In northern Sumatra, they crushed the rebellion of Suvarna in Samudra. These victories helped to assure a safe maritime route linking China with the countries of Arabian Peninsula and East Africa—via Sumatra and Sri Lanka. China was thus able to establish friendly ties with the Sultanate of Kilwa and was assured of a favourable prospect in developing economic relations with other Arab and African countries. Husain Ibn Sulaiman (1392-1416), the Sultan of Kilwa, responded to the visit of the Chinese fleet by sending his envoys twice to China in 1415. These ties were severed, after the sultan's brother succeeded him as the Sultan of Kilwa and then lost control of the state to the local rulers. Despite the discontinuation of Kilwa's ties with China, however, the Ming court was host to envoys from both of Mogadishu and Brava, both of which exchanged diplomatic delegates with China during the 17 years from 1416 to 1433.

As a result of the opening of direct maritime routes between the Samudra Harbour in north Sumatra and Maldives and Mogadishu, and between Belligame of Sri Lanka and Brava by Zheng He's fleet in 1414, Chinese ships were able to sail from Nanjing to Kilwa in a continuous voyage. This greatly shortened the distance between East Africa and China and reduced the 7,300-nautical-mile voyage from Wuhushan in Fujian to Mogadishu to about 60 days at sea. This was a record achievement in the history of navigation.

None of the three subsequent expeditions of Zheng He's fleet, (the fifth voyage from December 1417 to July 1419, the sixth voyage from February 1421 to August 1422, and the seventh or last voyage from December 1431 to July 1433) had ever matched the fourth voyage in scale and sailing range, although all reached the Benadir Coast of Somalia.

Within the brief period of thirty years, China had occupied a predominant position in the maritime trade of the Indian Ocean, thanks to the successful voyages of Zheng He's fleet. Particularly noteworthy was the historic episode of a Chinese sailing ship exploring the seas off South Africa and rounding the Cape Agulhas to reach the Atlantic in 1420.[1]

2. The Treasure Boat Fleet and Overseas Cultural Exchange

The size of Zheng He's fleet exceeded 100 ships during each voyage, and these included many so-called *Baochuan*—the large multi-mast sailing ships—which numbered 63 in the first voyage. There were more than 40 during each successive voyage.

The first voyage involved 208 ships and 27,870 men. Most remarkable was the 9-mast, 1,500-ton *Baochuan* measured 138 metres from bow to stern and 56 metres wide at its middle. It was far bigger than any of the 3-mast vessels then built in Europe to replace twin-mast ships. Later, after the end of Zheng He's maritime expeditions, the shipyards in Genoa—known as Europe's largest shipbuilder—started building large sailing ships with a loading capacity, ranging from 1,000 to 1,400 tons. In 1418, the English shipyard in Southampton was known to have

---

[1] Yusuf Kamal, *Monumenta Cartographia Africae et Aegypti*, Vol. X, pt. 4, 1409 Sq.

built a large ship *Gracedieu* with a loading capacity of over 1,400 tons. However, the ship was never actually commissioned. Then, 60 metres was the limit to a vessel's length, as observed by many shipbuilders in Europe. The outstanding size of China's *Baochuan* ships exceeded all others in the world during that historic period.

In addition to the large *Baochuan* sailing vessels, Zheng He's fleet boasted advanced navigation techniques and well-trained crews, who were known to have mastered the use of such instruments as astronomical direction-finder and course-setting compass. Moreover, the fleet had navigation charts to guide them to their destinations along the pre-set course in the shortest time and under most favourable weather conditions. The navigation chart and course-setting compass were under the responsibility of the *huo zhang* (chief navigator) of each ship. Preserved samples of such navigation charts have been found in such classical books as Wu Pu's *Du Hai Fang Cheng* (*Navigation Directory*) of 1537, the sea map in Volume 240 of Mao Yuanyi's *Wu Bei Zhi* (*Treatise on Armament Technology*), the handwritten copy of *Shun Feng Xiang Song* (*Bon Voyage*) preserved in the Oxford University, and the *Hai Di Bu* (*Notes of the Sea*) recently unearthed in Quanzhou. Among these relics, the map in *Wu Bei Zhi* compiled before 1413, which had been called "Zheng He's Navigation Chart," was a rarely-seen classical sea map showing the extensive maritime area from the mouth of Yangtze River in East China Sea to Cabo Delgado on the African coast in the Indian Ocean. This area was then well-known to the Chinese navigators.

Through a policy of sending gifts by its fleet to the overseas states in exchange for their tributes, the Ming court succeeded in re-activating international trade across the Indian Ocean and expanding exports market for Chinese products. On the other hand, by giving support to overseas Chinese businessmen, it improved their status in contacting with the Islamic traders in the area. Apart from sending gifts of silk, satin, gauze and embroidery to foreign rulers and officials, the Ming court also paid for all living and travelling expenses of foreign envoys during their stay in China, and even had them sent back home by special convoy. Furthermore, it also paid favourably for the goods of tribute brought by foreign envoys and allowed them to openly trade among themselves, without imposing any tax on such trade.

The Treasure Boat Fleet trade enabled the Chinese exports —silk, brocade, satin, blue-floral-patterned and glazed-red porcelain, blue porcelain utensils, coloured beads, herbal medicine and metalware—to reoccupy their overseas market, while bringing back large quantities of imported goods including spices, drugs, pepper, sapanwood, hardware, jewelry and cotton fabrics. These goods piled up in the official warehouses of the provinces in such a quantity that they were often used to pay government employees as part of their salaries in kind. Thanks to the new trade boom, many popular Indian cotton goods, such as the Bengal mahmal and sanahbaf, the Calicut saklat and betteela, the Coromandel guinea, percallen, salempoeres and mousseline—all of which were widely sold in Southeast Asia—became favourite items on markets across the Chinese coastal provinces. In the fifteenth century, spectacles were also introduced to China from Malacca; they were then called "aidai" or "aina," after the Arab name. Zheng He's fleet was also instrumental in bringing back experts from the Arabian Peninsula to help Chinese workers improve their glass-making technology and produce new glass products, which were durable and resistant to the change in temperature. Most of all, the fleet played a major role in restoring and further enhancing communication between China and the rest of the world.

There was marked progress in the cultural exchange between China and foreign countries in the early part of the fifteenth century. Through the expeditionary voyages of Zheng He's fleet, China was able to establish special diplomatic ties with many key states located in the vast area between Japan in the east and Calicut in the west. The Ming court issued decrees, through its maritime envoys, to grant princedom titles and jade seals to the rulers of Malacca, Samudra, Sirandib, Cochin and Calicut, where stone monuments were built to mark the event. The monument in Calicut had a stone tablet, bearing the engraved inscription written by the Ming Dynasty Emperor Yongle (Zhu Di) himself, which concluded with the phrase: "a country sharing similar life, culture and economy with China, some 100,000 *li* (50,000 kilometres) away." The stone monument built in Sirandib of Sri Lanka bore inscriptions engraved in three languages, with Chinese on top followed by Tamil and Persian. To these states, the Ming Dynasty court also issued "Da Tong" (Unified) Calendar, which recorded 62 important national political and social events. Diplomatic activities launched by Zheng He and his colleagues, along with the grant of generous gifts and treatment to these overseas states, prompted them to send envoys to China in rapid succession. When these envoys returned home, after having seen the prospering Chinese civilization during their visits to Beijing and elsewhere in China, they became more eager to introduce Chinese culture to their countries.

Chinese emigrants and traders overseas were, themselves, responsible for disseminating Chinese culture to regions around the Indian Ocean. It was said that the fishermen of Cochin had learned how to weave fishing net from the Chinese emigrants, who went there during the Zheng He expeditions. In his book, Indian writer Abdul Razzak said the sailors of Calicut were called Chini bachagan (Chinese guy). Local legends held that Calicut was once ruled by a Chinese, who was chosen as king after the old king died.

The Latin historian Juan Gonzalez de Mendoza wrote, in his *History of the Kingdom of China*, that the local residents of Calicut had told him that the many fruit trees in Calicut were planted there by Chinese immigrants. In Sarawak, wooden tomb pillars were found in the Dayak cemetery, with porcelain bowls inlaid upon them. Similar tomb pillars had also been found along the Kenyan coast and in Pemba Island off the East African coast, where pillars topped with porcelain vases or pottery bowls were found to date from the thirteenth and fifteenth centuries. They were believed to have been built by Chinese sailors of Zheng He's fleet. Moreover, in the jungles near Mombasa, there were a few old dwellings which were said to have been used by the Chinese visitors during those years. All these indicated that Zheng He's fleet had undoubtedly served as the emissary and bridge of Chinese civilization across the vast ocean.

As a diplomatic envoy of the Chinese people, Zheng He was

also a cultural ambassador respected by the local people. In Malacca, the tiles on the front roof of the royal palace were said to have been brought there by Zheng He. In Samut of Thailand, which was the entry of Chinese travellers to the Southeast Asian country, Zheng He had built an arch, bearing his inscription "Tian Zhu Guo" (Buddhist Kingdom). In Jakarta, it was said that Zheng He had left a stone anchor as his relic. According to the historical record left by Portuguese traveller Gaspar Correa, Chinese descendants had remained in Calicut, where they had built magnificent temples. Temples entitled "San Bao Shrines" were found in Java, Sumatra, Malacca and Bangkok to commemorate San Bao Eunuch (Zheng He). Bangkok's San Bao Public Shrine still attracts large crowds of worshippers. The name of San Bao was also used in many places in the area to designate harbours, palaces, wells, caves or walls, showing Zheng He was respected by local people long after his death. Tribute was given not just to commemorate this great Chinese navigator and diplomat, but to remind future generations of the magnificent maritime expedition of the Treasure Boat Fleet.

3. The Attraction of Blue-Floral-Patterned Porcelain

During the Yuan Dynasty, the Jingdezhen Kiln of Jiangxi began batch-producing blue-floral-patterned porcelain, using a cobalt-based colouring agent. The product, which featured a blue floral pattern on a white base finish, was marked for its bright colour, delicate design and fine texture, and it soon became a success on the export market. Yuan Dynasty blue-floral-patterned porcelain had since been found in many other countries, and was praised by the great medieval Chinese traveller Wang Dayuan. It was sold extensively in the Philippines, Malaysia, India, Iran, Java, Sumatra, Bengal, Mecca and Kenya. The production of blue-floral-patterned porcelain gained its greatest popularity in the Ming Dynasty, particularly, in the reign of Emperors Yongle (1403-1424) and Xuande (1426-1435), when it topped all other porcelain products on the export market. At that time, the Jingdezhen blue-floral-patterned porcelain already began using Arab and Sanskrit scripts in its pattern design. Brisk sales prompted other kilns in Leping and Ji'an of Jiangxi, Yuxi and Jianshui of Yunnan, Jiangshan of Zhejiang, Boluo of Guangdong and, Dehua and Anxi fo Fujian to produce blue-floral-patterned porcelain. In the reign of Emperor Zhengde (1506-1521) of the Ming Dynasty, many such porcelain products adopted the popular styles of Middle East or Near East in their designs, with scripts of Arab or Persian language on them to cater to the taste of the Islamic world. Al Ekber, an Islamic businessman, visited China in 1513. When he left China for home in 1516, he brought back two pieces of extremely exquisite blue-floral-patterned porcelain bowls as part of the imperial gifts from Emperor Zhengde to the Osman Sultan Selim I. The bowls were said to have complimentary notations in Arabic baked upon them.

During its maritime expeditions, Zheng He's fleet brought along large quantities of domestic products, including silk products, textile, copper ware and ironware, gold, silver, copper coins, black lead, umbrellas and porcelain, particularly, the most attractive blue-floral-patterned porcelain. During the Yongle and Xuande years—as was during the Yuan Dynasty—the production of blue-floral-patterned porcelain had involved the use of imported cobalt ore with a low manganese but high ferrous content, which was critical in producing greenish-blue floral patterns, in bright contrast with the glazed finish of the porcelain base. The imported cobalt ore, called Somali Blue, was a product of Somalia. Zheng He's repeated visits to the East African coast as far as the Mozambique channel were inspired by his desire to import from this area—in addition to gold, ivory, copper ore and high-quality timber—the Somali colouring agent for the attractive blue-floral porcelain products.

Timur, who ruled Central Asia and Iran during the Mid-and Late fourteenth century, took pride in the possession of Chinese porcelain. Other rulers in Central Asia, including Sultan Mirza Rustem of Esfahan and Sultan Mirza Ibrahim of Shiraz obtained valuable porcelain from China many times in and after 1419. Many early fifteenth century Persian handwritten copies, now kept in the museums of Calcutta and Paris, showed pictures of aristocratic families using Chinese blue-floral porcelain tableware and utensils. Relics of fifteenth century Chinese blue-floral porcelain have been unearthed in Dambaguh, Mashhad, Rayy, Esfahan, and Firuzabad to the south of Shiraz in Iran. A large number of similar relics were found in the Philippines. Sarawak, Punjab, Sudan and Somalia. Next to the blue-floral porcelain, the blue porcelain of the Ming Dynasty was favoured by the buyers of East Africa. However, relics of Chinese porcelain, dating from the fifteenth century, which have been unearthed in East Africa, comprised far more blue-floral than blue porcelain. The fact that a large number of coarse blue-floral porcelain bowls were among the relics unearthed there was strong evidence that such Chinese porcelain products had been widely used by various sectors of the local community at that time. The ancient city of Kilindini in Kenya had seen the largest discovery of Chinese porcelain relics in the East African coast; a porcelain vase unearthed there was considered a gift presented to the city by the Treasure Boat Fleet from China. Blue-floral porcelain was popular in Kilindini through the fifteenth century, and some of the relics unearthed there had Arabic scripts on them. The large quantity of Chinese porcelain unearthed in Tanzania could well prove that the Ming Dynasty porcelain had overwhelmed Arabian porcelain to become a daily necessity in the life of local residents in the Revuma region.

Chinese traveller Ma Huan noted in his *Ying Ya Sheng Lan* (*Reflections of Overseas Tours*) that he had seen the people of Java as highly favouring Chinese blue-floral porcelain and also musk, gold-threaded silk and coloured beads, which were sold on the market for copper coins. Fei Xin, member of the Treasure Boat Fleet, said in his memoirs that Chinese blue-floral porcelain was the rage in Bengal, Sri Lanka as well as in India. Countries in the Arabian Peninsula and East Africa, which were traditional porcelain importers, also rated the blue-floral porcelain high above the blue or blue-and-white porcelain products.

The Persian rulers of the Safavid Dynasty (1502-1736) were said to be enthusiastic collectors of blue-floral porcelain. This was revealed in 17 letters sent by the Persian King to the Ming Emperor. Four of the letters contained requests for porcelain gifts from the Ming court. In 1611, the Persian King Shah Abbas made offerings to the Safavid Family Shrine located in Ardebil of northwest Iran. Offerings included 1,600 pieces of Chinese potery and porcelain, of which 1,162 were porcelain. Some 805 pieces of the porcelain relics are now preserved in the Teheran Archaeology Museum, and most of them—618 pieces—were exquisite samples of the Yuan and Ming Dynasty blue-floral porcelain, including the Ming Dynasty blue-floral porcelain of the Yongle and Xuande eras, taken to Persia by Zheng He's expeditionary fleet. Those relics are now priceless treasure. The Seraglio Palace of Istanbul, originally used as bedchambers by the Osman sultans, has become a museum called Topkapu Sarayi Müzesi. Out of 10,000 pieces of porcelain relics preserved in the museum, 8,000 are Chinese porcelain. Half of this number are Yuan and Ming Dynasty blue-floral porcelain, the other half are Qing Dynasty porcelain products.

Having opened their maritime route to the Orient in the late fifteenth century, Portuguese explorers began placing orders for Chinese porcelain for shipment back to Europe. Most of the orders were for blue-floral procelain products. In 1604, the Portuguese sailing ship *Carrack*, loaded with Chinese porcelain, was intercepted by Dutchmen, who took the cargo to Europe and auctioned it off on the market, calling it Kraaksporselein. The sale sparked a rising demand for Chinese porcelain in Europe, and the Dutch traders began buying spree for both the blue-floral and coloured Chinese porcelain.

Also in 1579, Chinese blue-floral porcelain was shipped to Mexico by the Spanish sailing ship *Galleons* from Manila in the Philippines. The Ming Dynasty blue-floral porcelain of Wanli reign (1573-1620), which was unearthed from the tomb of a Miwok Indian in America, indicated that the Chinese blue-floral porcelain had indeed reached all the five continents in the world, winning the admiration of the whole international community for the Chinese culture.

Chapter Six
Chinese Science and Culture
Introduced Worldwide

I The Inventor of Iron Foundry and Tunnelling Techniques

China was known for its ancient iron foundry techniques, which flourished during the early era of the iron age, when the Chinese were already using both the pig iron and wrought iron in foundry work. Europeans had not begun producing pig iron until the fourteenth century. In 1380, iron was still cast in Europe with iron ingots.

It was also the Chinese who first knew how to use coal in smelting iron, and how to add phosphor to cast iron. Then, during the Han Dynasty, low-silica pig iron and nodular cast iron were produced for the first time in the world by Chinese metallurgists. The Chinese people in the Han Dynasty not only widely adopted the use of malleable iron, which was developed during the Warring States Period, but also invented a new process of decarbonizing pig iron to produce tougher steel through "broiling." All these developments preceded those in Europe by almost 1,000 years. As a result, the Chinese metallurgical technique was introduced to the West, as early as the beginning of the first century, and soon became known throughout the world. The ironware produced in China was first brought to the Roman Empire during the early Eastern (Later) Han Dynasty, and was described as "Chinese iron" by Pliny the Elder (23-79) of Rome.

When the Western Han troops occupied the area south of

the Tianshan Mountains, during the years before the Christian Era, the tribesmen of both the Se and the Tukhara began learning from the Han soldiers ways and means to improve their primitive weapons. The Han troops were armed with sharp 80 to 118 centimetre-long swords with blades made of tempered steel in addition to long-handled slashing sabres which were far superior to those used by the armies of Central Asian countries at that time. It was said that deserters from the Han expeditionary army later introduced the iron casting technique to workshops in the countries of Dayuan (Samarkand), Kangju and Parthia. In 104 B.C., when the Han army, under the command of Han General Li Guangli, attacked Dayuan and lost its first battle at the Ferghana Basin, a number of Han soldiers were taken prisoners by Dayuan troops and stayed on, working as ironsmiths. Hence, the Ferghananians of Uzbek were the earliest to master the iron-casting technique outside the Chinese territory. In Tadzhik language, the Chinese word "zhu" (casting) was used for cast iron; it was also used later in the Tatar and Russian languages.

Parthia and Kangju were countries which imported metal weapons from China. The Parthian border town of Meru (now Mary) was, then, the largest trade centre in Central Asia and the transit centre of Chinese arms. The Parthian cavalry soldiers used very sharp swords and sabres made of Chinese metal, which left a deep impression upon the Roman soldiers during battles between Parthia and the Roman Empire. The Romans only knew that the Parthians got their weapons from Meru, therefore, they were called "Meru Weapons" by the Greek biographer Ploutarchos.

In 36 B.C., a Han expeditionary army of more than 40,000 strong attacked the headquarters of Zhizhi Chanyu, the Xiongnu leader, who had occupied Kangju. The Han troops, coming from their bases in Wusun and Dayuan, under the command of General Gan Yanshuo and General Chen Tang, discovered that the Xiongnu defenders had built a Roman-style fortification around their walled camp site, using rows of heavy wooden barricades. They also noticed that hundreds of the Xiongnu infantry soldiers

were training in a Roman-style fish-scale formation. It was believed that the Xiongnu chief Zhizhi Chanyu had adopted
Roman-style defence tactics, or even had a Roman legion under
his command at Kangju, during the battle. The Roman soldiers
were either former troops under Roman leader Crassus (115-53
B.C.), defeated and captured by the Parthians during the battle
of Carrhae, or Kangju troops trained by the Roman officers.
Then, after Zhizhi Chanyu and his Xiongnu troops were defeated
by the Han Dynasty army, the reputation of China's excellent
weapons soon became known even in Rome.

Chinese ironware found its way into India also quite early. In
the year of 90, the King of Yuezhi in India dispatched an army
of 70,000 men, under the command of his deputy, Kshatrap, to
cross the Congling range and attack the Eastern Han garrison
under the command of General Ban Chao, in the Shache and
Shule area of western Xinjiang. Faced with a numerically superior enemy, Ban Chao withdrew his men and materials into
fortified strongholds, while attacking the invaders from their
rear. The battle ended in a major defeat for the Yuezhi army,
which retreated in humiliation. The Yuezhi commander, who was
the Western Kshatrap under King Gandhinagar (78-120), and his
army were defeated by the outnumbered Han troops because of
the latter's superiority in both tactics and weapons. Since then,
friendly ties were established between the Han Dynasty and
Yuezhi with regular exchange of men and materials each year
—including, naturally, the flow of Chinese ironware into India.
Chinese iron, then, had several names, one of which was the
Sanskrit term "Cinaja" (China-born), implying the product (cast
iron) was made in China. The Sanskrit term for red lead (Pb_3O_4)
was also connected with the prefix of "Cina," indicating it was
from China.

China's unique product of white bronze was a white or
silver-coloured alloy of copper with zinc and nickle. During the
Han Dynasty the alloy found its way into Parthia, where it was
called "Xar-Cini" in Persian or "Xar-Sini" in Arabic—both
meaning "Chinese stone." The Swedish scholar von Engestrom
remarked in his article, published in 1776, that a Chinese white

bronze, containing nickle, had been brought to Bactria from China in as early as the second century B.C., and was used to mint coins. The relics of such coins, unearthed in the area, were found to contain 77 percent copper and 20 percent nickle, similar to the Chinese white bronze. This kind of white bronze was called "ao" or "white gold" in Chinese books of the third century, and was produced mainly in Dongchuan of Yunnan Province. It was known in Persia that the Chinese used white bronze to make mirrors and arrow-heads, and that such arrow heads were "lethal."

Tunnelling and trenching techniques, which were connected with mining, had been known in China since the ancient times, long before they were used in India and West Asia. Such techniques, first applied in copper mining in inland China, were later adopted by the Se people of Xinjiang, after the seventh century B.C. In the ruins of an ancient Se copper mine, discovered in Nilka County in Xinjiang in 1983, there remained some mining and water-lifting devices, including a balancing weight made of cobbles. These devices, which were identical with those unearthed in the Tonglushan copper mine of Daye in Hubei Province, had obviously originated from inland China during the reign of Prince Li (878-828 B.C.) and Prince You (781-771 B.C.) of the Zhou Dynasty, when groups of skilled Chinese workers moved to and settled in the northwest ethnic minority region. Mining activities thrived in China during the Warring States Period, when the Chinese people should have mastered the necessary tunnelling and trenching techniques. However, historic literature of such examples did not emerge until the reign of the Han Dynasty Emperor Wudi in the second century B.C., when a new form of an underground trench, called Dragonhead Trench, was built in Dali of Shaanxi to control underground water and protect embankments along rivers. Sino-Persian exchange on the technique had begun since the middle of the third century B.C., resulting in the use of similar underground trench in Seleucid Persia, where the design was further improved. The device, which was called "hyponomoi" by Greek historian Polybius (200-125 B.C.), had existed in West Asia since 146 B.C. It was further developed in Oman, where it was called "Faraj." By the second century, the total number of such underground trenches reached 10,000 in the area. The author of the travel book *The Periplus of the Erythraean Sea* noted in his book that he had seen such a trench-well in Barygaza of India in the first century. The origin of the Indian trench was a controversial subject. Some people believed that it was built by the Greeks of Bactria after they had conquered Barygaza; but some argued that the Greeks had never actually controlled the area. Therefore, a more likely possibility was that the project was built by the Grecized Se people, who had migrated down along the Indus Valley from Central Asia in the first century B.C., introducing the tunnelling technique to this area.

II   China's Sericulture Spread Overseas and Silk-Weaving Skills

Most ancient people depended on natural fibres, such as jute, cotton and hemp, for making cloth, while only a small number used animal-hair for the purpose. But the Chinese were the first to discover that the cocoons of wild silkworms could be used to spin into silk-fibre for weaving. And they succeeded in breeding the silkworm (Bombyx mori) at home with leaves of mulberry trees raised on their farm, thereby developing silk producing and processing technology. This included mulberry farming, silk worm breeding, filament spinning to weaving and dyeing. Thus, silk industry became the most important sideline production in China's agricultural society throughout its history of several thousand years.

Chinese silk had long since been known abroad, following the appearance of Chinese silk goods on the international market. However, the technology of silk production, as China's secret treasure, had not been introduced abroad until the third century B.C., when a group of Chinese emigrants settled in southeast Korea Peninsula. These people, then, began planting mulberry trees and breeding silkworms in this new country, which they called Chen Han. Later, the State of Pathae was founded in the area, and Chinese culture was introduced through Pathae into Japan. In the classic Japanese history book *Nihon Shoki*, there was a story saying that in the year of 199, a man named Prince Gongman—who called himself the eleventh generation descendant of China's Qin Dynasty Emperor Shihuang—brought silkworm eggs to Japan from Pathae, whereby the Japanese people soon learned how to plant mulberry trees and raise silkworms, starting silk industry in that country. During the Three Kingdoms period of China, the Japanese court sent their emissary to China four times in ten years since 238 to learn from China the skills of silk embroidery and dyeing. They also brought back some Chinese silk craftsmen to Japan with them. Japan, which was already producing brocade and dark-coloured satin, saw its silk industry develop rapidly in the following two to three hundred years, eventually catching up with the pace. The growth of the Japanese silk industry was partly related to its importing of Chinese skills and technicians.

During the reign of Japan's Emperor Ojin Tenno (270-310), more silk-weaving and garment-making skills were introduced to Japan by technicians from Pathae, and the Japanese began to copy the dress and style of China's Wu Kingdom, located in areas south of the Yangtze River. In 308, an envoy sent by the Japanese Emperor Ojin Tenno came to China with a request for skilled silk-weaving and tailoring craftswomen to work in Japan. As a result, four experienced women weavers and tailors went from China to Japan and started working in the Japanese court. Although the Wu Kingdom, no longer existed in China, the Japanese still referred to China as "Wu," which was pronounced as "kure" in Japanese, meaning "sunset" as opposed to the "sunrise" that Japan called itself.

Later, in the reign of Japanese Emperor Yuryaku Tenno (457-497), more Chinese senior silk-weaving and tailoring experts sailed to Japan from China's Zhejiang Province, in response to Japan's invitation. This event marked the birth of Japan's traditional garment of "wafuku," (*kimono*), which originated from the "wufu" dress of south China. The "waku" in Japanese also carried the meaning of its national identity. During that period, a large number of Chinese emigrated to Japan and contributed to the development of Japan's silk and garment industry. They introduced sophisticated silk processing skills to workers in that country. In recognition of their service, they were granted honourable titles by the Japanese emperor and nominated as "Ayabito" or "Silkman."

The Chinese sericulture and silk-weaving technology were also being introduced to the West during the same period when they began to take root in Japan. In the border regions of Yutian and Qiuci, silkworm-breeding and mulberry-tree-planting began in the first century, and were soon followed by the growth of silk weaving industry. Such silk product as Qiuci brocade was mentioned in books of Turpan script dating back to the fifth century, when silk industry was also established in Gaochang by skilled Han emigrants. In Yutian, many Indian emigrants, speaking northwest Indian dialect, referred to silk as "kita" or "krmi," meaning made from worms. However, the Indians were using filaments of natural silkworms for weaving, producing fabrics resembling flax. As for the Romans, they did not even know how silk was produced.

In the first century, well-known encyclopaedist Pliny the Elder said in his *Natural History* that silk was produced in the forests of Seres State (China) and could be woven into glossy silk fabrics. This indicated that he knew silk only as something growing out of the trees, and had never even heard about silkworms. To the east of Rome, the Persians were, of course, better informed, and managed to obtain silkworm eggs quite early. In the beginning, they used the leaves of the local plant of black mulberry (morus nigra) to feed the worms, then tried to learn the weaving skills from the Chinese in Xinjiang region. Efforts were made through various channels with the help of the Ruoran and Tukuhun tribes in Xinjiang to seek the help of Chinese experts. The result was the emergence of Persian brocade in the fifth century, and such brocade was even sent back to China in 520 as a gift from the Tatar King to the Liang Dynasty court in Nanjing.

The Byzantine Empire, as a close neighbour of Persia, was

being troubled by continued wars, and lagged far behind in developing its silk industry. However, spurred by the boom of colourful silk products in Persia, the Byzantine Emperor Justinian I (527-565) issued a decree in 542 to enforce the state monopoly of silk industry. Ten years afterwards, two Indian monks came from Serinda to see the Byzantine emperor in his palace, and told him that they would help his country produce its own silk by transferring silkworms from Serinda to the Byzantine Empire which was depending on Persia for raw silk. Justinian I accepted their offer, and they brought silkworm eggs from Serinda and started breeding the silkworm with local mulberry tree leaves, thus making possible the country's own silk industry. This is a story told in the book *De Bello Gothico* by Byzantine historian Procopius. A similar story was told by Theophanes that the silkworm eggs were brought to the Byzantine Empire by a Persian, who hid them in his bamboo stick to escape notice. Both stories, however, corroborated each other in saying the silkworms were brought to the Byzantine Empire from Serinda, which was an area between southern Xinjiang and India, then belonging to the State of Yutian. Therefore, the growth of the Byzantine silk industry was again related with China. In fact, extensive exchange on silk-weaving technology had begun much earlier between China and such Mediterranean cities as Beirut, Tyre and Sidon.

The Byzantine silk industry played a pioneering role in the whole Mediterranean region. In the twelfth century, the troops under King Roger II (1127-1154) of Sicily abducted 2,000 Byzantine silk workers and re-settled them in south Italy to begin silk-weaving industry of Europe. After the thirteenth century, other Mediterranean cities in Spain and France began to have their own silk industry. China's great neighbour India set up its own silk industry about the same time. When the famous Monk Xuan Zhuang of the Tang Dynasty was on his pilgrimage tour to India, the Indian weavers were still using the silk of natural (wild) worms to make the Kauseya garments. But when maritime communication began to flourish in the twelfth century, silk goods were seen everywhere from the Sea of Japan to the Mediterranean.

III   Taoist Alchemy Originated in China

The Chinese Taoists advocated the principle of contemplation in peace and reticence—a doctrine which resembled the yoga of Hinduism, focusing on moral and physical disciplines as well as meditation. In ancient China, however, the Taoist craving for "self-cultivation" had led to a quest for "immortality" through the use of certain drugs. Such a trend, then, gave rise to alchemy, which was considered as the essential technique both to produce the "panacea of immortality" and to transmit base metals into gold. The book of *Zhou Yi Can Tong Qi* (*Kinship of the Three and Book of Changes*) written by Wei Boyang (born in Shangyu County of Zhejiang Province) in the early second century had thus become the first book in the world to dwell on alchemy. The origination of the Chinese alchemy art was dateable back to, at latest, the second century B.C.

In Europe, meanwhile, the Greek copy of *Manuscript of St. Mark* in the Museum of Venice was considered the oldest book available on the art of alchemy. The existing copy was made in the tenth century, several hundred years after the original was written. Europe, probably, had not had its own book of alchemy before the fourth century, when the Alexandria pastor Synesius first used alchemic terms and formulas in his book *Physics et Mystica*, revealing that the Grecized Christian priest had begun to come in touch with the technique of Oriental alchemists.

In *Zhou Yi Can Tong Qi*, there was a clear introduction on the theory of alloy, such as that the mercury could form alloy with lead and amalgam could be used to produce gold. The book also clearly stated the reason why gold could not be easily oxidized and also explained the ratio of some matter's interaction. The author Wei Boyang used only 6,000 words to explain the theory and practice of alchemy in his book. It was during this time when the Chinese Taoists discovered that artificial cinnabar could be produced through the sublimation of a mercuric sulphide compound (Hg + S → HgS). Such a cinnabar product was considered an "elixir," which could enable anyone who ate it to become a "celestial being." In the Chinese classic *Shen Xian Zhuan* (*The Biography of Immortals*), written by Ge Hong, a story described how Wei Boyang had himself become "immortal" by the same means. According to the story, Wei Boyang and his three disciples went into the mountains to devote themselves to developing the "elixir." When they finally succeeded in producing the "immortal drug," Wei tried to test the faith of his disciples by first giving the drug to a dog, which ate it and died right away. Next, Wei took the drug himself and he, too died instantly. Seeing that the drug, which they had worked so hard to produce, had actually killed both the dog and their master, two of the disciples lost their faith in the cause and left the mountain. But the third disciple, who remained loyal to his master, chose to stay on, ate the drug, and died beside Wei. Soon afterwards, Wei Boyang came to life again. He shared the real "elixir" together with his third disciple and the dog. Thus, all the three of them turned into "immortal beings," so the story went.

Ge Hong (284-364) was born in Jurong County of Jiangsu Province. His grandfather Ge Xuan was a veteran Taoist, who passed his Taoist art to his disciple Zheng Yin, and Zheng Yin, in turn, passed it on to Ge Hong. In his early twenties, Ge Hong travelled to Nanhai in Guangdong, where he learned alchemy from another Taoist Bao Xuan. At the age of 50, he gave up his official post in the government and devoted himself in alchemy in the Luofu Mountains of Guangdong Province, leading the life of a Taoist hermit. He was an unparalled writer of his time, having written 220 books himself in addition to compiling 310 other books before he reached 40. The most important of these works included *The Book of Master Baopu*. The book deals with alchemy in "Chapter of *Metallous Enchymoma*" "Chapter of Elixir" and "Chapter of Yellow and White."

In his works, Ge Hong presented a systematic record of the chemical process—as having been verified since the second century B.C.—"Cinnabar when heated yields mercury, which after many transformations turns into cinnabar again." He had also made experiments of the alternation of molysite and cupric compound in producing several alloys that looked like gold or silver. In his alchemic experiments, Ge had tested a large number of chemicals and minerals—such as mercury, sulphur, lead, lead oxide (Pb_3O_4), orpiment (As_2S_3), realgar (As_2S_2), as well as cupric sulphate, nitre, hematite and alunite—and fully mastered their interactions.

The Arab alchemist Jabir Ibn Hayyan of Cufa initiated the transition of alchemy from primitive to modern chemistry by integrating practice with theory, thereby separating chemistry from physics and medicine and gradually establishing it as a special discipline. However, Jabir and Ge Hong were alike in their rich chemical knowledge. The Arab alchemists, like their Chinese counterparts, also sought to produce their al-iksir (elixir). Since mercury was not produced in the Arab territory, Jabir learned from the Chinese how to transmit mercury into other metals, including gold. Like the Chinese alchemists, he believed that all metals were formed by mixing sulphur and mercury in various ratios. He was the first Western scientist to succeed in producing sulphuric and nitric acid and the *aqua regia*—the all-powerful solution that could melt gold. As a result of his successful research, he came to master all the chemical process involved in distillation, sublimation, and incineration, thereby improving alchemical equipment, some of which, such as the water bath pot and carbon bath plate, remained in use until the thirteenth century.

The alchemical theory and experience of Jabir Ibn Hayyan and his successor Rhazes (865-925) were later introduced to Europe, where they won the popular recognition by the medieval European alchemists. In fact, what Roger Bacon (1214-1292) —the founder of European alchemy—had craved was the compound of sulphur and mercury called "the sage stone," which had been produced in the form of *huan dan* (miraculous elixir) by Wei Boyang and the Han Dynasty Prince Huainan. Therefore, while the European alchemy led to the birth of modern chemistry, its origination had come from the Arab alchemy of the early medieval age as well as the efforts of the ancient Chinese alchemists. And this was why the word "chemistry" in English, "chimie" in French and "chemie" in German could be traced to the Arab word "al-kimiya" and Chinese phrase "chin-i" (gold solution).

IV   The Rapid Development of Porcelain Industry

The ever-increasing demand for Chinese porcelain on the international market prompted many other countries the desire to produce porcelain themselves. And it was Egypt that had first undergone to imitate Chinese porcelain products—in the same manner as China had once learned glass-making process from Egypt. The earliest imitation of Chinese porcelain began in Egypt during the rule of the Turkic slavery dynasty (868-905), featuring a process of applying glazed colourful finish on a pottery base, which marked an innovation in the ceramic technology, despite the fact that it was not an immediate success. The Egyptian initiative was soon followed by efforts made by the Arab pottery centres in Bagdad and Samarra of Iraq and Raqqah of Syria, to produce white porcelain after the models of the Song Dynasty porcelain in both pattern and style. The Bagdad pottery workers began producing imitation Tang Dynasty tri-colour pottery and white porcelain products in the ninth century, through a process of applying an opaque white glaze of tin oxide on a pottery base, producing a yellowish cream colour finish after baking it in the kiln. But they did not succeed in turning out pure white pottery until the twelfth century. Meanwhile, the Arab blue porcelain, hamstrung by a series of technical problems, had not been able to compete with products from the "motherland of porcelain" for a long time.

During the Song and Yuan dynasties, Chinese porcelain was exported mostly to the Southeast Asian and Islamic countries. Since much of the exports were shipped overseas from south China, the products of China's southern kilns attracted more attention in the Islamic countries. China's export of porcelain technology made headway during the Yuan and Ming dynasties, when Chinese workers travelled to other countries and helped the local people establish their own porcelain industry, turning out products quite similar to the Chinese design. For example, the old kilns around Hanoi in Viet Nam had produced creamy, green and brown mono-coloured glazed Song-style porcelain for export. Later, in the Yuan Dynasty, Vietnamese kilns began to use imported cobalt blue to produce blue-floral patterned porcelain. The style of Vietnamese porcelain had been strongly influenced by China's Jingdezhen products, and its principal kiln of Bac Ninh was set up by Chinese porcelain workers in 1465, after they moved there from Lao Cai. Thailand first produced its own porcelain in the early thirteenth century at the Sukhothai kiln. Then, after the Siamese King Khamtin visited Beijing in 1300 and brought back a number of Chinese porcelain workers, the porcelain products of Sukhothai were greatly improved in quality, catching up with the Chinese porcelain of Cizhou kiln in Hebei. The kiln also adopted the Chinese traditional baking method by placing the semi-finished ceramic base separately on supporting racks so that they would not stick together. Thirty years later when the quality of the ceramic clay of Sukhothai began to deteriorate, the kiln's Chinese workers built a new kiln at Sawank-halok to the north. Following the arrival of more Chinese craftsmen from the Longquan kiln in Zhejiang, the Sawankhalok kiln began producing a fresh style of Longquan blue porcelain and, particularly, blue-white floral patterned porcelain of a much better quality.

The fifteenth century saw Chinese porcelain becoming the most attractive and admired target of imitation in the world, as the country achieved spectacular breakthrough in its porcelain-making industry. The "learn from China" trend started from Egypt, spread over the entire Islamic world and crossed the Mediterranean to reach the Christian states of Europe.

Not long after the first appearance of Chinese blue-floral porcelain on the market, Egypt began to imitate such products in style and design, but using local ceramic clay. Some ceramic products bore their makers' names in Arab script. In the early sixteenth century, Abbas I (1587-1629), Shah of Persia, who was known as an ardent admirer of Chinese porcelain, recruited several hundred Chinese porcelain workers and made them settle down with their families in Esfahan, there to produce blue-floral porcelain. Not long after that, such porcelain was also produced for the first time in Syria. However, the Persian porcelain, which was produced under Chinese workers' supervision, emerged as products of high quality that could hardly be differentiated from the original Chinese products. The book *Sir Jean Chardin's Travel in Persia*, 1927, London, written by Sir Jean Chardin, a French traveller who visited Persia in 1671, told the story of a Dutch Company's representative Hubert de Laresse presenting to the Persian Shah in 1666 some gifts, which included about 60 pieces of Chinese ancient porcelain. When the Persian Shah looked at the porcelain, he chuckled and asked his guest where he had bought the porcelain, because the Shah discovered many of these so-called "Chinese" products were actually Persian porcelain exported to Europe.

In the mid-fifteenth century, when the Portuguese began placing orders for Chinese fine-grain porcelain, the Italians were planning to set up Europe's first porcelain production centre in their country. Having learned the skills from the Arab craftsmen, they began to trial-produce porcelain at Venice, Verona and Turin in succession. However, a large-scale production was never launched. During this period, the Venetian alchemist Antonio succeeded in developing a kind of light, thin and translucent porcelain vessel. Backed by the Grand Duke Francis I (1574-1587), Florence also succeeded in developing a kind of blue porcelain called "Medici," which featured blue-coloured Persian or Chinese pattern, drawn upon a layer of white enamel spread over the yellow ceramic base. The "Medici" blue-floral porcelain went into production in 1580, in small quantity; and its production continued for only three decades. In 1627, the Italian porcelain workers of Pisa successfully imitated the Arab blue-floral products; after that, they also produced imitation Chinese blue-floral porcelain.

Following the lead of Italy, the Netherlands and France launched their copy-production of Chinese porcelain. However, 300 years after the discovery of the Limoges ceramic clay mine in France, the European porcelain industry lingered at the stage of producing mostly the "soft" porcelain, which were more brittle and less durable. Earlier, the Dutch workers of Delft learned from the Italian to produce "soft" porcelain, which was like the yellow transparent porcelain produced in 1673 by the French in Rouen. In 1735, the Italian kiln in Florence, by mixing French ceramic clay with Chinese ceramic clay and using Chinese equipment imported from Southeast Asia, finally succeeded in turning out the first batch of white-coloured hard porcelain, featuring the pattern of the porcelain from Fujian's Dehua kiln.

The man who revealed the secret of "hard" porcelain was J.F. Böttger, a German technician, who came from Berlin to trial-produce porcelain in the Electorate of Saxony. Böttger succeeded in turning out the first batch of red porcelain in 1708. The next year, the German technician again succeeded in producing both glazed and unglazed "hard" porcelain in Saxony, marking an epoch-making event in the European porcelain-making history. In 1710, Böttger moved his pottery from Saxony to Meissen near Dresden, the first batch of coloured chinaware was produced, putting the product on sale in the market three years later. The Meissen porcelain, which has proved its vitality through the centuries, is still being produced today. And the Meissen Porcelain Museum, which enjoys a lasting reputation in Europe, has a colourful collection of various porcelain products.

The overseas sales of Chinese porcelain reached a new peak at the time, when the European countries began to trial-produce chinaware. Throughout the seventeenth century, hundreds of thousand pieces of Chinese porcelain were being shipped to Europe every year by both Portuguese and Dutch merchant ships. In 1639 alone, some 366,000 pieces of Chinese porcelain were delivered to the Netherland by merchant ships. Even when J.F. Böttger was beginning to produce coloured porcelain in Meissen, European countries continued to place orders for Chinese porcelain made in Western style—further enhancing the Westernizing trend of the Chinese products. Such Europe-oriented porcelain products were called *Yang Cai* (foreign patterned ware) in China. The widespread sales of Chinese porcelain on the European market began in the fifteenth century and reached a boom during the seventeenth and the eighteenth centuries; however, the techniques, style and designs of Chinese porcelain had influenced European porcelain industry for more than three centuries.

Interesting was the fact that the British Empire, which boasted of no sunset in its vast empire, was the last country in Europe to learn the making of porcelain. In 1745, the first British ceramic kiln was set up in Stratford northwest of London, which was followed by another kiln built in Plymouth (1768-1776) where the first batch of English "hard" porcelain was produced after the Chinese design, but bearing a Rococo style. However, in 1755, William Duesbury founded the Derby Pottery in Derbyshire, absorbing the Bow Pottery. The Derby porcelain soon became famous for its high quality. When the British special envoy, Lord Macartney visited China in 1792, the gifts he presented to the Qing Dynasty Emperor Qianlong included the Derby porcelain. The British delegation was elated over the ostensible admiration shown by the Chinese for the British clocks and Derby porcelain. But when the Chinese hosts asked them to compare the British porcelain with the Chinese products, the British delegates gave an indirect but tactful answer, saying that they would not have brought the Derbyware—as gifts for the Chinese emperor—if they had not believed that these were "the most valuable of their kind." However, they added that it could be easily seen from the large quantity of Chinese porcelain bought and shipped from Canton (Guangzhou) to London every year by the British merchants "how highly the British people appreciate the Chinese products."

V   Global Tour of the Paper-Making and Printing Techniques

1. Paper-Making Skills Introduced Across the Ocean

In ancient times, materials used for writing were of two types: bamboo, wood and silk fabric, which the Chinese used before they invented paper; the second involved bark, tree leaf, reed and

---

[1] H.M. Robbins, *Our First Ambassador to China*, P.289, London, 1908.

leather, used by people in the Arab, India and Egypt. Following
cultural and economic developments in the human society, there
was a rising demand for a light, convenient and durable, yet
cheap, material to replace the clumsy materials for people to write
on. This led to the invention of paper by the Chinese in the first
century B.C. Such paper, which was made of plant fibres, was at
first used as handkerchief or wrapping material.

In the book *Han Shu* (*History of the Han Dynasty*), the
material was described as *Xiti* made of used silkwool. However,
archaeological discoveries proved that it was made of jute fibres
—possibly with some old cotton fibre added to it.

Through further improvement made by Cai Lun, a craftsman
of the Han Dynasty imperial court, a new product made from a
mixed pulp of bark, jute fibre, waste cloth and useless fishing net
was turned into writing paper. This writing paper had many
advantages over the old writing material of bamboo and wood,
most importantly it could be easily produced in large quantities.
Hence, within three centuries after its invention, paper had
replaced all other previously-used materials for writing and came
into use across the country. Soon afterwards paper was also used
in the western border regions, owing to military and commercial
demand.

In 751, a battle broke out between an expeditionary army of
the Tang Dynasty and an Arab tribe at Talas in Central Asia,
resulting in the defeat of the Tang army and some 30,000 Tang
soldiers taken prisoners by the Arabs. Many of these war prisoners, who were specialists in some crafts, stayed in the Arab
occupied region to carry on their skills. These Chinese craftsmen
included paper-making technicians, who played a major role in
founding the paper-making plant in Samarkand. In the early
ninth century, the Arab writer Tamim Ibn Bahr quoted, in his
travelogue, from another Arab author Abul-Fadl al-Vasjirdi,
"The children of the previous captives are today in Samarkand
making top quality paper, weapons and tools." These very
Chinese craftsmen, who had settled down in other countries,
established the best paper mills in the Muslim world. The light
and convenient paper soon proved far superior to the expensive

goatskin or the cheap Egyptian reed mat used as writing pads. Paper-making mills were soon built in Bagdad, Tihamah and Damascus. In the late ninth century, paper-making was also launched in Egypt—the home of reed mat writing pads—paving the way for popularizing the new invention across the Mediterranean.

After the ninth century, while the Europeans gradually took to using the new paper imported from the Orient, the paper-making technique remained a secret monopolized by the Arab Muslim countries. When the Almoravids of Morocco withdrew from Spain around 1121, the first European paper-making plant was established in Shatibah and staffed by Arab workers. The first paper-making mill of the Christian world was built in 1189, in Guixols near the foot of the Pyrenees Mountains. The second did not appear until 1276, in Montefano of Italy.

Spurred by the need to print playing cards as well as coloured religious portraits, paper-making mills and printing shops sprouted in cities of Western Europe. In Germany, both Cologne and Nürnberg and set up their own paper mills in the fourteenth century, in order to supply paper needed by the local printing works. The fifteenth and the sixteenth centuries saw the final competition between the goatskin writing pad and the plant-pulp paper in the European continent. Until then, goatskin had been the main source of writing pads and printed copies used by churches, high officials, aristocrats and their schools in Europe. Inexpensive paper enabled books of knowledge to leap over the limitations of churches and Christian doctrines and travel at will in the world of free thinking.

After the invention of the movable type printing by Gutenberg, the demand for paper was no longer limited to playing cards and pictures, but spread far and wide following the need for printing books in volume. This prompted the remote areas of Europe to establish paper mills. During the sixteenth century, paper-making techniques were introduced from Germany as the centre to both the East and West Europe. In 1511, England in the west set up its first paper factory, followed by the Moscow paper mill founded in 1576. Then in 1582, Matteo Ricci, the Italian

Jesuit, arrived in China, carrying with him well-printed Italian books. The high quality of the European printing technique surprised the Chinese, whose craftsmen had invented both paper-making and printing. Also during his period, paper-making technique was introduced to the New World by Spain, when the first paper mill of the American continent was built in Mexico in 1575. And 115 years later, Philadelphia, the new port on the Delaware River, built its own paper-making mill.

Having crossed the Atlantic, paper-making techniques moved westward to the South Pacific and Australia where a paper factory was built in 1868. During those years the people of Madagascar off the East African coast also learned paper-making skills in the Chinese manner.

2. Printing Techniques and the Renaissance of Europe

It might sound almost as incredible as the fabulous stories in the "Arabian Nights" to some people, if they were told that an ancient invention had resulted—several hundred years later—in an epoch-making development, which symbolized the monumental importance of that invention in the history of human culture. Nevertheless, this was what actually happened, in the slow course of the historic tide of civilization.

Since the early Han Dynasty, Chinese Taoist sorcerers and alchemists had been wearing wooden seals, engraved with magic figures in order to expel "evil spirits." These engraved magic seals served as the catalyst to spur the invention of woodblock printing by people who wanted to print Buddhist pictures as gifts to religious adherents. The well-known Tang Dynasty pilgrim monk Xuan Zhuang had, since 645, been distributing printed copies of Buddhist portraits to his followers, marking the first use of woodblock printing in China. All Chinese printed matters, during that period, were connected with Buddhist pictures or scriptures. Gradually the device was used by people to print semi-religious matters, such as books of almanac, fortune-telling or astrology. The earliest literature that went into printing, in the ninth century, were the most popular poems written by Tang Dynasty poets Bai Juyi and Yuan Weizhi.

The Chinese invention of printing was soon introduced to Korea and Japan, where the technique was quickly adopted to print various Buddhist papers and scriptures. In the Islamic world, however, the printing technique, unlike paper-making skills, was not widely used for a long time—possibly, because local tradition prohibited the use of such tools as hog-bristle brush, which was needed in the process.

In the wake of the Mongolian occupation of Iran, however, printing techniques were introduced to the area. Such a development had not resulted—as was assumed by some people—from the Mongolian practice of printing paper money, but from the growing popularity of a paper card game in the Muslim countries. Card game was first seen in China during the tenth century, and continued to enjoy the favour of people in some cities in the twelfth century, when there were special card shops in the city of Hangzhou. Mongolians who brought the game to Iran at a time when the Il-Khanate was seeking to form an alliance with the Christian countries against the Mameluke Sultanate. The card game was thus introduced to the travelling Italian merchants visiting Iran. Through them, the game found favour for the first time in the Italian city of Viterbo, where the game was called by the Arab name, "naib." The time of its arrival in Europe was debatable because the historic record gave it as 1379; other evidence showed the game was officially banned in Germany two years earlier in 1377. Regardless of such bans, the infamous card game became the rage in Spain and France in less than 20 years, resulting in a mounting demand for such paper cards across Western Europe. Hence the production of the playing cards turned from handicrafters to printing shops.

From religious scriptures and incantation to popular playing cards, the printing technique completed its leap, first from China to Iran, then from Iran to the European Continent. The Italian workers who printed the playing cards also printed religious pictures. In Italy, printing industry made the greatest headway in Venice, which became the largest printing centre of Europe in the mid-fifteenth century. Following Italy's lead, Germany and the Netherlands also set up their woodblock printing plants. Almost at the same time, however, Gutenberg developed his movable-type printing—based on information acquired from the Orient, not by way of the Mediterranean but probably through sources in Russia. He succeeded in producing the first set of metal movable type in 1448, and launched printing with such type for the first time in 1452. First major production was the *Bible*, printed on goatskin pages. The complete volume of a printed *Bible* was finished in 1454, signalling the beginning of a cultural revolution in Europe. By 1480, some 110 cities in West Europe had set up their own printing factories. Armed with both paper and printing technology, Europe was ready for the religous reform of Martin Luther and the Renaissance emerging in the Italian Peninsula.

Since the invention of engraved woodblock printing, it took China nearly 600 years to switch to the movable-wooden-type printing, which was first used in 1298 by Wang Zhen in printing the 100-volume *Jingde County Annals*. This was a sharp contrast to the 50 years, needed by Europe, to complete its transition from its first knowledge of printing techniques to the publishing the *Bible* by movable-type printing. However, the European success would not have been possible without the earlier pioneering role played by Chinese inventors.

VI Mariner's Compass and the Revolution of Maritime Navigation

For ages, since people started sailing on the sea, the sailors had to depend on their luck, while hoping for the blessing of favourable weather that would allow a safe voyage. Sailing at sea, navigators relied on their experience during the day, and on their observation of the stars during a clear night to steer a safe course. In a storm, the crew would lose their confidence, and their ship would lose its bearing and run into trouble. Centuries later, navigators noticed that the point of a magnetic head might be used to determine directions on the boundless sea, thus guiding the ship on a fixed course. And it was the Chinese who first invented such a device.

The magnetic polar concept was found in ancient Chinese literature, dating back to the first century. Then 1,000 years later in the tenth century, the Chinese discovered how to magnetize steel needles, and began producing the compass. At the same time, they realized that there was a slight eastward inclination of the magnetic point. Shen Kuo (1031-1095), the learned Song Dynasty scientist, had conducted an experiment with four different types of magnetic compass, one of which was a magnetic needle attached to a rush stem floating on water. Such a floating compass was actually used in the shipping sector before Shen's time—possibly as early as the tenth century, according to a study by the British scientist Joseph Needham. Such was the earliest type of magnetic needle compass.

The earliest record of a mariner's compass in practical use was made by Zhu Yu, a relative of Shen Kuo. In his book *Ping Zhou Ke Tan* (*Pingzhou Table Talk*), Zhu recalled that his father Zhu Fu had seen the merchantship captains—who were familiar with both the geographic and astronomical guidance at sea in clear weather—depend on their mariner's compass to chart the sailing course in bad weather. Zhu Fu was then in Guangzhou, serving as a provincial official during the years from 1098 to 1106.

The mariner's compass originated from the old-fashioned square orienting-instrument used by classical Chinese geomancers in choosing favourable sites for a new house or a tomb for their clients. The square geomantic orienting plate had 24 marked directions, which were arranged according to the Chinese traditional Orders of the eight "stems," twelve "branches" and four "divinations." Once converted into a mariner's compass, it was remodeled into a circular instrument called "gyro" in the twelfth century. The original Chinese compass had 48 marked directions —doubling the original 24 positions by dividing each inter-space into two equal parts. Such a design had also been adopted by the Persian and Arab navigators, but was later simplified into 32 directions by the European mariners.

During the twelfth century, the Chinese navigators, aided by their mariner's compass, were able to sail to their overseas destinations along prescribed courses, under any weather condition. This made it possible to open several over 5,000-nautical-mile-long maritime routes across the Indian Ocean. The longest of these new routes was the line linking Guangzhou with Dhufar on the southern coast of the Arabian Peninsula, which needed only one stop at the midway port of Aceh of Sumatra to finish the voyage within a five-month period of the northeast trade winds. The economic value of this Chinese invention in navigation was immediately recognized by Persian and Arab navigation circles. Since the Chinese were employing some Persians and Omanians to serve as captains on their merchant ships, the new navigational innovation was soon mastered by these experienced sailors of the Indian Ocean.

Since the Crusades began the eastward expedition in 1097, the European Christian countries soon came to notice the new technical achievement made by the Oriental navigators. The Europeans, faced with the intensifying trade competition in the Levant and Mediterranean region, were keenly interested in adopting such a device as the mariner's compass. Therefore, apart from the Chinese records, the earliest known data concerning mariner's compass was found not in Arab or Persian literature, but in the writings of English and French authors. In 1195, in the book concerning the nature of materials, English author Alexander Nekam discussed, for the first time, the navigation device of "floating needle." According to his description, the navigational compass, which was to guide a ship's voyage under an overcast sky or on a dark night, was made of a magnetized iron or steel needle stuck into a wheat straw, floating on water surface and pointing to the north. The description was similar to that of the Song Dynasty's Shen Kuo. The French author Guiot de Provins, in his poem of 1206, described the mariner's compass in this manner:

"Through the magnet, an ugly brown stone to which iron turns of its own accord, mariners possess an art that can not fail them. A needle touched by it and floated by stick on water turns its point to the polestar, and a light being placed near the needle on dark nights, the proper course is known."

Following Provins, another Frenchman James Viderit also discussed the innovation in his works 15 years later. Story of the floating compass was also found in the *Thomas Encyclopaedia of Canterbury*. All this information appeared some two decades before the story of the "magnetic fish compass" emerged in the *Book of Stories* written by Muhammad al-Awfi. Then, the use of the mariner's compass was already spreading all the way from the Mediterranean to the Indian Ocean.

The Italian merchant ships were the first in Europe to master the new navigation device. And an Italian sailor from Salerno was the first seaman to learn the compass guiding technique. This led to the legend that Flavio Gioja of Salerno was the man who invented the compass in 1302—a story which was proven false by earlier information of the device shown in the English and French literature, and the detailed description of the device given by an Italian called Petro in 1269. The legend about Flavio Gioja, however, indicated that since the fourteenth century, the Mediterranean countries producing their own compass, and no longer depended on imported devices.

Chinese navigators were accustomed to using mariner's compass marked with 48 directions, spaced 7 degrees 30 minutes on centres, to ensure maximum precision. However, it was the European tradition to mark only 32 directions on their compass, which was shown in the famous Cantino Chart dated as late as 1502. Despite their more accurate mariner's compass, the Chinese were inferior to the Europeans in their navigational cartographic technique, a trend which was discernible in the fifteenth century. However, the Chinese invention of the navigational compass had been introduced across the world, and led to the development of modern navigation devices used in both aviation and maritime services.

Invention of the compass brought about a new era in world commerce. In China, it enabled merchant ships to sail to the coast of South Africa and the Atlantic. In the West, it helped Vasco da Gama succeed in opening maritime routes to Africa and Asia, and the Spanish to discover the New World and sail around the globe.

VII   Historic Changes Caused by the Invention of Gunpowder and Firearms

The emergence of gunpowder in the historic arena brought about the disintegration of the European knights and marked an important turn in the trend of civilization, pushing the world towards a unified market. But the root of this motivating force had originated in China's Yangtze and Yellow river regions—far from the centre of Europe, where the major changes took place.

Gunpowder was invented by alchemists, who mixed charcoal, sulphur and nitre according to a certain ratio to make a fire or explosive. Alchemists discovered the process during their chemical experiments designed to produce the miraculous "elixir." It was soon adopted by military planners, who used the product as a destructive weapon against the fortified enemy. In the battlefield, gunpowder was often tied to the arrows and shot into the enemy by the fighting troops during the early tenth century when wars continued between the Five Dynasties and invading tribesmen. Since the eleventh century, gunpowder became more powerful, as big guns were developed to hurl exploding shells, which looked like today's landmines.

When war broke out between the Song and Kin dynasties, weapons design was accelerated under the pressure of the military. In 1132 the Song Dynasty general Chen Gui, garrison commander of De'an City (Present Anlu County in Hubei Province), designed the world's earliest tube-shaped firearm, called "firegun," which was made of a large bamboo-pipe and carried by two soldiers, who would ignite the gunpowder in the bamboo-pipe and throw it at enemy troops. Such fireguns were widely used by Song Dynasty troops fighting against the Mongolian invaders in the mid-thirteenth century, along with a shorter but heavier powdered-pipe weapon, called "firepipe." In the defence of Shouchun (present Shouxian County in Anhui Province) in 1259, the Song Dynasty garrison used a weapon made of a huge bamboo-pipe, called "burst gun," which could fire "bullets" into the enemy, when the powder inside it was lit. The invading Yuan Dynasty troops, however, soon learned about these firearms from the Song Dynasty defenders, and changed their design by substituting metal tubes for the bamboo pipes, thus greatly improving their effectiveness. The new metal tubes were filled with iron or stone pellets and fired with the explosion of gunpowder, against the enemy. Their basic design was similar to today's short-barrelled firearms.

The Muslim countries learned to use firearms like the Chinese and the Mongolians, 100 years before the Europeans. The invention was introduced to them mainly through two channels. The first was their trade link with the Chinese coastal cities like Hangzhou, where there were many Muslim travellers and tradesmen, including the Mamelukes who were familiar with various kinds of firearms, including the use of nitre in making explosives. The second channel was through their military encounter with the Mongolian troops. Some of the firearms, used by the Muslim countries in the thirteenth century, were called by their Chinese names, such as "Qidan rocket" or "Qidan firegun." However, some of their weapons were improvised versions of the Chinese fireguns, including the "Madafi" or "Midfa," the "Mukhula" or "Naft." The "Midfa" was similar to the Chinese firepipe in design, but had an arrow put inside it to force out the metal or stone pellets, when fired. The Mukhula, which looked like the *zhen tian lei* (thunder shot) was once used by the Kin Dynasty troops. The *pi li pao* (blitz gun) later used by the Song Dynasty troops, was a ball or can-shaped metal shell, containing gunpowder. All these larger types of firearms were used in the armies of the Muslim countries in the early fourteenth century.

The Christian crusaders of Western Europe suffered heavy losses from the powerful firearms used against them by the Muslim forces during their expeditions in the late thirteenth century. In 1325, when the Muslim invaders attacked Baza in Spain, they used such weapons as catapults to hurl explosive fireballs into the town, inflicting heavy losses on people and properties. These cruel lessons taught the Europeans to catch up on the development and use of firearms. They emerged, eventually, far more efficient than the Muslims or the Chinese pioneers in advancing the new weaponry.

Italy, France and England were quick in making such firearm as shotguns. In 1345, the Italians used handguns in combat; such handguns looked very much like the Madafi of the Arab countries, as was shown in a classic mural of an Italian church. Also, according to a French record of the same year, the King of Toulouse had delivered to the army two iron guns, along with 200 lead pellets and eight pounds of gunpowder, which were obviously to be used as munition for the guns. In 1357, the British produced a small gun to shoot stone pellets, in more or less the same type as the Italian handgun or the Arab Madafi.

The pipe-shaped big guns were introduced, almost simultaneously, in both Egypt and Italy. The Egyptian event was recorded by the Islamic encyclopaedist Al-Kalkashandi, who said he had seen a bronze gun (midfa) firing a big shell in Alexandria in the 1360s. Also shown in an Italian painting, dating back to 1364, was an iron gun with a bamboo-shaped barrel, which differed from the bronze guns cast in China during the last years of the Yuan Dynasty and the early years of the Ming Dynasty. The Chinese bronze guns consisted of three parts—gun barrel, shell chamber and breech—joined into one piece. The European big guns had a bigger barrel in the shape of a ribbed bamboo, which was attached to a slenderer breech, also shaped like bamboo and accounting for one third of the gun's total length. Such ribbed-barrel guns were introduced quickly from Italy to all over Europe. In the *Chroniques d'Angleterre*—edited by Jean de Wavrin and finished in the fifteenth century—there was a picture of the Hundred-Year-War between England and France (1337-1453), which showed the English army using two iron guns and one bronze gun attacking a French fortress. The two iron guns had ribbed barrels and were mounted on wooden supports, while the bronze gun—also mounted on wooden supports—had a smooth barrel and a globe-shaped breech with a fuse cord at the end.

The relic of an early European copper handgun, made around 1390, is preserved in the Nürnberg Museum. It looked similar to the earliest Chinese cooper handgun, unearthed in Acheng County of Heilongjiang Province. The Nürnberg handgun was 33 centimetres long, and weighed 1.24 kilogrammes, while the Acheng handgun was 34 centimetres long and weighed 3.55 kilogrammes. The Acheng handgun was used in 1287, some 100 years before the Nürnberg handgun was produced, indicating the obvious lineage between the two. The Chinese handguns were easier to handle and had a longer range. The Europeans later made up the gap in shooting range by developing a long-barreled musket, which was followed by their invention of rifles. In the development of big guns, the Europeans achieved swift progress during the fifteenth century, while the Chinese made little headway through the 400 years from the fifteenth to the early nineteenth century.

The West European countries grew into leading world powers through the rapid development of their firearms. The widespread use of firearms, meanwhile, led to a fundamental reform in the establishment for army units and military operational planning, while the modernization of maritime weapons also resulted in the rapid growth of the European naval force. All these factors, eventually, contributed to the birth of a unified world trade market, in the course of which, the native inhabitants of Africa, America and Australia first saw "civilization" coming upon them, through the deadly bursts from blazing guns.

PART TWO

THE DEVELOPMENT OF MODERN SCIENCE AND THE REFORM OF CHINESE TRADITIONAL CULTURE

Chapter Seven

China's Access to Western Culture During the Ming and Qing Dynasties

I Matteo Ricci and His Collaborators Xu Guangqi and Li Zhizao

Although the Vatican dispatched John de monte Corvino (1247-1328), a Franciscan priest, to introduce Catholicism to China during the Yuan Dynasty (1271-1368), the Christian doctrine had created little impact in China; the influence of Western culture was limited to only such places as Beijing and Quanzhou. There were at that time fewer than 100 converts in the area to learn Greek and Latin from the Catholic missionaries. Their task was merely to preach and proselytize, their activities bound by their religious responsibilities. Medieval Europe, dominated then by the Roman Catholic church, was struggling with change and had not yet shown any new initiative. Therefore, the first impression given by the Western missionaries to the Chinese was only that there was a greater world of Christianity—in addition to the Nestorians—in a Europe dominated by the Roman Catholic church. And in the eyes of the Mongolians, Europe was the vanquished land during their westward expeditions.

The Christian church soon saw its influence completely disappear from China following the overthrow of the Yuan Dynasty. When Matteo Ricci (1552-1610) first arrived in China in 1582, Christianity was already a stranger in the country.

Matteo Ricci, of Mazzarino in Italy, came as a Jesuit to Macao on August 7, 1582. For decades afterwards, he had been a force in introducing Western culture to China, while reporting news of the great Eastern country to Europe. Indeed, he and his successors had played the historic role of building a new cultural bridge between China and Europe.

Why was Ricci so notable in his personal achievement, and what was his attitude and philosophy compared with his European predecessors? The best answer to the question was given by the Italian Jesuit himself in his book *Notes on China*, written in his late years. In the book, he pointed out that he and his colleagues were never tired of learning more about China, even though they had read much about that country from books while in Europe.

"We had lived in this country nearly 30 years, toured some of its most important provinces and became good friends with its aristocrats, high officials and the most distinguished scholars. We spoke its local dialects, and conducted firsthand study of their customs and laws. The last but not the least important thing was that we devoted ourselves to studying their literature, by day and by night." This was what distinguished Ricci during his fruitful 28 years in China. And such merits were just what many of those who had never entered this part of the world needed to acquire.

Matteo Ricci had come to China as a missionary, and the religious task had always been his primary goal and purpose. Like many other Jesuits, Ricci was well-educated before he came to China. In 1572, he was a student in the Rome Academy, where he studied astronomy, applied mathematics, geography, music and perspective art under the tutorship of Christopher Clavius. Then, upon his arrival in China, he spared no effort in learning the Chinese language, Chinese classics and China's customs and traditions. As a result of years of continued research, he designed a pragmatic approach of proselytizing among the Chinese compatible with the circumstances of China. According to such an approach, the missionaries should purse their religous proselytism first through introducing the advanced scientific knowledge of the Western world to their friends—members of the Chinese ruling strata—while respecting the Chinese heritage of Confucianism and other traditions.

In order to cope with the Chinese cultural tradition, Matteo

Ricci and his colleague Michael Ruggieri had, from the beginning, taken Chinese names, posing as travelling monks from India. Ricci also assumed another Chinese name, "Xi Tai" in addition to his formal Chinese name of Li Madou, to suggest he had come from a place west ("Xi" in Chinese) of India. However, from the first time they practised their religious missions in Zhaoqing of Guangdong, the two "Indian monks" found themselves facing an antagonistic public. Then, on August 10, 1583, Matteo Ricci and Michael Ruggieri obtained the local government's approval to stay as resident missionaries in Zhaoqing. This did not change the hostility of the local people, who considered them agents of the "foreign devils" in Macao and even attacked their houses.

Under such conditions, Matteo Ricci tried to make himself appear as an enthusiastic admirer of Confucian doctrine and a follower of Chinese traditional rites in order to win friends among local officials and intellectuals in Zhaoqing. He managed to attract the attention of Chinese scholars by displaying his attractive Western books, a world map drawn by himself and various astronomical instruments made with his own hands. The missionary library of Zhaoqing, set up by Ricci and Ruggieri as China's first Western language library, created an impression on many Chinese intellectuals who admired the printed and bound books displayed there. Of these, the book which drew most attention from the visitors was the two-volume *Canon Law* with its covers finished in gold letters. These impressively-finished books led the Chinese to feel a new respect for Western culture and science, sensing the superiority of the West in the field of knowledge.

In 1584, Matteo Ricci finished his drawing of a new world map, showing the five continents with places marked with Chinese names. At first, he was apprehensive that the Chinese might be angered for not seeing their country occupying a prominent position in the centre of this world map. On the contrary, the Chinese not only seemed quite aware of their country's geography as was shown in the map, but were delighted for Ricci's demonstration of Western map-drawing skill. The first geographic information brought to China by Matteo Ricci, through his map, was the existence of the continents of North and South America. Not knowing that China had, in the fourteenth century, produced its own relatively accurate map of the world—consisting of the three continents of Asia, Europe and Africa—Ricci had believed at first that the Chinese were ignorant of the true size of the world and considered their country the only respected nation on earth. Ricci's world map became so popular among the officials and intellectuals in China, that it was reproduced many times, under the auspices of the Zhaoqing prefectural magistrate Wang Pan, and even engraved upon a stone stele in Suzhou by order of the Suzhou prefectural magistrate Zhao Kehuai. When Matteo Ricci was asked to add his remarks on the maps reproduced by Wang Pan, he included in his notes an introduction on the religion and rites of the different countries. This way, he managed to present an explanation on the Christian faith and practices, as a part of his remarks, on the map. Thus, an introduction of the Christian creed which had been virtually unknown to the Chinese was, for the first time, transmitted to many parts of China through Matteo Ricci's world map.

Following his successful production of the world map, Matteo Ricci went on to make a number of astronomical instruments, including a metal celestial globe, an earth globe, astronomical sphere and vertical sundial. His celestial globe was probably designed after the one invented by Hieronymo de Boncompagni of the Rome Academy in 1575, which was very popular in Europe; his earth globe was made after the design by Emmanuele Filiberto of the Rome Academy. These sophisticated instruments as well as the delicate timepiece and triangular prism, which he put on display in an exhibition impressed the visiting Chinese officials and scholars, who began to view the Italian Jesuit as a great astronomer.

Following these accomplishments, Ricci came to realize the reason he was able to win such keen admiration for the Western civilization from a nation, which had always boasted of its superior cultural heritage, was because he had demonstrated things these people had never seen before. In his memoirs, he criticized the conceit of those Chinese, who had once looked down on any other kingdom, dynasty or culture in the world. Attributing the Chinese egoism to their ignorance, he assumed that once these people realized their inadequacy under the new circumstances, their superiority complex would give way to inferiority complex. Nevertheless, he had found the Chinese not at all reluctant to accept new knowledge and understand the changing world. They appreciated the information of Western culture, which Ricci had brought to China, because it was a blessing they had not expected to come from overseas—sources that were blamed for troubles and disturbance over the past 200 years. Such a blessing, for most Chinese friends of Ricci, had emanated not from his Christian creed but from his impressive knowledge of science.

In 1589, the new Ming Dynasty governor general of Guangdong and Guangxi, Liu Jiwen, became hostile towards the Christian church, forcing Ricci to move from Zhaoqing to Shaozhou in northern Guangdong, where he came to know Qu Taisu, son of Qu Jingchun, former Minister of Rites in the Ming court. An ardent student of alchemy, the young Qu asked Ricci to be his tutor, and studied algebra and geometry from the Italian Jesuit for two years. During this period, he was also obliged to study the Christian creed, at the behest of his tutor. Qu Taisu proved to be a brilliant student in quickly mastering whatever the tutor taught him, including the essentials of mathematics, the theory of Christopher Clavius' Sphere of Earth and Book I of Euclid's *Elements of Geometry*. He even translated the geometry book into a fluent Chinese text and wrote lectures on arithmatic calculations done with pen and paper. The widespread introduction of these publications across the provinces further enhanced the reputation of Ricci as a mathematician. Qu Taisu had also learned from his Italian tutor how to make delicate astronomical instruments with bronze, silver and wood, and succeeded in making such items as celestial globe, planetary template, quadrant, compass and sundial with perfect precision and attractive finish. Qu's works of drawing and graphics won high praise from his tutor, who described them as comparable to the best work found in Europe.

With a view to winning cooperation of Chinese authorities,

Ricci accepted Qu Taisu's advise and forsook his former practice of calling the church "temple" and calling the missionaries
"monks." Instead, he began adapting to the customs of Chinese
scholars to grow long hair and beard, and to wear silk gowns in
place of the robe or *kasaya*. In 1595, Ricci arrived at Nanchang,
where he lived for three years and acquainted himself with such
local dignitaries as governor of Jiangxi Province Lu Wangai,
Prince of Jian'an Zhu Duojie and renowned Confucian scholar
Zhang Huang. By presenting the Prince of Jian'an with such gifts
as astronomical instruments, table clock, world atlas and his book
On Winning Friends written in Chinese, Ricci became an hon-
oured guest of the prince. He emerged as a new member of the
upper class, and his new friends were found in 10 out of the 15
provinces of the Ming Dynasty. This marked the beginning of the
"full bloom" of Ricci's social career in China, putting him in a
very favourable position to pursue his religious mission.

Posing as an amateur "Confucianist" and assuming the identity of a "naturalized Chinese," Ricci made rapid progress in his
mission work through his newly-acquired influence in the elite
circle. Ricci relied as much upon the help of the Chinese high
officials as he did on the help of God. In furthering his church
mission, he hoped the Chinese people would follow the example
of their officials and become devout converts. While making the
best of his new successes, Ricci now began working towards his
ultimate target of going to Beijing and getting the emperor's
approval for him to proselytize across the whole China. His
efforts paid off, and the Italian Jesuit arrived in Beijing on
January 24, 1601, with baskets of presents. Three days later, on
January 27, Ricci was granted an audience by the Ming emperor,
to whom he offered 31 items in 19 kinds of gifts, including one
each of the portrait of Christ and the Holy Mother and a copy of
the *Bible*; a variety of coloured glassware; a world map; a large
and a small clocks; a big Italian violin; eight mirrors and glass
vases; two sets of sand timepiece; a compass; four rolls of Italian
coloured silk piecegoods; five rolls of European muslin and flax
and four European silver coins.

The Ming Dynasty Emperor Wanli was pleased with the gifts

offered him by Ricci, who took up residence in Beijing with
imperial approval, and stayed until his death on May 11, 1610.
During his 10 years in the Chinese capital, Ricci came to know
such influential friends as Shen Yiguan and Ye Xianggao, both
Grand Secretary of the Ming court, and the Minister of Personnel
Li Dai; Ye Xianggao, leading member of the elite Donglin party,
an organization of Chinese scholars critical of the corrupt officials, especially the powerful eunuchs in the Ming court. But his
two most faithful aides, in both his religious and cultural activities, were Xu Guangqi and Li Zhizao, low-ranking officials who
were enthusiastic followers of the Italian Jesuit.

Xu and Li both ardently admired Western sciences, as introduced by Matteo Ricci. Xu Guangqi (1562-1633) was baptized
by Jesuit Joannes de Rocha in Nanjing in 1603; Li Zhizao
(1565-1630) was baptized by Ricci himself in Beijing in 1610. In
Beijing, Xu helped Ricci translate the first part of the Euclid's
Elements of Geometry, which was considered the fundamentals of
Western mathematics. The translation, which was based on the
notes of Clavius and covered only half of the 15 volumes of the
original, was finished in 1607. However, it contained the essential
part of the universally-acclaimed book of classic mathematics,
and stood out as the first ever Chinese translation of the Western
natural sciences. It would not be an overstatement to describe it
as an opener to the store of Western sciences.

In addition to his works on the Euclid's geometry, Xu also
helped Ricci translate in 1607 the *Science of Survey*, which was
the first ever introduction of Western triangular surveying technology to China. In the same year, Li, absorbing the Western
astronomical theories as contained in the *Astrolabium* by Christopher Clavius of Rome, published in 1593, wrote two volumes
of astronomical books, elaborating on the ancient Chinese theories of *gai tian* (hemispherical dome) and *hun tian* (celestial
sphere), as first brought forth in the classic Chinese book of *Zhou
Bi*. The year of 1607 marked the beginning of introducing Western science to China by Chinese academic circles.

In 1608, Li helped Ricci finish his geometric book of *Yuan
Rong Jiao Yi* (*Study of Circles and Volumes*), which was followed

in 1614 by the publication of *Tong Wen Suan Zhi* (*Mathematical Handbook*)—Ricci's first book to introduce the European calculations on paper to China, as written by Li according to Ricci's dictation. The second book was based on Clavius' *Epitome Arithmeticae Practicae*, with revisions made by Li, who had compared it with Chinese traditional calculation methods as well as the book *Suan Fa Tong Zong* (*Systematic Treatise on Arithmetic*) written by Cheng Dawei in 1592.

Xu, on his part, had also translated in cooperation with another Jesuit, Sabbathinus de Ursis six volumes of *Tai Xi Shui Fa* (*Western Hydraulic Engineering*), which were revised by Li and published in 1612. The books represented the first introduction of Western hydraulics to China by the Chinese scientists for the purpose of improving the irrigation work in northwest China. In addition to the books on hydraulics, Xu wrote two more books on survey methods and Pythagorean theorem, based on Ricci's teachings and other mathematical publications.

In their introduction of the Western sciences, the Chinese scholars had, from the start, paid attention to comparing the Western technology with the Chinese heritage, in both theory and practice. While absorbing the advanced knowledge of the West, they would try to adapt it to the Chinese tradition and update the domestic practice to meet the modern standard. These Chinese scholars, Xu Guangqi and Li Zhizao, had helped lay the cornerstone for Chinese modern science. Xu was, in a way, comparable to his contemporary European statesman and scholar, Francis Bacon (1561-1626), as both of them were outstanding in pavig the way for modern experimental science—one in China, the other in Europe. Bacon was widely acclaimed for his vision in proposing a reorganization of human knowledge as seen in his books of *Novum Organum* (1620) and *De Augmentis Scientiarum* (1623). During this same period, Xu—in the wake of introducing a variety of Western sciences to his home country—raised a comprehensive proposal to develop modern sciences in China and update its traditional culture. He proposed that efforts be made to modernize the following 10 scientific departments: meteorology, hydraulics, music, defence, statistics, architecture, physics and mechanics, geography and cartography, medicine, and time-piece. His ambitious programme was aimed at helping China catch up with the West in scientific development.

Xu was also responsible for introducing the plane and spherical trigonometry to Chinese students, through his work of *Da Ce* (*Grand Survey*), compiled and translated during his service in reforming the Chinese calendar. Later, he again introduced to China the newly-developed trigonometric functions from the West, through the mathematical tables translated by several Jesuits and finalized by himself. A prolific scholar, Xu completed a large amount of works covering wide-ranging subjects in politics, poetry and literature, classics, linguistics, caligraphy, polemics and sciences. His scientific works comprised 32 varieties, including 5 on agriculture, 10 on astronomy, 10 on mathematics, 1 on geography, 3 on military science, 1 on medicine and 2 on hydraulics. He was, indeed, the founder of China's modern sciences and the first bridge-builder between Western sciences and Chinese scholars.

II   Xu Guangqi's Reform of the Chinese Calendar System

Xu Guangqi, who had been responsible for introducing such Western sciences as astronomy, mathematics, survey, hydraulics and gunnery to China, was given credit for reforming the Chinese calendar system after the Western model.

During the reign of the Ming Dynasty Emperor Wanli (1573-1620), there were more than a dozen instances of solar eclipses, none of which had been correctly predicted by the Imperial Board of Astronomy. In 1610, the year Matteo Ricci died in Beijing, another solar eclipse occurred in November without any prediction by the board officials. The Ministry of Rites then proposed to the Ming court, on recommendation of Xu, to appoint Didacus de Pantoja, Sabbathinus de Ursis and a few other resident Jesuits as officials responsible for translating the Western calendar and revising the Chinese calendar. Although the proposal was not adopted by the Ming ruler, Xu and Sabbathinus de Ursis proceeded to work on making such advanced astronomical instruments as the celestial sphere and earth template. Then in 1613, Li Zhizao again formally recommended Jesuits Didacus de Pantoja, Nicolaus Longobardi, Sabbathinus de Ursis, and Emmanuel Diaz to the Ming court, stating that these Jesuits had made 14 significant renovations in the astronomical observation system, which should be adopted to reform the existing calendar. While the Ming ruler was slow in deciding on the calendar reform, Xu, Li and the Western Jesuits went ahead with their renovations in astronomical observation and produced positive results. Their persistence in the reform effort, however, offended the conservative vice-minister of Rites Shen Que, a high official based in Nanjing. He attacked the Western Jesuits in China, and had several of them, including the Italian Jesuit Alphonsus Vagnoni, arrested in Nanjing. The opposition continued until 1623, with Xu boldly defending the reform cause. Although he was compelled to resign a few times in the 1620s, because of strong opposition from the conservatives, Xu had never given up his effort to introduce advanced sciences to China. He saw it as the only way to save the waning Ming Dynasty.

His dream finally came true in 1629—the year after the new Ming Emperor Chongzhen was enthroned and eradicated the powerful clique of the notorious eunuch dictator Wei Zhongxian. Xu was re-appointed as a high official in the Ming court by the new emperor. A solar eclipse occurred on the first day of May in that year, and was again not correctly predicted by the officials of the Board of Astronomy, who used the traditional calendar in their calculations. However, another prediction made by Xu, based on his reformed method, proved accurate in both the anticipated time and duration of the eclipse. This experiment proved the need to reform the traditional Chinese calendar system after the superior Western model. It was as important an event as the introduction of Indian calendar to China in 733 in the history of China's calendar reform.

On July 14, 1629, the Ming Emperor Chongzhen issued an edict, approving the founding of the Bureau of Calendar Reform with Xu Guangqi as its director general. And at Xu's recommendation, Li Zhizao and Nicolaus Longobardi and Joannes Terrenz (both Jesuits) joined the official staff of the bureau, which was formally established on September 22 in the same year. Reform of the traditional calendar was then put on course, beginning with the translation of Western calendars and astronomical observations, just as Xu had planned to do. Thus began the most significant calendar reform in the history of the Chinese astronomy, which was basically accomplished in the last six years of Xu's lifetime, with the publication of the Chongzhen Calendar in 1635.

The compilation of the new calendar was done, mainly, by Xu, Jacobus Rho and Joannes Adam Schall von Bell. The Italian Jesuit Jacobus Rho was originally based in Kaifeng, while the German Jesuit Joannes A.S. von Bell was in Xi'an; both came to Beijing at the request of Xu, after Xu's colleague Joannes Terrenz died in May of 1630. Rho and Bell spared no effort in translating and preparing the necessary data, some of which were gathered by them from the Italian Academy of Lineci and L'Universite de Montpellier and also from other colleges in Germany and Austria. Xu, for his part, served as the chief editor, while checking the data by personally conducting celestial probing at the astronomical observatory. Already in his seventies, Xu carried on the work relentlessly—even after his leg was injured in December, 1630, while he was climbing the stairs leading to the observatory. By the time he ceased breathing on November 24, 1633, Xu had already finished editing 60 volumes of the new calendar.

In his final hours, Xu, who had been appointed to the high position of Grand Secretary and concurrently Minister of Rites since 1632, recommended Li Tianjing as his successor in heading the Bureau of Calendar Reform. It took Li two more years, after Xu's death, to accomplish the work which Xu had longed to do to finish in his lifetime. The Chongzhen Calendar, also called Calendar Based on "New Western Method," had a total of 137 volumes, and was first published in the last year of the Ming Dynasty. The publication—introducing such essential concepts of calendar science as the "circular measure," "definition of survey,"

"stellar index," "stellar directory," and "quintile" to China
—was instrumental in injecting theories of "spherical earth"
and longitude-latitude system, as solid basic concepts, into the
Chinese astronomy, thereby establishing the method of global
computation based on the longitudinal and latitudinal system.
Such a development was most essential in the design of astronomical instruments, as it adapted the traditional Chinese calibra-
tion of the celestial sphere by "365 and a quarter degrees" to the
"360 degrees" as used in the Western calendar system.

Xu was enthusiastic about introducing modern astronomical
instruments to China. He was responsible for procuring, in 1629,
21 pieces of new instruments for his calendar reform project,
including quadrants and celestial globes, in addition to three
timepieces and three astronomical telescopes. The telescopes were
the latest models developed by Galileo in Venice, and for the first
time introduced to China and mounted on a Chinese-built framework. In 1634, Joannes Adam Schall von Bell, the German Jesuit,
brought another new telescope from Europe to China, along with
its gilded framework and bronze accessaries. The telescope was
installed on an observatory platform, built in the Ming palace, by
the German Jesuit, under the supervision of two imperial eunuchs Lu Weining and Wei Guozheng. When completed, the Ming
Emperor Chongzhen inspected it and praised their job. Joannes
Adam Schall von Bell was known to have introduced Galileo
telescope to China several times, including the one brought in by
him, when he first arrived in the country on June 22, 1622.
Western Jesuits had often spoken of the efficiency of such telescopes in their books. Then, in 1634, von Bell and Jacobus
Rho produced China's first domestically-made telescope, drawing compass, miniature celestial sphere and ivory sundials, which
helped the astronomical observatory in its work during the last
years of the Ming Dynasty. However, to the last day of the Ming
Dynasty, the Bureau of Calendar Reform was still separated from
the Board of Astronomy, and had to depend on its own observatory.

In 1644, the Ming Dynasty was overthrown, and the Qing
Dynasty army entered Beijing by way of the Shanhaiguan Pass.

The new dynasty took over the Bureau of Calendar Reform, which was being looked after by von Bell alone, who managed to preserve most of its instruments. Joannes Adam Schall von Bell was given immediate support by the ruler of Qing court, who expressed keen interest in the reform of the traditional Chinese calendar system and the new calendar worked out by von Bell and his colleagues. The German Jesuit further enhanced his prestige in the new dynasty by correctly predicting—with his new calendar system—the solar eclipse on the first day of the eighth lunar month in 1644, and also the lunar eclipse on January 15 in the following year. The accuracy of his prediction contrasted sharply with the incorrect forecast made by others, who used the Islamic calendar. As a result, the Qing Dynasty Regent Dorgon (1612-1650) approved and made official the new calendar system; his hand-written edict "Let the Western New Calendar Be Observed" was printed upon the title page of the new calendar published in the second year of Shunzhi (1645).

The newly-printed calendar listed the name of Xu Guangqi on the top of its editing staff, followed by the two Western Jesuits Joannes Adam Schall von Bell and Jacobus Rho in both its first and second impressions. In 1645, von Bell was appointed president of the Board of Astronomy by the Qing Dynasty ruler. Since then, for a continuous period of nearly 200 years until 1838, the post had always been held by an European Jesuit—following the precedent set by von Bell. Thanks to his success, the Western calendar system was legalized in China. Joannes Adam Schall von Bell was also responsible for compiling the Yongnian Calendar in the reign of the Qing Emperor Kangxi, and also the book *Differences in the Calendar Systems* which listed the Western calendar's 42 advantages as well as the shortcomings of the traditional Chinese calendar system. In his another book *Introduction to the New Calendar*, he summed up the essentials of the Chongzhen Calendar and, for the first time, presented a systematic introduction of the Western calendar system, thereby accomplishing finally the task which Xu Guangqi had initiated but was unable to finish in his lifetime.

III Western Missionaries and Emperor Kangxi of the Qing Dynasty

1. Emperor Kangxi and Western Science

The 61-year-long reign (1661-1722) of the Qing Dynasty's Emperor Kangxi was remarkable as the period when the Western culture was being extensively introduced into China. It is also interesting to note that Emperor Kangxi reigned in the same era as the French King Louis XIV (reigned 1643-1715) and the Russian Czar Peter the Great (reigned 1682-1725), and that the three monarchs all played significant roles in world history.

The controversy of calendar reform was the first issue faced by the young Emperor Kangxi, when he was enthroned at the age of eight. The issue first surfaced in 1658, when the aging Joannes Adam Schall von Bell was promoted to the top rank of official-dom, under the patronage of Emperor Shunzhi (1644-1662) who treated the German Jesuit like his Godfather. Wu Mingxuan, the Chinese official in charge of the Islamic calendar order, was the first to accuse von Bell of committing errors in his astronomical observation, but the accusation was proven groundless.

In 1660, another Chinese scholar from Xin'an Prefecture, Yang Guangxian, criticized the calendar reform conducted by the Western Jesuits as contrary to the teachings of the ancient saints of China. However, such an accusation was again ignored by the emperor. Then, after young Kangxi's succession to the throne, the power of the Qing court was briefly held by his regent-chancellor Aobai, who had long since borne a grudge against the favoured Jesuits in the court. Seeing this as an opportunity, Yang Guang-xian again launched attacks on the Western Jesuits, by publishing two booklets entitled *Clearing away Heresies* and *A Must*, in which he accused the Christian church—which called Adam the ancestor of mankind—of trying to convert Chinese into "descend-ants of the Westerners," and that the Western Jesuits were using Macao as their base to seek control of the whole China, with von Bell as the most dangerous leader of the plot. Thousands of these booklets were distributed in the country, arousing heated debate between Yang and an Italian Jesuit Ludovicus Buglio. Yang followed it up in 1644 by formally accusing von Bell and the Western Jesuits in the provinces of "sedition." As a result, von Bell and his colleague Ferdinandus Verbiest were arrested and thrown into jail. Yang did not stop there; he went on to accuse von Bell of causing the untimely deaths of Emperor Shunzhi and his queen, because the Jesuit had earlier chosen "an ominous date" for the funeral of the emperor's infant prince—who had died only three months after birth. At this point, the 73-year-old von Bell suffered a stroke and could not defend himself at the trial. He received a special pardon granted by the late Emperor Shunzhi's Queen Mother, and was finally released on bail, in 1665. But more than 30 Chinese officials involved in the calendar reform—with Li Zubai as their leader—were all tried as criminals; most were sentenced to jail or even death, with the remaining few dismissed from their posts. A year later, von Bell also died.

After the arrest of von Bell, Ferdinandus Verbiest and other Western missionaries, the calendar reform was completely revoked, and the old Ming Dynasty's Da Tong Calendar was reinstated for some months; but it proved to be so deficient and inaccurate that the Qing court had to replace it again with the Islamic Calendar. At the same time, Yang Guangxian—who knew nothing about astronomy—was appointed president of the Board of Astronomy, with Wu Mingxuan as his deputy to take charge of the Islamic Calendar. The two men made a chaotic mess of the country's calendar system.

In 1668, the 14-year-old Emperor Kangxi, got rid of his notorious regent-chancellor Aobai, established his personal rule and soon began to re-examine the case of the controversial calendar reform. In winter of that year, he sent one of his trusted officials to preside an open debate between the jailed Jesuit Ferdinandus Verbiest and the Chinese officials in charge of the Board of Astronomy. Then, at the beginning of the following years, the young emperor ordered an experimental observation, held at the imperial astronomical observatory, to check both the celestial phenomena and calendar-related solar terms, which was again presided over by one of his top aides.

The results of the experiment proved that the calculations by Ferdinandus Verbiest were correct, and that Wu Mingxuan, then president of the Board of Astronomy, was at a loss to offer any authentic information on the astronomical condition. Faced with the evidences, Yang Guangxian had to admit before the emperor that both he and Wu Mingxuan knew nothing about astronomical observation. However, when the young emperor demanded why he had fabricated such groundless accusations against the Jesuit astronomers, Yang retorted, "How could a majestic emperor, who professes the principles of the ancient saints of Yao and Shun, turn against such tradition to believe in the calendar of the Catholics?" Yang, then, went on to say that Ferdinandus Verbiest's reform of the astronomical observatorial apparatus was aimed at destroying all the traditional instruments left by the nation's ancestry beginning with Yao and Shun, and also at annulling all the traditional cultural system founded by the nationa's ancestors after Yao and Shun. Ferdinandus Verbiest, for his part, had written several articles, such as *On the Truth of Calendar* and *On Groundless Prediction of Fortunes*, to defend himself during the controversy. In the year 1670, Emperor Kangxi again gave the task of calendar reform to Verbiest, who had been engaged in improving the old astronomical instrument after he was released from jail. Then, the emperor agreed to Verbiest's suggestion on shifting the intercalary month from the twelfth month to the second month of the next year (1671), which was then the ninth year of Kangxi's reign. Corresponding changes were also made in the schedule of related solar terms in the calendar.

In August 1669, Emperor Kangxi dismissed Yang Guangxian and Wu Mingxuan from their posts. Joannes Adam Schall von Bell was rehabilitated and Ferdinandus Verbiest was appointed vice-president of the Board of Astronomy, and became president four years later. Western calendar system regained a footing in China. In the same year Austrian priest Christian Herdtricht, Italian priest Philippus Maria Grimaldi and Portuguese priest Tomas Pereira were all invited back to Beijing to participate in the work of the Board of Astronomy, which went all out again to promote Western calendar.

Following the footsteps of his predecessor von Bell, Verbiest carried on the promotion of a new calendar system in China, in coordination with the rapidly progressing astronomical research in the world. It was also in 1667 that French King Louis XIV invested millions of francs in building the Paris Astronomical Observatory, a project in which such famous scientists as Auzout, Picard, Couplet and the learned Cassini all took part. When completed, the Paris Observatory enrolled Huyghens of Italy and Roeumer of the Netherlands in its research staff, and procured a number of top-precision astronomical instruments.

In China, meanwhile, Verbiest and his colleague Philippus Grimaldi—under the patronage of Emperor Kangxi—restored and developed a series of astronomical instruments in the Beijing Astronomical Observatory after 1674, including the celestial sphere, transit instrument, theodolite, altazimuth, and the quadrant. For each, they prepared specific graphs and operation manuals in a book called *Register of New Instruments for the Heavenly Observatory*. Eventually, Ferdinandus Verbiest finished the work of compiling the new Qing Dynasty calendar called Kangxi Yongnian Calendar, thereby concluding the Chinese calendar reform in this historic era.

Verbiest was also a machine-building expert. His talent was discovered by the Qing Dynasty rulers, who ordered him to design new guns for the army after 1674; and he succeeded in developing two types of lightweight but more powerful cannons. Under his direction, 440 pieces of the first type and 240 pieces of the second (heavier) type were built for the Qing army, who used them in the battles to suppress rebel troops in Shaanxi, Hunan and Jiangxi provinces. In 1682, Verbiest wrote a booklet to illustrate the new cannon, which was, obviously, developed by him based on European technology, and for which he was rewarded with the high post of junior vice-president of the Board of Works. But Verbiest's talent did not stop at these achievements; he had also produced a book on geographic cartography, in addition to a world map and three Western-style "perspective" paintings, all drawn by himself. Also remarkable was his experiment on driving a four-wheeled wooden carriage with a primitive steam turbine developed by the Italian mechanist Branca. This experiment, carried out in Beijing, was the first time anyone ever tried to move a wooden carriage with steam power.

In the reign of Emperor Kangxi, astronomical research was carried out not only in the large Beijing Astronomical Observatory, but also at such major cities as Nanjing and Shanghai with the help of the local missionaries. And progress in such research work sparked keen interest in the young Qing Dynasty emperor about Western sciences. His interest soon extended from astronomy to include mathematics, physics, survey and cartography and pharmacology. The Chinese emperor's craving for scientific knowledge and his fondness of Verbiest had greatly encouraged the French Society of Jesus to intensify their missionary operations in China. Therefore, the Paris Astronomical Observatory's director Cassini and the French king's confessioner de la Chaise suggested to French King Louis XIV that he should send a missionary group, comprising mainly scientists, to China, with a view to expanding the cause of the Jesuits in that country. The French king adopted their suggestion. And, as a result, a five-man French Jesuit group, headed by Joames de Fontaney, a mathematics professor, left France in 1685 for China, arriving in Beijing in 1688.

The French Jesuit group was favourably received in the Chinese capital. Later, Joames de Fontaney, Claudus de Visdelou and Aloysius Le Comte went on to work as missionaries in Nanjing, Shanxi and Shaanxi, while Joachim Bouvet and Jean-Francois Gerbillon were ordered to stay in the Qing court as tutors to lecture the Qing Emperor Kangxi on Western sciences, regularly, each week. The two French Jesuits took pains to learn the Chinese and Manchu languages, and within a year were able to speak both fluently. Thus they no longer had any difficulty in communicating with the emperor or the court officials. The Jesuit tutors first taught the Qing emperor geometry, which Kangxi studied with enthusiasm, not only during the lectures but after the tutors had finished their lessons. In five months, he had fully memorized the theories of Euclid's geometry. Several textbooks, originally written or translated into Manchu language by the two French Jesuits during their tutorage in the Qing court, had been found in the old collections of the Peking Palace Museum. These included a Manchu translation of Euclid's *Elements of Geometry* and its seven simplified textbooks, in addition to lecture notes on trigonometry, astronomy and philosophy.

Emperor Kangxi was known to like applying his acquired scientific knowledge, especially on astronomy and survey, to practical matters. On February 25, 1689, when the emperor arrived in Jiangning (Nanjing) during an inspection tour of east China, he personally took part in the observation of Canopus in the night sky, and consulted local Jesuits Joannes de Gabiani and Joames de Fontaney on the result of observation. In 1711, during an inspection of the Yellow River, the emperor walked up to the embankment on the west bank and started measuring the distance and position of the embankment with the help of a transit and surveyor's rod. He explained to the princes and officials the importance of these instruments in land survey, as well as in astronomical observation to predict solar and lunar eclipses. He also told his sons and aides that with these methods it was really not difficult to work out such measurements and calculations.

The two Western Jesuits, Tomas Pereira and Jean-Francois Gerbillon, who were quite conversant with the Latin language, were appointed by the Qing court as interpreters to take part in the Sino-Russian talks held in Nerchinsk in 1689. Enjoying the confidence of the Qing officials, the two Jesuits played an active role in the negotiations, attracting attention internationally.

With his interest in the Western sciences growing continuously, Emperor Kangxi, in 1693, sent the French Jesuit Joachim Bouvet back to Paris, bringing a letter from him to French King Louis XIV, requesting the French king to dispatch more learned French Jesuits to China to introduce Western sciences and arts to the oriental country. Bouvet remained in France for four years, and returned to China in 1698, in the company of new French Jesuit group composed of 10 missionaries, headed by Dominicus

Parrenin and Joannes Bapt Regis. The arrival of these new French Jesuits led to the Qing emperor's enthusiastic study of Western medicine and music, and to marked progress in China's capacity for geographic survey.

A learned scholar of extensive knowledge, Dominicus Parrenin specialized in mechanical and civil engineering, as well as anatomy. It had not taken him long to learn the Chinese and Manchu languages after arriving in Beijing; and he became a close aide to Emperor Kangxi for more than 20 years, accompanying the Qing monarch even during his inspection to the border regions. During all these years, Parrenin served as the emperor's teacher on anatomy and physiology. And through the decades, he had translated more than a doezen famous Western scientific works into Manchu for the Qing emperor, including the French book "L'anatomie de l'homme suivant la circulation du sang, et les nouvelles decouvertes par Dienis" by Dienis. The translation of the first eight volumes of the book done by Joachim Bouvet was read and approved by Emperor Kangxi. The following nine volumes of the book took Parrenin more than five years to translate from French to Manchu, and were carefully studied by the emperor himself. The translated book, which showed all the original well-delineated drawings and graphs on blood circulation, muscular and nervous system of the human body—with translated notes by Joachim Bouvet and Dominicus Parrenin —became a standard science textbook in the Qing court. The translation of the Dienis' book marked a major step forward in the study of anatomy in old China, since the science was first introduced to China by the two verteran Jesuits, Joannes Terrenz and Jacobus Rho, in the last years of the Ming Dynasty.

During those years, the attention of Emperor Kangxi was also attracted by the initial success of the Western physicians and Western drugs in treating some unusual ailments in the country. As a result, he allowed the Western doctors to practise in the Qing court. Once the emperor himself fell sick with malaria and was cured by the French Jesuits—Joames de Fontaney, Jean-Francois Gerbillon and Joachim Bouvet—with quinine. Since then the emperor had become all the more impressed with the value of

Western medicine. Quinine, then called *jin ji na* in China, was first introduced from India, only a few decades after its special function was first discovered by scientists in Peru in 1638.

Since he was cured by the medicine, Emperor Kangxi had taken special interest in studying the use of quinine, and introduced it to some of his trusted aides, including Gao Shiqi and Cao Yin. Cao Yin—grandfather of Cao Xueqin, author of the classical novel *A Dream of Red Mansions*—who was, then, serving as the influential superintendent of the imperial silk factory in Jiangning (Nanjing), fell ill on July 1, 1712. When his illness was diagnosed as malaria, he implored the emperor—through another high official Li Xu—to save his life with the "wonder drug." When Emperor Kangxi received the message, nearly three weeks later, he immediately dispatched a special messenger to bring the medicine and his personal message to Cao Yin in Nanjing, "by express horse." In his message, Kangxi not only specified the dosage of quinine for Cao Yin, but also warned him not to use it, if the disease had turned into dysentery or some symptom other than malaria. However, despite the emperor's order that the express message should be delivered to the patient in Nanjing within nine days, it was not received by the sick official's family, until some three weeks after Cao Yin had passed away.

In 1708, Emperor Kangxi formally appointed a Western physician to serve as a court doctor. The direct cause of this decision was the fact that the Qing emperor was seized with heart disease in September of that year, when he was deeply disturbed by the outrageous behaviour of his son Prince Yun Reng, designated heir to the throne. The emperor abolished the heir title of Prince Yun Reng—bestowed since 1675 when the prince was only two years old—because Yun Reng had become increasingly unscrupulous over the years and had flagrantly abused his power in the imperial court. The incident caused deep sorrow to the 55-year-old Emperor Kangxi, who was soon bedridden with tachycardia. Bernardus Rhodes, the French Jesuit from Toulouse, was called to the palace to treat the sick emperor, who had earlier been favourably impressed by the French Jesuit's successful treatment of several seemingly uncurable cases in the Qing capital. Rhodes, who was conversant with both Western surgery, pharmacology and the Chinese pulse-testing diagnostics, treated the emperor's illness and restored him to health in a matter of days. Rhodes was appointed by Emperor Kangxi as his court doctor; shortly after that, he was credited again for successfully treating a tumour which had grown on the emperor's upper lip. Having won the personal confidence of Kangxi, Rhodes became the emperor's travelling companion, throughout all the 10 more lengthy inspection tours, which the aging emperor made during the late years of his reign. Rewarding Rhodes' outstanding service as a court physician, Emperor Kangxi gave the French Jesuit gold ingots valued at 200,000 francs.

Apart from Rhodes, another Jesuit named J. Joseph da Costa, who came to China in 1717, had also been called to the court to treat ailing aristocrats or high officials. Jospeh da Casta had, until his death in 1740, been working as both a surgeon and a preacher in China for 30 years. Experienced in surgery and pharmacology, he had set up a clinic of his own, giving free treatment to poor people. Emperor Kangxi was known to have joked with da Costa —in front of the papal envoy called Carol—saying, laughingly, "You have probably killed more people in your clinic than I ever had!"

There was still another Jesuit-physician Stephanus Rouset, who had accompanied Emperor Kangxi as his personal physician during Kangxi's last few inspection tours. Rouset, who came to China in 1719, was known to be a very amiable preacher; and during the years when the Christian church was banned in China, many Chinese believers had come to his place, posing as patients, to say their prayers. Rouset died in 1758 from a malignant tumour.

Western music was yet another major gift brought by the European Jesuits to Emperor Kangxi, who had since expressed keen interest in the Western rhythm. The Portuguese Jesuit Tomas Pereira was summoned by the emperor to Beijing, after Ferdinandus Verbiest had recommended him to the emperor as a "musical expert." Tomas Pereira was particularly remarkable in his memory of music. He could remember every Chinese song and its Chinese lyric, after listening to it just once, and then play it on the instrument—thereby winning the favour of the Qing emperor. Once, after Philippus Grimaldi told Kangxi that Pereira was well conversant with music notes, the emperor took up an instrument himself and played together with several Chinese musicians, in front of the Portuguese Jesuit. When the performance was finished, Tomas Pereira had already made a record of the music in Chinese traditional notes, and filled in with the Chinese lyrics.

In March of 1699, nine newly-arrived French Jesuits, including Dominicus Parrenin, Ludovicus Pernon and Philibertus Geneix, were ordered by Emperor Kangxi to accompany him on an inspection tour of southern China. On March 12, when the emperor was cruising down the Yangtze River near Jinshan of Zhenjiang City on a dragon-boat, he discussed Western music with the Jesuits and heard their performance on some instruments. On the third night, Emperor Kangxi again invited these Jesuits to his boat to discuss music with them and listened to their playing of the Western themes. That was when the Qing emperor first cherished the thought of reforming the Chinese music with Western-style instruments.

When Emperor Kangxi returned to the capital from his tour in June of that year, he called all the Jesuits together to hold a musical performance before him, with Tomas Pereira as the conductor, using a wide variety of musical instruments. However, the impromptu performance was a total failure because the numerous Jesuit musicians simply could not produce any harmonious sound with their violins, clavecins, bassoons and cellos. In fact, they created such a discord that the emperor had to cover his ears with both hands and ordered them to stop the performance. Later, Emperor Kangxi again summoned the four Jesuits of Tomas Pereira, Ludovicus Pernon, Dominicus Parrenin and Gherardini to hold a small concert for him in the palace. The four Western Jesuits who were good at a variety of musical instruments, including both stringed and wind music, played in perfect unison and harmony. After that, the Qing emperor often heard them play together before him for hours each time. Once, the emperor was so fascinated with their beautiful performance, that he let the concert continue for four hours without interruption, until the performing Jesuits—who had to remain kneeling while playing—were exhausted. Ludovicus Pernon, while serving in the court, conducted Western music lessons for the emperor and also made some musical instruments, including clavecin, éspinette and timpanon. The éspinette was said to be the same as the one offered to Ming Dynasty Emperor Wanli by Matteo Ricci, when the Italian Jesuit first came to China; the instrument was known to have as many as 72 metal strings and had to be played with a small plate. In the final years of the Ming Dynasty, the Jesuit Joannes Adam Schall von Bell was known to have repaired the original éspinette, offered by Matteo Ricci, and played it for Ming Dynasty Emperor Chongzhen. For his part, Qing Emperor Kangxi heard a performance of the newly-made éspinette by Ludovicus Pernon.

Tomas Pereira, before his death in 1708, contributed to China's study of Western music by elaborating on the theory of harmony and temperament. He was succeeded by the Italian Jesuit Derek, who was remarkable in analysing the relationship between the Western musical rhythms and the Chinese musical melodies, which he illustrated in graphs. The two Jesuits' musical works were later included in the supplement to the *Lü Lü Zheng Yi* (*Definitions of Music*) compiled in Kangxi's name in 1713. The book, in five volumes, contained works by Chinese musicians in its first four volumes and devoted its supplementary fifth volume to Western musical works. Tomas Pereira's book was first written in Chinese under the title of *Excerpts of Music*, which was later translated into Manchu, upon the order of Emperor Kangxi, and given the translated Latin name of *Musica pratica et Speculativa*. The Italian Jesuit Derek also gave music lessons to seven students in the Qing court, including Kangxi's second and third sons, all of them learned from their Italian teacher, not only Western music theories, but also how to play clavecin.

A major feat accomplished by Emperor Kangxi during the last years of his reign was a national atlas of China compiled through the cooperation of Chinese and foreign scientists, under his sponsorship. The national map, called "A Complete Atlas of the Imperial Territory of Emperor Kangxi," was finished in 1718, on the basis of an on-the-spot survey covering the nation's 18 provinces of Zhili, Henan, Shandong, Shanxi, Shaanxi, Gansu, Hunan, Hubei, Jiangsu, Anhui, Zhejiang, Jiangxi, Fujian, Guangdong, Guangxi, Sichuan, Yunnan, and Guizhou—in addition to the Tibet, Korea, Taiwan, Hami and Ryukyu regions.

It was said that the compilation of a national atlas was first suggested by the Jesuit Jean-Francois Gerbillon, and that the two other French Jesuits Joannes Bapt Régis and Petrus Jartoux made remarkable contribution in the surveying task. The completion of the atlas was a great satisfaction to the then 66-year-old Emperor Kangxi, who revealed to his close aide, sub-Chancellor of the Grand Secretary Jiang Tingxi in 1719, that he had tried for more than 30 years to have such an atlas compiled. The remark indicated that the Qing emperor had first cherished the idea of compiling a national map after the Sino-Russian Border Talks of Nerchinsk in 1688, when the interpreter Jesuit Jean-Francois Gerbillon showed an atlas of Asia to Emperor Kangxi and explained to him that the lack of a border map had given the Russian expeditionary force an excuse to infiltrate Chinese territory. The practical importance of maps in defence and military use, as pointed out by the French Jesuit, left a deep impression on the perceptive Qing emperor, who had since made up his mind to have such an atlas compiled—as one of his strategic objectives.

In 1696, Emperor Kangxi took personal command of his troops in quelling the Dzungars revolt, and followed it up with an inspection of the Zhangjiakou, Datong and Ningxia areas. Then in 1699, he set out for another inspection of areas south of the Yangtze River, in the company of Jean-Francois Gerbillon and Tomas Pereira, with whom the Qing emperor discussed such issues as geographic survey and astronomical observation, indicating that he was concerned with both. Large-scale land survey actually began nine years later in 1708, first along the Great Wall, to meet defence need. Jesuits Joannes Bapt Régis, Petrus Jartoux and Joachim Bouvet took part in the survey, which was completed a year later in the form of a four-metre long survey map, showing all the mountains, waterways, fortresses and towns in and along the Great Wall areas. Emperor Kangxi was pleased with the finished map because it had surpassed all his previous maps in both quality and content.

One month after the completion of the Great Wall map, Emperor Kangxi, on December 10, 1709, ordered his Jesuits to cross the Great Wall and start a survey of western Manchuria, northern Korea and northern Zhili areas. The Jesuits finished the job and drew a map of the areas in about six months. Then, they were ordered to continue their survey in northern Manchuria, in the Hami area of Xinjiang and Shandong Province. In 1712, Joannes Bapt Régis first finished a survey map of Shandong, while Petrus Jartoux was still working in areas to the northwest of the Great Wall. The emperor, then, sent four more Jesuits to help Jartoux, boosting the size of the surveying team to 10 Westerners, greatly accelerating the surveying work. Of the 10 Western surveyors, nine were members of the Society of Jesus, and only Bonjour was an Austin friar. Following the completion of their work in the north, the surveying team moved on to the southern part of the country, extending their cartographic project to coastal Taiwan and the inland provinces. Most outstanding among the Jesuit-surveyors was Joannes Bapt Régis, who first took over the Yunnan surveying job, after Bonjour died while working in Yunnan's border town of Mengding in 1715 and when he had just finished his own work in Fujian. Then, immediately after completing his work on the Yunnan map, Régis proceeded to take over the Sichuan surveying job from the ailing Xavier Fridelli, and finally finished the maps of Sichuan and Guizhou for him. Eventually, Joannes Bapt Bégis also took over the last unfinished part of the national survey—the two provinces of Hubei and Hunan—and accomplished the final phase of the great task. It was in the year 1717, that Régis finally returned to Beijing, where he and Petrus Jartoux began checking on the map of Tibet, as done by two lama surveyors. The two Tibetan lamas were science graduates from the Mathematics Institute of the Qing Imperial Changchunyuan's Mengyangzhai School. The Mengyangzhai School was founded by the Qing court specially for the offsprings of Manchu aristocratic families to study such scientific subjects as mathematics, physics, astronomy and music. Its Mathematics Institute was set up in 1713 for the purpose of training surveying and map-drawing technicians. The two lama technicians were sent to work in Xining and Lhasa as map surveyors, immediately after graduation. These Chinese technicians were responsible for compiling the map, covering the entire plateau region with an average altitude of 3,000 metres above sea level, and they succeeded in producing such a map with excellent precision. Two other Chinese mathematicians Ping An and Feng Sheng'e, who accompanied Qing Dynasty envoys Hai Bao and Xu Baoguang in their mission to the Ryukyu Islands were also graduates trained by the Mathematics Institute. They undertook the survey of the Ryukyu Islands, adding it to the Kangxi Atlas as a supplement a year after it was finished. The "Complete Atlas of the Imperial Territory of Emperor Kangxi," in its trial edition published in 1718 for examination by high officials of the Qing court, comprised 32 maps drawn at the scale of one to 1.4 million, in addition to 15 provincial maps—one for each province.

The Jesuit-surveyors, who worked in the provinces, were dispatched by the emperor as his personal representatives with corresponding authority. They were empowered to examine the local data and annals and gather all necessary information from the provincial officials. But their most important role was to visit the key locations and organize on-the-spot triangulation as a part of the nationwide surveying network. Through triangulation, in addition to astronomical observation, they were able to redefine the distance between the different cities and their longitudinal and latitudinal positions, disregarding all previous maps and measurements. In their survey, they used Beijing as the meridian point of longitude and adopted the Chinese *li* of 1,800 *chi* (600 metres) as the standard of measurements. And their finished map, showing every major Chinese city with its correct position, was then the best available map in the world.

A copy of the Kangxi Atlas was sent by Xavier Fridelli to Paris, where it was revised by the French royal geographer J. B. Bourguignon d'Anville and published in several editions during the period from 1729 to 1734. Each edition of these Chinese maps comprised 42 drawings, which were the same as the European copperplate edition, based on the copy brought back to Europe by the Italian Jesuit Ripa. The French geographer Bourguignon d'Anville, himself a research fellow of the Russian Academy of Sciences in St. Petersberg, later used the Chinese maps—with Russian translated notes—to exchange data with the Russian Academy of Sciences, in an apparent politically-oriented practice.

The geographic survey and compilation of a national atlas of China was an important achievement, which superseded such geographically-advanced countries as France, Belgium and Italy, in both the scale of land survey and the scientific value of the finished map. In fact, none of these nations had then accomplished a nationwide map survey. Through this project, China was able to train its own technicians, with the help of the Western experts, and integrate these talents with its huge financial and political resources in accomplishing the gigantic task of surveying a territory of some 10 million square kilometres within a period of 10 years. The work of Kangxi Atlas also set an example in defining geographic longitudinal and latitudinal positions through triangulated survey, which was an unprecedented technical success. Joannes Bapt Régis and Petrus Jartoux discovered, in the course of field survey, that the length of longitudes differed on both ends, thereby providing evidence for the oblate spheric shape of the earth. Their discovery was an affirmation of Newton's theory on the shape of the globe, as against that of Cassini. Such a valuable contribution to scientific research, as yielded by the making of Kangxi Atlas, was something even Emperor Kangxi had not expected.

2. The Catholic Crisis

When Matteo Ricci opened the way for Catholic missionaries in China, during the final decades of the Ming Dynasty, he followed an approach of adapting Catholic rites for Chinese converts by fully respecting Chinese traditional rituals and heritage. This way, he was able to absorb members of the elite into his circle of followers. Ricci and his Jesuit colleagues tried their best to find "common ground" with their Chinese converts, from the teachings of the Chinese sages and classics. As he stated in his book "Truth of Catholicism" published in 1595, Ricci tried to adapt Catholicism to Confucianism—"in order to convert Confucianists into Christians," as Xu Guangqi had put it. Ricci was quoted as saying that the Chinese Confucianists, while refraining from discussing supernatural beliefs, were, however, adhering to the same moral principles as the Jesuits. Therefore, Ricci claimed that his missionary approach was fully practicable among the vast Chinese intellectuals who observed Confucian and ancestral rituals under the imperial official examination system.

After the death of Ricci in 1610, his missionary approach was continued by other Jesuits, including Joannes Adam Schall von Bell, Ferdinandus Verbiest, Martino Martini, Philippus Maria Grimaldi, Tomas Pereira, Jean-Francois Gerbillon and Joachim Bouvet. But it was opposed by a number of other missionaries, particularly the Dominican and Franciscan priests in China, who condemned the practice of allowing the Chinese converts to continue their worship of Confucius and ancestors. Their controversy was reported to the Vatican in 1635 by the Archbishop of Manila. After investigating the Vatican acknowledged the Chinese missionary approach. The Manila Archbishop, in 1638, withdrew his objection to the approach, accordingly. However, the Dominican missionaries in China continued to complain to the mission department of the Vatican over the Jesuits' tolerance of such practice by their Chinese converts, as participating in activities worshiping Confucius, observing state rituals, holding temple festivals and hanging banners or setting up steles in the church to hail the monarch. They asked the Vatican to restrict "such uncatholic activities" of the Jesuits. In response to the Dominicans' protests, the Jesuits in China sent their Italian colleague Martino Martini back to Vatican to defend their cause, finally winning a de facto approval of their missionary approach. It was contained in the Directive of 1656 issued by the Vatican, which allowed the missionaries to exercise their discretion in allowing the converts to participate in Chinese rituals.

However, the protests of the Dominicans were fueled by a

series of disputes between churches and the Chinese public, and in 1676 they launched new charges against the Jesuits' "accomodation to Chinese rites" in the missionary approach. This caused the Jesuits to write a series of articles to explain that the Chinese respected Confucius as their "great teacher" and that their tribute paid to the ancestors was not idolatry. The intensified controversy between the Dominicans and Jesuits spurred the Europeans to pay increasing attention to the rites and customs of the Chinese, giving rise to a heated debate among different factions of the Catholic Church and scholars of the major universities in Europe, centering on the "Rites Issue." Their arguments covered such subjects as whether the ancient Chinese religious beliefs had anything in common with the Christian creed, and also the authenticity of ancient Chinese philosophies and the values of Chinese ethics.

During the years between 1676 and 1679, the book *Tractados históricos, politicos, éticos y religiosos de la monarquia de China*, written by the Dominican Domingo Navarrete, was published in Madrid. The two-volume book expressed the Dominicans' view of the Chinese culture; its explanation of China's history and its system of rites created a powerful impact in Europe.

Navarrete was one of the 23 Catholic missionaries, who had been detained by the Qing Dynasty authorities in Guangzhou for violation of Chinese rites. They eventually reached a 42-article agreement among themselves on January 26, 1668, to abide by the Vatican's Directive of 1656 in their missionary practice. Navarrete, the only one who refused to sign the final agreement, fled back to Europe in 1669. After his return to Europe, Navarrete continued his attacks on the Jesuits in speeches and writing; his arguments fanned the ongoing debate of "Rites Issue" (Quaestio de Ritibus) to focus on the Church's authority over the Jesuits in China.

Originally, the Catholic Church's authority over its missionaries in the Far East was under the protection of the Portuguese monarch; however, according to a Vatican statement in 1608, Franciscan or Dominican missionaries going to the Far East did not have to pass through Lisbon, but could take orders directly from their own organizations. In 1680, the Vatican began to ordain administrators in China by direct appointment of the Pope, upon the recommendation of the Portuguese monarch. Then, following its appointment of Bishop Pallu as the first priest-administrator in China, the Vatican's circular department issued an order, requiring all missionaries in the China diocese to take an oath to obey the Vatican administrator. However, Bishop Pallu did not take office until he arrived in Fujian in 1684, when he formally assumed the authority of the China diocese. The order of the new administrator created a dilemma for the Western missionaries in China, who belonged to different organizations. The missionaries of Franciscan and Dominican orders based in Guangzhou, who were Spanish, promised their obedience only to their archbishop of Manila and refused to swear to obey the new administrator from Vatican. As a result, they were required by church discipline to leave the China diocese. After the death of Bishop Pallu, his successor Bishop Charles Maigrot issued orders forcing the missionaries to take oaths, resulting in a clash first with the French Jesuits. Recognizing that its order had caused chaos among the Catholic missionaries in China, the Vatican's circular department made a concession in 1688, rescinding its requirement for oath-taking, demanding only their obedience to the new administrator. Since the Vatican, which now assumed direct control over the missionary activities in China, differed with the French Jesuits—who had the backing of both French King Louis XIV and Qing Dynasty Emperor Kangxi—in their stance regarding the Chinese traditional rites, the Roman Pope dispatched his special envoy, Carlo Tommaso Maillard de Tournon, and later Carlo Ambrogio Mezzabarba, to Beijing to visit the Qing emperor in a bid to enhance the Pope's prestige among the missionaries in China.

In a solemn ceremony held on December 31, 1705, Emperor Kangxi received Tournon for the first time, but the papal envoy did not have the courage, then, to formally notify the Qing emperor of the Pope's order of 1704 on banning the "accomodation process," as practised by the Jesuits. However, when the Qing emperor received the papal envoy Tournon for the second time on June 29, 1706, Emperor Kangxi, having realized the intention of the papal envoy, stated in clear terms that only those missionaries "who respect Chinese traditional rites" would be allowed to proselyte in China. Since Tournon had openly declared his support for Vatican administrator Charles Maigrot, the Qing emperor banished the papal envoy from the court. Then, in 1707, Emperor Kangxi formally notified all Western missionaries in China that anyone of them, who refused to follow the established practice of Matteo Ricci, would not be allowed to stay in China but should be expelled from this country. The imperial notice further stated that in the event the Pope should disapprove of their practice, the missionaries could stay on in China "as voluntary missionaries" and continue their religious career in the country. The Qing emperor made it clear that China had no intention to ban Catholicism in the country, but it could not adapt the Chinese traditions to suit the Vatican's missionary policy, as demanded by the Pope.

On March 15, 1715, Pope Clement XI issued his Ex illa die, reiterating the papal order of 1704 and forcing the Catholic missionaries in China to take oaths and pledge their obedience to the order. This resulted in a resurgence of the clash between the Qing Dynasty and the Roman Pope, who again sent his special envoy Carlo Ambrogio Mezzabarba to Beijing for negotiation with the Qing emperor. Emperor Kangxi, having already seen the translated version of the papal Ex ille die, reaffirmed his denunciation of the papal order, throughout his 13 meetings with the papal envoy. He condemned the papal ban of Chinese rites—as "You Westerners know nothing about the Chinese tradition, so how could you take the liberty to criticize the Chinese rites?" —during the first meeting with the papal envoy. Whereby, Emperor Kangxi issued a formal decree, banning Vatican missionary activities in the country, stating that the reason was because such activities ran contrary to Chinese rites, and therefore would cause disputes and chaos. Thereafter, the Catholic missionaries could only work among the poor people in China and were unable to make any conversions from among the intellectuals or officials. As a result, the cultural exchange between China and Europe

—through the bridge of Western missionaries—virtually came to a standstill; so did the hitherto rapidly-expanding introduction of Western technology into China, despite the Qing government's policy of welcoming specialized Western missionaries to work in China—"provided they respected Chinese rites." Consequently, this adversely affected the cultural and scientific development in China.

IV   A Chinese Visitor to the Original Site of the Renaissance

The Western Jesuits, while contributing much to cultural and scientific exchanges between Europe and China, had, however, failed to bring any information about the important event of Renaissance from Europe to China. The Renaissance was beginning to spread from Italy to Western Europe at the time, when Matteo Ricci and Michael Ruggieri, the two Italian Jesuits, came as missionaries to China.

But a century later, as the Renaissance had become a past event in Europe, a Chinese Christian convert came from China to Italy—there to pay tribute to the Vatican and visit the city of Florence, where the Renaissance had first originated. The man's name was Fan Shouyi, also called Fan Shuohe.

Fan Shouyi (1682-1753) went to Europe at the age of 25, and returned to China when he was already 38. During this period, he spent 11 years—the prime of his youth—in Italy. He first arrived in Lisbon in August of 1708, where he was received by the Portuguese monarch. The next year, he went to Italy and was enrolled there in a Jesuit school and joined the Society of Jesus. He finished his studies in 1718, then went again to Lisbon to pay his tribute to the Portuguese king, before returning to China in March of 1719. Shortly after his arrival back in Guangzhou on June 13, 1720, he went to visit Emperor Kangxi in the imperial summer palace in Rehe (now Chengde). The emperor received him on September 11 of that year, and asked him many questions about the Roman Catholic Church and conditions in the European countries. Being the first Chinese Christian, who had visited and become acquainted with Europe, Fan Shouyi was able to brief the Qing emperor on the European situation, and provided Emperor Kangxi with important background information the emperor needed in his negotiation with the papal envoy Carlo Ambrogio Mezzabarba.

In the wake of the visits to China by two papal envoys in the early eighteenth century, the Catholic missionaries in China faced the problem of whether they could carry on their missions independently. Until then, adapting their Catholic rites to the authority of the Chinese emperor and the Chinese traditions had already become an accepted practice of most Western missionaries in China—whether they were Jesuits, Augustinians or Franciscans. That such a practice was "in keeping with the Christian Creed" was also the conviction upheld by the Chinese Christian Fan Shouyi, who had just returned from Catholic Italy. It was his explicit view that had further encouraged Emperor Kangxi to sustain the country's religious policy based on nationalistic considerations.

As China's first Christian pilgrim to visit the Vatican, Fan Shouyi later published a 5,000-word memoir of his travel to Europe, devoting one quarter of its content to describing the sights of Rome. He also gave his remarkable impressions of such Renaissance centres as Florence and Siena and such trading centres as Genoa and Naples in Italy. According to his memoir, he was stunned by the magnificent palace structures, fascinating gardens and colourful treasures, which he had seen in Rome and Lisbon.

Fan began his tour of Europe from the Portuguese capital of Lisbon, his first port of arrival, where he stayed for four months and was received by the young Portuguese monarch who was still in his teens. While in Lisbon, he participated in the king's birthday celebration and had toured the royal court, where he was dazzled by the luxurious decoration and exquisite furnishings of the palace. Then, before leaving Europe, he again visited Lisbon and was received again by the king, who granted him one hundred gold coins as a farewell gift.

During his ten years in Italy, Fan Shouyi spent most of his time on religious studies in Rome, but he did find time to tour many nearby cities and harbours. On the second day of his arrival in Rome, he was received by Pope Clement XI (1700-1721) and given the opportunity to visit the myriad of elaborate palaces, variegated gardens and the voluminous collections in the Vatican Library. The literary treasures in the library left an unforgettable impression on this Chinese pilgrim. As the first Chinese eye-witness of the magnificent Graeco-Roman artifacts, which marked the cultural revival of the Renaissance, Fan Shouyi was also the first Chinese messenger to introduce the information of the European Renaissance to his home country. In his memoir, Fan stated how he had marvelled at the luxurious lifestyle, extravagant pageantry and splendid mansions and gardens of Roman aristocrats. He also noticed that Rome had built a "via-duct" of nearly 50 kilometres long to draw water from a remote spring into the city, where there were also such attractions as rockeries and stone statues built in fountains, which were found everywhere in the paved streets. Business establishments were full of colourful commodities. He was impressed with the numerous beautiful churches, cathedrals, convents and shrines in the Italian capital. As for the scenic wonders of Fra Scati and Tivoli in the suburbs of Rome, they were described as what the Chinese pilgrim "had never seen before."

Fan Shouyi gave a vivid description of the impressive historic relics of Rome, such as the remains of temples in the Forum, the Trajan's Column of marble (98-117) and the marvellous Colos-seum, which he said had been used to "breed lions" in ancient Rome. He mentioned the Angels Bridge over the Tiber, which was lined by 12 stone angels, guarding the road to the Tomb of Roman Emperor Hadrian (117-138).

But it was the grandeur of St. Peter's of Vatican that filled Fan Shouyi with awe. He realized that it was this great religious structure which symbolized the prime of the Roman Renaissance, and to which, dozens of celebrated sculptors and architects dedi-cated the dream of their talents. Since the reign of Pope Nicholas V (1447-1455), efforts were launched to renovate St. Peter's as well as the city of Rome. Such great talents as architect Bramante (1444-1514), painter Raphael (1483-1520), and sculptor Michelangelo (1475-1564) all devoted the prime of their years and skills to perfecting this grand religious monument. By the time the first Chinese Christian pilgrim paid his tribute to the magnificent basilica, the remodeling of the monumental structure was already completed by architect Bernini (1598-1680) who designed the Portico of St. Peter's. Fan was probably the first Chinese visitor to the just-finished masterpiece of the Renaissance.

Rome, cultural centre of the Italian Peninsula, had four universities, in addition to a well-designed and managed multi-department hospital, containing some 1,000 rooms of high sanitary standard. It also had such public amenities as an amply-provided orphanage, all of which indicated that post-Renaissance Rome had emerged as a modern city marked by both flourishing arts and rapid cultural and scientific developments.

During his visit to the birthplace of European humanism —Florence—Fan Shouyi toured the Ponte Vecchio, Palazzo Vecchio, and the Baptistry with keen interest. But what impressed him most was the unfinished St. Maria del Fiore Cathedral, which had been under continuous construction for 200 years. The mighty religious structure was linked with such famous names as Giotto (1266-1337) and Filippo Brunelleschi (1337-1446), the two great architects who had worked on it and made it known around the world. It was in the city of Florence that the Renaissance first unfolded, and here the Chinese pilgrim visited the palaces, art galleries, gardens, and was received by its ruler and answered his queries. From Florence, Fan Shouyi went on to visit several other Italian cities, including Siena, Pisa, Parma and Milan, where he saw the myriad spires overlooking the unfinished great Gothic cathedral, under construction since 1386.

Fan Shouyi's memoir, however, had not produced a complete record of the climate, life, politics and rites of Italy, as witnessed during his 11-year visit to that country. Much of his information about Europe was contained in his verbal report to the Qing emperor. But since he was the first Chinese who had met with the Roman Pope, the Portuguese king and rulers of several Italian states in addition to the Qing emperor, he played the role of a Chinese messenger between the monarchs of the East and the West. Information about Europe introduced to the Qing Dynasty ruler by Fan Shouyi superseded the limited communications provided by the Western missionaries travelling between China and Europe. Fan's memoir, viewed in this context, was more remarkable than the books written by Italian Jesuit Julius Aleni (1582-1649) to introduce Western culture to China. Fan Shouyi was also the first Chinese to return Marco Polo's epic trip to China, by conducting a lengthy tour of his home country and studying its Western culture, as Marco Polo had done during his 17 years in China. Fan's 11-year tour of Europe coincided significantly with the period of negotiation between the Qing Dynasty's Emperor Kangxi and the Roman Pope Clement XI on the final phase of the "Rites Issue."

Chapter Eight
Missionaries and the Turning Point of European Culture

I The Enlightenment Movement of Europe and the Political Ideology in China

1. The Mode of an Open-Minded Monarch in the Orient

The early eighteenth century in France saw the end to the autocracy of King Louis XIV and the unfolding of the Enlightenment movement, which was led by such figures as the talented historian and philosopher Francois-Marie Arouet Voltaire (1694-1778). Voltaire, a follower of the philosophies of Issac Newton (1642-1727) and John Locke (1632-1704), believed in the "natural religion," and used it as his weapon of materialism to combat the absolute authority of the Catholic Church. In political ideology, Voltaire advocated the "natural rights" of human beings and sought for an "ideal society" built on the basis of the "order of nature," as opposed to the absolutism of the Christian Church and Monarchy. From this point of view, he became keenly interested in the political system of the Oriental monarchs, particularly, in the Chinese cultural heritage and its influence upon other ethnic nationalities. This was just when the controversial "Rites Issue" had created a stir in Europe, attracting renewed attention of the European scholars to the religion, philosophy and social system in China. Then, following the publication of a series of Jesuits' reports on China, Voltaire wrote an anecdote about China in his *Lettres philosophiques* in addition to the first two chapters in his other work *Essai sur les moeurs et l'esprit des nations*. These were followed by the *China's Autoc-*

racy written by Francois Quesnay, which described China's feudal system as a model system of open-minded monarch.

According to the Confucian principle of "education through power," the monarch was supposed to play a "model role" for the whole nation, which looked to him for the example in observing moral and legal principles that served as the basis of his government. In Europe of the early eighteenth century, when the structure of autocratic monarchy had become the stumbling block impeding economic development, the pioneers of the Enlightenment movement were pinning their hopes on the open or liberal force in the monarchism to bring about the reform of political structure, marked by the introduction of constitution and parliament, so as to enable the new bourgeoisie to rank among the ruling classes. Like many other reformists in the Enlightenment, Voltaire hoped for the emergence of an open-minded monarch who could coordinate the interests of the feudal aristocrats and the middle class. And, therefore, he used the story of "Princess of Babylon"—in his *Lettres philosophiques*—to describe his ideal ruler as a respectable and wealthy monarch, who was all-powerful to do good things but powerless to do any evil, had thus become the ruler of a free, strong, businesslike and open-minded state. Voltaire's illusion for a free, equal and rationalistic France under an "open-minded" monarchy, had its root in the lengthy autocracy of Louis XIV, when the French court was involved in continued clashes, overtly or covertly, with the Roman Pope. However, Voltaire had declared that he did not advocate Lutheran or Calvinist revolution, but favoured a revolution within the human spirit itself. And so, he discovered the mode of such an "open-minded" monarch in the form of a Chinese emperor, who adhered to the Confucianist doctrine—or the principle of "natural religion."

The introduction of Chinese philosophical and political thoughts to Europe began with the publication of *Confucius Sinarum Philosophus* in 1687, a book published in Latin by the Belgian Jesuit Philippi Couplet. The book also had a Chinese name, *Western Interpretation of the Four Books*; however, it contained only the translations of three books, namely, *The Great*

Learning, *The Mean* and *Analects*—with the fourth book, *Mencius,* missing. Returning to Europe in 1681, Philippi Couplet presented 49 categories of Chinese classic literature to French King Louis XIV, and then compiled the book on Confucius, which was actually a reproduction of the three classic books of Confucianism translated in China by Italian Jesuit Prosper Intercetta and Portuguese Jesuit Ignatius da Costa. The book of *Confucius Sinarum Philosophus,* which was published for the first time in Europe, contained also Philippi Couplet's letter to the French King Louis XIV and an introduction written by Couplet himself, in which he explained the distinction between China's Confucianism, Buddhism and Taoism and also the "64 Diagrams" contained in the *The Book of Changes.* In the eyes of the Jesuits, Confucius stood as the model of ethical principles and the teacher of political philosophies.

Apart from the book on Confucianism, two other books, written in French by the Jesuits, were directly responsible for creating an ideal image of the Chinese monarchism in the eyes of the Europeans. They were the *Nouveaux mémoires sur l'état présent de la Chine,* 1697, by Jesuit Ludovicus Le Comte, and the *Histoire de l'Empereur de la Chine,* 1699, by Jesuit Joachim Bouvet. Le Comte came to China in 1687, and arrived in Beijing via Ningbo. He was later sent to work in Shanxi and Shaanxi, until 1692, when he returned to Paris and then to Rome to report on the mission work in China. Le Comte had since stayed in France, and finished his two volumes of the book *Nouveaux memoires sur l'état présent de la Chine,* which comprised 13 letters introducing the situation in China—eight in Volume I and five in Volume II. The letters covered such aspects as China's language, science, economy and arts, and lauded the Chinese monarchism as "the most perfect" such system in the world. And Joachim Bouvet, for his part, produced a vivid picture of Emperor Kangxi in the *Histoire de l'Empereur de la Chine,* which lavished the finest possible descriptions to praise the physical, mental, ethical, scholastic and personal merits and attraction of the "most brilliant" Qing emperor—who had already reigned for 36 years at the age of 44. The book created an impact on the

European readers, who later became admirers of the spectacular monarch of the Orient.

Then, in 1735, Du Halde collected the reports, literature and translations written by 27 Western missionaries, and compiled a four-volume book in Paris, called *Du Halde, Description géographique, historique, chronologique, politique et physique de l'Empire de la Chine et de la Tartarie Chinoise*. This so-called "Encyclopaedia of the Chinese Empire" soon became a popular publication across Europe, even having its Russian translation published in Moscow. At the time, when the Enlightenment thinkers—heralding "freedom, equality and philanthropy " —were attacking the absolutism of the Christian Church in Europe and seeking a greater role for the middle class and masses of the people, the image of a great and higly-civilized empire ruled by a brilliant open-minded emperor provided them with a practical model of a "perfect open monarchism." And following the continuous growth in trade and the demand for Chinese goods, the prestige of China—as an Oriental "open monarchy" in contrast with the autocracy of pre-revolution France—had become very high in the eyes of a number of European thinkers, who were seeking a just and rational society.

2. The Chinese and Western Views of "Comtemporary China"

Baron Gottfried Wilhelm von Leibniz (1646-1716), well-known German philosopher and mathematician, had been acquainted with the Jesuits. In 1686, he met in Rome with Philippus Maria Grimaldi, the Italian Jesuit who was then on his way to Petersberg as an emissary of the Qing Dynasty Emperor Kangxi. Their meeting provided an opportunity for Leibniz to learn much first-hand information and perceptive views from the Jesuit to help him in studying China. And this led to the publishing of his book *Novissima Sinica* (in Latin) in 1697, which was followed by his Latin translation of *Historie de l'Empereur de la Chine*, published as a supplement to the second edition of his *Novissima Sinica* in 1699.

Leibniz, in his book, expressed deep admiration for the great achievements of Chinese culture, describing it as a model for

Europe in its exemplary ethical standard. He also concurred with the Confucian doctrine of politics, in believing that rationalization of power would bring about a "sagacious government," leading to "Herrschaft der Besten." The German philosopher had been interested in China since his early years, and had at the age of 21 read the book *China Monumentis Illustrata*, 1667, by Kircher. Then, in 1669, when he proposed the founding of a German Academy of Sciences, he listed China as a country to be studied. Later, after he had read the *Confucius Sinarum Philosophus* by Philippi Couplet, Leibniz began to consider himself a follower of Confucianism, calling Confucius the leader of Chinese philosophers. As a great German scientist, Leibniz was very interested in the new information coming from China, and spared no effort in studying Chinese theories. He was particularly attracted by China's "natural religion" and moral and political practices, as well as by the "binary scale" theory as first indicated in the Chinese classic *Book of Changes*.

Leibniz's *Novissima Sinica (Contemporary China)*, as indicated by its lengthy sub-title, was an introduction of the history of contemporary Chinese nation as well as a revelation of some "untold" facts related to the missionary work in that country. It also covered the Sino-European relations, China's keen interest in the heritage and sciences of Europe and also the Sino-Russian border war and the consequential peace treaty of Nerchinsk.

In his nine-page preface for the book, Leibniz elaborated on the comparison of Chinese and European civilizations. In his view, China was superior to civilized Europe in the size of both territory and population, and was not at all inferior to it in other aspects. He pointed out, in particular, that if a war did break out between China and Europe, it was difficult to predict who would emerge as the victor. According to his analysis, the two sides each had its own merits in the skills of essential subsistence and empirical science. While Europe led China in science of thinking and ideology—as a result of its inherent development in logic and metaphysics, and its advancement in material and abstract science such as mathematics and physics—China was far ahead of Europe in social practice, and especially, in ethical behaviours, because the Chinese upheld the preservation of public order as their top social responsibility. The Chinese ideal of human conduct—beginning with "self-cultivation," "putting one's family in order," and finally contributing to the "success of the nation and the whole world"—was completely consistent with Leibniz's conviction that "freedom is a force which obeys reason."

Leibniz spoke highly of the fine morality of the Chinese nation, and described it as an essential merit which enabled the Chinese to continue absorbing the best of foreign cultures and always standing at the fore of the changing world. Therefore, he predicted that if the Saint wished to award a nation for its outstanding merits, then this "golden apple" would certainly fall into the hands of the Chinese.

The German philosopher wrote in his book: The Chinese nation appeared to be superior in their ethics. While the two sides matched each other in skills and technology, Europe, despite its relative advantage in the science of thinking and dialectics, was beyond comparison with China in the philosophy of practice, i.e. the ethics and politics reflected in human life. (And this is a grievance which we have to accept.) Because the Chinese nation has always tried their best to unite themselves in order to realize mutual security and order in the human society. This is where they are superior to the legal structure of any other nation.

Leibniz was an admirer of ancient China's legendary "model monarchs" of Yao and Shun and also a worshipper of Confucius and Mencius; but he was particularly impressed with the then incumbent Qing Dynasty Emperor Kangxi, praising the Chinese monarch as an unprecedented sage of wisdom and generosity, and an extremely perceptive ruler who was so open-minded as being always ready to absorb the technology and science from Europe. The German philosoper even defended Emperor Kangxi's decision to deny the Christian Church's right to continue its operation in China, for the Church's objection to the inviolability of the Chinese heritage. He was convinced that the Chinese emperor was a man of great vision, and well-learned in both the Chinese and Western knowledge.

These remarks made by Leibniz reflected the perceptive

views of some European scholars, who believed that European and Chinese cultures were complementary to each other and that cultural exchange between them would benefit both sides. And such an exchange—at least in the eyes of Leibniz and those scientifically and politically-enlightened Jesuits—had already been practiced by Emperor Kangxi, way ahead of the Europeans. That was, indeed, the reason why China had then been able to further enhance its prestigious ancient civilization and win renewed respect from the Europeans.

3. Francois Voltaire and His Play *L'Orphelin de la Chine*

On August 20, 1755, the play *L'Orphelin de la Chine* was put on the stage for the first time in Paris. The presentation of such a drama, featuring a Chinese background, was unprecedented in the theatre of the French capital, which was considered the cultural centre of Europe.

The play's author was none other than the celebrated Francois Voltaire, who had chosen to focus on Chinese ethical merits in this play and also in his novel *Zadig*, in an attempt to educate the European community. He wrote the first three acts of the play in 1745, and then expanded it into a five-act drama in 1753. When the drama went on the stage in Paris, Voltaire had already resigned, indignantly, from his post of Chamberlain in the court of Prussian King Frederick II, and taken residence in Ferney of Switzerland.

His frustration with the Prussian court life had further spurred his longing for the ideal ethics of China; therefore, Voltaire tried to make his play an exemplary reflection of his desire to seek social peace and tranquillity, through the restraint of human selfishness by the universal sense of reasoning. That was why he wrote these words: "A five-act play based on Confucianism" under the title of his drama. When Voltaire first accepted the invitation of Frederick II and joined the court of the Prussian monarch in Berlin, he had hoped that, under the patronage of a relatively open-minded monarch, he could now vent his anger against French King Louis XV. But in a few years, he had to again break away from the Prussian monarch, fleeing to

Switzerland, where he finished his play *L'Orphelin de la Chine*.

Voltaire's drama originated from the story of *The Vengeance of Zhao's Orphan* written as a Yuan Dynasty operetta by Chinese classic writer Ji Junxiang, which was translated into French in 1732 by the French missionary Joseph de Prémare, then included by Du Halde in his *Description geographique, historique, chronologique, politique et physique de l'Empire de la Chine et de la Tartarie Chinoise*. This story, which was adopted by Francois Voltaire as the theme of his drama, dated from the ancient Spring and Autumn Period (770-476 B.C.), when Zhao Dun—chancellor of the State of Jin—and his whole family of some 300 people were massacred by his rival Tu Anjia, another high official of Jin, in a power struggle. Zhao Dun was, however, survived by his infant grandson, who was rescued by Cheng Ying, a faithful hanger-on of the Zhao family. Tu, knowing of the escape of Zhao's orphan, decided to kill all the infants in the country, thereby preventing any possible revenge by Zhao's descendant in the future. Cheng Ying, in an attempt to save the thousands of innocent infants from the massacre, sought the help of his close friend Gongsun Chujiu, who agreed to take over Cheng's own child disguised as Zhao's orphan and hid him in his home. Cheng, then, went to see Tu Anjia with the "information" that Zhao's orphan had been concealed by Gongsun in his house. As a result, Tu had both Gongsun Chujiu and Cheng's own son killed, but all the other infants in the country were saved from a possible bloodbath. The surviving Zhao's orphan, who had been kept by Cheng as his own "son," won the favour of the powerful Tu, and was adopted by Tu as his son with the new name of Tu Cheng. Under the patronage of his adopted father, Tu Cheng grew into a fine young man 20 years later. It was then that he learned from Cheng Ying the tragic fate of his true parentage, and made up his mind to avenge them. The story ended with Tu Anjia dying at the hand of his "adopted son"—the true orphan of Zhao Dun, the man slain by him 20 years before.

In his play, however, Voltaire remodelled the villain Tu Anjia into a liberal-minded Genghis Khan, who was "moved" by the exemplary virtues of his enemy and forsook his unholy desires. Voltaire's drama began with the army of Genghis Khan storming into Yanjing (Beijing), and the vanquished Chinese emperor entrusted his only child to his loyal official Shang De before he died. Then, after the conqueror Genghis Khan had killed all the remaining members of the imperial family, he discovered that there was still a child missing and so ordered an immediate search. Shang De, fearing that the hidden child might be found by the guards, decided that he should hand over his own son, in lieu of the late emperor's orphan, to Genghis Khan, so that the orphan could escape. But when his wife Yi Shi heard of his decision, she went straight to the conqueror herself and told Genghis Khan the true story, begging his pardon for her husband and the orphan. Impressed by the woman's courage and beauty, the Mongolian conqueror told Yi Shi that he would forgive them —only if she would agree to become his consort. The woman refused Genghis Khan's offer, but asked the conqueror to let her see her husband once again, before arresting them. At their last meeting, Yi Shi, after encouraging her husband to live up to his loyalty for the country, asked Shang De to slay her on the spot so that she could keep her chastity. While Shang De continued to hesitate, Yi Shi entreated him so impassionedly that the Mongolian conqueror, who was watching them from behind the curtain, was deeply moved. And in the end, Genghis Khan, feeling himself shameful in the face of the noble virtues of the couple, decided to pardon them both and also the child.

Through the story of the Chinese orphan, Voltaire praised the ethics advocated by Confucius, in the hope that an open-minded monarch would emerge in Europe to realize his dream of a constitutional monarchy and bring about a society of equality and harmony.

As a celebrated poet, playwright, historian, a proponent of science and an opponent of Church rule through his lifetime, Francois Voltaire spent the last 20 years of his life in Ferney of Switzerland. He continued his praise of the Confucian education doctrine, calling it a powerful force to combat religious superstition. He once said that he had heard enough of the story that the Christian Church was founded by the 12 Apostles. "I really wanted to prove to them that it needed only one man to destroy it," he was quoted as saying. And Voltaire kept reminding people that they should remember the teaching of Confucius: "Don't do to others that you would not wish others do unto you."

4. The Chinese Monarchism and the European Physiocrats

In the wake of the decline in mercantilism in the eighteenth century France, coupled with the financial crisis caused by the policy of King Louis XV, the physiocrats began to stage a comeback in this European country. In 1758, Fancois Quesnay (1694-1774) published his famous *Table of Economy* to rally a group of followers around him; then, in 1767, they formally announced themselves as "physiocrats," advocating the economic theory that land was the source of all wealth and that it alone should be taxed. They carried on their economic study into the industrial sector to explore the root of surplus value; whereby these physiocrats became another branch of the Enlightenment movement.

The physiocrats had also pinned their hopes on an economic reform initiated by an open-minded monarch from above. Francois Quesnay, who had once served as a court physician himself, was the author of the two books *Laws of Nature* and *China's Autocracy*. In Quesnay's view, the order of nature sought by him was the root of reasoning, whereas reasoning was what man relied upon in his study of the laws of nature. He thought China was a model in building its national economy on the basis of agriculture, while adhering to the reasons and principles regulated by "Lord Nature" or "Heaven," which symbolized its belief in the order and law of nature. He lauded China's autocracy as a "rational autocratic government," which was responsible for stipulating rules within the scope of the law of nature; and that even the monarch had to adhere to such rules, and obey the "rules of Heaven" as his guidelines. Then, upon Quesnay's suggestion, Louis XV decided in 1756 to follow the example of the Chinese emperor to hold ceremonies on the occasion of ploughing and harvesting. Francois Quesnay was so ardent in propagating the Confucian doctrine that he had once been called the "Confucius of Europe."

Another outstanding French physiocrat was Anne Robert Jacques Turgot (1727-1781), a man known for his extensive knowledge and political practices. He was the governor of Limousin in 1761, when he first carried the physiocratic reform by abolishing the levy of labour duty on farmers and replacing it with taxation. Then, when Louis XVI was enthroned in 1774, Turgot joined the cabinet and served as minister of navy, and later as controller general of finances, until he was dismissed in May, 1776. Advocating a monarchism based on law, Turgot went further than Francois Quesnay's ideal of economic regulation founded upon the order of nature to consider such regulation as the reflection of "personal mentality." Thus, his physicratic thinking showed a marked capitalistic trend.

Turgot was, nevertheless, keenly interested in China's developments in economy, taxation and technology, viewing the Oriental nation as a practical model of "order of nature," as did Quesnay. While he was governor of Limousin, Turgot came to know two Chinese students, Gao Leisi and Yang Dewang, and asked the two young men to stay one more year in France as his visiting guests. Then, he prepared for them a 52-question outline of investigation, entitled "Instruction on the Study of China for Two Chinese," which covered such subjects as the roles of land, rental and capital in the agricultural economy and the technological achievements in China's paper-making, textile and porcelain industries. When the two Chinese youths were ready to return home in 1764, Turgot again wrote the book *A Study on the Making and Distribution of Wealth* for the two men to understand his theory and be able to help him with his study of China. The book, which was published as a continuous serial in the physiocrats' periodical *National Review*, since late 1776, explicitly elaborated on the physiocrat theory constituted the most authoritative explanation of its doctrine, and further developed the ideology of Francois Quesnay. It was interesting to note that the book was a product of Turgot's persistent admiration for China —originating from his desire to introduce his physiocrat views to the two young Chinese students. Such a keen interest and admiration for Chinese ideology and technology in France had emerged, just 80 years after the French Jesuit group arrived in Beijing in 1688 to introduce information of Western sciences to the Qing Dynasty Emperor Kangxi. Such a trend—which was interrupted by the French Revolution of 1789—had, nonetheless, symbolized an epilogue to this era of Sino-European relationship, in the form of a Franco-Chinese cultural ensemble.

II   New Creations of the Western Fine Arts

1. The Different Genres of Chinese and Western Fine Arts

The Chinese and Western fine arts represented two entirely different trends in the world history of fine arts. They differed from each other not only in art style but in the artists' painting skills. Chinese classic paintings focused on the vivification of a conception but not the true image of the scene or object in the picture—in short, not a physical resemblance but a more refined, spiritual resemblance of what they painted. As a result, no matter whether they were painted in colour or in black and white, the persons, objects or landscapes in the pictures were often unrealistic or even out of proportion and scale. On the other hand, the Western classic paintings stressed the creation of real and lively images of the people or objects in the picture. And they were often marked with the effect of light and shade and the contrast of colour and size, whether in oil or in water colour, resulting in a "true to life" style.

During the thirteenth century in Italy, new Florentine and Siena painters including Cimabue and Giotto moved forward to displace the rigid and grave Byzantine style with naturalistic oil paintings, playing a pioneering role in the Renaissance and paving the way to a new epoch of Western fine arts. In China, however, there was no breakthrough in the style of traditional fine arts during this period as the artists still adhered to line-drawing in their portrayal of persons and produced few masterpieces to reflect social life, despite marked progress in the painting skills of flowers and birds or landscape. Moreover, the Chinese elite painters locked themselves in their own circles, leaving the decorative art and religious murals to the "folk-artists."

Following the lead of Western missionaries, the Western religious art began to emerge in China. Matteo Ricci was the first to introduce portraits of the Holy Mother and Jesus into China, surprising many Chinese who had never seen a Western painting. Jiang Shaowen, who was one of Ricci's Chinese friends, was deeply impressed with the picture of Virgin Mary and praised its vivid image as being lively as a picture from the mirror, beyond the reach of any Chinese painter in beauty and elegance. Another Chinese, Gu Qiyuan, noted that the picture's unique rendering of light and shade had given it a true to life feeling. When Ricci was asked to comment on the difference between Chinese and Western paintings, he explained that the Chinese paintings showed only the light but not the shade of persons, therefore they looked "flat" in the picture. The Italian paintings showed both the light and shade in their presentation, and the persons in the picture looked more real with distinct facial features and rounded arms, as their contours could be clearly seen through the contrast of light and dark tones. He told his Chinese friends that the Italian artists were able to paint persons in their real image, because they had mastered the skills of light and shade presentation. Ricci's explanation of the Western drawing skills was the first ever introduction of the Western theory of fine arts to China. Since then, nearly every Western missionary, coming to China's Beijing or Nanjing, would bring many religious pictures with him. These pictures constituted the first collection of Western fine arts seen by the Chinese.

The Christian Church paintings were later widely copied and reproduced in China, and many of them were somewhat "Sinicized" in the process. One example was the four religious pictures given by Ricci to Cheng Dayue and later reproduced by Cheng's friend in engraved type and included by Cheng in his *Collection of Ink Paintings*. These reproductions, albeit well engraved, showed the images in much simplified lines, more or less after the traditional Chinese style.

The first Chinese painter, who adopted the Western art style to greatly improve the Chinese portraiture skills, was Zeng Jing. As a painter of the Jiangnan (south of the Yangtze River) School, Zeng changed the traditional method of adding water colour to sketchy ink-lines to a gradual rendering with ink strokes from the start, producing a more vivid image of the persons he portrayed. His ingenuity revitalized the Jiangnan style paintings, and was passed on to his students. By the time Zeng's student's student, Xu Yaopu, became known, the Jiangnan style artists had fully absorbed the Western perspective painting skill in their drawings of persons or buildings, and their students had demonstrated such painting skill in places like Tianjin, Hangzhou and Yangzhou. Most remarkable was the Yangzhou painter Zhang Shu, whose paintings had featured such a perfect perspective presentation of persons and objects that could well match the Western paintings.

Along with the introduction of Western painting skills among the private artists, a number of painters serving in the imperial court also began to adopt the Western painting techniques with remarkable success in their works. One of the most famous among such court artists was Jiao Bingzhen of the Imperial Astronomical Observatory. Thanks to his close contact with the Western missionaries serving in the observatory, Jiao managed to learn from these Jesuits how to apply the theories of geometry and trigonometry to painting. As a result, his paintings of persons and landscape were marked for their effective illustration of distance, dimension, and clear contrast in tones. His works were represented by a series of 46 paintings of "Farming and Weaving Work," finished in 1696 in Western style and based on the Song Dynasty theme. Despite these notable successes, the Western perspective painting skill was not widely used in the court paintings of the Qing Dynasty because of the strong influence of the traditional artists, who had stubbornly adhered to the heritage of the celebrated classical Chinese painters of the Yuan Dynasty, such as Huang Gongwang and Ni Yunlin. The conservative art critics of that period also viewed the Western painting skills as not up to the refined taste as cultivated by the ancient art style of the classic Chinese painters, although the skill of light and shade presentation could be used. Zhang Pushan in his book of *Accounts of Paintings* made this critical observation. Another Chinese art critic, Zou Yigui, in his book, *Xiaoshan's Painting Review*, said the Western paintings focused excessively on the scale of angles and dimensions and were, therefore, only good for occasional adaptation to add attraction to the picture, but certainly could not be rated as the real art. The difference in painting skills was then treated as the basic difference between the two traditional art styles, which became the strongest pretext used by the Chinese painters to boycott Western paintings throughout the seventeenth and eighteenth centuries. During this period, the technically-advanced Western paintings, in the eyes of the celebrated classic Chinese painters, were attractive and true-to-life but lacking the inner conception of art then considered most important by the elite painters.

In spite of the unfavourable comments, Western paintings had, nevertheless, appeared on the Chinese stage of art, bringing new blood and vitality to the age-old convention of the traditional Chinese fine arts. Once they were introduced to China, the Western art style, however, had to adapt itself to Chinese themes and style to survive in the country. Such an adaptation of art style was seen to develop gradually, through the 40 years when the Italian painter Giuseppe Castiglione (1688-1766) was serving as a court painter in the Qing Dynasty.

Castiglione, who began his service in the Qing court around 1722, had been trained as a painter in Italy since his childhood. During his service with the imperial court, he worked on the paintings in the Ruyi Lounge of Haidian in daytime and rested in the Eastern Catholic Church in Beijing. At first, he was rebuked by the Chinese emperor for painting in the Western style of light-and-shade rendering, and was told that he should learn to paint "the Chinese way." Consequently, the Italian painter had to learn how to use the Chinese painting brush and pigments to paint on tough-silk scrolls. In the end, Castiglione was able to combine his Western painting skills with the Chinese style, thereby creating a new genre which served to revitalize the traditional Chinese fine arts and also brought a new look to the Western paintings. The Italian painter's unique achievement in renovating the classic

Chinese painting won high praise from the Qing Dynasty Emperor Qianlong, thereby making him one of the most favoured persons in the Qing court. In 1757, when Castiglione marked his seventieth birthday, a magnificent celebration was held in the court by order of the Qing emperor to show his special regard for the Italian artist. In that year, Castiglione painted two murals —showing the triumphant return of the Roman Emperor Constantine the Great—for The Nantang Catholic Church in Beijing. He also painted two other exquisite perspective oil paintings for the church's inner chambers, both of which were acclaimed for their perfect resemblance to reality. His oil paintings were done in the Western style of line drawings.

However, Castiglione's mixed art style in paintings had drawn criticism from some Westerners, who described them as purely Chinese and had nothing in common with the Western art. When the British envoy Lord Macartney and his entourage toured the Yuanmingyuan Palace during their visit to China in 1793, two members of the British delegation pointed out that the two landscape paintings there (by Castiglione) had lost their identity as Western art, because they had shown neither the contrast of light and shade nor the perspective scale of distance. When the British envoy offered a portrait of oil painting to the Qing emperor, a Chinese official pointed out that the picture's shady rendering on the nose was a "stain" on the otherwise perfect artwork. Recriminating remarks between Chinese and Western art critics were common during the early phase of the exchange of painting art; nevertheless, the introduction of a Sino-Western mixed art style was an interesting exploration in the exchange of fine arts between China and Europe. While the Italian painter in the Qing court had to obey the order of the emperor to adapt his Western art to the Chinese style, he had nonetheless, brought about an evolution in the style of the classic Chinese paintings. The silk scroll painting of "A Hundred Stallions," finished by Castiglione in 1728, was done with Chinese painting tools and mounted in Chinese fashion, but it was painted strictly according to the Western rules. This early masterpiece impressed the Chinese court artists. Castiglione's works consisted mainly of pictures of persons, flora and fauna, but he was best known for his paintings of horses. In 1755, a group of Chinese and Western painters, headed by Castiglione, completed the two major paintings of "An Imperial Banquet in the Wanshu Palace" and "Equestrian Art Show" to depict the story of the surrender of an ethnic Mongolian nomadic tribe.

Castiglione had been a leading figure among the court painters patronized by Emperor Qianlong and his father Emperor Yongzheng. During his service in the reign of the two emperors, he had taught oil painting skills to three groups of students. Emperor Qianlong's court painters Dai Zheng, Zhang Weibang and Ding Guanpeng had all been the Italin painter's regular students; and their works of oil paintings were seen in the Qing Dynasty court art collections. Apart from Castiglione, there were several other Western painters serving in the Qing court, including the Bohemian painter Ignatius Sickelparth (1708-1780), who came to China in 1745 and was an outstanding student of Castiglione, and the French oil painter J. Denis Attiret, who arrived in the Chinese capital in 1738. Emperor Qianlong, while telling Attiret that he could do some portrait with his oil painting skills, expressed dissatisfaction with the French painter's water colours. As a result, Attiret was obliged to start learning water colour skills, using Chinese landscape and buildings as his themes. Through their four decades of continuous service in the Qing court, Castiglione and Sickleparth led the court art into full bloom, marked by the emergence of a new generation of Chinese court painters, who had surpassed their famous teachers. Jiao Bingzhen and Chen Mei were particularly noteworthy for their mastery of the Western perspective drawing and oil painting skills. Other talented artists included Zhang Weibang, Ding Guanpeng, Wang Youxue, Dai Zheng, Jin Tingbiao and Luo Fumin, who were responsible for introducing a fresh art style to China and setting an example for the renovation of the traditional Chinese paintings.

2. Samples of the Rococo Architecture

Chinese and Western artists had started contacts with each

other during the seventeenth century. Early contacts were often met with criticism, even hostility. The arrival of the eighteenth century saw the two totally alien art schools joining forces to create new forms of vitality in each other's territory.

Europe of the seventeenth century knew little about Chinese paintings or sculptures. However, through the import of highly popular Chinese porcelain to the European market, many Europeans began to appreciate the natural and serene beauty of the Chinese pictures and the exotic attraction of the Chinese sculpture art; but very few of them knew anything, then, about the Chinese classic paintings of the literati. Nevertheless, the genre and conception of the Chinese arts served to open the eyes of the European artists to a new horizon, enabling them to free themselves with more ease from the grandiose and pompus art style of the Louis XIV era. The Rococo trend which developed in Western Europe in the eighteenth century was somewhat related with the introduction of the Chinese art style into Europe in the same period.

The beauty of European architecture was known to China when the Rococo trend had just emerged in Europe, thanks to the exchange of such information through the Italian and French Jesuits. The Chinese Christian pilgrim Fan Shouyi had also brought back news about European palace, church and garden architecture to China. Then, the beautiful palaces in Vatican and Tivoli of Rome, Vecchio of Florence, Versailles and Saint-Cloud of Paris had become images of the popular Western paradise in the minds of many people in the Chinese court. Following the enthronement of Emperor Qianlong (1736-1795), new palace buildings and fountains, designed in the Roman style, were first constructed in the young emperor's former prince villa of Changchun Xianguan (Eternal Spring Villa) located in Beijing's suburban garden of Yuanmingyuan. The newly-enthroned Emperor Qianlong then renamed the villa "Changchunyuan" and expanded it by building a complex of Westernized villas and gardens to its north, which later became a part of the world-famous Westernized Palace of Yuanmingyuan.

In 1736, the second year in the reign of Emperor Qianlong,

court artists Giuseppe Castiglione, Tang Dai, Shen Yuan and Zhang Weibang were ordered to design a master plan for the new Yuanmingyuan Palace. In 1747, Emperor Qianlong again asked Castiglione to design "Western houses" and fountains, after the examples shown in the European paintings, which had attracted the notice of the emperor. A variety of European-type buildings had since been built north of the old Changchunyuan Villa. Upon recommendation of Castiglione, the emperor appointed French Jesuit Michael Benoist as the designer of the fountains in Yuanmingyuan. Benoist, who had been working on revising the calendar since coming to China three years earlier, had to give up his work to design a pumping device for the fountains in the Yuanmingyuan Palace. Benoist, who was responsible for the construction of fountains in the new palace, borrowed the technique of French garden-designer Alexandre le Blond, alias Antoine Joseph Dezalliers d'Argenville, who was the author of *La Theorie et Pratique du Jardinage*, 1709, a book introducing the types and designs of fountains. Fountains were very popular in Europe during the seventeenth century, when such structures had spread out from palaces and gardens to the cities' squares and streets, especially, in cities of Italy and France. Alexandre le Blond had been hired by Peter the Great of Russia to design the Summer Palace of Petersburg, modelled after the Palace of Versailles in France. The Petersburg Palace, completed in 1711, had as great a variety of gardens and fountains as the Palace of Versailles. The first Western-type building "House of Exotic Interest," built north of Changchunyuan Villa, was designed as a complex structure with hexagonal wings to accommodate performers of Xiyu (Western Regions) music, in addition to a pump-house for the fountain, a Westernized garden and a "cage house for birds." Like most European gardens of the medieval style, the design of the compound was basically symmetrical. In Europe, meanwhile, the Sans Souci Palace of Potsdam, designed for the Prussian King Frederick II (1740-1786) by Knobelsdorff, was also just completed in 1747.

The rococo architecture, emerged in Europe in the 1740s on the basis of the baroque style, featured an ornate use of curved lines and elaborate scrollwork, which could be traced to the Oriental art style. The new rococo-style building design had then appeared, almost simultaneously, in the palaces of Europe and China. The chief designer of the Yuanmingyuan Palace in Beijing was Castiglione, the Italian missionary-artist; his two assistants were Ignatius Sickelparth, the Bohemian missionary-painter, and J. Denis Attiret, the French missionary-painter. The Bohemian and French missionaries also undertook the sculptural work. While all the fountain design and construction work were handled by Benoist, and the two other court missionaries, Thebauet and Adeodat, were responsible for the structural and technical projects of the entire palace. Castiglione also organized all his Chinese students and many Chinese craftsmen to work with him. Under the guidance of the missionaries, the Chinese craftsmen and workers managed to overcome a series of difficulties in the construction and erection of devices and structures, completely new to them, and eventually succeeded in building up a magnificent garden-palace, designed in the Franco-Italian style. This marvellous achievement in the history of architecture was a joint effort of both Chinese and Western artists and workers.

Following the completion of the complex of the "House of Exotic Interest," Western-style expansion of the former Changchunyuan garden continued in a rectangular layout towards the east. In 1760, most of the new projects were completed, including Fangwaiguan Pavilion, Haiyantang Hall and Yuanyingguan Pavilion as well as a Grand Fountain—the centre of attraction in the whole palace flanked by Haiyantang Hall and Yuanyingguan Pavilion. Farther east, a rockery hill, a square lake and more picturesque landscape were built in the style of a Chinese garden, adding an Oriental finishing touch to the basically Western-styled Yuanmingyuan Palace. The design of the magnificent Haiyantang Hall and the scenic centre of "Shuimumingse" (Mirrorlike Water and Rustling Trees) were an architectural masterpiece, featuring Western art style and fountain techniques. Known as the largest building in the Palace of Yuanmingyuan, Haiyantang Hall had two stories with eleven bays on each floor and a large elevated porch, which led through a pair of symmetrical winding stone stairways down to the terrace. The stairways' walling handrail was designed after the villas of Rome with a jet of water and forming a stepped cascade. In front of Haiyantang Hall was a pool, which was lined with six water-spouting cast-bronze animals on both sides, as substitutes for the nude nymphs seen in the Western pools. The twelve animal statues were designed after the Chinese traditional symbolic animals representing the twelve "Earthly Branches," and were set to spout water in turns every two hours, one after another; all twelve of them should spout at the same time at noon.

Located close to Haiyantang Hall was an I-shaped building of eleven bays to house the "Archimedes' Screw," which supplied water to the fountains and cascade. In the centre of the building was a fish pond called "Tin Pool," which was wrapped in tin plates to prevent leakage. To the east of Haiyantang Hall was the grand stonewall fountain, which together with the cascade and pool of Haiyantang Hall, formed the centre of attraction in the Yuanmingyuan Palace. The fountains' designer, Benoist, had even tried to adapt the technique of the famous "water-powered wind music instrument" of Villa D'Este in suburban Rome to the fountains of the Yuanmingyuan Palace. Such a device was earlier introduced in the book *Stories from Abroad* written by Julio Aleni, the Italian missionary who came to China in the Ming Dynasty. Devices using water-power to report time, at noon, or to play music were also seen in the book "Les Raisons des Forces Mouvantes," published in Germany in 1619. And when fountains of similar designs were being unveiled in the Versailles Palace by French King Louis XIV, they were also emerging in the Palace of Yuanmingyuan in Beijing. Regrettably, however, there was no one to take over the management of the fountain devices after Benoist's death in 1774. He had designed, then maintained them to the last day of his life. As a result, the "Archimedes' Screw" stopped running and the fountains ceased their jets, except when Emperor Qianlong came to visit the palace. At that time, buckets of water would be carried by men to the top floor of the pump-house—as a substitute for the "Archimedes' Screw"—to keep the fountains working for a while.

The "pictorial screen" at the east end of the Changchunyuan Villa was a structure, comprising ten wall-screens covered with oil paintings, which showed ten different views of the Muslim buildings in Aksu of Xinjiang—the homeland of Xiangfei, Emperor Qianlong's favourite consort. These paintings were drawn with excellent perspective effect, giving one the illusion of being in the real scenario. Perspective art style had been successfully used in the design of gardens to create like-real landscape, since it was initiated by the Italian painter Paolo Uccello (1397-1475) first in paintings. Giuseppe Castiglione had been an expert in perspective art. He was known to have introduced the theory of Western perspective drawing first to Nian Xiyao, junior vice-president of the Board of Works in the reign of Emperor Yong-zheng (1723-1735). Based on Castiglione's teaching, Nian wrote China's first book on the theory of perspective *Science of Vision*. The design of the Yuanmingyuan Palace was worked out by Castiglione, in a perspective light, guided by the backdrop of the stage of the Vicenza opera house designed by Andrea Palladio in Italy. It was composed of a three-tier carved-stone arch, which marked the first instance of applying perspective art to the design of stage setting. Castiglione, who had earlier demonstrated his perspective skills in the two mural paintings done by him for the Nantang Catholic Church in Beijing, made good use of his perspective art again, in the design of the Yuanmingyuan Palace.

The plan of the Changchunyuan garden featured the symmetrical design of the French parks and adopted many Western decorative styles such as topiary, parterre and maze. But different from the European hedged layout of intricate paths, the maze in Changchunyuan was built with a complex network of 1.5-metre-high patterned brick walls crowned with clipped bushes, and was called the "Scene of Shining Bloom." The design of the Western-style palace buildings featured such ornaments as gables and pitched roofs, paved with cylindrical or scale tiles and decorated with floral ridges or vases with fish and birds patterns. Apart from the European-style pools and fountains, the gardens were also fitted with rockeries, bamboo pavilions and other Chinese-style sceneries. The Sinicized characteristics in the garden design further emphasized the primarily Western rococo art style of the overall design of the Yuanmingyuan Palace.[1]

As the Qing emperor's autumn and summer villa, the Yuanmingyuan Palace had been known for its magnificent scale, luxurious architecture, intricate gardens and beautiful scenery, which had won it the title of "Jardin des Jardins." Particularly attractive was its Changchunyuan Garden which was marked by a unique integration of the Western (French) artificial garden design with the traditional Chinese "natural gardening," making it a dazzling star in the whole Yuanmingyuan Palace. Franciscus Bourgeois had said, in his letter of October 1786 to the French artist L. F. Delatour, that he had been ordered by the Qing emperor to make 20 engraved brass pictures of the European-style palace buildings in the Yuanmingyuan Palace. The brass pictures, which were engraved by Castiglione's Chinese students, had eventually found their way to Europe, where Delatour in his "Essais sur l'Architecture des Chinois, sur leurs jardin, Paris, 1803" had first mentioned the design of these European-style palace building in China. Sadly, however, this splendid "Garden of All Gardens"—Palace of Yuanmingyuan—was totally destroyed in a fire set on October 19, 1860, by the Anglo-French Forces during their invasion of Beijing in the second Opium War.

As much as the Palace of Versailles was viewed as a typical example of the baroque architecture of the eighteenth century, the Western-style palace buildings of Yuanmingyuan could be described as samples of the rococo architecture.

3. The "Anglo-Chinese Gardens"

In 1747, the first Western-style building, "House of Exotic Interest," was being built in the Changchunyuan garden of Beijing, and the Palace of Sans Souci and its Oriental structure were completed in Potsdam near Berlin. In England, meanwhile, a Chinese-style garden was being designed for the Duke of Kent, by the royal architect William Chambers. Within three years, a

---

[1] E. Danby, *The Garden of Perfect Brightness*, 1926; Georges Soulie de Morant, *Histoire de L'art Chinois*, 1928, Paris.

unique Kew Garden was completed in the Kew district outside London, as the first of its kind.

The Kew Garden, which has now become the London Botanical Garden, was designed to produce a natural yet picturesque landscale—far different from the symmetrical pattern of artificial neatness as seen in a French-style garden. The centre of attraction in the Kew Garden was a nine-storey Chinese pagoda towering over the gateway leading into the garden. The inconspicuous decors of little bells and dragon patterns around its outstretched eaves added to the charms of the pagoda. Inside the garden, ornate Chinese-style pavilions, with their red wall, black tile and engraved railings, intermingled with luxuriant evergreens —a scene which seemed to give one the illusion of being in China.

Chambers, architect of the Kew Garden, acquired his knowledge of Chinese garden design not only from literature but also from his visits to China during the years he worked for the Swedish East Indian Company. That was the time when Western Europe was fascinated by the exotic Chinese arts and articles, as more and more people enjoyed drinking Chinese tea, furnishing their houses with Chinese porcelain and lacquerware and adorning themselves with Chinese silk and even Chinese folding fans. And in the art of garden design, while the popular trend in Europe was still the French style of artificial beauty with its neat pattern of symmetrically-planned buildings, fountains, flowerbeds and hedgerows—all arranged in order—there were some people who became interested in the natural beauty of the Chinese-style garden design, in which every artificial scene or structure was intended to enhance the attraction of the natural growths or landscape. All such exquisite features in a Chinese garden—bamboo groves, winding paths, undulated terrace, overlapped rockeries, and winding streams running through arched bridges against a backdrop of scattered towers and pavilions —were designed and arranged to produce the maximum beauty of an imaginary natural landscape. English poets and artists were among the first to appreciate the art of Chinese garden design.

The formalistic trend of Western garden design, as represented by the French artist Le Notre, was at its peak in the reign of the French King Louis XIV. At about the same time, the art of Chinese garden design was being introduced to Europe by the French missionary Ludovicus Le Comte, through his book of *Nouveaux mémoires sur l'état présent de la Chine*, 1697, which drew strong response first from among English scholars and artists. The English essayist Joseph Addison wrote in the *Spectator* of July 1712 a commentary, criticizing the uniform geometric layout of European gardens as void of art, and praising the unique creative design of Chinese gardens as truly artistic. Addison's comments and his praise for Chinese garden art further spurred a reform in the garden design during the rococo trend.

After the completion of the Chinese-style "Trianon de Porcelaine," built by the French King Louis XIV for Madame de Montespan in 1670, Chinese-style structures such as teahouse, pavilion, bell-tower, stone bridge, rockery and grille became fashionable among the aristocrats in the eighteenth century Europe, and emerged as fashionable ornaments in France, Germany and the Netherlands. By the time the Kew Garden of London was built, the Chinese-style garden design had finally established itself in Europe. In 1757, William Chambers again summed up the experiences of his second visit to China in his book *Designs for Chinese Buildings, Furniture, Dresses, Machines and Utensils*. In the book, he praised Chinese artists for their remarkable garden designs, pointing out that the ideals embodied in such designs were just what the English had been craving for in vain for a long time. In his view, the Chinese art of garden design had created a natural landscape—totally different from the artificial embroidered flower farm or green sculpture—but far more interesting and picturesque. And the Chinese gardens were closer to nature's original form and possessed such a depth in visionary image, as to supersede their actual size or space.

The art of Chinese garden design dated from many centuries ago, and today many gardens in Yangzhou, Suzhou and Beijing are typical of the classic design of the twelfth or thirteenth century. The largest of such gardens was the imperial summer palace of Yuanmingyuan, which was first expanded in 1725 as the palace villa for Emperor Yongzheng. The summer palace, which

included 28 scenic areas, was further expanded by Emperor
Qianlong, who added into the Yuanmingyuan many river-side
sceneries typical in the south of the Yangtze River, increasing the
number of scenic areas to 40. A silk album of 80 coloured
pictures and captions called *Yuanmingyuan in Pictures*, in two
sandalwood-folded volumes, were stolen from the palace in 1860
and kept in the French National Library of Paris. The expanded
Yuanmingyuan, eventually, became the largest garden in the
world, and had been acclaimed by the French missionary J. Denis
Attiret as superior to any other garden "he had ever seen." In his
letter dated November 1, 1743, addressed to M. d'Assaut, Attiret
lavished praise on the artistic achievement of this Chinese garden,
saying that he—as a French painter—was "filled with admiration" for the unforgettable natural sceneries in this palace garden.
And he admitted in the letter, "I feel that our gardens would seem
shallow and lifeless, when they are compared with theirs." Praise
like these had, undoubtedly, prompted the English and German
architects to seek a new approach to the rococo design of gardens.

William Chambers, having studied more than two decades on
the subject, had been a pace-setter in the new approach, in theory
and practice. In 1772, he finished his last book *Essays on Oriental
Gardening*, which was followed, a year later, by *Uber die Chine-
sischen Gärden* by the German architect Ludwig A. Unzer, who
called on the Germans to follow the English example in their
absorption of the Chinese gardening art. In the same year, Germany sent F.L. Sekell to England to study Chinese-style gardening. Soon afterward, the Moulang Garden—designed after a
Chinese garden in the south of Yangtze River—was built in
Germany's Wilhelmshöhe by Count Kassel. In 1774, this type of
Chinese-style garden, as introduced to Europe by the English, was
named "Anglo-Chinese Garden" by the French garden designer
Georges L. Le Rouge. He published his collection of more than a
hundred copperplate pictures of Chinese gardens in the book *Le
Jarden Anglo-Chinois*, thereby marrying Chinese gardening with
English landscaping art. Such an artistic trend was a brilliant
achievement in the rococo architecture of garden designing,
which had borrowed from the Oriental gardening of China,

especially, China's Yuanmingyuan Palace and gardens south of the Yangtze River. Today, when the glory of Yuanmingyuan Palace lingers only in the minds of nostalgic historians, the brilliance of Chinese gardening still shines in some parks and villas of England and Germany.

III　Sinology and the Chinese Cutural Boom in Europe

When the European Jesuits came as missionaries to China, they first had to study the language, Chinese script and Confucian classics in order to understand China's ancient philosophy, religion, history, politics, ethics and customs. Thus, they became the earliest group of Europeans acquainted with Chinese culture. During the period 1664 to 1671, the Catholic missionary work in China suffered a setback, as a result of a sweeping anti-Catholic campaign initiated by a few Chinese officials in the Imperial Astronomical Observatory. And the year of 1671 marked the end of the first phase of the Catholic Church mission, and the beginning of its second phase in China. The Jesuits, who were involved in the first phase of missionary work in China, were mostly learned in Chinese language, characters and the Confucian classics. They included Matteo Ricci, Michael Ruggieri, Julio Aleni, Alrarez de Semedo, Ludovico Buglio, Martino Martini, Ferdinandus Verbiest, Philippi Couplet and Prosper Intercetta. All contributed to the exchange of Chinese and European cultures, particularly in the coordination of Catholicism and Confucianism. Most of these Jesuits wrote their books in Chinese in a bid to convince the Chinese readers that Catholicism and Confucianism were quite conciliatory with each other, thereby winning more Chinese converts through the accommodation process.

Meanwhile, however, missionaries also published their books in their home countries to introduce Chinese culture to the Europeans. Martino Martini, the Italian Jesuit, was the first to publish his works on China's geography and history in Europe, breaking ground for the birth of Sinology in Europe. Martini, who returned to Europe in 1653, had his *De Bello Tartarieo*, written in Latin, published in 1654 in Amsterdam, Cologne, Milan and Anvers of Belgium. The next year he published his *Novus Atlas Sinensis* in Amsterdam, which was followed by his *Sinicae Historiae Decus Prima* published in Munich in 1658. In the 10-volume book on Chinese history, he gave a thorough and accurate introduction to China's ancient and contemporary history, geography, economy, medicine, astronomy, religion, philosophy, marriage and social life. It was done in such detail that the book was acclaimed as the "father" in the Westerners' study of China's geography. His *De Bello Tartarieo*, which focused on the war history of the Qing Dynasty, saw its original Latin edition reprinted many times across Europe; later it was translated into Italian, German, French and English. There was also a Dutch translation. The book was enthusiastically read by Europeans, who were deeply interested in this first book on contemporary history of China written in Western languages.

Then, during the earlier "Rites Issue," some Europeans heard for the first time, in 1643, the name of Confucius, who was described—by Dominican missionary Jean Morales to the Pope—as a person idolized by all Chinese, from the emperor down to every commoner. In the context of Morales' report, Confucius and his followers were the leading foes of the Catholic Church in China. Then, when the "Rites Issue" was rekindled after 1684, there was a new desire in Europe to study China's politics, ethics, philosophy and history. That was after the publication of Athanasius Kircher's book *China Illustra* in 1667. Within five years after it was published in Amsterdam, the well-written Latin book with illustrations, was translated into French and German and viewed by many as an "encyclopaedia on China." It was read by many, including Leibniz and Voltaire. This was the first comprehensive book about China, written by a European scholar, and it represented a milestone in the development of Sinology in Europe.

Also noteworthy were the study on Confucianism by Philippi Couplet and the introduction of the *Book of Changes* to Europe by Joachim Bouvet. Both created deep impact upon France and Germany during the seventeenth century, and contributed to the gradual advance in Sinology. The study of Confucius fueled the political enthusiasm of the French enlightenmentalists in their quest for government of an open-minded monarch, whereas the research on the *Book of Changes* prompted European philosophers to seek for the conciliation of the East and West cultures.

Joachim Bouvet had, since his arrival in Beijing in 1688, been engaged in teaching Emperor Kangxi on Western sciences almost every day, while devoting himself to studying the Chinese classics. He returned to France in 1693, and gave a lecture in Paris in 1697, in which he praised the *Book of Changes* as much of a rational and perfect philosophy as that of Plato and Aristotle. In refutation of the views of most Jesuits, who looked upon the book as full of groundless theories and superstition, Bouvet insisted that it represented the ideology of China's first philosopher and the creator of its monarchism, Fuxi, and so could guide readers to understand the truth of Chinese philosophy. Bouvet said he believed that the theories of the book, openly attcked by Charles Maigrot, were "the very truth." The study of the book in Europe was initiated by Joachim Bouvet against the background of the "Rites Issue." As Bouvet stressed in his lecture, there was nothing else in the world which could match the *Book of Changes* in its predominance over the mentality of the Chinese people as to enable them to absorb the holy creed of Catholicism. And the only way to achieve this was by "allowing them to understand our religion as being consistent with their own ancient philosophical truth." Bouvet's views, which were further reflected in his other writings, won the support of Gottfried Wilhelm von Leibniz in Europe, and the backing of Emperor Kangxi in China.

Bouvet and Leibniz began their correspondence in 1697, when the French Jesuit was still in Paris, and continued even after Bouvet had returned to Beijing. From Beijing, Bouvet sent a copy of the *Book of Changes* to Leibniz, sparking the German philosopher's interest in the culture of ancient China. In 1702, when Leibniz noticed in the *Book of Changes* the ancient graphic circle of the "64 Diagrams" as restored by Shao Kangjie of the Song Dynasty, he discovered that he could explain the secret of the ancient book by means of the binary scale which he invented in 1679. This discovery seemed to vindicate his earlier presumption that it was possible to find the philosophical symbol of "Caractéristiques Universelles," through numerical or algebraic deduction. And he thought that he had found the very evidence in the *Book of Changes* to prove his idea, because he believed that the book's use of the two symbols of *yin* (female or negative) and *yang* (male or positive) to indicate all things on earth coincided, mysteriously, with his binary scale of using only the two digits of "1" and "0" to represent all other numbers. Through his mathematical intuition, Leibniz had thus found a vital link between the cultures of the East and the West, in the convergence of his own brilliant initiative with that of an ancient Chinese talent. Such a discovery led the great German philosopher and mathematician to believe that the ancient Chinese were not idolatrous but worshippers of the supreme truth. Therefore, Leibniz considered the European accusation—resulting from the "Rites Issue"—that "the Chinese were idolatrous," as completely meaningless.

Leibniz's discovery of the Chinese "binary theory," as contained in the *Book of Changes*, was attributable to the thorough research on the ancient Chinese book by Bouvet, who first studied the *Book of Changes*, with the encouragement of Emperor Kangxi. The Qing emperor had personally lectured Bouvet on the theories of the book and encouraged him to write his essays on the Chinese classic, when the two of them discussed it in 1710. Emperor Kangxi urged the French Jesuit to study all literature connected with the book without any preconception or prejudice. In order to achieve an understanding of the book, Bouvet tried to explain its themes by means of mathematical theories and diagrams contained in the Chinese classic book *Suan Fa Tong Zong* (*Systematic Treatise on Arithmetic*). Thus the controversy over the Chinese religion and rites had prompted European missionaries like Bouvet to devote themselves to the study of Chinese philosophy and mathematics. In 1712, Bouvet finished his Latin book of *Idea Generalis Doctrinae libri I-King* and sent it back to Europe. However, it was never published but preserved in the National Library of Paris.

The study on the *Book of Changes* had focused on the point

of whether or not its doctrine was consistent with the Catholic Creed. As a result of their study, Bouvet and his assistant Jean Francois Foucquet finished their work of "General Doctrines of the *Book of Changes*" in Chinese, in which they summed up the book's consistency with the Catholic principles, and submitted it for review by Emperor Kangxi. Their work also included the result of their mathematical study of the book. But their conclusion on this point was contradicted by two other European missionaries Claudus de Visdelou and Joannes Bapt Régis. Visdelou stated his own views in his book "A Review of the *Book of Changes*," which was formally published in 1770 in Paris, as a supplement attached to the French translation of the *Shu Jing* (*Book of History*) by Antonius Goubil. But Visdelou also sent his book to the Vatican in 1728, and won approval of the Roman Catholic Church for its support of the Church's argument on the "Rites Issue." It had, therefore, been widely circulated among the Catholic missionaries.

The European Sinology had originated in France, with S. Fourmont as its founder. He was helped by the research on China done by Jesuit Joseph de Prémare. As one of the ten Jesuits sent by French King Louis XIV to China, Joseph de Prémare possessed rich knowledge in both the Chinese language and Chinese classics; as such, he had contributed much to the European study on China. In 1728, Prémare finished his book *Notitia Linguae Sinicae*—a comprehensive introduction to the Chinese language —and sent it back to Paris for revision by Fourmont. Fourmont took the liberty to include it in his own book *Linguae Sinicae Grammatica*, which was widely acclaimed in literary circles after its publication in 1742. It was not known at that time that Prémare should be credited for the research work.

The growth of Sinology in Europe was, from its beginning, closely linked with the study of Chinese culture by the Jesuits in China. And in Europe, the establishment of Sinological courses was due, primarily, to the efforts by A. H. Francke, a student of Leibniz. Francke founded the Academy of Oriental Theology in Halle in 1707, first with a department for the study of Chinese philosophy. After that, his lectures and literary works on the subject attracted more attention to the study of Chinese philosophy in European academic circles. Later, Italian Jesuit P. Ripa set up the Collegium Sanctae Familiae in Naples in 1732, with the help of Chinese Catholic converts, marking the founding of the first Chinese school in Europe. By 1913, when the school had changed its name to the Oriental Royal Institute, it had enrolled 106 Chinese students. These schools had served as the breeding centres of Sinology in Europe.

The study of Sinology through the eighteenth century was inseparable from the work of the European Jesuits in China. Until the turn of the century, Beijing served as the frontier of the European Sinologists, whose base was in Paris. The existing communications link between Beijing, Guangzhou (Canton) and Paris made it possible to pass the Jesuits' research work from Beijing on to Paris. It was under such favourable conditions that the French Jesuit J. B. Du Halde was able to publish in 1735 his four-volume compilation of an encyclopaedia of Chinese culture. It bore this impressive title: *Description Géographique, Historique, Chronologique, Politique et Physique de l'Empire de la Chine et de la Tartarie Chinoise.* The voluminous book about China was published 16 years before the publication of the 28-volume *Encyclopaedia*, edited by the French encyclopaedist Diderot. After its publication, the book by Du Halde was soon translated into German and English and circulated across Europe, stimulating the European quest of "food for thought" from the Orient. As a Jesuit close to the imperial court of the Qing Dynasty, Du Halde's book created a far greater impact than he had anticipated. This was because the systematic introduction of China's philosophy, social system, literature, science, language and arts was tantamount to transfusing new energy to Western Europe on the eve of its revolution. As a result, Western Europe was intrigued with the image of a "wonderful and disciplined China." Du Halde's book became a landmark in the development of Sinology in Europe.

Chapter Nine
China's First Attempt to Understand
the Western World

I The New Maps and New Knowledge

1. Wei Yuan and Xu Jishe and Their Works on Knowledge
of the World

The "Rites Issue" initiated by the earlier Jesuit missionaries in China led to a standoff in the eighteenth century between China and the European Catholic countries. Later, China became involved in a dispute with the Western powers over trade. Eventually, this ancient Oriental country was forced—at the point of guns by British warships—to re-assess and re-understand the world.

The surge in imports of opium in China's coastal areas, since the early nineteenth century, had resulted in a mounting trade deficit for China and almost depleted its currency reserve of silver, at the same time causing widespread damage to the people's health. The Qing government, worried by the situation yet not knowing what to do about it, dispatched a high official Lin Zexu (1785-1850) to Guangzhou in early 1839 in an attempt to stop the flourishing opium trade. Upon his arrival in Guangzhou on March 10 of that year, Lin started gathering information on the trade situation and foreign parties involved; he organized the translation of the English-language publication *Eastern-Western Monthly Magazine*, foreign geographic journals and the *The Law of Nations* written by the Swiss lawyer Emerich de Vattel. Lin, who was the first Chinese intellectual to realize that China must arm itself with modern military equipment to cope with the menace of technically advanced Western aggressors, managed, in 1840, to purchase 380 Western cannons plus a ship, through Portuguese and American merchants. Lin urged his officials to build more cannons and ships "as good as these foreign products." Lin's ideas represented the eager desire of China's new generation of intellectuals to understand the Western world. They foresaw that a clash between the Chinese and the Western cultures would inevitably erupt in their home country in the near future.

After the Qing government suffered its first setback in the first Opium War, Lin Zexu was sacked by the emperor and sent into exile in the border province of Xinjiang. In June of 1841, when Lin stopped over in Jingkou (now Zhenjiang) on his way to Xinjiang, he was met by his friend Wei Yuan (1794-1857), a patriotic intellectual serving in the provincial government. Lin gave Wei the manuscript of his unfinished "Four Continents" as well as his collection of maps and blueprints of guns and ships, asking Wei to write a book to tell the Chinese people about the changing world situation and the need to learn advanced technology from the West. Wei Yuan accepted Lin's request with enthusiasm, and finished the 50-volume *Hai Guo Tu Zhi* (*Illustrated Record of Maritime Nations*) in December of 1842.

This book was the first encyclopaedic handbook of the five continents on the globe compiled by a Chinese author, based on contemporary Western historical and geographical publications. The book provided separate coverage for each country and each continent in the world, clearly illustrating the worldwide expansion of the Western powers. Five years after publication of the first edition of the 50-volume book in Yangzhou, Wei Yuan published yet a new edition of the same book in 60 volumes, which included much more about Western technology—his favourite subject. The publication of Wei's book received warm response from patriotic intellectuals in China, especially, when the first Opium War ended in 1842 with a humiliating defeat for the Qing government, causing widespread concern among many Chinese over the future of the feudalist empire of the Qing Dynasty. The "Middle Kingdom," which boasted a civilization of many thousand years, was "powerless" to defend itself in the face of an invading British fleet, yielding to the guns of the foreign "barbarians." Enlightened Chinese realized the need to learn from the West and introduce advanced technology to their own country. As a leading thinker in this enlightenment drive, Wei Yuan went on to collect more information from all possible sources and, eventually, finished expanding his *Illustrated Record of Maritime Nations* into a 100-volume book in 1852, which included more details on the industry and economy of the Western countries with more maps added.

In the preface of his book, Wei Yuan pointed out his purpose was to let the Chinese nation know that the only way to defend itself against foreign aggression was "to learn from the foreigners." This was because he realized that China was faced with the immediate danger of foreign enslavement, unless an all-out effort was made to catch up with the Western powers in industry and technology. He summarized his ideas in the chapter on the Atlantic and European countries, warning: "Only those who were good in learning from the foreigners could overcome the foreigners; those who refused to learn from the foreigners would be overpowered by the foreigners." Wei Yuan pointed out that the superiority enjoyed by the Western powers lay mainly in their warships, weaponry and military training. In the 100-volume edition of his *Illustrated Record of Maritime Nations*, he devoted 10 volumes to information on the design and function of Western ships, cannons, firearms, mines and telescopes, and his suggestions on the building of China's own shipyards and arsenals. Moreover, he pointed out that the British troops were not only better-armed but also "better-paid, better-trained and better-disciplined" than the Chinese troops. He appreciated the importance of military organization and training and the significance of technical advantage. Wei Yuan was also aware that technical advancement played a vital role in the betterment of living standards of the Western countries, which further covinced him that the future of his country and his people depended on the introduction of industrial technology. However, neither Wei Yuan nor his followers realized that the materialization of their dream would be so costly for their country, as history later proved. Nevertheless, Wei Yuan and his precursor Lin Zexu were the forerunners of China's "Learn from the West" campaign of the late nineteenth century.

During the years when Wei Yuan was continuing to add new information to his book, another Chinese intellectual Xu Jishe had also initiated a similar project in Xiamen (Amoy) where he was working as a foreign trade official. Xu Jishe, first saw a volume of world maps at the place of his friend Ablee, an American Presbyterian missionary, and was deeply impressed by the rich information contained in the book. With Ablee's help, he made a hand-drawn copy of more than 20 maps from the book, with Chinese translation of the captions. Then, in 1844, he added more information to these map copies and had them compiled into a book called *An Outline of Global Geography*. The book, published in September of 1848, could not compete with Wei Yuan's book in scale or content, but it was well received by many intellectuals as an introductory book on world geography because of its clear, concise illustrations. Both *Illustrated Record of Maritime Nations* and *An Outline of Global Geography* had emerged as excellent introductory handbooks for Chinese readers to learn about the outside world, especially when the perceptive Chinese intellectuals were in dire need of new "food for thought" to revitalize the country's aging civilization. As a result, both books became popular soon after their publication, and were reprinted many times.

2. Li Shanlan and Xu Shou, and Their Cooperation with the Missionaries

In the face of growing foreign aggression against China, a patriotic campaign of "learning from the West to save the country" swept entire China, and was particularly strong in the coastal provinces. Many patriotic intellectuals gave up opportunities to join the officialdom—through taking examinations held regularly by the Qing government—and threw themselves into the quest for scientific knowledge from the Western countries. The campaign gave rise to new challenges against the traditional Chinese culture, as conservative ignorance was blamed for scientific backwardness while superstition was blocking creativity. Similarly, the obsolete official examination system and the practice of "eight-legged essay" writing were attacked as the root cause which led to protracted stagnation of China's culture.

A number of Chinese intellectuals soon distinguished themselves as pioneers in the patriotic "New Knowledge" movement first initiated by Lin Zexu. In open defiance of the Chinese tradition of "placing ethics and reasons above arts and crafts," and regardless of the conservatives' criticism of Western technology, they dedicated themselves to the cause of introducing modern scientific knowledge to China. Li Shanlan (1811-1882) and Xu Shou (1818-1884) were two representatives in the movement.

Li Shanlan was born in Haining of Zhejiang Province; Xu Shou was a native of Wuxi in Jiangsu Province; and they were both well educated in traditional sciences. But when the country confronted with the strong impact of the Western culture, Li and Xu, like many other Chinese intellectuals, perceived the superiority of the Western pragmatic sciences based on experiments. Their enthusiastic efforts in absorbing and introducing advanced Western technology to China helped pave the way for Chinese scientists to catch up with their counterparts in other countries.

An outstanding mathematician, Li Shanlan started working on translation of Western mathematics, soon after he arrived in Shanghai in 1852. In cooperation with British missionary Alexander Wylie (1815-1887), he translated the last nine volumes of Euclid's *Elements of Geometry*, completing the unfinished work of Xu Guangqi and Matteo Ricci, who had translated the first six volumes of the mathematics classic in the seventeenth century. His final completion of the translation work in 1856 marked the conclusion of a 250-year-long effort by Chinese intellectuals to introduce the masterpiece of Western mathematics into China, thereby putting Li Shanlan in the fore of Chinese academic circles just as his predecessor Xu Guangqi was in the early seventeenth century. Then, again in cooperation with Alexander Wylie, Li translated the *Elements of Algebra* written by the British mathematician Augustus De Morgan, giving China its first mathematical textbook which used symbols to represent numbers. Algebra was first known in China during the early Qing Dynasty, when Emperor Kangxi was known to have discussed mathematics with then Zhili provincial governor Zhao Hongxie in 1711. Although the Qing emperor mentioned that algebra had originated in the Orient, Li Shanlan was, nonetheless, the first Chinese to have introduced algebra, as applied mathematics, to China. Li had received help from another British missionary, Joseph Edkins, and finished translating the 20-volume *Mechanics* by William Whewell, with Edkin's assistance.

Li Shanlan was conversant with most mathematical subjects, including geometry, algebra and logarithm, and had written many books about them, of which 13 were included in the *Mathematical Collections of Zeguxizhai Studio* series. These books, mostly finished before he came to Shanghai, proved his extensive knowledge of these subjects, which contributed to his successful translation of such important Western mathematic works, in cooperation with the British missionaries. Li was re-markable also for giving accurate definitions to numerous math-ematical terms, through his translation work. Many of such terms, as translated and defined by Li, are still in use today. These include *wei ji fen* (differentiation and integration), a pertinent Chinese definition given by Li himself.

Li's translation works included a wide range of scientific subjects in addition to mathematics, including astronomy, me-chanics, physics, and botany. He was responsible for guiding the Chinese students to new developments in such basic sciences. Apart from algebra and the integral and differential calculus, Li was credited with giving the Chinese readers the first complete explanation of celestial mechanics of Copernicus and Newton, through his translation of the *Outlines of Astronomy*.

In a matching contrast with Li Shanlan, his contemporary Xu Shou made outstanding contributions in physics and chemistry. He was among China's first engineers to master the design and construction of steam engines. He undertook the task of trial-producing a wooden steamboat in the Anqing shipyard, built by Qing Dynasty high official Zeng Guofan. He was especially keen on scientific experiments, and was known to have insisted on "proving truth through tests" throughout his 30-year scientific career. It was in 1855 that he came to Shanghai in the company of Hua Hengfang (1833-1902), a mathematician from Xu's home town of Wuxi. He first came into contact with modern Western science through the book written by British missionary Benjamin Hobson, entitled *Introduction to New Knowledge*. Since then he had devoted himself to reading and translating Western scientific works, while engaging in one experiment after another to prove the new technology which he had learned.

In 1867, Xu Shou joined the newly-founded Kiangnan Machine Building Works in Shanghai, and continued working there until 1884, when he died at the age of 66. During the 17 years with the Kiangnan Machine Building Works, Xu was responsible for translating scientific publications from abroad, and translated 13 Western books into Chinese. In 1872, Xu Shou compiled China's first Periodic Table of Chemical Elements, based on a translated version by a British scientist. Because it was then impossible to define in Chinese all the 64 elements by their specific nature, Xu wisely chose to name the new elements by the Chinese phonetic version of the first syllable of their original names. Thus he created many new Chinese characters to translate the sound of such new elements as sodium, manganese, nickel and magnesium, which have been universally used in China ever since. His translation of the Periodic Table proved to be much simpler and more useful than the old 1882 orally-translated Table by M. A. Billequin, a French scholar of the Tung-Wen Kuan (Tongwen Institute). Xu Shou took great pains in deliberating and verifying the chemical terms, while translating the chemical publications. Owing mainly to his dedicated work, the "Chinese-English Names of Chemical Materials" and the "Chinese-English List of Western Medicine" were finally compiled and published after his death.

It was because of Xu Shou's translation of the most essential works of chemical science of the late nineteenth century that chemistry became an independent discipline in China. His translation of the works of the German chemist Fresenius on chemical quality and quantity became China's first publication on the qualitative and quantitative analysis of chemical elements. He conducted a systematic translation of the latest works of basic chemistry and introduced them to the Chinese. He was so highly regarded that Japan sent its scholars to Shanghai to seek advice from Xu Shou on chemical research. Xu Shou stood out as an example of the self-taught perceptive Chinese intellectuals, who had grown up in the mid-nineteenth century. His valuable translation works, while prevented by historic and social conditions from producing greater effect in the country's economy, had, nevertheless, created a major impact in enhancing the scientific awareness of China's academic and intellectual communities.

3. The Kiangnan Machine Building Works and Its Publications

The "Learn from the West" campaign, launched across China since 1861, was a part of the Westernization drive sponsored by the ethnic Han officials under the Qing government. The campaign was aimed, primarily, at developing a munition industry after the example of the Western powers, so as to provide the country with weapons and warships to match those of the foreign countries. The Kiangnan Machine Building Works founded in Shanghai in 1867—with machinery bought from America by Rong Hong at the behest of Zeng Guofan—was a major achievement of the Westernization group among the Qing officials.

One of the first actions taken by the Kiangnan Machine Building Works, after it was founded, was to set up a Translation Agency in June 1868; and John Fryer, a British working in the Chinese newspaper *Shanghai Xinbao*, was enrolled to oversee the translation work. The first three books translated by the agency were *Theory of Mechanics* by John Fryer and Xu Zhonghu, *Steam Engine* by Alexander Wylie and Xu Shou, and *Identification of Materials* by Daniel Jerome MacGowan and Hua Hengfang. Later, the Shanghai Guangfangyan Language School also moved into the Kiangnan Machine Building Works, and the American missionary Young J. Allen was employed by the Translation Agency. While continuing to teach in the school he also translated books.

Of the Chinese staff in the Translation Agency, Xu Shou and

Hua Hengfang were the most outstanding. Other proficient translators included the medical specialist Shu Feng, who had studied in the United States, and the alchemist-turned surgeon and physicist Zhao Jinghan. The Chinese mathematician Li Shanlan had also served briefly in the Translation Agency, before he was summoned to Beijing and appointed dean of mathematics in the capital's Tongwen Institute in 1868. Li had given valuable help to the staff of the Translation Agency, many of them being his close friends while he worked there.

The Translation Agency of the Kiangnan Machine Building Works began publishing books in 1871, the third year after its founding. Its first two publications were *Yun Gui Yue Zhi* (*Theory of Mechanics*) and *Kai Mei Yao Fa* (*Essentials of Coal Mining*) which were followed by wide-ranging translation works on mathematics, survey, steam engine, chemistry, astronomy, navigation, natural sciences, medicine, industrial technology, military science, shipbuilding, history, international law and annals —totalling some 163 kinds, published over a period of 25 years until 1895. Western knowledge was then introduced into China, through three main channels, namely, the official agencies, the Church and the civilian sector. Of these, the official agency of the Kiangnan Machine Building Works in Shanghai and the Tongwen Institute in Beijing played a predominant role. Since its publication of the *International Law* (*in Chinese*) in 1864, Tongwen Institute had published nearly 200 varieties of translated works, mostly concerning diplomacy, current affairs, history and geography. The Church sector was late in introducing translated Western publications to China, while their focus was primarily on theology and medicine. The Kiangnan Machine Building Works, meanwhile, put more emphasis on translating natural sciences, technology, applied techniques, military science and various maps, whereby, it had surpassed all others in the introduction of Western science and technology to China in the nineteenth century and exerted strong influence on the country's academic community.

In the choice of subjects, the Translation Agency gave top priority to applied techniques related to coastal defence, navy, gunnery and mining, while paying attention also to natural sciences, mathematics, astronomy and chemistry publications. This marked an improvement on the previous overemphasis on defence and military science, which prevailed during the early years of the Westernization drive. The correct approach in the translation work of the Kiangnan Machine Building Works paved the way for the coordinated development of both the basic and the applied sectors of natural sciences in China.

The Kiangnan Machine Building Works lay emphasis on both the translation of practical natural sciences and the dissemination of scientific knowledge in the public. In 1876, it launched the country's earliest scientific periodical *Ge Zhi Hui Bian* (*Chinese Scientific Magazine*)—first a monthly, then changed to quarterly —which, until its publication ceased in 1890, continued to report on the progress and new developments of sciences in Europe. The magazine was financially independent, without getting any subsidy from the Kiangnan Machine Building Works. In addition to the magazine, the Translation Agency also published a four-volume *Ge Zhi Qi Meng* (*An Introduction to Sciences*), compiled by Young Allen, specially for the beginners.

The various scientific publications of the Kiangnan Machine Building Works had been widely used as textbooks by the non-traditional Chinese schools and the mission schools run by the Church in China. One of these books was the four-volume *Chemistry* translated by Wang Runan. Another book was the *Wu Li* (*Physics*), written by Iimori of Japan, whose publication by the Kiangnan Machine Building Works led to the universal use of "Wu Li" as the standard name for physics in China. The Gezhi Institute of Shanghai, with John Fryer as its principal and Xu Shou as its dean, had also adopted science books published by the Kiangnan Machine Building Works as its reference or lecturing materials. Mathematical publications from the Kiangnan Machine Building Works had also been used as textbooks by public schools in Nanjing, Xiamen, Yantai and the American mission school in Dengzhou of Shandong Province.

II   Schools Teaching Western Sciences

1. From Tongwen Institute to Military Academies

The Qing government was forced to open its capital of Beijing to foreign diplomatic corps since 1860, and a treaty was signed to allow the foreign envoys to have permanent residences in Beijing, thus creating a need for more interpreters. Upon the suggestion of the British official Robert Hart (1835-1911), who was then serving in the Qing government, Yixin (the Qing Dynasty Prince Gong in charge of foreign affairs) asked the local governments in Guangdong and Shanghai to recruit teachers to teach foreign languages at Beijing. However, since there were no applicants to fill such qualification in either Guangdong or Shanghai, Prince Gong was obliged to hire foreigners to teach the Chinese students, at the country's first foreign languages school Tongwen Institute (Tung-Wen Kuan), which opened in Beijing in June of 1862. The school opened with English-only courses in the first year, followed by French and Russian courses in the second year, absorbing the Russian Language Institute which was set up in the Qing court since 1757.

The founding of the Tongwen Institute ran into opposition from conservative officials in the Qing court, who condemned it as an attempt to convert China into a part of the foreign culture, claiming China should stick to its principle of depending on rites and popular support for the monarch, not on tricks and techniques of the Western culture. In spite of strong criticism from the conservatives, Tongwen Institute eventually survived with the full backing of the Ministry of Foreign Affairs, headed by Prince Gong.

In 1866, Tongwen Institute developed from a foreign languages school into a polytechnic institute by establishing an astronomy and mathematics department, and began to train Chinese students specialized in Western scientific subjects. This marked the starting point of a systematic training of advanced science students in China, which compared favourably with such Western countries as the United States, where systematic science education had begun in the 1850s. Tongwen Institute had thus proved itself as the pace-setter of China's higher education on sciences. Prince Gong, who sponsorded the founding of the first science department in the institute, outlined his purpose as seeking to develop the country's machine building industry through training specialists in mathematics and sciences. He rebuked the conservatives' criticism by citing examples set by the late Emperor Kangxi in introducing Western techniques and appointing a Westerner to run the astronomical observatory; he also told these officials that Japan was then sending its students to study in England, while the Western countries had been learning from each other in the sciences over the decades. Therefore, he declared that learning the sciences from the West was "nothing shameful" and had nothing to do with "superseding the Chinese heritage with the Western culture."

As soon as the new Astronomy and Mathematics Department was set up in Tongwen Institute, Li Shanlan was called from Shanghai to Beijing to serve as the dean of the new department. As a learned scholar, Li was well-acquainted with the Western sciences and also with many of the missionaries, enjoying their respect. The appointment of Li to the job was, therefore, welcomed by all the relevant parties. Then, professor Dr. W.A.P. Martin of international law, an American missionary, was appointed president of the newly-expanded Tongwen Institute, where he had since served continuously for 25 years. The number of students in the institute increased to over 100, and the length of their study was extended to eight years, during which they studied foreign languages the first two years and started learning astronomy, mathematics, chemistry, physics, medicine, foreign history and geography—while practising translation of books —beginning the fourth year. In 1888, Tongwen Institute set up German Department, followed by a Japanese Department in 1895. Through the years, Tongwen Institute trained many Chinese diplomats. Among its graduates were some who served as important aides to leading officials of the Westernization group. The founding of this Westernized institute in Beijing also marked an infiltration of sciences into the traditional official examination system, leading gradually to a nationwide reform of the education system in China.

The new Western-type institutions, set up by the Westernization group in the Qing government, were called "schools" (xuetang) to distinguish themselves from the traditional "study halls" (shuyuan) which used to teach only Chinese language, classics, and official doctrines. In the initial stage, these schools were built to train military technicians for the various arsenals or shipyards founded by these Westernization group officials. One of these early-type schools was the Shipbuilding School founded in June 1866, as a part of the Fuzhou Shipbuilding Administration in Fujian. The school first had only a foreign languages department, teaching English and French; it was expanded to include departments of drawing, navigation and engineering, under the name of Shipbuilding School, and became known as the first government-founded military academy in China.

After 1870, more military academies were established in China, along with the Western-type departmental institutes, in such major cities as Tianjin, Shanghai, Guangzhou, Wuchang and Nanjing. These included the telegraph school and munition school in Tianjin, the military institute in Guangzhou and the army school in Nanjing. The earliest Westernized departmental college was the Zhengmeng Shuyuan of Shanghai, which—albeit its old-fashioned name—was organized with separate departments teaching different subjects, such as Chinese literature, geography, history, politics, physics, mathematics and music. Most of the courses in the Zhengmeng Shuyuan covered scientific or political education, and the school's name was soon changed to Meixi School. However, the first official departmental institute was the Zhiqiang School founded by the leading West-oriented official Zhang Zhidong, governor-general of Hubei-Hunan-Guangdong, in Wuchang of Hubei in October of 1839. This new-fashioned school comprised four separate departments of language, mathematics, physics and commerce, observing a strict departmental education system, seen for the first time in China.

The founding of the new Western-type schools marked a sharp departure from the old education system represented by the traditional *shuyuan* (study hall), which had been sending classic-oriented, conservative bureaucrats to the Chinese society for centuries. "To shift China's education from such an obsolete system to a new science- and profession-oriented course, learn from the Western countries and train thousands of competent scientists and technicians" had been the common wish of numerous reform-minded or West-oriented Chinese officials and intellectuals throughout the Westernization drive and the Reform Movement in the second half of the nineteenth century. During this period, many graduates from Tongwen Institute and other new-fashioned schools became important government officials and diplomats or served as key staff members in machine building works, shipyards, telegraph agencies or military academies, giving powerful support to the social status of specialized professionals in the country, as against the traditional disrespect for such persons. Entry of new-type school graduates into the officialdom also served to break the centuries-old tradition of winning official titles through writing "eight-legged essays."

While the Westernization group officials hoped only for establishing new industry and a modern army through the training of specialized professionals in the new-type schools, some radicals among the reformists had, however, perceived that reform of the old system could not be achieved by merely promoting Westernized schools and factories, without replacing the traditional feudal system with a modern democratic system.

In the view of these reformists, the key to the problem was a total reform of the education system. Liang Qichao, a leading reformist, declared in his article "Integration of the Official Examination and the Schools" that the traditional official examination system should be abolished and be replaced nationwide with schools to train professionals from primary schools at the grassroots to colleges at the highest level and choose future officials from among the graduates. Liang's views caused heated debate and ran into a wall of conservative opposition for some years. Nevertheless, his ideas symbolized an irresistible historic trend, which eventually led to the official abolition of the traditional examination system, giving way to the modern school education in August 1905.

2. The Missionaries and Mission Schools

There was a marked difference between the Western and the traditional Chinese education systems in curriculum, teaching method and length of study. The initial introduction of the Western-style education to China was closely linked with the activities of the Western missionaries during the early nineteenth century, when the Anglo-American Protestant missionaries first visited this country. These Western missionaries, whose religious activities in China were not protected by treaties or law, had entered the coastal provinces often in the guise of merchants, physicians or teachers. They would then sometimes set up schools to teach English or other subjects to the Chinese students, all the while preaching the Christian creed. These so-called mission schools, operating on a limited scale and with only a score of students, relied on giving free education and other favours to attract poor children to study in them. However, they were the first Western-style educational establishments to have appeared in China to train a different kind of students, who were then called foreign-style students in this country, as opposed to the traditional Chinese students.

Missionaries of the Congregational, Presbyterian and Methodist Episcopal churches were the first to found schools in China. The British Congregational Church missionary Robert Morrison moved his Yinghua Shuyuan (Anglo-Chinese School) from Malacca to Hong Kong in 1842; with James Legge as its principal, the school taught Chinese students Christian creed, Chinese and English, marking the start of English-teaching in a school for the Chinese.

In the wake of the Opium War, missionary activities were legalized in China; and more mission schools soon emerged in such coastal cities as Ningbo, Fuzhou, Xiamen (Amoy), Guangzhou (Canton) and Shantou. In 1844, the Oriental Women's Education Society of Britain sent Miss Alden to set up a women's school in Ningbo—the first of its kind in China. Later the same year, two other Anglo-Chinese schools, one for men and another for women, emerged in Xiamen. According to the old Chinese custom, maidens were not allowed to participate in public activities before marriage. The founding of women's schools symbolized a breakthrough—though still insignificant—in the old Chinese society. Thereafter, more mission schools for women were set up by churches in Fuzhou, Beijing, Shanghai and Suzhou, in accordance with the missionary policy of non-coeducation. Mrs. Elijah Coleman Bridgeman, who was the earliest American missionary in China, founded the Bridgeman School for Women in Beijing in the 1860s, then moved it to Shanghai. Dr. W.A.P. Martin, another American missionary, came from Shanghai to Beijing in 1864 and set up the Chongshi Middle School in the east city of the Chinese capital. All these were the early mission schools in China.

The Catholic Church moved slower than the Protestants in launching their misson schools, the earliest of which was the Xuhui Public School founded in 1850. However, the Catholics later established the Aurora University in Shanghai and the Fujen Catholic University in Beijing.

According to a survey in 1900, most of the mission schools in China were elementary schools. Out of a total of 3,000 in 1899, only 300 were middle schools. The mission schools all stressed Christian theological lessons, and practised a conversion policy linked with exerting economic pressure on the non-converts. Then after the 1880s, the churches readjusted their education programme, reinforced their funding and teaching staff for the mission schools, whereby the first group of mission colleges began to emerge in China. These mission colleges and universities appeared as the first such higher education institutions in China, apart from the government-run colleges. Of these mission institutes, St. John's University in Shanghai was the earliest, founded in 1879 by merging the two Episcopal mission schools of Peiya (founded in 1865) and Du'en (founded in 1866) in Shanghai. Since the beginning of the twentieth century, many secondary mission schools began merging with each other into colleges, leading to the establishment of such famous institutes as University of Soochow in Suzhou, Qilu University in Jinan, Lingnan

University in Guangzhou, Zhijiang University in Hangzhou, University of Nanjing, Huaxi University in Chengdu and Yenching University in Beijing, in addition to other institutes of arts, science and medicine. American churches alone set up 13 universities in China. Then, as a result of the Washington's decision in 1909 to refund part of China's silver reparation—imposed by the Treaty of 1901 at the end of the Boxer Uprising—to set up a foundation for funding Chinese students studying in America, a large number of Chinese college graduates went to study postgraduate courses in the United States. These returned scholars further reinforced the teaching staff of the mission institutes, and upgraded their standards of education.

The mission schools of the nineteenth century, whose graduates consisted mainly of new intellectuals trained in foreign languages and certain scientific areas played a limited role in the country's modernization. The mission colleges and universities of the twentieth century were able to produce many well-educated specialists and scholars, including returned scholars, who later filled key posts in the government or industrial, financial, academic, educational, religious, scientific and medical establishments, while still maintaining technical or personal links with the West, particularly, Britain and the United States.

III   The Transplanting of Modern Science and Ideology

1. The Theory of Evolution by Natural Selection as Reflected in *Outlines of Astronomy* and *Principle of Geology*

The achievement of the Kiangnan Machine Building Works in publishing many important translated works of natural sciences was attributable primarily to the dedicated effort of the perceptive Chinese intellectuals, who were driven by a strong sense of patriotism—with the help and advice of Western missionaries. The new generation of Chinese scientists—represented by Li Shanlan, Xu Shou, Hua Hengfang, Zhao Yuanyi and Xu Jianyin—were the first to realize that the only way to develop China into a strong world power during the "Epoch of Sciene" in the nineteenth century was by transplanting the advanced science and technology from the West. Insomuch as they were well-learned in both languages and sciences, they could translate Western scientific works into Chinese, in a more accurate and readable form than even the bilingual missionaries. In fact, these Western missionaries had to rely on the Chinese scientists like Li Shanlan, Xu Shou and Hua Hengfang to help them in the translation work. The Chinese scientists were remarkable not only for their dedication to research work, but also for their enthusiasm in introducing Western science and technology to China.

The publishing of the Chinese edition of *Tan Tian* (*Outlines of Astronomy*) and *Di Xue Qian Shi* (*Principle of Geology*) represented the outstanding efforts of Li Shanlan and Hua Hengfang in introducing the latest Western scientific developments to China. The nineteenth century Europe was marked by its spectacular technological achievements, particularly, in astronomy, geology, biology and physics, thanks to the application of experiments based on qualitative analysis and scientific induction. In fact, it was the new creative development of celestial mechanics and palaeontology—based on inductive inference and scientific experiments—that had made *Outlines of Astronomy* and *Principle of Geology* so popular among the Chinese intellectuals.

The book *Outlines of Astronomy* was translated from the book written by John Herschel (1792-1871), who was the president of the British Astronomical Society since 1827. His original book was published in 1856; three years later, Li Shanlan and Alexander Wylie cooperated to have it translated into Chinese. The translated version was revised by Xu Jianyin in 1871—the year the author died—by adding new discoveries about planets into its content.

The 18-volume book of *Outlines of Astronomy* covered a wide range of subjects, including geodesy, celestial sphere, planets, comets, fixed stars, time difference and calendars, using the heliocentric theory to explain the movement of heavenly bodies. The introduction of the book to China was of particular significance at that time, when the heliocentric theory had not yet been universally accepted in the country, despite its newly-achieved predominance in the astronomical research in Europe. Li Shan-lan, in his preface to the translated book, emphasized that the heliocentric theory and the assertion of the elliptical orbit of planets had, at first, encountered strong opposition from the conservatives. However, facts had finally proved that such opposition was based on nothing but "unfounded and unimaginative dogmatism." Li went on to list the contributions to the development of celestial mechanics by such Western scientists as Nicolaus Copernicus, Johannes Kepler and Issac Newton. Li declared that both he and Alexander Wylie were believers of the celestial theories, including the planetary motion and the elliptic orbit. He reiterated all these theories in the preface of the translated book to convince the readers their authenticity.

Li Shanlan admired Newton and his scientific achievements. He had translated Newton's *Philosophiae Naturalis Principia Mathematica*, first in cooperation with Alexander Wylie, then finished the first volume with the help of John Fryer, while he was serving in the Translation Agency of the Kiangnan Machine Building Works. Fryer was impressed with Li's knowledge of mathematics and his understanding of the complexity involved in Newton's works. Li was, indeed, the first Chinese scientist to introduce Newton's works to China.

The other important book published by the Kiangnan Machine Building Works was *Di Xue Qian Shi*, a translation by Hua Hengfang and the American missionary Daniel J. MacGowan from the original book of *Principle of Geology* by the British geologist Lyell. Lyell's book, first published in 1830, was acclaimed as a landmark in modern geology based on the theory of continuous evolution of nature, and had been reprinted 12 times in 40 years. Explainng why he had chosen to translate the book, Hua Hengfang stated in his preface that his recent translation of the book *Identification of Materials* had enabled him to understand the important relation between geology and minerals and the need to study both of them in the same light. Therefore, he said he had tried to use all the time he could spare from his daily work to have the book translated. The book, which focused on the basic knowledge of geology, covered the classification of rock formation, and the fossil remains of ancient creatures in aqueous rocks which could be used to identify the age of such stratum. It also explained the difference between the variation in nature and that of flora and fauna, thereby introducing the process of evolution in clear-cut terms. The book, brought more than just the latest developments in geology to the Chinese intellectual; it represented the first attempt to introduce the theory of evolution, systematically, to the Chinese community.

Both *Outlines of Astronomy* and *Principle of Geology* provided theoretical ground for progressive ideologists of the 1880s to seek historic reform in the country's age-old tradition. Indeed, the two books were partly responsible for creating momentum comparable to the Opium War on China's ideological trend, guiding the country to the road of reform and renovation.

Kang Youwei, a leading reformist, was the first to draw inspiration from the book *Outlines of Astronomy*. He realized the metaphysical nature of the traditional view of universe and accepted the theory of celestial evolution, thereby freeing himself from the bondage of traditional classics to become an open-minded thinker. In 1885, he wrote the book *Zhu Tian Jiang (On the Celestial System)* to elaborate on the theories concerning the origin of the solar system and the relation between the sun and the planets. Like Li Shanlan, he was also an admirer of Nicolaus Copernicus and Issac Newton, the two great scientists, who led the civilized world into a new awareness of the universe. Developments in palaeontology and celestial mechanics convinced him that human society—just like nature itself—was continuously developing and changing. In the light of the continuous evolution of the earth and creatures, he divided the history of the earth into the three eras, wild ancient, far ancient and near ancient. In the wild ancient era, he contended, there were only plants; then in the far ancient era, there appeared birds and animals; finally in the near ancient era, there emerged the human race. He described this as the process of evolution of the earth, plants and animals and mankind. He told his students there was not a permanent "Rule of Heaven," because the rules would change following the changes in heaven. It was on this ground that he developed his idea of reform; he believed that a gradual transition from pure monarchy to constitutional monarchy and then gradually to a republic was in keeping with the theory of evolution.

Tan Sitong, a radical in the Reform Movement of 1898, was known in 1895 to have proposed, in a 10,000-character essay, establishing a mathematics education centre in his home town of Liuyang in Hunan Province. He accepted the theory of Western natural science and wrote another article, proposing the abolition of the traditional education in classics and the old examination system. He studied the Western sciences of geometry, astronomy, physics, chemistry, geology; he read *Principle of Geology*, and embraced the theories on evolution of the earth, plants, animals and mankind. Based on such theories, he wrote many articles criticizing the ossified Confucian philosophy of the "unchangeability of heaven and truth" and expounded the materialistic views of Wang Fuzhi on the "changeability of both materials and truth." In February 1896, Tan Sitong came to Shanghai, where he met John Fryer, and was impressed to see, for the first time, the fossils of ancient animals, which convinced him of the inevitable decaying process of the old and obsolete and their giving place to the new and modern. As a result, he was more determined than ever to spearhead the country's reform movement. It also made him realize more keenly the impending national crisis, and strengthened his determination to learn more from the West. His articles during this period included "On Ether" and "On the Advantages of Electric Light." And in 1898, he gave a lecture in the Nan Xue Hui (Southern Society), focusing on saving China through studying sciences, which, according to him included politics, law, agriculture, mineralogy, industry, commerce, medicine, military, sound, light, chemistry, electricity, graphics and mathematics. The scope of these subjects indicated that he was including the truth of the "heavenly monarchy" in the category of the science of evolution. Such an ideology was formed through his absorption of the Western scientific theories, which played a catalyzing role.

2. The Widespread Introduction of Darwinian
and Spencerian Theories

The ideological weapon of the Chinese reformists of the late nineteenth century was not the materialist theory of Wang Fuzhi on so-called "changeability of (truth) according to changing conditions," but the Western theory of evolution based on research results in the natural science.

The Origin of Species, written by Charles Darwin (1809-1882) to sum up the theory of evolution, was published in 1859, but had not been translated into Chinese. Many Chinese had heard of it, only through a brief report about Darwin finishing a book on "biological evolution," and learned about "vulgar evolutionism" used by Herbert Spencer (1820-1903) to explain the progress of the human society.

The first Chinese publication, which offered an introduction of Darwin's theory of evolution to the domestic readers, was Yan Fu's translation of *Evolution and Ethics* by Thomas Henry Huxley (1825-1895). Yan Fu (1854-1921), a returned Chinese scholar from England, first published his translation of a part of Huxley's book in the Tianjin newspaper, *Guo Wen Bao* (*National News*), 國 报 which attracted immediate attention of many Chinese readers. The translated book on evolution was embraced by the young revolutionaries as their ideological weapon against the old guards of the traditional system. Liang Qichao, the noted reformist, was one of the first to read Yan's translation, even before it was published in 1896. Then, when the complete Chinese translation was formally published in 1901, it became a best seller among the intellectuals in China and created a tremendous impact on the thinking of a whole generation.

Encouraged by his initial success, Yan Fu continued his translation effort, thereby becoming the leading Chinese scholar in introducing modern ideology to China. In an introduction written for the translation of *Evolution and Ethics*, he said evolution was an "objective existence," which was specifically reflected in struggle for survival by all living things and in the natural selection of the fittest. The publication of his translation was soon adopted as a text by many new-fashioned schools in the country. It led many students to become exponents of the theory of "struggle for existence and survival of the fittest." In an era of upheaval, such a theory was immediately interpreted as a message to warn each individual, nation and state that they must strive for their own survival. Dr. Hu Shih, a noted Chinese scholar, was one of the young Chinese students, who had early been impressed with the translated *Evolution and Ethics*, while studying in Beijing's Chenghai School. In his memoir, Hu recalled that after Beijing was ravaged by the foreign invading forces which crushed the *Yi He Tuan* (Boxer Uprising) in 1901, the theory of survival of the fittest struck the hearts of many youngsters like a thunderbolt and soon spread like a prairie fire across the country.

Through his translation of the *Evolution and Ethics*, Yan Fu opened the door for Western ideology. He then went on to introduce to his country more Western works on philosophy, economics, sociology, logic and politics, moving with the prevailing trend among West-oriented reformists, who were shifting their attention from absorbing more Western technology to introducing the Western political doctrines and the parliamentary system to China. As a result, more and more Western social and political ideologies worked their way into the Chinese community. These included Herbert Spencer's *Study of Sociology*, whose theory of a gradual evolution of society soon became popular among the Chinese readers. Another Chinese scholar Ma Junwu followed up in translating more of Darwin and Spencer's works on evolutionism, including *On the Origin of Species by Means of Natural Selection* (published in 1902), a combined edition of Spencer's doctrine on women's rights and Darwin's theory on survival of the fittest (published in 1902 and also Spencer's *The Principles of Sociology* (published in 1903). When the original works of Charles Darwin were introduced through Ma Junwu's translations, it was already in the twentieth century.

Yan Fu and Ma Junwu had both contributed to the historically significant cause of introducing Darwin's theories of evolution to China, but the two of them were completely different in their political paths. Yan Fu was among the earliest West-oriented scholars, advocating enlightening the people with Western education and invigorating the nation by adopting Western technology. He suggested the adoption of a parliamentary system in Beijing as the key to achieving the goal of a civilized, prosperous and democratic country. However, he had remained a believer of Confucianism, and gradually moved away from the stance of an early reformist to become a monarchist politically. His knowledge of Western ideology had failed to spur him on in the course of China's social reform, for he had adhered to Spencer's idea of a gradual path in democratic reform, believing it as the inevitable outcome. On the other hand, Ma Junwu had discovered a new path for himself in the prevailing tide of revolution, which convinced him that it was impossible to build a democratic system, through the limited reform under the feudalist system. The examples of these two leading Chinese scholars reflected the entirely different responses among the Chinese intellectuals to the impact of the Western ideology.

3. The Democratic Ideologies of Zheng Guanying and Liang Qichao

The Westernization drive of the late nineteenth century in China, which had prompted the growth of modern industry and schools in the old country, was posing an inevitable challenge to the decaying system of its autocratic monarchy and traditional education, forcing them to undergo major reform. At this juncture, a number of individuals distinguished themselves as pioneers in the popular drive for progress in Chinese society. One of them was Zheng Guanying (1842-1921), a native of Macao, who had learned English from John Fryer in Shanghai, where he first served as a compradore in a foreign firm and then became a modern Chinese entrepreneur himself. He was author of several books, advocating a strong China through drastic reform in politics and education. In his 20-article book of *Yi Yan* (*Suggestions of Change*), written in 1875, Zheng argued that such a reform should be "completely free from traditional constraints or precedents, but guided by practical needs and benefits." Then in his *Sheng Shi Wei Yan* (*Warnings to a Prosperous Society*) written in 1894, he echoed the indeas of reform voiced by Zhang Shusheng, "Let the parliament decide on politics and let the schools educate the youths." Thus, he became the first "reformist" to openly call for the full-scale introduction of the Western education system and parliamentarianism to replace China's traditional education and feudal autocratic monarchism. And through his extensive contact with the Western circles, Zheng had conceived the idea that the reform should include not only a mere importing of the Western technology, but also an extensive introduction of Western arts and sciences, politics, education, law, trade, industry and commerce.

As an industrial entrepreneur in a government-owned firm, Zheng had been pushing for a constitutional government in the belief that only a constitutional political system could make the people wealthy, and only with a wealthy people could a country become strong. His idea was further expanded in his *Supplement to Warnings to a Prosperous Society*, written in 1920, when he wrote, "A nation has to become wealthy, before it could become strong; and a wealthy nation would be impossible without a wealthy people. Yet the only way to make the people wealthy is through industrialization, evidence of which is clearly shown in the history of Europe and America." Zheng Guanying drew this conclusion from the historical experiences of the Western powers. His view of democracy was to protect the rights of the national bourgeoisie, for he believed that the country would become powerful only with the backing of that powerful group. He had realized from his personal experience that only a political reform could bring about the protection needed for the cause of national bourgeoisie, and yet, as an entrepreneur Zheng was under the control of big bureaucrats and unable to press such a reform from his position.

Liang Qichao (1873-1929), another outstanding reformist ideologue, was, however, directly involved in the political upheavals at the turn of the century. A well-educated Westernized scholar and politician, Liang Qichao distinguished himself first as a leading participant of the abortive 100-Day Reform of 1898, but then turned into a monarchist in the wake of the

Wuchang Uprising, which spelled the end of the Qing Dynasty. Liang began his political career as an early student and follower of the reformist Kang Youwei. After the failure of the Reform of 1898, Liang fled to Japan, where he again studied the Western political theories and formed his own democratic ideology, focusing on the pursuit of free political rights under a constitutional monarchy. Liang was an admirer of the French writer Jean Jacques Rousseau, and wrote the essay "On Rousseau's Case of Education" in November 1901, to support the French writer's theory that freedom and equality were the ultimate goal of all legislature. In his essay entitled "The Opposite and Complementary Relations of Ten Virtues," Liang stressed that freedom stood as the "symbol of right, which represents the spiritual life." He accepted Spencer's theory of vulgar evolutionism in "the natural selection of power politics," and advocated the self-cultivation and solidarity of the weak in their struggle against the strong to force them to concede, as was indicated in another essay "Outlines on the Theory of Political Science." In his opinion, China was then on the course of drastic change, and the key to solving the problem was the introduction of political freedom. In his essay of "On New People" written in 1902, he proposed the citizens' participation in the government.

In view of the pervasive lack of education and courage among the Chinese people, Liang suggested that since such an ignorant and submissive people provided an optimum condition for a corrupt government, it was essential to cultivate a new generation of bourgeoisie citizens with national consciousness, sense of right and obligation to serve as the founders of a new system, new government and new nation. Thus, he looked upon the upbringing of new citizens as the key to the birth of new system and new government in a new country. For this reason, he wrote the essay "The Revolutionary Evolutionist Kidd" in October 1902 to introduce the book *Theory of Western Civilization* by the British scholar Benjamin Kidd. The book stressed the point that all social, national or ethical ideology would have no value or significance unless it was based on the future of such society or nation. In Liang's view, the world was then in a period of transition from the autocratic to the constitutional system, and China, hampered by the "underdevelopment in the people's ethical, intellectual and physical standards," should therefore best adopt the system of a constitutional monarchy. Liang claimed this would eventually lead to the future goal of a constitutional democracy.

Liang Qichao, however, favoured an integrated absorption of several Western political ideologies not an unconditional acceptance of any one of them. For instance, he advocated the *Du contrat social* (1762) of Rousseau, the theory of social organism of Spencer and the utilitarianism of Jeremy Bentham (1748-1832). He never claimed that any one of these principles could be wholly applied to China. During his 13-year (1898-1911) stay in Japan, Liang was a leading protagonist in introducing Western bourgeois political ideology to China. His ideas of a democratic government were actually founded on the integration of the Confucianist view of "people being the backbone of a state," Mohist doctrine of "practical utility" and the Legalist theory of "state authority"—the three major schools of classic Chinese political ideology. Based on such thoughts, he had continued to absorb the Western political theories of rights, freedom and utilitarianism, and constantly readjusted his pace and rhythm of political thinking according to the changing circumstances, in a bid to seek the ultimate realization of his goal of a constitutional monarchy in China.

IV   Western Democratic Politics and Its Influence on Chinese Revolutionaries in the Late Qing Dynasty

1. Dr. Sun Yat-sen's Revolutionary Ideal and the Western Sciences

Dr. Sun Yat-sen (1866-1925), Chinese democratic revolutionary, was born in Xiangshan (present Zhongshan) of Guangdong Province, but received his early education in Honolulu. As he stated later in his memoirs, he became deeply interested in the Western sciences from the very beginning, and devoted himself to studying mathematics, physics, chemistry, biology, physiology and modern social sciences, while he was a student in America. Sun returned to China in July 1883 at the age of 17; and at the end of that year, he was baptized by an American missionary of the Congregational Church and became a Christian. Then, he believed that Jesus Christ had preached a revolutionary cause. A few years later, he went to Hong Kong to study medical science. There he had opportunity to read more about Western philosophy and became keenly interested in the theory of evolution, which gradually replaced his religious doctrine. It was based on his conviction of evolutionism, that he eventually developed the theory of "three phases of world evolution" in his *National Development Strategy*—published 1919 in Shanghai. According to the theory, the world had gone through the first two phases of "material evolution" and "species evolution" to reach the final phase of "human evolution," thereby providing a new explanation for the progress in the natural and human world.

Throughout his persistent preaching of the revolutionary ideal, Dr. Sun had constantly sought to support his political theories with new discoveries in the field of natural sciences. And he believed that both the Eastern and Western civilizations had emanated from education, and the success of a revolutionary cause also depended on the education of political ideology. Therefore, he adopted Abraham Lincoln's doctrine of "government of the people, by the people, for the people" and gradually developed it into his Three People's Principles, namely, Nationalism, Democracy and People's Livelihood. His proposal of the Principle of Nationalism and Principle of Democracy was prompted by the impending national crisis of the late nineteenth century. And after he went to Britain in October 1896, he was struck by the wide economic gap between different social levels even in the prosperous and democratic European countries. This moved him to propose the Principle of People's Livelihood, in the hope that it would remove the cause of social upheaval once and for all. The proposal of the Three People's Principles by Sun—though seemingly unrealistic at a time, when the very existence of China as a nation was threatened by the imperialist aggressors—had, nevertheless, served the purpose of setting a goal for the social development of the country. And based on such a revolutionary goal, Dr. Sun declared that it was China's future responsibility to extend assistance to other weak and oppressed nations in the world and form a solidarity with them—after it had itself become a free and prosperous country. Under the guidance of this ideal, Sun Yat-sen, in his later years, decided on allying his party with the Soviet Union and the Chinese Communist Party and giving support to peasants and workers. This marked a major turn in the history of the old China. As a perceptive revolutionary, Dr. Sun realized that the self-emancipation of an oppressed nation was impossible without the backing of a coalition of revolutionaries in the world.

In the eyes of Dr. Sun, China was plagued by weakness and poverty, while the imperialist powers—despite immense wealth amassed from exploiting other weak nations—were, nevertheless, troubled by the social injustice of having most of their people still unable to make ends meet. Based on his personal observation of such problems prevailing in the Western society, Dr. Sun, therefore, brought up yet another proposal. This called for China to become a prosperous and strong country just like the Western powers, at the same time, avoiding their social problems. This proposal, aimed at "forestalling social problems through political and social revolutions in one integrated operation," led Dr. Sun to set forth the two major policies of China's economic development as "equal distribution of land" and "restriction of capitalism," both of which reflected his wish to steer China away from the Euro-American type capitalist society. In his words, the idea was, "Since China has not yet developed its capitalism, we should take necessary precautionary measures so that it will not repeat the same mistakes seen in Europe and America." Sun stated in clearest terms his opposition to allowing the people's livelihood to be manipulated by a limited number of business conglomerates, as was seen in some Euro-American countries. As an early student of Western political and social sciences, Sun Yat-sen had worked to develop a new political route different from the Western route of capitalist economy—a revolutionary route character-

·ized for its socialist tendency.

A physician by profession, Dr. Sun Yat-sen was naturally interested in the epoch-making achievements of the Western sciences in the nineteenth century, and was able to absorb much of it during his extensive contacts with the Western world through the decades. This was obviously responsible for his evolution-guided view of the materialist world, on which his theory of the "three-phase evolution" of the world was based. Sun believed that the publication of Darwin's "On the Origin of Species by Means of Natural Selection" had created a tremendous impact on the academic world. In his words, "The publication of Darwin's book has enlightened the world with his brilliant science of evolution, giving rise to a sudden turn in the trend of thought in the human society and causing every school of science to follow the guidance of evolution." Sun then expanded the theory of evolution, which Darwin used to explain the law of nature, into a universal concept applicable to the development of all matters. He added to it with his own specific interpretation, "While other species are governed by the principle of competition, human beings are guided by the principle of mutual assistance." This indicated that his view of the development of human society was influenced by the then very popular idea of "mutualism."

In his essay of "Sun Wen on 'It Is Easy to Do but Hard to Know'," Dr. Sun proposed his theory on *sheng yuan* (biogen) on the basis of the theory of cell, which was one of the three great discoveries in natural science during the nineteenth century. He used *sheng yuan* instead of cell to explain the origin of human beings and all matters, and attributed the wisdom and feeling of mankind as well as the various strange images of flora and fauna to their respective *sheng yuan* structures. He quoted the biogenic theory to explain the phenomena which could not be explained by philosophers, scientists, evolutionists or psychologists. Dr. Sun described his theory of *sheng yuan* as originating from the latest discoveries of scientists, particularly, the research results of German and French scientists of the late mid-nineteenth and early twentieth century. Dr. Sun was an admirer of the 1912 Nobel Prize winner French biologist Alexis Carrel (1873-1944) and applied Carrel's description of the "intelligence" of the cell to his own *sheng yuan*, which were a group of self-conscious and cooperative partners capable of "thinking, feeling, acting and planning." Dr. Sun Yat-sen had, indeed, acquired all such unique concepts, through his constant concern and close contact with the latest achievements of the Western scientists.

2. Anarchism and Populism

China's revolutionary movement, during the last years of the Qing Dynasty, was influenced by tides of Western ideology coming through Japanese schools by way of Chinese students, who went to study in Japan after the official examination system was abolished by the Qing government in 1902. Many of the revolutionary students paid particular attention to the surge of social upheaval in Russia, which had more similarity with China than the Western powers. As a result, Russian-style populism and anarchism began to spread—hand in hand—among Chinese students in Japan.

At the beginning of the twentieth century, Chinese students studying in Japan began publication of China's earliest modern magazines, which mainly covered social revolutionary movements and ideological tides in the Western world. Based on Japanese reports, the Chinese students described the Russian populists as "nihilists" in their magazines. The word "anarchy" was first used by Liang Qichao in the Japan-based newspaper *Qing Yi Bao*. In 1903, Chinese student Zhang Ji translated the book *Anarchism* by the Italian author Errico Malatesta, from its Japanese translation and published it in Shanghai. At about the same time, Zhang also compiled the book *Socialism*, in which he listed Marxism and anarchism as two parallel factions of socialism.

In 1903, six books were published in Shanghai to introduce socialism and nihilism; all of them were translated from Japanese publications. These included the *Anarchism* translated by Zhang Ji, the *Socialist Party* by Mitsujiro Nishikawa, the *Review of Socialism* by Saburo Shimata, the *Socialism* by Tomoyoshi Murai and *Contemporary Socialism* written by Junzo Fukui and translated by Zhao Bizhen. The last book by Fukui was the first such book which gave a systematic introduction to Marxist theory. In Japanese books, Russian populism and anarchism were often viewed as identical to each other. In the book *Blood of Freedom* rewritten by Jin Yi in 1904 from the *Contemporary Anarchism* by Sentaro Kemuyama, the history of Russian nihilists was introduced along with the Russian anarchist activities. Jin's book published in Shanghai marked the first Chinese-compiled introduction of the populist and anarchist ideology in Russia.

In 1905, the *Tong Meng Hui* (Chinese Revolutionary League) founded its organ journal *Min Bao* in Tokyo. It introduced the revolutionary movements and history of the Russian populists, expressing keen interest in their assassination of the Russian feudalist autocrats in their fight to topple the czarist regime. In fact, the acts of assassination taken by the Chinese revolutionaries against the Qing Dynasty rulers after 1904 were the Chinese imitation of the revolutionary activities of the Russian populists. Such activities created immense impact on the whole country, shaking the roots of the already badly-battered Qing regime. Revolutionary martyrs, such as Wu Yue, Xu Xilin and Ms. Qiu Jin—all returned students from Japan—who gave their lives to dealing a fatal blow to the feudalist regime, would be remembered forever for their contribution to enhancing the success of the Revolution of 1911, which marked the end of the Qing Dynasty.

Chapter Ten
An Open China and
the New Culture Movement

I   China with Wide Open Doors

1. The Footpath of the Missionaries

Missionaries, who brought Christian culture to China, had been the colonists of the Christian Church. In fact, the Christian missionary activities had been outlawed by the Chinese authorities—as a result of the controversy over the "Rites Issue" between the Chinese emperor and the Roman Pope—long before the Opium War. Nevertheless, the active contact and exchange between the two different cultures in China continued behind the scenes in various forms. In the West the main sources of such activities had, since the nineteenth century, shifted from the European continent to the Protestant countries in British Isles and North America. Such activities began with the arrival in China of the London Congregational Church's Robert Morrison in the early nineteenth century. Missionary activity flourished across China in the wake of the Nanjing Treaty of 1842, as the Protestant missionaries flocked to China's coastal ports, then spread out from Guangdong, Fujian, Zhejiang and Jiangsu into such inland provinces as Henan, Hebei, Shaanxi, Shanxi, Sichuan, Guangxi, Hunan and Hubei.

The Catholic Church, which had almost ceased its activities in China following the "Rites Issue," also staged a comeback after 1842 with the Jesuits taking the lead. The Jesuit missionaries first started activities in Jiangsu, Anhui and Hebei provinces. In 1858, the Millenarian missionaries set up their centre in Henan, and were followed by the Augustinians who also came to the province some 20 years later. Then, in 1885, St. Paul's Church founded its chapel in Shaanxi Province.

However, in the nineteenth century China, activities of the Catholic mission were on the wane, as compared with the bustling Protestant missionaries seen all over the Yellow River region and the Yangtze River valley. These missionaries had come from many other countries, besides Britain, the United States and Canada; they included Germany, Sweden, Norway, Finland, Denmark, Italy and Australia. Gradually, they became organized into the *Nei Di Hui* (Inland Church) under the sponsorship of the British missionary Hudson Taylor in 1865; and by 1876, Christian churches had appeared in Shanxi, Shaanxi and Gansu provinces. In 1877, they had opened parishes in Guangxi, Guizhou and Yunnan to preach among the ethnic Miao and Zhuang minorities.

The footpaths of the Western missionaries seemed to coincide with the ambitious prowling of the European aggressors against China during the period. While Britain, France and Russia were showing keen interest in China's southern and northern border regions, their missionaries began to appear in Yunnan and Xinjiang areas. In 1876, British missionary Margary entered Yunnan Province from Burma, and was joined there by members of the Inland Church in China. Then at the missionaries' convention in 1890, it was openly proposed that the Western countries should send 1,000 more missionaries to China to fulfill the ambitious goal of "converting China to Christianity." The Western powers —mainly, Britain, France and Russia—were, meanwhile, engaged in dividing China into their "spheres of influence," and gathering whatever interest or information they could for such purpose. The missionaries, at this juncture, also stepped up their work, travelling far and wide across the country. A missionary named Cameron had been to every part of China (except Hunan), including even Inner Mongolia and Tibet.

Missionaries also undertook such activities as publishing newspapers and magazines or opening schools and hospitals, while many of them travelled from place to place to proselyte.

From these ubiquitous missionaries, it was impossible for China to keep any secrets.

2. The Follow-Up Explorers

Following the footsteps of such pioneer missionaries as Elijah Coleman Bridgeman and Robert Morrison, came batches of foreign explorers to the border regions of China. Many of them had come to China in the 1860s with assignments given by the governments of Britain or British India, Russia, France, Germany, Japan or the United States, and their primary aim was to explore the roads leading into China from Central Asia, India, Mongolia, Burma or Viet Nam. Later, their exploration penetrated further into Chinese border provinces, where they conducted surveys of hydrology, meteorology, geology, economy, nationality and languages, following the first step of their systematic archaeological research in these areas.

As the door to China's northwest was thrown wide open in the years after 1860, the ruins of the ancient Silk Road once again became a major attraction, this time to the Western geographers and archaeologists, who were now interested in exploring the hidden treasures there. As a result of years of surveys by dozens of Western explorers and scholars, extensive data on the region became available to the countries concerned, facilitating their political, economic and diplomatic activities in the area. At the same time, some valuable academic achievements were registered.

Noteworthy was the Russian explorer N. M. Prjivalsky, who had travelled deep into Mongolia, Xinjiang and northern Tibet —along different routes on four separate trips—during the 17 years from 1871 until his death in 1888, winning the reputation of an outstanding explorer of Central Asia. His studies produced impressive information on a region, which had earlier been considered the "land of mystery" by many scientists.

After Prjivalsky, many other Western explorers came, one after another, to the area. They included the Russian P. K. Kozloff, the Swedish Sven Hedin, the French J. L. Deutreuil de Rhins, the British Aurel Stein and the American W. W. Rockhill. All sought to find the "hidden truth" of the vast region that ran across Inner Mongolia, Xinjiang, Hexi Corridor (Gansu) and the Qinghai-Tibet Plateau. The activities of Western explorers in this area continued unabated after the turn of the century. With assignments given them by the British government, F. E. Young-husband, F. M. Bailey, H. R. Davies and F. Kingdom Ward all yielded favourable results in the geographic resources, topographic and hydrological surveys conducted in Sichuan and Tibet, and on the Yunnan-Guizhou Plateau.

Sven Hedin, the Swedish geographer and explorer, was best known to the Chinese academic circles for his adventures in China. His 1938 publication of *The Silk Road* was also well-known. In 1900, he had been credited with new discoveries on the historic location of the Lop Nor, which was retold in his book *The Wandering Lake* in 1940. During his geographic exploration, Sven Hedin had come across many ancient Chinese relics, including the ruins of Loulan Kingdom, known to be situated on the west bank of Lop Nor across the Silk Road during the Han Dynasty. This discovery attracted world attention to the East-West communication link dateable from the second century B.C. In 1927, Hedin came again to China to organize a Sino-Swedish joint research group for another exploratory expedition in northwest China. The group left Beijing for Ningxia, along the upper reaches of the Yellow River, and travelled as far as interior Xinjiang to the south of the Tianshan Mountains, where they discovered numerous ancient relics dateable from the Han and Tang dynasties. Their exploration work continued until 1931.

3. The Surprising Discovery of the Dunhuang Treasures

Dunhuang, a land-locked county located near the east end of the ancient Silk Road at Yumen Pass, was a religious centre when Buddhism flourished 1,500 years ago, but it had since fallen into oblivion. Suddenly it became the focus of worldwide attention when twentieth century explorers learned of the priceless relics to be found there. A sensational discovery was made on May 26, 1900, when Taoist monk Wang Yuanlu of the Mogao Grottoes was digging away the sand silt in the cave to finish his regular clean-up of the grotto, of which he was the care-taker. Unexpectedly, he discovered that there was another sealed cave at one end of the tunnel which led to the No. 16 Cave of the Mogao Grottoes. Plaster on the tunnel wall had partly peeled off, exposing the hidden door to the sealed cave. When Wang opened it, he was stunned at the sight of a "treasure house," which was fully packed with colourful ancient relics, including scriptures, classic books, silk embroideries and paintings.

Situated on the eastern cliff of Mount Mingsha, 25 kilometres to the southeast of the county seat of Dunhuang, the Mogao Grottoes were composed of a group of stone caves—arranged in five vertical tiers—on the face of the cliff. Also called the Thousand-Buddha Caves, these grottoes were, indeed, the treasure house of arts, remarkable for their unique architecture and their rich contents of valuable paintings and sculptures. In the beginning, Wang's surprising discovery of the hidden Scripture Cave had only attracted the attention of a few elite Chinese scholars. Ye Changzhi, who was the Qing Dynasty's Education Commissioner of Gansu in 1902, managed to obtain a few pieces of the relics found in the Scripture Cave from the Dunhuang County's magistrate. He made a record of these relics later in his book *Yu Shi*. The Qing government, two years after the discovery, ordered Wang Zonghan, the Dunhuang County's magistrate, to make a careful registration of the scriptures, classics and paintings found in the cave, with the help of the Taoist monk Wang Yuanlu. The historic value of these rare relics had then apparently aroused the attention of the Qing authorities, who were, nevertheless, unable to find a safer place to store them, due to limited funding.

And so the priceless relics remained in the Mogao Grottoes' newly-discovered Scripture Cave (Cave No. 17), under the care of their finder Wang Yuanlu—until the arrival from Europe in 1907 of Mark Aurel Stein (1862-1943). Stein, who was one of the first Western explores to visit Dunhuang Grottoes, managed to take away from the cave depository 29 boxes of ancient relics, including scriptures, classics, scrolls, murals, fabrics and printed manuscripts—by paying a small amount of silver to the Taoist monk Wang Yuanlu. The spectacular discoveries of Dunhuang

Grottoes thus became a worldwide sensational event, which was acclaimed as a great achievement of archaeology in the twentieth century. While Stein should be credited with the remarkable "large-scale looting" of the the ancient relics from the Dunhuang Grottoes, it was inconsistent with historical facts to acclaim him as the discoverer of the "archaeological value" of the Dunhuang relics, because these relics had already caught the attention of Chinese scholars and their government long before Stein's arrival at the Dunhuang Grottoes.

In fact, history had proved that Aurel Stein—who was seen by some people as the "founder of Dunhuang Science"—was not even the first "thief" of the Dunhuang relics. According to the Moscow 1963 publication of the collections of Chinese Dunhuang relics preserved in the Asian Nationality Research Institute under the Soviet Union's Academy of Sciences, V. A. Obrucheff, a member of the Russian exploratory team in the Pamirs, went to Dunhuang in October 1905—soon after he heard of the new cave discoveries—and traded "some cheap Russian commodities" for a large amount of valuable Chinese ancient scriptures, classics and other relics, in a deal with the caretaker Wang Yuanlu. This story was told in the foreword of the first volume of the contents (in Chinese) of the collections, indicating clearly that another Western explorer had visited the Dunhuang cave and carried away ancient Chinese relics before Aurel Stein came to call on the Chinese Taoist monk Wang Yuanlu in 1907.

The fame of the Thousand-Buddha Cave in Dunhuang had long since been known in academic circles in Europe, where many scholars had looked on it as another ancient cultural wonder—as magnificent and mysterious as the Gandhara art in present northwestern Pakistan. The Hungarian orientalist Béla Széchenyi paid his visit to this "Chinese Gandhara" in 1879. In 1880, during his third tour of Central Asia, the Russian explorer N. M. Prjivalsky visited Dunhuang's Thousand-Buddha Cave. In 1899, the Frenchman Charles Etudes Bonin left Beijing for an exploration in Central Asia; he arrived at the Thousand-Buddha Caves in Dunhuang in 1900 and took away four woodcut pictures which he tore from an ancient book there. Since that was the very year that

Wang Yuanlu first discovered the Scripture Cave in the Mogao Grottoes, Bonin probably got the woodcut pictures from Wang.

In 1902, after Aurel Stein had returned to his home from his first exploratory trip to Central Asia, his old Hungarian friend Professor L. de Loczy, who was then president of the Hungarian Geographic Society, suggested that Stein should pay special attention to the art treasure of Dunhuang during his next trip to Asia. As a member of an exploratory team led by Béla Széchenyi, Loczy had been to China before. Three years later, Stein departed on April 2 from Srinagar of Kashmir to start his second exploration of Central Asia, determined to gather and excavate ancient relics in northwest China. The exploration was financed entirely by Britain, with the British-Indian government paying 60 per cent and the British Museum paying the rest of the expenses—on the condition that part of the collected art pieces or relics should be given to them as compensation. Stein achieved spectacular success during his second exploration, which included his large-scale looting of the ancient Chinese classics and relics from the Dunhuang Grottoes.

When Stein first arrived at the Mogao Grottoes of Dunhuang, he was dazzled by the myriads of inscriptions and murals in the numerous stone caves there. He was amazed to find that those ancient murals, dateable from the sixth century, were still preserved in perfect condition in the caves, despite the harsh climate of the desert. He decided to carry out a detailed study of Dunhuang Grottoes, and stayed there for three months, during which time he scored a major achievement by learning the secret of the Scripture Cave from the Taoist monk Wang Yuanlu. Through his Chinese interpreter, Stein succeeded in persuading Wang to open the hidden cave of treasures for him. There he saw stacks of ancient handwritten scriptures tied in bundles, and piled to a height of three metres in the stone chamber. These ancient books, which had been lying undisturbed through the centuries, were now brought before the foreign explorer by the Chinese caretaker, for the curious Stein to examine carefully. Sitting in a small room nearby the hidden cave, Stein was amazed by the colourful ancient pictures painted on paper, silk or brocade; the embroidered banners and portraits contained in the bundles which, to his surprise, further displayed countless sheets and volumes of Chinese scripts, letters, account books and Buddhist scriptures. Some of these were written in other languages, including Sanskrit, Tibetan, Uighur, Turkic and even some Manichean scripture written in Syrian. The contents of these relics indicated that they had been hidden in the secret cave for 1,000 years. Stein was overjoyed to think that he was the first explorer to discover the truth of the hidden Scripture Cave in the Dunhuang Grottoes.

It had cost Aurel Stein only 40 silver pieces (then equivalent to some 5,000 rupees) to make Wang Yuanlu let him take away 24 boxes of scriptures plus five boxes of paintings, which were carefully selected by him from among the ancient relics. Then, when Stein revisited Dunhuang seven years later in 1914, in the wake of earlier visits to the Scripture Cave by French and Japanese explorers, he again collected five boxes of ancient relics from among those left over by the French and Japanese looters, saying that he was buying them on behalf of the British Museum. Thus, Aurel Stein had taken more than 10,000 ancient relics from the Dunhuang Scripture Cave, including some 8,000 pieces of Chinese classics and scriptures and more than 2,000 Tibetan scriptures and other literatures plus numerous pictures, paintings on silk and paper and embroideries.

Paul Pelliot (1878-1945), the French Sinologist, visited Dunhuang in 1908, only months after Aurel Stein had returned to Srinagar, by way of Xinjiang, from his first exploratory trip to the Mogao Grottoes of Dunhuang in June 1907. Pelliot went into the hidden cave and looked through the remaining relics there, with "the eyes of an expert," and picked out more than 5,000 volumes of literature—including 2,000 volumes in Tibetan language—plus a number of classic Chinese paintings on silk and paper, and had them shipped away in boxes, just as Aureal Stein had done before him. These priceless relics found their way into the museum of Paris. Pelliot had made many friends in Beijing, but what he had done became known to the Chinese public and it caused indignation among the country's officials and scholars, who urged the government to take measures to protect national treasures from theft by foreign explorers.

The French explorer was followed by his Japanese counterpart Tachibana, who started his second trip to Central Asia in August 1910, and travelled on from Xinjiang to Dunhuang, where he was joined by another Japanese explorer Koichiro Yoshikawa. Together the two Japanese visitors bought some 300 volumes of the Chinese ancient scriptures from the Taoist monk at the Dunhuang Grottoes, and carried them away to Japan in January 1912.

Next came in 1914 the Russian adventurer S. F. Oldenburg, who succeeded in carrying away some 3,000 volumes of ancient scriptures, in addition to a number of murals he had removed from the Dunhuang Grottoes. Like his predecessor V. A. Obrucheff, Oldenburg hid his lootings in Petersburg, and never displayed them in public.

In 1910, the Qing government finally issued an order to ship all the remaining relics in the Scripture Cave of Dunhuang to Beijing for preservation in the Capital Library. More were lost in the process, and only 8,600 volumes actually reached the library in Beijing. Through years of efforts to recover the lost relics, the Beijing Library (the Capital Library) eventually registered a total collection of 10,000 volumes of ancient scriptures, originating from the hidden Scripture Cave of Dunhuang. However, this was but one fifth of all the ancient scriptures and relics discovered by Wang Yuanlu. And of the 40,000 volumes of Dunhuang scriptures scattered in other parts of the world today, about 50 per cent were kept in the museums in London and Paris, according to a recent study.

4. Havoc in the Art Caves of Xinjiang Grottoe

Since January 1896, when Sven Hedin first discovered ancient ruins underground in the desert of Tarim Basin and near the Hotan River of Xinjiang, a great variety of ancient relics had been unearthed. These successive discoveries served to reinforce the image of ancient culture in the Xinjiang area, and further spurred an influx of foreigners to explore in the region. In 1900, Aurel Stein, the British explorer, set out from Srinagar in Kashmir to Xinjiang, by way of the Pamirs, in his first visit to the area. After a large-scale excavation in the ancient Hotan area, Stein had unearthed for the first time in history, symbols of the ancient language of Hotan; they were in the form of written scripts in Brahmin, and wooden scripts in Kharosthi letters. Further discoveries of clay sculptures, wooden pictures, engraved wooden decors and paintings, dateable from the third to the eighth centuries, proved that close links existed between the ancient culture of Hotan and the Buddhist and Hellenic arts of northwest India. The discoveries indicated that Hotan could have been another centre of Indo-Greco arts located to the north of the Himalayas. Following Aurel Stein, more British, German, French, Japanese and Russian explorers flocked into Xinjiang and the Hexi Corridor area of Gansu during the decade, plundering both places of the underground and cave deposits of ancient relics that had remained undisturbed for more than a thousand years.

The large volume of Chinese ancient scriptures and relics on display today in the museums of London, Paris, Berlin, Tokyo and Petersburg had been brought there by the foreign travellers or explorers, who had secretly shipped these priceless relics from China to their home countries. The worst case of such relic-theft was the removal of the precious ancient murals from cave walls by the German explorers, who designed a special technique for the purpose. In 1902, a year after the discovery of the Loulan ruins in Xinjiang, a German exploratory team, led by A. Grünwedel, was sent by the Berlin Ethnological Museum to excavate the Idikutschari ruins in Turpan of Xinjiang. The ruins of Idikutschari or Karakhotcho indicate that it had been the capital of the ancient Gaochang Kingdom in the fifth century. The second German exploratory team, led by A. Von Le Coq, visited the area again in 1904 and this time took many ancient Turpan scriptures, including scriptures written in Tocharian and Turkic, cave murals from Turpan and sculptures from Kuqa area—all of which were shipped to Berlin. Le Coq developed the technique for removing murals from cave walls. Using adhesive tape and scissors, he peeled the murals from the ancient temple walls at Murtuq, Bazakliq and Karakhotcho in Turpan. Some of the murals were destroyed in the process. Having finished his job at Turpan, Le Coq was ready to move on to Dunhuang to carry on his mural theft when he received orders to join the third German exploratory team, led by A. Grünwedel, in Kaxgar. From Kaxgar, Le Coq returned to Germany with his loot, by way of Karakorum and India, while A. Grünwedel continued his exploration in China until 1907. These two German teams, led by Le Coq and Grünwedel, had been responsible for the unprecedented looting of the grottoe arts of Xinjiang—an atrocity that caused profound resentment of every Chinese. As a result of these two "explorations," the cave murals of Turpan, the Buddha statues of Kizir Grottoe and the famous coloured Buddha sculptures of the Qilin Cave of Baicheng were removed from Xinjiang to Berlin.

The big coup of the German explorers in Xinjiang further prompted Aurel Stein, Tachibana and others to revisit the region, time after time, searching and excavating the grottoes, ancient tombs or ruins found in the area. Their unearthed objects later became exhibits in the museums of Europe and Japan. The Americans came a little later in 1923, when L. Warner, the Oriental Department curator of the Fogg Museum of Art in Harvard University, visited Dunhuang Grottoes, where he succeeded in peeling off some two dozens of ancient cave murals from inside the grottoes—by using cloth and glue—and carried them over a long journey of 18 weeks, back to Harvard University in Cambridge, Massachusetts. In his book, entitled *The Long Old Road in China*, Warner gave an account of his inglorious adventure in China.

The unscrupulous looting of China's ancient relics by foreign explorers and researchers provoked national concern after the country was reunited in the wake of years of internal strife. In 1925, the people of Dunhuang succeeded in stopping Warner's plan of peeling off all the remaining cave murals in the grottoes. Then, in May 1930, when Aurel Stein came to Nanjing to begin his proposed fourth exploration in Central Asia, the strong objection raised by Chinese patriotic circles foiled his plan to launch yet another looting of China's hidden ancient treasures. His fourth expedition to Central Asia never materialized.

II   The May Fourth Literary Revolution and
the Tide of Social Revolution

1.   The New Literature Movement and the Western Literature

The Revolution of 1911 had not only resulted in the over-throw of the feudal dynasty and a crushing defeat of all attempts to restore monarchy in the country, but also dramatized the need for an in-depth cultural revolution to enable the people to be mentally prepared for a new political system and modern think-ing. Soon, a heated debate on the cultural controversy between the East and the West erupted between the *New Youth* magazine and the *Orient* magazine in 1915, thus unfolding the inevitable China's New Culture Movement, which reflected the desire of Chinese people to seek their own unique approach to realizing cultural modernization.

New Youth first published Chen Duxiu's articles challenging Chinese traditional culture, provoking strong opposition from such defenders of the "quintessence of Chinese culture" as Du Yaquan and Gu Hongming, as well as other "old guards" of Confucianism. As a leader in the New Culture Movement, Chen Duxiu first called for introduction of science and democracy to reform Chinese traditional culture, criticizing the authority of the country's ancient heritage for its lack of scientific attitude and democratic spirit. Such calls became the theme of the ensuing May Fourth Movement in 1919. Pioneers of the May Fourth Movement formally broke with the "heritage of tradition," adopt-ing the slogan "Down with Confucianism." They initiated the national drive to replace blind submission to medieval rites with respect for modern science, and substitute obsolete autocratic rule with new democracy.

Once the cultural revolution was on the move, the denuncia-tion against traditional culture began to turn from ethical and moral concepts to literature. In January 1917, the *New Youth* published an article by Hu Shih who was studying in the United States, proposing a reform of the Chinese literature. Such a reform, according to Hu, should focus on eight points: 1. No more empty talk, 2. No more copying of classics, 3. No more ignorance of grammar, 4. No more aimless "complaints," 5. No more cliches, 6. No more literary quotations, 7. No more emphasis on antithesis, and 8. No more shunning of vernaculars. Well educated in Western literature, philosophy and logic, Hu Shih had proposed such points as the primary targets in reforming the obsolete "eight-legged essays" and classic literary style favoured by the old-fashioned Chinese writers. A month after Hu Shih published his article in *New Youth* in February the same year, the magazine released yet another article written by the more radical Chen Duxiu, then studying in Japan, calling for a "literary revolution." In his article, Chen openly urged Chinese writers to: 1. Replace rhetorical and eulogistic aristocratic literature with simple and lyrical people's literature; 2. Replace obsole.e and exaggerated classic literature with fresh and sincere realistic literature; and 3. Replace pedantic and obscure hermit literature with straightforward and popular social literature. In the spring of 1918, Hu Shih, having returned from the United States, published an article entitled "On the Constructive Literary Revolution," calling for the introduction of a "living literature" (vernacular literature) and "truthful literature" (realistic literature). Thus, a literary revolution, initiated by Hu Shih and Chen Duxiu, led to the swift development of a translation-based vernacular literature, which first emerged after the inception of the twentieth century. During the early phase of the translated-literature in China, Lin Shu, who did not understand English himself, but had started translating English novels since 1899 with the help of a bilingual assistant, finished as many as 180 books of translation over a period of more than 20 years, all written in classical Chinese. Some other translators, such as Zhou Guisheng, initiated translation of Western literature in vernacular Chinese. However, Zhou's translations were mainly detective novels, with little value as literature. Another early translator was Su Manshu, who was known for his translation of the works of Victor Hugo and George Byron, had played a unique role in the development of modern Chinese literature before the Revolution of 1911. New novels and poems, written in vernacular Chinese, began to mushroom in

China, absorbing the style of the Western literature, in the wake
of the open call for a "literary revolution" by Chen Duxiu. More
serious translated works also began to emerge in vernacular
Chinese, which were done by such outstanding writers as Hu
Shih, Zhou Zuoren, Lu Xun and Liu Dabai, whose own literary
compositions were also deeply influenced by the Western literary
style. Meanwhile, many Japanese translations of Western literature had also served as an important channel for introducing the
Western literature to the Chinese writers. In June 1918, *New
Youth* published a special issue on the "Works of Henrik Ibsen,"
which contained the translation of Ibsen's *A Doll's House*, jointly
done by Hu Shih and Luo Jialun. The translation set an example
of realism in literature through the introduction of Ibsen's works,
and stimulated interest in sponsoring an ethical revolution in
China.

Introduction of vernacular literature brought criticism from
the classic writers, notably strong opposition voiced by Lin Shu
in his letter addressed to Cai Yuanpei, then president of Beijing
University, in 1919. In his letter of reply, Cai rebuked Lin's
criticism, pointing out that Western literature was originally
written in the vernacular, and that translations by Lin Shu and
Yan Fu—in classic Chinese—were "not, in anyway, an improvement of the original work." Cai further quoted, in his letter,
paragraphs from Lin's translations of the works of Alexandre
Dumas (Dumas fils), Charles Dickens and Thomas Hardy to
prove his point that the classic Chinese verses used by Lin in his
translations "could not correctly reflect the ideas of the originals."
While the use of classic Chinese had soon receded from the scene
of Chinese literature, it continued to exist along with the vernacular versions in the other publications, including those of philosophy, history, political science, law and journalism—for as long
as another 30 years.

In 1920, China's first literary organization, the Literary Research Society, was founded in Shanghai; since then, a number
of similar organizations, such as Creation Society, New Moon
Society, Wilderness Society and the Sun Society emerged, one
after another. Members of these literary groups were usually

engaged in both writing and translation works. And since most of them had been influenced, directly or indirectly, by Western literature, their own writings were often marked by Western styles in both structure and expression or the use of Western historical quotes. However, each of these organizations advocated a particular genre of their own. For example, the Literary Research Society upheld realism, the Creation Society eulogized romanticism, the Sun Society followed the line of Left-wing writers and warmly applauded "proletarian literature." The modernist poets were, however, seen as pursuing the writing styles of the Western symbolists.

The growth of new Chinese poetry—in a major departure from the centuries-old tradition of the classical Chinese poetry —stood out as an example of a full-scale adoption of the Western style in one sector of the Chinese literature. Such cases were seen in the free-style poems of the Creation Society poets, the stress on rhymes by the New Moon Society poets, and in the individual Chinese poets' absorption of the English sonnet, the French triolet and villanelle in their own compositions. And once the Western style of poem writing appeared in their Chinese forms, they became Sinicized in their expression. An exception was the translation of *Rubaiyat*—originally a poem written by the Persian poet and astronomer Omar Khayyam by the Chinese scholar Guo Moruo in four-lined stanzas, which, as a modern conversion of the traditional style of classic Chinese poems, also attracted the attention of the literary circles.

On the other hand, Lu Xun, a leading figure in the New Cultural Movement, was influenced by the thinkings of a number of European authors, especially such Russian realist writers as Nikolai Gogol, Anton Chekhov, Leonid Andreev and others. Lu Xun was credited with translating nearly 30 foreign literary works, many of which were written by writers of Russia or of other poor and oppressed nations. The new literature after the May Fourth Movement had absorbed mainly Western literature that reflected struggles for national independence and social progress. These subjects also constituted the bulk of the Chinese translation works during that period.

2. The Choice of the Socialist Ideology

As forerunners of the May Fourth Movement launched their challenge to Chinese traditional culture inspired by Western thinking, socialism was emerging as an important modern ideology, introduced to China along with other Western thought. Following the outbreak of the World War I, the European capitalist countries were in serious trouble, signalling a decline of the Western civilization; all these had made the socialist ideology all the more attractive to the Chinese pioneers of the New Cultural Movement.

Then, as socialism became popular among the Chinese thinkers during the May Fourth era, the new ideological trend was soon split into a myriad of different factions.

The anarchist theories of Russian Prince Pëtr Kropotkin (1842-1921), marked by his "mutualism," became popular for a while among the Chinese intellectuals. Believers of his theories held that the human race could evolve into the communist society of "to each according to his need," once they practised the doctrine of "mutualism." The trace of such thought was found even in the essay "Class Struggle and Mutual Aid," written by the veteran Chinese Marxist Li Dazhao in July 1919.

Also popular was "pan-labourism" initiated by Leo Tolstoy (1828-1910), which introduced the ideal of popular education through work-study programmes. This thought was the principle advocated by the *Labour* monthly with Wu Zhihui as its chief editor; it was, however, published for only five months—from March to July, 1918. The publication of this magazine marked the increasing importance attached by the Chinese intellectuals to the role of labour following the May Fourth Movement, when they began to write more articles to introduce the government of the working class in Russia.

There was also extensive response among Chinese intellectuals to the "new village" theory sponsored by the Japanese writer Saneatsu Mushanokoji (1885-1976), through his *White Birch* magazine published in Tokyo. In December 1918, Japanese "new village" idealists acquired a tract of some three hectares of land in the beach of Nikko in Kyushu, where the 22 idealists built their first "new village" of three houses, and started an idyllic life. They had "no government, no exploitation, no power of authority, no oppression, and no difference between mental and physical labour." Such an example was soon imitated by a Chinese intellectual Wang Guangqi, the executive director of the Chinese Youngster Study Society, who designed an intellectual mutual-aid organization called Work-Study Mutual-Aid Group, which worked for creating an "urban new village" for the intellectuals to work, read and translate together, under mutual aid.

At the end of 1919, the Work-Study Mutual-Aid Group was formally established, with some three dozen members divided into three squads. This was followed by the drafting of a programme to set up such organizations across the whole country. The Mutual-Aid Work-Study Movement spread among the Chinese intellectuals who believed in the "ideal society," in which, "everyone works, studies and are paid according to their need."

These idealists were unaware that such an imaginary or "utopian" society was but the illusion of people living in an underdeveloped economic system. And so the Work-Study Mutual-Aid Group specified the work and study hours and the compensation for each member, down to their miscellaneous needs such as spectacles and shoe-polish. However, such an experimental communism-style mini-society was unable to overcome the economic difficulty resulting from their failure to be truly "self-sufficient." The Work-Study Mutual-Aid Group, which was originally designed as a combination of cooperationism, "new village" theory and the pan-labourism, existed in Beijing for only three months. Similar groups in other cities also closed down, one after another, before the end of 1920. The failure of such an experiment taught the country's "socialist dreamers" that they had to be realistic and serious in considering the approach to realizing their ideals of communism.

It was the powerful impact of the October Revolution in Russia that awakened China's progressive intellectuals to the truth of Marxism, and turned many of them into Marxists. One of them, Professor Li Dazhao of Beijing University, published several essays in 1918 and 1919 to analyze the world situation after the October Revolution, and raised the question of reconsidering the road of China's social revolution, according to the experience of the Russian proletarian revolution. These views were stated in Li's "Triumph of the Common People," "The Victory of Bolshevism," "Youth and Rural Villages" and other essays written during this period. Another leading intellectual, Chen Duxiu, perceived that a society would evolve along the course of "from feudalism to republic, then from republic to socialism." In his view, not only the republic would give place to socialism, but—based on the experience of the Russian revolution —even an underdeveloped feudal society could leap into socialism through revolution, as shown in the example of "Russia's shortlived republic being replaced by socialism, only six months after it had overthrown feudalism." Similarly, Li Dazhao also pointed out, in his "The Fundamental Difference Between the East and West Civilizations," that the Western Marxism would, as a result of the success of the Russian October Revolution, "become the new trend of world thought and give rise to a gigantic change in world civilization."

The failure of the Work-Study Mutual-Aid Group and the success of the Russian October Revolution caused the progressive Chinese intellectuals to rally around the revolutionary calls of the *New Youth* and the *Weekly Review*, evolving into a fervent mass pursuit of the ideal of scientific socialism. The *Weekly Review* published in 1919 a translation of excerpts from the *Communist Manifesto*, written in 1848 by Karl Marx and Friedrich Engels; despite its short text of only some 1,000 Chinese characters, it was the first ever introduction of the works of Karl Marx to China's reading public. The next year, the forerunners of China's New Culture Movement and its earliest advocates of Marxism organized a "Marxist Theory Research Society" and formed the first Communist Group in Beijing. At the same time, groups of young Marxist activists began to emerge from among the Chinese students studying in France and Japan. Then, in July of 1921, the Chinese Communist Party was formally founded as the party of

China's proletariat. A complete Chinese translation of the *Communist Manifesto*, from its Japanese translated version, was published—just before the founding of the Chinese Communist Party —by the Shanghai Socialist Research Society. Since then, more and more Marxist literature was translated and published in China, leading to a widespread introduction of the ideology of scientific socialism in the country through the upcoming decades.

The New Culture Movement, which resulted from the May Fourth 1919, had started as an anti-feudalist campaign focusing on the cause of democracy, science and vernacular literature. But it had, in a matter of months, developed into an anti-imperialist movement, introducing Marxist theory, Russian revolutionary experience and the proletarian revolutionary literature in China. In fact, the New Culture Movement had grown from an all-out camapign against feudalism into a powerful tidal wave of socialism, which closely followed the ideological trend of the world to guide China's intellectual community in their quest of a modern culture to serve the need of social revolution.

3. China's New Art Movement

China's art sector, particularly, its disciplines of fine arts and music, were the first to see marked departures from the traditional culture, as a result of the influence of Westernized reforms in the education system and the emergence of modern schools.

The mission schools, in their musical lessons, used Western piano, pipe organ and staff to teach the students hymns, which were first published in Shanghai by the Meihua Press in an edition called "Holy Hymns Music" in 1872. After the turn of the century, Western music and musical instruments became more popular in China's coastal areas, and the Chinese musicians began to translate various kinds of piano or reed organ études from Japanese publications. In 1919, the first *Organ Textbook* written by a Chinese musician was published. Lessons on vocal music started in the schools during the last years of the Qing Dynasty; since then, the use of numbered musical notations became fashionable among music students.

In the wake of the Revolution of 1911, Western travelling

music theatres from Russia, Britain and Italy visited China and gave concerts in such cities as Beijing, Shanghai and Harbin, to perform Western operas, vocal and instrumental music before Chinese audiences. The founding of China's own music organization was first sponsored by Chinese students in Tokyo and Yokohama of Japan. In 1914, the "Sino-Western Music Society" was founded in Beijing, as the first Western music group to emerge in the country with the intent of reforming Chinese traditional theatre music by introducing Western skills. The celebrated Chinese educator Cai Yuanpei was known for his keen interest in and important contribution to promoting the education of music and art "to substitute religious education." Believing that education of art and music could help cultivate the fine qualities of human character and disposition, Cai was responsible for a marked enhancement of art and music education in China during this period. Several organizations were set up by leading Chinese educators to introduce Western music and art teaching to this country; these included the Beijing University Music Research Society, sponsored by Cai Yuanpei, and the China Art Education Association, founded in Shanghai, by Wu Mengfei and Feng Zikai.

Another Chinese educator, who had made a significant contribution to the composition and education of Western-style music in China, was Xiao Youmei (1884-1940). Xiao went first to study piano in Japan in 1901, and then went on to study music theories in the Leipzig Music Conservatory of Germany, before returning to China in 1920. After his return, Xiao had taught music in the universities in Beijing, then Shanghai, where he was responsible for setting the pace of the Chinese modern music and training a large number of young music talents, who later became China's leading modern music composers. In 1927, Xiao established China's first music institute, the National Conservatory of Music, which was subsequently re-named the National School of Music; and Xiao served as its president for many years. Also noted for his music achievement was Wang Guangqi, who went to study music in Germany in 1920, and earned the degree of Doctor of Music at Berlin University for his dissertation on "The

Operas of Ancient China." Wang contributed significantly to the introduction of Western music to China and the reform of Chinese traditional music. He was known for his study on the comparison of Chinese and Western music as shown in his report of "The Study on the Structure of Oriental and Western Music."

Many of Wang's works served in the exchange of music between China and the West, by opening "the window of Chinese music" to the Europeans; they also symbolized his effort in music reform by conducting a theoretical research on the Chinese traditional music. Both Xiao and Wang were marked for their Westernized orientation; but neither of them took a negative view towards Chinese traditional music. In fact, they both advocated a simultaneous development of traditional and modern music, which eventually became the fundamental guideline of the Chinese music circles.

Meanwhile, Western fine arts first became part of the school curriculum in China during the last years of the Qing Dynasty, when painting lessons were initiated by Japanese teachers at the Liangjiang Teachers Institute in Nanjing and the Beiyang Normal Institute in Tianjin. In 1912, Chinese artist Liu Haisu founded China's first school of fine arts, the Shanghai Academy of Fine Arts, which was later re-named the Shanghai Training School of Fine Arts. Liu, who served as its president, introduced—for the first time in China—the use of nude models in painting of human figures. Liu, a master of both Chinese traditional painting and European oil painting, was known as an "art rebel" for his arbitrary art style, a style between romanticism and impressionism. Another talented Chinese artist was the realist painter Xu Beihong (1895-1953), who was noted for both his Chinese and Western works of fine arts. He was also the first Chinese artist to exhibit his works in the Salon des Artistes Francais in France. After returning from France, Xu taught fine arts courses in Beijing and Nanjing, where he served as the head of the Central University's Art Department. During this period, he was responsible for selecting many talented Chinese art students to study abroad, and holding Chinese modern fine arts exhibitions in France and Germany.

In 1928, the National West Lake Art Institute was founded in Hangzhou, and Lin Fengmian—a Chinese artist known for his pro-French-impressionist art style—was appointed as its president, who then openly called for "creating an epoch-making art by integrating the Chinese and Western arts." It was at this time that several Chinese traditional painters, who were then studying in Japan, created some new art style in Chinese painting by absorbing the Western painting skills.

Apart from fine arts and music, the Western-style performing art—the modern drama—was also introduced to the Chinese stage. These dramatic performances, which featured a certain theme expressed through the dialogue between players, were different from the traditional Chinese theatrical performances marked by singing, dancing and sometimes martial art displays. *La Dame aux camélias* by Alexandre Dumas was the first modern drama staged by the Chunliu Drama Club, organized in 1907 by Chinese students studying in Japan. Their second performance was the drama of *Uncle Tom's Cabin* by Harriet Stowe, which was such a success that the performance continued in the theatre, through the winter of 1907 till the spring of 1908.

In Shanghai, the modern drama emerged in a more localized style called Civilized Drama, which featured domestic revolutionary themes, with the players wearing modern clothing and talking in vernacular on the stage. Such dramas became popular since it was first introduced in 1906 by the Wenyou Club. In 1914 the cub joined with the Chunliu Drama Club to form the Chunliu Theatre in Shanghai, which then presented a series of Western dramas, including *La Dame aux camélias* by Alexandre Dumas, *Resurrection* by Leo Tolstoy and *A Doll's House* by Henrik Ibsen on the Chinese stage. In later years, the vernacular Civilized Drama gradually developed into vulgarized comedies and became completely separated from the modern dramas.

In north China, meanwhile, modern drama was introduced by the students' drama club of Tianjin's Nankai College. The club, named "Nankai Modern Drama Troupe," was best known for its performance of Henrik Ibsen's *An Enemy of the People*. In 1923, modern drama was performed for the first time on the stage of Beijing, where both men and women performed the roles of their own sex—breaking the tradition of men acting as women in Beijing operas. The performance of modern dramas hit a climax in Shanghai, when Eugene O'Neill's *The Emperor Jones* was adapted into a Sinicized drama called *Zhao, the King of Hell* by Hong Shen who returned from the United States to present it at Shanghai's Xiaowutai Theatre. After that, the Chinese public became more and more familiar with the dramas of such popular Western authors as Henrik Ibsen and Oscar Wilde, as their works were frequently presented in theatres of both north and south China.

In 1930, a New Drama Campaign was launched in Shanghai by a number of Chinese dramatists, including Zheng Boqi and Yang Chunren, who staged dramas written by the French writer Romain Rolland and the American writer Upton Sinclair, attracting the attention of foreign press. Dramas of William Shakespeare and Anton Chekhov also appeared on the Chinese stage. However, as the country sank deeper into national crisis, more and more short dramas—marked with strong political themes—were produced. Certain liberal Western dramas, such as *The Storm* by the Russian dramatist Aleksandr Ostrovsky, enjoyed continued popularity throughout the War of Resistance Against Japan (1937-1945), after it was first presented in January 1937 in Shanghai. During the war years, it was the most popular drama performed by the New China Drama Club in the theatres of Guilin, Changsha and Kunming. In 1946, the first year after the anti-Japanese war, the performance of the drama *Night Inn* by the Russian writer Maxim Gorky in Shanghai was also a remarkable event.

4. Introduction and Translation of Western Literature

Since the May Fourth Movement, Western literature had been playing a catalytic role in promoting in China a literary revolution, which turned gradually into a movement of revolutionary literature. Many literary organizations had undertaken to introduce Western literature to this country. Mao Dun (Shen Yanbin), founder of the Literary Research Society, stated in his article—"The Responsibility and Endeavour of the New Literature Researchers" —that an important purpose to be achieved through the introduction of Western literature was to introduce to China modern thoughts in the world. Many Chinese translators of the progressive foreign literature—as represented by the famous Chinese writer Lu Xun—tried to absorb "food for thought" from the Western literary works to help enhancing the growth of China's new literature. Such desire was shared by most Chinese writers at that time.

(A) Literature of the Weak and Small Nations

Because many progressive Chinese writers were motivated by the desire to seek the awakening and liberation of the Chinese nation, they had set store by the translation of literature of the weak and small nations. They found their desire for national liberation was echoed in the works of the Polish, Bulgarian and Greek writers, whose nations suffered the same foreign oppression as China had. Lu Xun was noted for his early admiration for such Western poets and writers as Byron, Ibsen, Petöfi, Sienkiewicz, and Pushkin, who were distinguished for their pursuit of national independence and liberation of peoples. Byron was admired as much as Petöfi and Sienkiewicz, for his selfless dedication to the cause of Greek national liberation. The fact that Russian and the oppressed nation's literary works accounted for more than half of the translated stories contained in *A Collection of Out-of-Country Fictions* edited and translated in 1909 by Lu Xun and his brother Zhou Zuoren, also reflected such a tendency. Lu Xun had stated, in his autobiographic story "How I Became a Novelist," that his eyes turned to East Europe, including Russia, Poland and the small nations of Balkan Peninsula, because he was seeking for the "literature of struggle and resistance." It was the literature of these small oppressed nations and Russia that had served to shape Lu Xun's writing career just as they had guided the early Chinese literary translators to their brilliant achievement in the new literature movement.

In 1922, Lu Xun and Zhou Zuoren again cooperated in publishing *A Collection of Translated Modern Novels*, which contained 30 translated of foreign novels, written mostly by

Polish, Bulgarian and also the Russian writers Chekhov and Andreyev. The works of Polish writers Sienkiewicz and Mickiewicz had earlier been introduced to China, by both Lu Xun and other Chinese translators. The Chinese readers were, particularly, interested in the talented literary style of and the praise for "self-sacrifice" in the writings of Sienkiewicz, whose historic novel *Quo Yadis?* was also translated into Chinese in the 1920s in addition to *Yanko the Musician, The Lighthouse-Keeper* and others. And the celebrated verse of the Hungarian poet Petöfi —Life is a treasure, Love even dearer; But to win freedom I would throw both away!—had long since become the motto of many young Chinese intellectuals, and guided them to dedicate themselves to the cause of revolution.

Another popular collection of translated works was the *Tao Yuan (Peach Garden)*, edited and translated by Mao Dun, which contained the literature of nations under oppression. After 1940, more and more Polish and Bulgarian long novels or long poems were translated into Chinese.

(B) Works of the Renowned European Writers

In the years before the May Fourth Movement, *A Collection of Short Stories by Famous European and American Authors* in three volumes was translated by Zhou Shoujuan, in classic Chinese style resembling that of the old translator Lin Shu. The collection included stories written by English, French, American, German, Russian, Italian and many other Western authors.

During the new literature movement, most of the Western novels translated by Chinese writers were either English or French. The best known of these was Victor Hugo's *Notre Dame de Paris*, which had been translated into many Chinese versions, under different names. His other works, such as the *Quatre-vingt-treize* and *Hernani*, were also re-translated many times. The literary works of Alexandre Dumas and Guy de Maupassant were also very popular among Chinese readers, who were especially interested in the various Chinese translations of Maupassant's short stories, including *Ball of Fat* and *Necklace* which were as well-known in China as they were in France. His long novels, including *Bel Ami* and *Two Brothers*, had also been translated into Chinese.

To the Chinese readers, the works of Emile Zola, noted for his naturalist style, were even more attractive than those of Honoré de Balzac. In addition to his novels of *Germinal, Nana* and *L'Assommoir,* many of Zola's short stories had also been translated into Chinese. Other French writers, admired by Chinese readers included Alexandre Dumas ("Dumas pére"), Gustave Flaubert and Alphonse Daudet; Romain Rolland also became one of most favoured Western writers in China, for his outstanding pursuit of peace and progress.

The introduction of English literature to China took place at quite an early date; the literary works and unique styles of such English writers as Charles Dickens, John Galsworthy, Robert Louis Stevenson, and Thomas Hardy enjoyed lasting popularity among the Chinese readers. The name of Charles Dickens was as well-known in China as the translated stories of his *A Christmas Carol, The Pickwick Papers* and *David Copperfield.* John Galsworthy was first known in China, through the translation by Guo Moruo of his dramas, when the Creation Society of Chinese writers was first founded. The fascinating *Treasure Island* and *Strange Case of Dr. Jekyll and Mr. Hyde* made Robert Louis Stevenson one of the most admired Western writers in China's literary circles. Stories about his poor health, travelling life and creative talent were often featured in the Chinese literary journals. Thomas Hardy, for his part, was widely viewed as a leading pace-setter of realism by the Chinese writers; and his *Tess of the D'Urbervilles* and *The Return of the Native* were ranked with the most popular literature in China. Of the classic English writers, William Shakespeare commanded much respect in the Chinese literary and art circles. In addition to translation and publication of his complete works,—there were various translations of his *Romeo and Juliet, Hamlet* and *The Tempest.* The works of Shakespear had been chosen as an essential subject in the English literature courses of the Chinese universities.

Other English novels and short stories, such as Daniel Defoe's *Robinson Crusoe,* Jonathan Swift's *Gulliver's Travels* and the fables of Oscar Wilde or the stories of Charles Kingsley had all captured the interest of Chinese readers for their rich imagination and witty styles.

Bernard Shaw was popular among the Chinese progressive writers, who favoured his rebellious attitude against the social traditions, and so translated many of his dramas and essays into Chinese. Then, when the 77-year-old Shaw visited Shanghai in 1933—during his round-the-globe tour—he was warmly welcomed by the Chinese people who were impressed with his sincere advice to "Rely on yourselves for your own survival," offered during his brief visit.

The works of the celebrated German writers Johann von Goethe, Johann von Schiller and Heinrich Heine were introduced to China by the noted Chinese writer Guo Moruo, who was their ardent admirer. The well-known novel *Immensee* by Theodor Storm, another German author, was translated time and again into Chinese by domestic writers. Also popular among the Chinese readers were the works of Gerhart Hauptmann and Erich Remarque, whose *All Quiet on the Western Front* was one of the best-selling translated books and had been adapted for the stage. Chinese translators were also favourably impressed by the literary wit of the Austrian writer Stefan Zweig, whose historic novels and biographic literature, including the biography of Romain Rolland, had been translated into Chinese.

The translated works of many more Western writers—Italian Alighieri Dante (1265-1321), Belgian Maurice Maeterlinck (1862-1949), Norwegian Henrik Ibsen, Danish Hans Andersen, and Spanish Miguel de Cervantes and Vicente Blasco Ibanez —had been produced by Chinese writers and won acclaim of the domestic readers. Even more important was the fact that the brilliant wit, style and themes of these Western literary masters had greatly enhanced the creative capacity of the Chinese writers themselves, thereby further accelerating the growth of China's new literature.

(C) The Popular Russian Writers

The realism of Russian literature in the nineteenth century had much in common with the Chinese literature, in their social background and their quest for social reforms. The similar struggle against feudal shackles, anguish of the groping intellectuals and growing urge for social revolution all helped in tying them together, in the wake of the May Fourth Movement.

After the introduction in 1903 of works by such Russian literary masters as Aleksander Pushkin and Mikhail Lermontov, more Russian literary works written by Leo Tolstoy, Anton Chekhov, Maxim Gorky and Leonid Andreev were translated into Chinese—at first from translations in other language, then, directly from Russian originals after the May Fourth Movement in 1919. Much of the work was done by such veteran Chinese translators as Geng Jizhi and Qu Qiubai, who were the earliest Russian linguists in the country. In 1921, the Shanghai Gongxue Institute began publishing its *Russian Literature Series*, which included the works of Aleksander Pushkin, Nikolay Gogol, Ivan Turgenev and Leo Tolstoy; the first book in the series was Pushkin's *The Captain's Daughter*. Also published by the Gongxue Institute was the *Collection of Russian Dramas*, which comprised 10 volumes, including complete versions of *The Government Inspector* by Gogol, and The *Storm* by Aleksander Ostrovsky. The Shanghai magazine *Xiao Shuo Yue Bao* (*Short Story Monthly*), which was taken over by the Literary Research Society in 1921, published an extra issue of "Russian Literature Study," which presented, for the first time, introductory comments of the Chinese writers on Russian literature and authors —in addition to some selected translated Russian literary works —to the Chinese readers. These essays and commentaries were written by such noted Chinese writers as Zheng Zhenduo and Mao Dun.

Translations of Russian literature exceeded any other foreign literary works in China through the 30 years after 1921. Almost all the novels written by Ivan Turgenev and Feodor Dostoyevsky and most works by Leo Tolstoy were translated and published in Chinese. As a result, Chinese readers became well-acquainted with such fictitious characters as Pazalov in Turgenev's *Fathers and Sons*, Maslova in Tolstoy's *Resurrection*, Anna Karenina in Tolstoy's book of the same name, Oblomov in Ivan Goncharov's story and Chichikov in Gogol's drama. Many short stories written by Chekhov had been translated into Chinese, in a continuous series during the 1930s and 1940s, as part of a plan to publish his complete works in China.

Maxim Gorky, as an outstanding Russian writer who joined the 1917 October Revolution and laid the cornerstone for the new Soviet literature, naturally, became the model of China's progressive and pro-socialist writers. Since 1928, many new translations of Gorky's works, in vernacular Chinese, were done by Geng Jizhi, Qu Qiubai and Cao Qinghua, directly from the Russian originals. After Gorky's death in 1936, the six-volume *Selected Works of Maxim Gorky* was published in Shanghai, in addition to the translations of his separate works published in other parts of the country. Translations of the new Soviet literature flourished, following the popular drive to "learn from the Soviet Union," launched by China's art and literary circles after the 1930s. By the time war broke out between the Soviet Union and Germany, the volume of translated Soviet literature had topped translations of all other foreign literary works in China—the same way classic Russian literature had done in the wake of the May Fourth Movement.

(D) American Writers Known for Their Outspoken Praise for Democracy and Progress

American literature distinguished itself at a later stage in the Western world, but their two "pioneers"—Washington Irving and Mark Twain—were among the earliest American writers to attract the attention of the Chinese translators. Mark Twain's merciless ridicule of the American "democratic society" was matched with his satire for the new "Empire of Wealth," which aroused the interest of Chinese writers. *The Adventures of Tom Sawyer* and *The Gilded Age* were both best-sellers in China. Many of his other novels and short stories had also been translated and published by Chinese. The renowned American progressive writer Upton Sinclair was admired, especially, by Chinese writer Guo Moruo, who undertook to translate his works, *The Jungle*, *King Coal* and *Oil!* into Chinese. For some time, *King Coal* was viewed by Chinese literary critics as the symbol of proletarian literature in capitalist countries.

Among the progressive American poets, Walter Whitman had created considerable influence in the Chinese literary circles for his rugged and impassioned "celebration of democracy." His many works, such as *Leaves of Grass* and *Democratic Vistas* had been translated into Chinese, winning him more fame in China than his compatriot Henry Wadsworth Longfellow.

The works of American dramatist Eugene O'Neill were introduced to the Chinese readers soon after the May Fourth Movement; many of his dramas had since been absorbed into the repertoire of the Chinese drama circles.

Since the 1940s, modern American writers, such as Jack London, Ernest Hemingway, John Steinbeck and Theodore Dreiser became well-known to the Chinese readers, through the publication of many of their works in Chinese translations. Then, in March 1949, a collection of *American Literature Series* was published in Shanghai by a Sino-American joint venture, introducing the works of 18 American writers.

III The Widely-Circulated Theories of the Western Society

1. John Dewey and His Positive Philosophy

The May Fourth Movement, which touched off a widespread interest in science and democracy in China, also gave rise to the gradual intellectual trend, marked by an enthusiastic absorption of modern philosophical ideas from the Western world. The Chinese ideologists began to show a keen interest in the scientific approach of the Western philosophers, and they studied these Western ideas with eagerness and enthusiasm. The Chinese intellectuals were no longer satisfied with the theories of "social evolutionism," based on Darwin's "evolution by natural selection," but wanted to move forward in ideological research in response to the call for social progress.

Following the lead of American philosopher John Dewey, who came to lecture in China in 1919, British philosopher Bertrand Russell, German biologist Hans Driesch and Indian poet Rabindranath Tagore visited China to deliver lectures on their theories in Shanghai, Beijing and other cities. Introduction of their philosophical views and theories to Chinese audiences forged the link between the Chinese academic and cultural circles and their Western counterparts, and helped to draw Chinese culture closer to the West.

John Dewey (1859-1952) was remarkable for having influenced the Chinese intellectuals more than any other Western philosopher. The American philosopher stayed in China for more than two years, during which time, he gave lectures in Beijing. He also visited Fujian, Guangdong, Liaoning and Hebei provinces to introduce his pragmatic education theories to the local communities. Upon the request of Chinese scholar Hu Shih, who was his host in China, Dewey delivered major speeches in Beijing, under titles of "Philosophy of Education," "Groups of Thoughts," "The Three Modern Philosophers," "Speech on Ethics." His speeches were interpreted in Chinese by Hu Shih, who had been awarded a doctorate by Columbia University. These speeches were later printed and widely circulated in China. In his speech on "The Three Modern Philosophers," Dewey tried to introduce the ideas of Bertrand Russell, Henri Bergson, and William James to China. Then, when Bertrand Russell came to China in 1920, he also gave five major lectures in Beijing, focusing on his theories of mathematical logic, which were received enthusiastically by such Chinese scholars as Zhang Shenfu. The success of his lectures won him instant fame in China, and his mathematical logic became popular among Chinese scientists and philosophers. The works of Henri Bergson, through Dewey's introduction, were later translated into Chinese by Zhang Junli and Zhang Dongsun, and ranked among the best-read Western philosophic works in this country.

Dewey's theory of positivism, also translated as pragmatism, had been advocated wholeheartedly by Hu Shih as the scientific approach to education. Initiated by C.S. Peirce, the doctrine was first called "instrumentalism" and later developed by William James and John Dewey, before it was introduced to China, where it was known in the beginning as "experimentalism." Since the doctrine of pragmatism emphasized a "scientific approach to assessing situation" and advocated "testing truth by its practical consequences," it soon became known as the most scientific school of philosophy in China. Dewey was widely admired and respected by such leading Chinese scholars as Cai Yuanpei, Hu Shih and Jiang Menglin, during his stay in China. At a party held in Beijing to celebrate Dewey's 60th brithday, Cai, in his toast to the American philosopher, praised his success in "formulating philosophic theory on the basis of scientific achievements of the nineteenth century and the development of the positivism of Auguste Comet, the evolutionism of Charles Darwin and the pragmatism of William James." He added, "We dare say that his philosophy represents the new civilization of the Western world." The introduction of his principles to China had resulted in the emergence of a new school of philosophy, which was marked by the merging of pragmatism, experimentalism and positivism.

The philosophic ideas of John Dewey formed the root of the pragmatic philosophy of Hu Shih. And the theory of "education through experience of life" as advocated by John Dewey was, for quite some time, the popular mode upheld in Chinese education circles.

2. The Philosophies of Friedrich Wilhelm Nietzsche and Georg Wilhelm Friedrich Hegel

The German idealist philosophy, as represented by the theories of Immanuel Kant, Arthur Schopenhauer and Friedrich Nietzsche, was first introduced to China by their ardent Chinese admirer Wang Guowei, who was known as a leading researcher of history, archaeology and literature. However, Wang was so deeply influenced by the profound expression of pessimism in the philosophy of Schopenhauer, that he eventually sank into an irrevocable mental dilemma, then committed suicide in 1927 by drowning himself in a lake in Beijing.

The ideas of Friedrich Nietzsche (1844-1900), including that on the breeding of a new aristocracy or the "superman," was first introduced to China also through the effort of Wang Guowei. The basic content of Nietzsche's "superman philosophy" was formed on the basis of the positivism of Auguste Comte, the evolutionism of Darwin and the anthroposophy of Rudolf Steiner. According to the introduction by Wang Guowei, the philosophies of both Nietzsche and Schopenhauer had originated from the same doctrine. While they were also identical in the concept of "will is the key to reason" and the "denial of the existence of God," their only difference was shown in Nietzsche's "unscrupulous will to defy the authority." (See *Schopenhauer and Nietzsche* by Wang Guowei.)

The discussion of Nietzsche's philosophy reached a climax in 1920, when the Beijing-based *Minduo* magazine published a special issue on Nietzsche, which focused on the German philosopher's doctrine, related literature and his biography. His doctrine was also a point of debate among people of different political tendencies, during the 1930s and the 1940s in this country. In 1932, Chinese writer Gao Han translated Nietzsche's *Ecce Homo* into Chinese, and wrote an introductory prelude to his translation, praising Nietzsche's work as "a book from the sky"; Gao Han further compared the "superman philosopher" Nietzsche to the "decadent poet" Samuel Butler—in the same manner as Ivan Turgenev had once compared Don Quixote to Hamlet—and described the German thinker as a "rebel of the capitalist society" and a philosopher aspiring after a society of supermen. "To look at Nietzsche in this light will enable people to avoid underrating or over-exploiting Nietzsche's ideal, and help readers to refrain from viewing it from a biased or prejudiced angle," concluded the Chinese translator in his prelude.

The philosophy of Georg Wilhelm Hegel (1770-1831) was introduced to China, at almost the same time as that of Friedrich Nietzsche, amid a spate of criticism. The essence of Hegel's dialectical theory and philosophy of history was not correctly understood and appreciated in China until after 1927, when the philosophies of Marx, Engels and Lenin were extensively translated and introduced to this country. While his *Philosophy of History* had long since been translated into Chinese, an in-depth study on Hegel's theories began around the 1940s by Chinese scholar He Lin. The study on Hegel's "Logic" constituted the mainstay of subsequent research into and introduction of Hegel's philosophy by Chinese scholars. However, many domestic readers were interested in the German philosopher's comments on Chinese culture and its ancient sages, as contained in his book *Philosophy of History*.

3. Sociology and the Culturists

Sociology was a new discipline for the Chinese students, who had not begun looking into it until 1927—90 years after the science was formally established by the French philosopher Auguste Comte (1798-1857) in 1838. And it was a group of Chinese students in the University of Chicago, who first organized a forum on sociology to discuss the subject among themselves.

Of the various factions of sociology, the geologists and psychologists had little or no influence in China, while the culturists and biologists both enjoyed considerable following in the Chinese academic circles. In fact, the culturists held the respect of most Chinese sociologists, whose research into cultural sociology, national sociology and comparative sociology helped promote the study on ethnology and cultural sciences in China.

Sun Benwen, a returned Chinese student from the University of Chicago, was most remarkable in introducing culturist sociology to China. In 1927, the Beijing-based Pushe Press published his book *The Cultural Theories on Sociology*, in which Sun introduced the culturist theories of the American sociologists, especially the ideas of Frank Ward, as discussed in the book *Changes of Society* published in 1923. In it he attributes the changes in society to cultural changes as the principal factor. The American sociologist blamed cultural disharmony for many social problems, and stressed the need for the human community to adapt itself to the existing social culture. He covered up the objective need of cultural reform in today's world. The book *Theories of Sociology*, written by Sun Benwen himself, was also centred on a theoretical exploration of sociology from the culturist angle.

The introduction of comparative sociology in China was conducted by Chinese scholars, under the influence of the theories of the British functional anthropologist B. Malinowsky. The comparative sociology was first brought up by the Functionalists, who sought to find out the inner links between the different social phenomena. In 1936, the Chinese scholar Fei Xiaotong conducted a survey of Wujiang County's Jiangcun Village in Jiangsu Province. He then went to England and wrote his report "Peasant Life in China," under the tutorship of Professor Malinowsky. The report was widely acclaimed, winning Fei instant fame. Since then, the subject of rural survey in China had attracted worldwide interest. In 1939, Fei wrote a book *A Field Study of Country Life in the Yangtze Valley*. After his return to China, Fei undertook to organize a group of sociologists to carry out grassroots surveys and wrote their reports in English, and had them published in the United States. In his book *Rural China*, Fei offered an analytical study of the structure of the Chinese rural society.

4. Eugenics

Eugenics, as the subject of study by the socio-biologists, was first established as a discipline by the English scientist Francis Galton (1822-1911), through biological experiments and his research into the ancestry of the British upper class. Among the Chinese researchers of the subject, there was a group of scholars who advocated the theory of heredity as expounded by the Austrian botanist Gregor Mandel and American biologist Thomas Morgan, while there were also a number of academics—as represented by Professor Pan Guangdan—who studied eugenics wholely in the light of socio-biology.

In 1922, Pan Guangdan went to study in the United States, first at Dartmouth College, then at Columbia University, where he studied zoology, genetics, anthropology and eugenics. After returning to China, he taught eugenics and sociology in China's universities, and tried to introduce the American practice and theories on eugenic administration to China, in the hope of "improving China's ethnological quality."

The most remarkable achievement of Pan Guangdan was shown in his book, *A Study on the Consanguinity of the Chinese Opera Performers*, which summed up his research into the blood relationship of this unique stratum in the Chinese society—as was characterized by both their outstanding artistic talents and their traditionally deprecated status in the society. His research, conducted after the example of the *Hereditary Talents* written by Francis Galton, was an attempt to open a window in the study of eugenics in China's society, from the socio-biological angle. During the research, Pan conducted an analytical study of the ancestry and family trees of such famous Chinese Beijing Opera actors and actress as Mei Lanfang, Gao Shenglin, Ma Fulu, Ye Shenglan and Meng Xiaodong. His conclusion was that, for these people, as long as the health of both their parents were guaranteed, the I.Q. of their descendants would be above average.

Through the years, Pan Guangdan continued his lecturing on eugenics in the light of physical anthropology, ignoring the reality of social inequality between the different classes. His works were, therefore, introduced merely as theoretical study of eugenics in academic circles, but viewed as unfeasible ideas under the country's existing circumstances. Among his works was the book *Ethnic Character and Ethnic Health,* which introduced the theory of the American anthropogeographer Ellsworth Huntington's book *The Character of Races.* During the War of Resistance Agaisnt Japanese Aggression, Pan wrote the book *An Outline of Eugenics,* which was followed by his *Theory of Eugenics* published in 1949. Both these books, which were marked either by theories introduced from American publications, or an overstress on the effect of blood relationship, had little impact on China at a time when the country was in the process of a drastic social transformation.

5. Anthropogeography

In the wake of the May Fourth Movement, a large amount of anthropogeography literature was introduced to China, mainly, by the returned students, who then began to study and teach geography in an anthropographic light, viewing the geographic distribution of man as the basic factor which determines human relationship in a society. Numerous works on anthropogeography, "human geography," "cultural geography" and "relationship between man and geography" had since emerged in China's geographic circles, mostly expounding the theories as introduced by the American anthropogeographer Ellsworth Huntington in his *Theories on Human Geography* and the French anthropologer-geographer Jean Brunhes in his *Theories on Anthropography*. Both of these books had been translated into Chinese.

The book *The Effect of Geographic Environment* by the American geographer Ellen C. Semple was translated into Chinese in 1937, and her views were widely accepted by Chinese geographers. According to the American scholar, geography was but a discipline of "human ecology," which only allowed human beings to adapt themselves to the geographic environment, with little room of choice. The American geographer Isaiah Bowman's book *The New World: Problems in Political Geography*, which was translated and published in China in 1927, had been seen as an authoritative publication on world geography after the First World War. The predominant view among the Chinese geographers, then, was that the geographic environment determined the destiny of a nation and also the physical and cultural development of mankind. Many of these scholars had since written to analyze the poverty, backwardness and population problems of China in this light.

The American geographer Prof. Glass, who had taught at a university in Shanghai, was the author of *The Geographic Foundation of China* (1934) and *The Land and Man of Asia* (1944), both of which had been translated into Chinese and seen as valuable literature on the subjects. However, the American geographer claimed in his books that China had little deposits of the essential minerals, therefore not much hope of becoming industrialized. These biased views were proved to be unfounded by later developments.

6. The Culturist Trend of Comparative History

To interpret historical events in a subjective light had long since been a well-established stand of the Chinese historians. Theoretically, such a stand was based on the *Method of Historical Study* written by the German scholar E. Bernheim and translated into Chinese. The original version, revised and reprinted in 1908, was named *Textbook on Historic Method and Historic Philosophy*. Another book *An Introduction to the Study of History* written by two French scholars C.V. Langlois and Charles Seignobos in 1897 was also translated into Chinese and accepted by Chinese historians as their reference of research in the early twentieth century. Guided by these European theories, they accepted the method of "textual research plus comprehensive survey" as the scientific approach to historical research. However, their "comprehensive survey" was not aimed at studying the law of historic development, but at seeking the linkage of "cause and effect" in specific events. Such an approach had first been stated by the Chinese scholar Liang Qichao in his essay "On Method of Chinese Historic Research" published in 1921. It was subsequently expounded by He Bingsong in his *On Historic Research* (1927) and *New Concepts on General History* (1929). He Bingsong, like his German and French predecessors, held that historic developments followed no laws, because the human society and lifestyle kept changing so quickly that they could not possibly be governed by any law "which was based on generalization and repetition of the same pattern." His conclusion was, therefore, that since history would not repeat itself in a generalized pattern, it was impossible to find any law governing its development. Thus all a historian could possibly do was to conduct textual criticism and find out the linkage between various historic events.

He Bingsong's *New Concepts on General History* was actually compiled and translated from the French scholar Charles Seignobos' book, *Approach to Historic Research on Social Science* (1905), with a prelude by himself added to it. He Bingsong was also an exponent of *The New History* by the American scholar James Harvey Robinson who advocated historic pluralism and applied John Dewey's pragmatism to historic research, introducing such an approach in his *The New History*. The book was translated into Chinese by He Bingsong in 1923. Other books written by authors of the new history school were also introduced by He Bingsong and his colleagues as textbooks for Chinese university students. Two other American authors of the new history school, Charles A. Beard and his wife, were known for their works on "economic determination" and "historic relativi-ty"; their book, *The History of American Culture*, was used also as a university textbook in China.

Historic pluralism had eventually resulted in the introduction of the culturist approach to historic research. Such an approach was theorized by British historian Arnold Toynbee (1889-1975), whose 12 volume *Study of History* was an attempt to analyze history in terms of the growth and decline of civilizations. Ac-cordingly, he divided human history into 21 types of civilizations, "among which a certain type would dominate the world while it was at the peak of its growth." Toynbee claimed that of the existing five major types of civilizations, "only the Western Christian Civilization still possessed creative vitality." And, based on the historic examples of the Greek, Roman, Arabian and Mongolian civilizations, he predicted in his book that the United States would eventually dominate the world. Similar culturist historic theories had been introduced openly in China's Chongq-ing (wartime capital) in 1942. In 1946, there was a book published in China, entitled *The Theory of Culturist History*, which was an abridged translation of Toynbee's *Study of History* and contained some critical comments on the views of the British historian.

IV   China's Modern Science and Its Returned Students

1. The Enthusiastic Trend of Going Abroad to Study

China began sending young people to study abroad, during the last years of the Qing Dynasty, as a part of the official-sponsored Westernization drive. It was Rong Hong, a returned Chinese student from the United States, who first suggested it to the two Qing Dynasty high officials Zeng Guofan and Li Hong-zhang. Then, in July of 1871, Zeng and Li formally proposed to the Qing court that the country should send youngsters to Amer-ica to study such subjects as geographic cartography, mathemat-ics, astronomy, navigation, shipbuilding, manufacturing and oth-er courses connected with naval and military training. The Qing government approved the proposal, whereby Chinese students began travelling to other countries to study on official expenses. Rong Hong, the man who originated the idea, had studied at Yale University in the United States, before returning to China in 1855. Since then, he had openly called for a drive to learn from the West, as an essential step to turn China into a strong world power. He had once even tried to persuade the revolutionary leaders of the Taiping Uprising to accept his idea, but had finally turned to join the staff of Qing high official Li Hongzhang. It should be noted that among the first group of China's students abroad, sent by the government, was the celebrated Chinese engineer Zhan Tianyou, who designed China's first self-built Beijing-Zhangjiakou Railway, and whose bronze statue now stands before the railway's tunnel at Juyongguan Pass. The government-sponsored overseas studying drive led to the gradual emergence of a new generation of Chinese intellectuals, who were marked for their knowledge of modern Western science and technology as well as their consciousness of Western democratic ideas.

After China's defeat in the Sino-Japanese War (1894-1895), it became a national urge for the Chinese people to catch up with their main rival Japan; this led to the spate of Chinese students going to Japan to study at the beginning of the twentieth century. Then in 1908, the United States—in a move to compete with Japan in attracting more Chinese students to go there to study —initiated the policy of offering scholarships to Chinese students, with funds drawn from the cash indemnity paid to it by the Qing government since 1902, based on the Treaty of 1901. According to this policy, the U.S. Government promised to refund the said indemnity—which the Qing government was paying to the 14 foreign powers involved in the invasion of Beijing to crush the Boxer Uprising in 1900—from 1908 and until the expiry of the said indemnity in 1940. And the money would be used, partly, to set up Qinghua (Tsing Hwa) School in Beijing as a preparatory college, and, partly, to subsidize the Chinese graduates from the preparatory college to continue their study in American universities. This was an ingenious idea to train Chinese students in

American institutes with Chinese money—in the hope that these Americanized Chinese returned students would eventually introduce American ideas to China's political, economic, cultural and educational life. The American initiative was later followed by Britain and France, which also set up agencies to organize the Boxer indemnity refunding projects. In 1924, the China Educational and Cultural Foundation was established, as a Sino-American joint agency, to manage the projects financed by the U.S. refund of China's indemnity, extending its influence over a large number of education and academic establishments in China. Similar Sino-British and Sino-French joint agencies were set up soon after that. In 1939, the Sino-French-Belgian-Swedish Cultural Association was also founded with similar funding from these countries' refund of such indemnity.

The Qinghua School in Beijing later became China's Qinghua University, which, however, continued to maintain a close link with a number of American universities. Moreover, many church-sponsored mission schools and colleges in China also served as principal West-oriented channels for Chinese students to study abroad, while maintaining their own particular connections with the Western countries, especially the United States. And these connections were reflected in the curriculum, textbooks, faculty, funding, teaching facilities and the education system of these schools or colleges. In fact, the reform of China's education system, after the Revolution of 1911, was basically an imitation of the American pattern. Then in January 1922, the Chinese government formally stipulated the country's new education system, featuring the American-style mono-rail three stages of "primary, intermediate and higher education." According to such system, the higher educational establishments were divided into two separate categories, namely, universities and colleges or institutes. Only those, which had at least three schools (colleges) in the same establishment, could be named as "universities."

Japan, which featured such advantages as shorter travelling distance, cheaper living expenses, more convenient environment and a language which was easier to learn for the Chinese students, had hosted far more Chinese students than any other foreign country until 1928. Since then, however, more and more Chinese youths, encouraged by the new government policy and foreign subsidy from the Boxer indemnity refund, travelled to the West to study. Academies or postgraduate schools in Britain or the United States were preferred because of their fame and prestige. The West-oriented study boom lasted some 20 years, from 1929, throughout even the years of the War of Resistance Against Japanese Aggression (1937-1945). During this time the Sino-American ties were further strengthened, while the outflow of Chinese students to Japan, France and Germany virtually ceased.

2. The Inception of China's Modern Sciences

Since the Chinese first began to introduce Western sciences to their country in the 1860s, it took China some 50 years to absorb and digest the imported technology—through the help of foreign advisers and its own returned students—before it set out on its own path of modernization.

The earliest group of returned students played a pioneer role in promoting China's modern sciences, following the trend of world development. Nearly all the early Chinese scientific organizations were sponsored by the Chinese students abroad; one of them was the "Europe Branch of the Chinese Chemistry Society" founded in Paris on December 25, 1907—50 years after the founding of the French Chemistry Society in 1858. This Chinese Chemistry Society of Europe held its first convention in London in June the next year, which was attended by Chinese students in France, Belgium and England. They discussed the formulation of Chinese chemical terminology and the development of the country's chemical industry to produce articles for daily use. However, this student-sponsored science society soon ran into financial difficulty and ceased operation.

The slogan "Save the Nation with Science" was also initiated by the earlier Chinese science students overseas. And it was such an ideal that led Chinese students in Cornell University in the United States to set up "The Science Society" in 1915, as the first ever Chinese organization of sciences in general. The sponsors of the society included Zhao Yuanren, Bin Zhi and Hu Shih, who began publishing their own *Science* magazine in Shanghai, using —for the first time in Chinese printing history—Western punctuation marks for horizontally-lined Chinese text in the magazine. Three years later, the Science Society moved its headquarters from the United States to Shanghai, and made the *Science* magazine its official monthly publication to introduce translated Western scientific literature to the Chinese readers in a systematic way. It also organized lectures on scientific subjects, and contributed to the establishment of libraries, museums and research laboratories, thus becoming a key element in the country's modern science promotion effort.

The growth of China's modern sciences was directly related to the efforts of the returned Chinese students. Many of these Chinese scientists, who had been trained in Western universities, became leading faculty members of the domestic universities and played an important role in the renovation of the country's higher education system. Then, when the country founded its first two science research institutes in the 1920s, they became the first generation of Chinese researchers, as members of either the Nanjing-based Central Research Academy or the Beijing-based Peiping (Beijing) Research Academy. The noted Chinese educator Cai Yuanpei, who was known to have called for "substituting education for religion" in the early years of the Republic of China, began recruiting young returned Chinese science graduates from Western universities to lead new research projects in the Central Research Academy, during the period when he was president of the academy. A most remarkable example was the archaeological project of a massive excavation of the ancient Yin Ruins of the Shang Dynasty (sixteenth to eleventh century B.C.) in Henan Province, which was planned in 1928 as an essential step to the systematic research of the Shang Dynasty culture. "Who should be the right man to lead the job?" was then the centre of controversy in the Central Research Academy, as people argued over whether to appoint an experienced traditional scholar with well-established cultural background, or a young returned scientist who had been trained in the West on field archaeological research, to head the excavation team. It was Cai, who made the final decision to appoint Li Ji, a young returned scientist, who had received the Ph.D. from Harvard University, to lead this important project. The excavation resulted in the discovery of a large amount of cultural relics of the ancient Shang Dynasty, which served to erase the past ambiguity in this period of Chinese history. Under Cai's leadership, the research institutes in the Central Research Academy were mainly staffed with young Chinese scientists from the West. Such a policy led to the academy's success in producing breakthroughs in astronomical, physical, electrical, geological, biological and mathematical research, winning respect in international academic circles.

The West-trained Chinese scientists were also responsible for opening many new disciplines in the domestic universities and institutes. These included departments in meteorology, anthropology and plant pathology which were instituted in the universities in the 1930s. In the decade that followed, departments were established in shipbuilding, soil fertilization, insectology, agricultural machinery and aviation engineering. Many of the returned young scientists distinguished themselves as teachers and researchers. An outstanding example was the Chinese physicist and electrical engineer Sa Bendong, who was a returned Ph.D. in physics from the United States in the 1920s, and author of the new textbook on physics used in Chinese universities. In 1935, when he was a guest professor in the American University of Illinois, he published his book *Dyadics Circuit Analysis*. When anti-Japanese war broke out, he returned to China and served as the first president of the National Xiamen University. In 1944, he went again to the U.S. on a lecture tour, and published his book on electric engineering, *A.C. Dynamo*, which was introduced as textbook by a dozen U.S. universities. In 1948, not long after he was appointed president of Central Research Academy, Sa Bendong died of illness.

In China, a number of universities were established after the mode of American universities, especially, Massachusetts Institute of Technology (MIT), which had been seen as their model by the Chinese polytechnic institutes. One of these was the

Peiyang University, which was first founded in 1895 in Tianjin, with departments similar to those at MIT, in addition to their own hydraulic and physical laboratories. The Qinghua (Tsing Hwa) University, which was moved to Kunming from Beijing during the war years, merged with two other universities, Beijing University and Nankai University that had also moved there, to form the Southwest Associated University. In 1938, China's first Aviation Engineering Department was set up in the Southwest Associated University, with the department under the same name at MIT as its model. In fact, China and the United States had —until 1949—maintained close ties, in both engineering and basic scientific subjects. Such ties had not only brought hope to the Chinese in realizing their dream of modernization, but also served to regulate the pace of China's scientific development.

3. The Riddle of the Peking Man

Of the many achievements seen in the history of China's modern sciences, the most spectacular and yet most mystifying was the discovery and "disappearance" of the fossils of Peking Man.

What was the prehistoric ancestor of the Chinese people? Were they the so-called "ape-men"? And who were the original creators of China's ancient civilization? Were they the natives who lived in the Yellow River and Yangtze River valleys since tens of thousand years ago? These had long since been major subjects of controversy among numerous Chinese and foreign scholars. A French scholar had suggested, in the mid-eighteenth century, that the civilization of ancient China was created by the Egyptian immigrants from Africa. But still, none could find an answer to the question: How did the Chinese nation and the Chinese culture come into being?

However, following the rapid progress in the research on anthropology, paleontology and geology, people began to see a gleam of light in the long tunnel which might lead to the final answer to these questions.

Located in Beijing's southern suburbs was a place called Zhoukoudian, which had been known for the many ancient fossils found in one of the hills there. Since the old Chinese folks believed the fossils to be remains of ancient "dragons," they called the hill "Longgushan" (Dragon-Bone Hill). Then, in 1926, the excavators found in the hill two pieces of unearthed fossils, which looked like human teeth. These fossils were sent to the prestigions Peking (Beijing) Union Medical College, where they were examined by Dr. Davidson Black, head of the college's anatomical department. As a result, the fossils were found to be the remains of ancient human being, which belonged, however, to an unknown species that was different from all known species discovered elsewhere in the world. And, therefore, this species of primitive man was named *Sinanthropus pekinensis* or "Peking Man." The limestone cave in Zhoukoudian, where the fossil teeth of Peking Man were unearthed, had since become the focus of attention for both geologists and paleontologists, upon whose suggestion, the Beijing (Beiping) Geological Survey decided to launch a major excavation in the area, in a bid to unveil the secret of Peking Man.

As a result of the continuous excavation through five years since 1927, a variety of fossil bones and fossil teeth of the Peking Man were unearthed from some 10 strata of subsoil under the area of Zhoukoudian. An active member of the excavation team was Pei Wenzhong, a young geological graduate from Beijing University, who joined the Zhoukoudian project in 1928 right after graduation. Pei, who became the leader of the excavation team after 1929, often stayed on his job round the clock. Then, on the afternoon of December 2, 1929, he discovered—in the dimness of the evening glow—a fossil, which looked like the skullcap of an ape-man, at the bottom of a newly-dug pit. He worked through the night to unearth it carefully, wrapped it up with cotton quilts for protection and brought it back to the Beijing Geological Survey at dawn the next day.

Pei Wenzhong's report "The Discovery of the Fossil of *Sinanthropus Pekinensis* was published on the Chinese *Science* magazine (issue 8, vol. 14); and the news soon spread throughout the country and then to the whole world, opening a new page in the human knowledge of their own primitive image. In Beijing, meanwhile, the Beijing Geological Survey again turned the Peking Man's fossil skullcap over to Dr. Davidson Black of the Peking Union Medical College for further research. At the conclusion of his research, Dr. Black published his book *The Skullcap of Adult Sinanthropus Pekinensis* in 1931, which contained many photographs of the unearthed fossils.

Similarly *Australopithecus* and *Pithecanthropus* were then also unearthed in Java and elsewhere in the world; and despite their slight variation, they all indicated the history of the primitive man who had existed much earlier than men had first thought. A few years later, in 1936, Chinese excavator Jia Lanpo again unearthed many fossils of the Peking Man, which were all turned over for preservation in the safe of the Peking Union Medical College, where the Swedish anthropologist F. Weidenreich was responsible for conducting research on these fossils in the medical college.

The fossils of the Peking Man remained in the care of the American-owned Peking Union Medical College until late 1941, when war appeared imminent in the Pacific Ocean. In an attempt to save these valuable fossils from falling into the hands of the Japanese, they were secretly removed from the safe in the medical college, packed into two large boxes and delivered to the American Embassy in Beijing—some two weeks before the Japanese attack on Pearl Harbour. The two boxes, which contained a total of 147 pieces of Peking Man fossils—including five skullcaps, 15 skull fragments, 14 jawbones, in addition to more than 100 pieces of fossils of shoulder, thigh and arm bones and teeth—were supposed to be carried to the United States by the evacuating U.S. Marine Corps. However, all these fossils vanished from view, and no one seemed to know where they had gone.

The whereabouts of the Peking Man fossils once again became the focus of attention, in the wake of World War II. Rumour had it that the two boxfuls of Peking Man fossils were loaded into the American liner *S.S. President Harrison* at Qinhuangdao Harbour, but the ship was later either sunk or seized by the Japanese navy. So the boxes were either lost in the bottom of the sea, or seized by the Japanese. Then, after the U.S. army occupied Japan, they launched an extensive search for the fossils without success. Finally in 1972, an American business tycoon offered a huge cash reward for information on the Peking Man fossil, but again no clue was found.

Then, in as late as 1984, someone offered a new clue to the whereabouts of the lost fossils of the Peking Man. According to the information, an old man recalled that he had seen—on an evening just before the outbreak of the Pacific War—two persons carrying a heavy box into the backyard of the then American Embassy in Beijing; then he saw the two dig a pit in the yard and bury the box in it. Judging from the circumstances, it could very well be a box full of Peking Man's fossils. Of course, it was already impossible to verify the belated information, because the alleged site of the hidden box has, since years ago, become the location of buildings.

But, if it was true that a box full of Peking Man's fossils, maybe including his skullcap, was buried in the soil of Beijing, then, the Peking Man has at last returned home—to where he had lived and thrived hundreds of thousand years ago.

V   Chinese Culture and the Western World

1. The Rediscovery of Chinese Culture

Their new expansion projects in the Eastern world rekindled the West Europeans' interest in the Oriental culture during the nineteenth century. British colonialists took pains to study Indian culture in the hope of consolidating their control of India. The Germans were also interested in the Indian ideology and literature, in an effort to trace their ancestral heritage. And the Western visitors went farther east to China and Japan to widen their knowledge of the Orient. Their influx was further bolstered by introduction of "open door policy" in China, with missionaries, diplomats, sailors and merchants flocking into Chinese ports and cities for different purposes. Many of these European visitors prepared by studying the Chinese language and culture, finally becoming outstanding Sinologues themselves. Noteworthy were the French explorer and diplomat Paul Pelliot, the British soldier and diplomat Thomas Wade, who had taken part in the first Opium War, and then became a Sinologue and distinguished himself by establishing the Wade System of Romanization of Chinese characters. The two American Sinologists Samuel Wells Williams and W.W. Rockhill had also been known to have written several books on Chinese culture, apart from their careers as U.S. diplomats in China. Another British soldier named Beal, who served in the Royal Navy during the second Opium War, was known to have translated Chinese Buddhist literature, including those concerning the medieval Chinese monks Fa Xian and Xuan Zhuang.

In the eyes of these Western Sinologues, who took part themselves in the political activities through the years—when China was being ravaged and humiliated—there seemed to be no convincing link between the past glory of the Chinese civilization and the present ignorance and humility of the Chinese nation. But things began to change at the turn of the century, as a new tide of revolution swept across the old country, bringing aspiration for rebirth to the whole nation. The first Western observer, who noticed the glittering spark rising through the hazy mist shrouding the old China, was the German philosopher Hermann Keyserling (1880-1946), then travelling through China during his round-the-world tour of 1911-1912. In his book *The Travel Diary of a Philosopher* written at the end of his tour Keyserling spoke, particularly, of the wisdom of the Orientals. In 1912, during his stopover in Shanghai, the German philosopher gave a lecture at the Shanghai International Research Society, under the title of "The East and the West and Their Search for the Common Truth," in which he said that the Westerners' interest in the Orient was based, in the past, upon curiosity, but still some of them conducted serious study of the Eastern culture. Keyserling said he felt the Westerners emphasizing more the means of material life, while neglecting the meaning of life itself. Concluding his lecture, the German philosopher pointed out that the wisdom of the Orient was like the rising sun at dawn—which surpassed the boundary between the East and the West, offering the people a key to open their minds.

At about the same time, Vladimir Lenin, who was leading Russia to its initial victory in the revolution, had perceived an advancing Asia through the revolutionary struggle in China—as opposed to Europe, which was becoming the headquarters of the backward conservatives.

Some Western thinkers were able to perceive—through China's democratic revolution—that the secret in the survival of an old nation was in the preservation of its cultural foundation throughout the process of modernized reform, but not to copy the Western culture per se. It was again Hermann Keyserling to issue the warning that China would be doomed, if she forsook her own cultural heritage to seek Westernization.

The voices of critical philosophers grew still louder, in the disillusionment in Europe brought on by the First World War. This was especially true in Germany. The book, *The Decline of the West* written by Oswald Spengler (1880-1936), predicted the end of Western civilizations in light of historical analogy. Past belief in the omnipotence of science was now shaken by the holocaust of war, giving way to widespread cynicism. Such a drastic turn in European thinking at that time was observed by the Chinese scholar Liang Qichao, who toured Europe for two years between 1918 and 1920. Liang, who had been active in China's politics since the abortive 100-Day Reform of 1898, published his book called *Impressions from a Tour of Europe*, pointing out that Europe was then in a quandary as to where its road should be—"waking up from the dream of an omnipotent science, the Europeans are now openly denouncing their science; this is the key to the recent change in the trend of their thoughts," he noted.

The anticlimax of European civilization, as preceived by Liang, made him realize that China could still play an important role in re-vitalizing world culture. And, in his book, he offered this advice to Chinese youths:

"First of all, everyone of you should have a sincere respect and affection for your own national culture. Secondly, you should study your culture in the same serious manner as the Westerners do in their search of knowledge. Thirdly, it is not enough to know your own culture, because you need to know also the culture of other countries, so you can integrate them into a new comprehensive cultural system. Finally, when you have done all these, then, you should expand this new cultural system to other parts of the world to serve the interest of the entire human race."

As a Chinese thinker, Liang Qichao had perceived that the future of China's cultural reform lay in its significance to the world civilization. Another Chinese scholar Liang Shumin went even further in suggesting that the Western civilization should be remodelled after the Chinese style so as to adapt itself to the Chinese heritage. In his view, the Western material civilization was simply irreconcilable with the idealistic civilization of the Orient. And Liang Shumin pointed out explicitly in his book, entitled *The Eastern and Western Cultures and Their Philosophies*, that while China could not refuse to receive the introduction of Western culture, "she should, nevertheless, try to absorb it and improve it according to her own heritage." These controversial views of the Chinese intellectuals reflected their widely divergent stance on how to reform China's traditional culture. It was, indeed, nothing less than a historic tragedy that the age-old traditional thoughts, which had dominated the Chinese feudal society through more than 2,000 years, were then still upheld by many as the "quintessence of the Chinese culture."

2. China's Classics and Traditional Literature

The nineteenth century Western Sinologists first began their study on China by translating and introducing Chinese classics —just like their predecessors, who tried to introduce Chinese culture to Europe, had done in the previous century. Then, gradually, they extended their scope of research to include the Chinese language, phonology, literature, philosophy, religion and art. Most remarkable was the British Sinologist Dr. James Legge from the University of Aberdeen and president of the Anglo-Chinese College in Hong Kong. He translated into English the famous Four Books of *The Great Learning, The Doctrine of the*

Mean, The Analects of Confucius and *Mencius,* in addition to *The Book of History, The Spring and Autumn Annals, The Book of Rites* and *The Book of Changes,* all of which were published by 1885. Legge was noted for his painstaking research into the Chinese classics and books and his careful deliberation of their meanings, before launching into the translation. As a result, his works emerged as the best ever Western translation of the Chinese classics. In 1876, Legge was appointed by Oxford University as professor in their Chinese language programme. But the university gave no degree to their students majored in Chinese until 64 years later in 1940, when Chinese scholar Yang Xianyi, a well-known English language translator of Chinese literature, was awarded such a degree by Oxford University. Then, in 1888, Cambridge University also established a course on Sinology, with Herbert Allen Giles as its professor. Giles (1845-1933), had served as the British consul in Shanghai and Ningbo, was a prolific writer and translator of books concerning the Chinese language, religion, poems, literature, history, personalities and other aspects of Chinese culture. His better known books include *The Civilization of China, A History of Chinese Literature, Religions of Ancient China, The Remains of Lao Tzu* and also a three-volume *Chinese-English Dictionary* (Shanghai, 1892). His two-volume *A Chinese Biographical Dictionary* (London and Shanghai, 1898), which listed as many as 2,579 names of Chinese celebrities, was a major achievement for an English writer. Giles was, however, most proud of his *A History of Chinese Literature,* calling it the first ever history book written on the subject. His other contributions to Sino-English exchange on literature included *Chinese Poetry in English Verse* (1898), *Strange Stories from a Chinese Studio* (1880), *Gems of Chinese Literature* (1884), *Chuang Tzu: Mystic, Moralist and Social Reformer* (1889), and *Chinese Fairy Tales Told in English* (1911). As a British diplomat, Giles had also tried to whitewash the British government's infamous role in the Opium War in his *Some Truths about Opium* (1923); nevertheless, to many Chinese scholars he had been the best known Sinologue.

The accomplishments of the French Sinologists were also

remarkable in their research of China's culture, religion, history and art. The famous French Sinologue Emmanuel-Edouard Chavannes (1865-1918) was known for his translation of the Chinese classic *Records of the Historian*. He had travelled to China to study its ancient grottoe art, and conducted research on the Han Dynasty bamboo scripts unearthed in Xinjiang by Aurel Stein. Chavannes was succeeded in his Sinological studies by his three students, Paul Pelliot (1878-1945), Henri Maspero (1883-1945) and Marcel Granet (1884-1940), each of whom had helped introduce Chinese culture to the world. The French distinction in its Sinological research continued through the College de France, which had, after its founding in 1814, conducted study on China in its Institut des Hautes Etudes Chinoises, under the guidance of noted Sinologues such as Louis Hambis. Similar Sinological research was also carried out by the Ecole Franciase d'Extreme-Orient, which was founded in Hanoi of Viet Nam in 1900, later moved to Paris in 1956—making Paris the centre of French Sinological studies.

Apart from the well-known British and French Sinologists, there were many other European and American writers, who had distinguished themselves in their study and translation of Chinese classic literature, such as the Swedish scholar B. Karlgren, noted for his research on Chinese phonology and his book *The Study on Truthfulness of Zuozhuan* (*Zuoqiu Ming's Chronicles*), and the German writer Otto Francke, known for his extensive translations of Chinese classic dramas and novels. Even more famous was the twentieth century English writer Arthur Waley, who was acclaimed first for his translation of the *A Hundred and Seventy Chinese Poems* (1918), which included 60 poems written by the famous Chinese Tang Dynasty poet Bai Juyi; this was followed by his other translations of *"The Temple" and Other Poems* (1923) and *The Book of Songs* (1937), *The Analects of Confucius* (1938), and finally *The Monkey*, which told the story of the Tang Dynasty's monk Xuan Zhuang's pilgrimage to India. Equally popular was C.H. .Brewitt-Taylor's translation of the Chinese historical novel *The Romance of the Three Kingdoms* and Pearl S. Buck's *All Men Are Brothers*, both of which were faithful translations of the original Chinese classical novels.

A few Chinese scholars, who lived in America, also made special efforts after the 1930s to introduce their country's literature to the Western world. Wang Jizhen (Wang Chi-chen) was known to have translated into English, *Dream of the Red Chamber* (London, 1929) and *Ah Q and Other: Selected Stories of Lusin* (Lu Xun) (New York, 1941). Another Chinese scholar Lin Yutang chose to write his own books in English to introduce China to the Western readers, as he did in his *The Wisdom of China and India* (New York, 1942).

3. The Reevaluation of the History of Chinese Sciences

Of the many Chinese traditional sciences, astronomy and pharmacology were the two branches most interesting to the Western scholars. While Chinese astronomy was studied mainly by the Jesuit missionaries working in China, Chinese pharmacology was introduced to the European continent and created a tremendous impact there, accelerating Sinological studies in France. It was said that when Abel Rémusat (1788-1832), the founder of French Sinology, was a young botanical student, he found a copy of the Chinese *Compendium of Materia Medica* in a convent. Although Rémusat did not understand the Chinese text, he was impressed by the large amount of illustration of flora contained in the book. It was then that the young French botanical student decided he should start to learn the Chinese language. The *Compendium of Materia Medica* was written by the celebrated Chinese physician Li Shizhen (1518-1592) and published in 1596, four years after his death. It was known to be the most comprehensive pharmacopoeia in the world, containing specifications of 1,892 medicinal herbs and a total of 11,000 prescriptions —all identified by Li himself. And through years of painstaking study, Rémusat finished the thesis on his research of the Chinese pharmacopoeia at Paris in 1812. The thesis, written in Latin under the title of "Dissertato de glossosemiotice, sire de signis morborum que à linguâ sumuter praesertim apud Sinensis etc." won him a doctorate from Paris University. Soon afterward, Rémusat was appointed professor in the French Academy.

The research and application of Chinese medicine in Europe touched off considerable reaction in Europe and Britain as to the value of Chinese sciences. Then, in 1813, the French writer F. A. Lepage published his 103-page book in Paris entitled *Recherches historique sur la médicine des Chinois*, which was followed by other essays, published by French missionaries, Sinologues and Russian pharmacologists, to introduce Chinese medical science to European readers. Especially noteworthy was Daniel Hanbury, a member of the British Royal Society, who devoted half of his 543-page voluminous *Science Papers, Chiefly Pharmacological and Botanical* published in 1876, to introduce contents of the *Compendium of Materia Medica*. The Russian scholar Emil Bretschneider, during his stay in China, published his book written in English *Botanicum Sinicum: Notes on Chinese Botany from Native and Western Sources*, in which he provided a well-considered classification of the plants and medicinal herbs listed in Chinese literature and specified their scientific terms. The results of all this research on Chinese botany and pharmacology prompted Charles Darwin to repeatedly quote—in his various works beginning from the *On the Origin of Species by Means of Natural Selection* in 1859—the *Compendium of Matera Medica*, calling it the "Ancient Chinese Encyclopaedia."

Since the beginning of the twentieth century, the reevaluation of the history of Chinese sciences became a subject of study by both Western and modern Chinese scientists. And a marked success was achieved in their joint study on the *Compendium of Matera Medica*. The study was led by British medical doctor Emms Read, who took over from the American physician Ralph Mills in 1920, while serving as a professor in the medical colleges of Beijing and Shanghai. Read explained most of the herbs mentioned in the 44-volume "Compendium," through his close cooperation with his two Chinese assistants, Liu Ju-Chiang and Li Yü-thien. They published a series of research papers on the subject between 1923 and 1941. Their work represented the most thorough study on the 52-volume masterpiece of Chinese pharmacology.

The study on Chinese alchemy was an important part of the

reevaluation of the history of Chinese science, and also a matter of world significance. During the nineteenth century, Western scientists believed in the suggestion of the French chemist M.P.E. Berthelot that Chinese alchemy had originated from the Arab countries. Such a view had prevailed in the West, despite the fact that the British missionary Alexander Wylie had pointed out, in his book *Notes on Chinese Literature* published in 1867 in London, that the Chinese book *Zhou Yi Can Tong Qi* (*Kinship of the Three and the Book of Changes*) written by Wei Boyang of the Eastern Han Dynasty was the earliest known book on alchemy. In 1901, the American missionary W.A.P. Martin also stated in his book *The Lore of Cathay* (New York, 1901) that the introduction of Chinese alchemy to Arabia was the earliest root of modern chemistry. However, it was not until the 1920s that Berthelot's suggestion was finally denounced by evidence produced by the Chinese chemist Wang Jin and British chemical historian Partington, who were finally able to convince the world that true origin of alchemy was in China. Then based on these findings, the American scientist T.L. Davis succeeded—with the help of Chinese scholars—in translating many famous Chinese alchemists' works into English, adding his own explanatory notes. The publication of these translations served to prove the ancient Chinese alchemists' achievement in chemical innovation to the world. In 1930, the essay on Chinese alchemy co-authored by Chinese chemist Wu Luqiang and T.L. Davis was published in the *Scientific Monthly* magazine. In 1932, the magazine "ISIS" again published the English translation of the ancient Chinese alchemical literature, written by Wu and Davis, under the title of "An ancient Chinese treatise on alchemy entitled Tsan Tung Chi." Subsequently, Wu and Davis again translated together two chapters from the book *Bao Pu Zi* written by another ancient Chinese alchemist Ge Hong of the Jin Dynasty. Davis also cooperated with another Chinese chemist Chen Guofu to translate yet two more chapters from the same Chinese book.

The effort of the Western scientists in re-studying Chinese sciences prompted the Chinese scientists to give more importance to the past achievement of their own ancestors. A Western scholar who played a major role in this respect, was Sinologist professor T.F. Carter of Columbia University in the United States. The book, which was later revised by L. Carrington Goodrich, became a popular publication focusing on the introduction of Chinese inventions to the West. It was the publication of such books in the West that moved the Chinese scholars to point out that paper-making, gunpowder and the compass were invented in China, thereby restoring the Chinese people's sense of national pride.

Years later in 1954, research on the history of Chinese sciences entered a new phase, which was marked by the publication of the first volume of *The Science and Civilization in China*, compiled by Professor Joseph Needham assisted by Chinese scholars at Cambridge University in England. The book was remarkable in placing Chinese sciences, from the very beginning, in the world arena so that it could be compared on equal terms with contemporary sciences worldwide. The publication of this book had further encouraged other scholars and Chinese scientists to explore the scientific heritage of China to a greater length, so as to more thoroughly and correctly reevaluate the Chinese cultural heritage.

VI   The Rejuvenation of Chinese Arts

1. Dr. Mei Lanfang and the Reform of Beijing Opera

Dramatic performance was a powerful art that could capture audiences and stir the emotions, thereby influencing the attitudes of the people. China was known for its rich variety of dramatic performances as regular public entertainment. People enjoyed watching stage shows, regarding them as a desirable pastime. Of the variety of Chinese dramas, which were distinguished by different ethnic or provincial characteristics, Beijing Opera ranked above all others because of its unique integration of dialogue, singing, dancing, music and martial art.

However, as a result of the New Culture Movement of May

1919, there was a general negation of the old-fashioned dramas, while new plays, featuring modern themes, gradually came into the limelight in the coastal cities. This led to the growing demand for a reform of the traditional local dramas as well as Beijing (Peking) Opera, despite its undiminished prestige and popularity in the country.

At this point, a young Beijing Opera actor Mei Lanfang (1894-1961), who specialized in the female role of "dan" (young woman), became a pioneer in sponsoring reform of the traditional performing art. He took his lead from the new art style of modern plays, exchanging knowledge and experience with the Western artists.

Mei carried out a series of reforms in Beijing Opera, focusing on improving both the artistic content of the operas while devising more colourful and meaningful acting and dancing styles to enhance the dramatic effect. In a major move to liberate Beijing Opera from its traditional role of entertaining the elite class only, and freeing the actors and actresses from their past status of being the servile entertainers of their patrons, Mei organized his own troupe and led it on performing tours across the country. His goal was to make Beijing Opera a popular dramatic performance for the public. In 1919, he led his troupe to perform in Japan where he performed regularly. His second performance in Japan, in 1924, was a great success, thus boosting his confidence that Beijing Opera could succeed on a foreign stage, as it did in China. His confidence was further enhanced when the foreign diplomats and a Swedish prince, who watched his performance in Beijing, unanimously acclaimed his superb art on the stage. So, in 1929, the 36-year-old Chinese artist decided to let his 24-person troupe make a daring performing tour in the United States.

The Mei Lanfang Art Troupe set out for America by way of Japan in January 1930; their ship arrived in Seattle on the west coast on January 31. Two weeks later, on February 14, Mei's troupe gave its premiere at a theatre in Washington D.C. before an American audience which included the host country's vice-president and other top officials. The premiere was a complete success, as the three operas—including "Chang'e Flees to the

Moon," "The Rocky Hill" and "A Smile at All Cost"—performed by Mei himself won a standing ovation from the audience. Mei and his troupe went on to perform on Broadway in New York for two weeks; each of the performances was accompanied by an introduction in English plus booklets on backgrounds of Beijing Opera, its facial makeup, costumes, and art style. As a result, his performance had not only brought himself fame and honour, but also contributed to introducing Chinese dramatic art to the American people.

The success of Mei Lanfang's overseas performance was attributed to his long-cherished determination to reform the old Chinese drama, especially, after he had been given strong support by the Beijing Chinese Dramatic Institute. And he had also made clear his ambition of promoting international cultural exchange through the performance of Chinese dramatic art. This was indicated in his farewell speech in Shanghai before his departure for the United States, "I realize the wide cultural gap existing between China and America; however, it is my ambition to make the best of this opportunity to build a bridge over such a gap through the exchange of dramatic art. And that is why I am travelling to America with my troupe, which should serve as an essential introduction of Chinese culture."

His trip to the United States had fully realized his wish, for the performance of his troupe was so successful and the audiences so enthusiastic that the schedule was extended for 72 days, with performances in New York, Chicago, San Francisco, Los Angeles, San Diego and Honolulu. The splendid Beijing Opera art style and its Oriental orchestra and paraphernalia fascinated American admirers, bringing them a surge of fresh exotic air. And suddenly, the dazzling art of Beijing Opera appeared to many Americans as the key to understand Chinese culture. Mei Lanfang was invited by both Columbia and Chicago universities to give lectures on the art of Beijing Opera. Finally, Mei was awarded the degree of Honorary Doctor of Literature by both Collegii Pomonensis and the University of Southern California. Mei Lanfang's popularity, following his highly successful performing tour, led to the emergence abroad of songs and flowers dedicated to his name. And

Mei's overseas success further boosted his prestige at home.

In 1935, Mei Lanfang travelled to Moscow, Paris and London, on a tour aimed at studying the European dramatic art. His performance in Moscow deeply impressed the German dramatist Bertolt Brecht (1898-1956), who was then in the Soviet Union. And in London, Mei became a close friend of George Bernard Shaw. Mei Lanfang's continued successes in promoting cultural exchange between China and other countries was convincing evidence that the Chinese traditional dramatic art, which had won recognition and respect of the whole world, would enjoy an even greater future on the road of reform.

2. Colour Ink Paintings and the International Popularity of Chinese Art

There was a growing interest in the research of ancient Chinese arts, both at home and abroad, following the 1920s. Such a rediscovery of classic Chinese arts developed side by side with the new art movement in China.

Foreigners' enthusiasm in the Chinese arts was attributed, primarily, to the three factors:

Firstly, the discovery of the "treasure house" in the Dunhuang Grottoes and the ancient cave murals and sculptures in Kuqa, Baicheng and Turpan of Xinjiang attracted worldwide attention to China's ancient art relics.

Secondly, the systematic excavation and archaeological research of the ancient Shang and Zhou Dynasty relics had resulted in the unearthing spectacular ancient Chinese bronze and jade sculptures that glorified the Chinese civilization in the eyes of the whole world.

Thirdly, the independent Chinese traditional art of painting and architecture had drawn increasing interest from the foreign art critics, who were beginning to study the Chinese classic art —viewing it for the first time as a unique school of the Oriental fine arts. This was an important development, because until then, there were only three schools of Oriental fine arts, namely, Egyptian-Arab fine arts, fine arts of the Indian sub-continent and finally, Japanese fine arts, which had been popular in the West since the middle of the nineteenth century. The rediscovery of the Chinese fine arts led the Western art and cultural circles to recognize the existence of a new world in Oriental art. As a result, study of Chinese fine arts became a favourable subject for the Western art and academic circles.

The discovery and research of the art treasures of Dunhuang and Xinjiang grottoes were a major contribution to the world history of arts. This was reflected in Paul Pelliot's voluminous *Les Grottes de Touen-houang: peintures et sculptures bouddhiques des époques des Wei, des T'ang, et des Song*, which was published, successively, from 1914 to 1924. These were followed by Sir M.A. Stein's *The Thousand Buddhas: Ancient Buddhist Paintings from the Cave Temples of Tunhuang (Dunhuang) on the Western Frontier of China* (London, 1922). Added to them was A. von Le Coq's five-volume *Die Buddhistische Spatantike in Mittel-Asien* (Berlin, 1922-1933). The dramatic discovery of these spectacular ancient Chinese arts created a major impact around the world, making the Chinese grottoes more famous than the well-known relic centres of Gandhara and Amaravadi in the Indian sub-continent. As a result, art enthusiasts around the globe began turning their eyes towards the western frontier of China, stirring interest and admiration in the Chinese painting, sculpture, architecture, gardening and porcelain.

There were many British, French, German, American and Belgian scholars, specialized in the research of ancient Chinese art. Their better-known works included *A Survey of Chinese Art* by Ferguson and the four-volume *Histoire des arts anciens de la Chine* by O. Siren. Their books served as a key to open the gate to the Chinese art house for the Western readers.

While the attention of the Western artists was attracted by the dazzling discovery of the ancient Chinese art, many modern Chinese artists were drawn by the Western art, hoping to learn from the post-Renaissance achievements of the artists in France, Italy and Britain—as a light to guide the future development of the Chinese fine arts. They realized then that even the highly expressive Chinese colour ink painting needed improvement to meet the challenge of the modern world. An important event was the "Exhibition of Chinese Contemporary Fine Arts" held in Paris in May 1933. The opening of this exhibition, which was organized by the well-known Chinese painter Xu Beihong then studying in France, marked the first ever introduction of the Chinese colour ink painting to the Western art world. Among the exhibits, the more unconventional poetic artworks of Chinese painter Qi Baishi won praise from foreign artists; the French government bought 12 Chinese paintings from the exhibition for display in a newly-opened Hall of Contemporary Chinese Paintings in the French National Gallery of Foreign Fine Arts. Encouraged by his success in Paris, Xu Beihong travelled through Europe to hold similar exhibitions in Brussels, Milan, Berlin, Moscow and Leningrad, introducing the contemporary Chinese fine arts to more Westerners and encouraging them to shift their interest from the ancient Chinese art to the modern art of China. The success of these exhibitions indicated they had achieved the desired effect.

Europe saw a flourishing of Chinese art two years later in 1935, following the opening of another "Chinese Modern Fine Arts Exhibition" in London. The exhibition, organized by famous Chinese painter Liu Haisu, president of the Shanghai Fine Arts School, was accompanied by a series of lectures on the latest trend of modern fine arts. The climax came in September of that year, when the magnificent "International Exposition of Chinese Arts" —of unprecedented scale and splendour—was opened in London's Burlington House. The exposition, co-organized by the Palace Museum and Ancient Relic Display Centre in Beijing and the Central Research Institute in Nanjing, displayed a variety of cultural relics from the collections of these Chinese institutions, ranging from 3,500-year-old Shang Dynasty bronzeware to colourful enamel and cloisonne objects produced in the last imperial dynasty. The impressive display of Chinese civilization in the exposition created an interest throughout Europe, leading to a basic change in their opinion of Chinese culture.

At about the same time, the performance on the British stage of a Beijing Opera item "Wang Baochuan"—featuring the legendary story of a chancellor's daughter, who was disowned by her parents for marrying a poor soldier, but remained faithful to her husband through the ten years while he went to fight in a border war. He finally came back as the monarch of a small kingdom and crowned her as his queen. The production was directed by the noted Chinese dramatist Xiong Shiyi, and was warmly received by English audiences and continued for two years in the London theatre. In 1936, Xiong was again invited by an American theatre to stage the show in New York. Throughout these years, the presentation of Chinese culture—from theatrical performance to arts and crafts, and from ancient to modern—was acclaimed on both sides of the Atlantic, as a new stimulus and tonic to help reinvigorate the then disenchanted Western world in the wake of depression. Such unexpected success of the Chinese artistic activities abroad also gave impetus to the country's cultural development at home.

During the war years against Japanese aggression, Chinese artists continued their activities abroad, holding art exhibitions in Singapore and New Delhi to help the war victims at home. Chinese painters also went to show their works in the United States and presented them to President Franklin D. Roosevelt. After the end of World War II, another "Chinese Ancient Relics Exhibition" was held in London in 1947, and was seen as an refreshing stimulant in Western cultural circles in the aftermath of a destructive war.

The celebrated Chinese painter Zhang Daqian (1899-1983) was noteworthy for bolstering the reputation of Chinese fine arts abroad. In 1933, his works were bought by the museums of Paris and Moscow for display as part of their collections. Later, he held exhibitions in London, Geneva and Paris, where he was acclaimed, particularly, for his exquisite presentation of louts flowers in both coloured and black ink. After 1949, Zhang travelled to Brazil and the United States, where he succeeded in adapting the skills of the Western impressionists to his works; then he again showed them to the Western world at more than 50 exhibitions, held in Tokyo, Paris, Cologne and New York. In 1958, Zhang was elected as the top contemporary painter by the International Society of Arts, ranking him equal to the Western art master Pablo Picasso (1881-1973), as the Oriental art master. Through the efforts of Zhang, China's traditional paintings became compatible with the Western fine arts in their artistic attraction, and proved a brilliant part of the international art. Truly, the success of the Chinese traditional fine arts symbolized both the pride of the perennial Chinese culture and its promising future.

Epilogue
The Outlook of Chinese Culture

Chinese culture has gone through a lengthy course of development—following the twists and turns of the Yellow and Yangtze rivers—in its history of some 6,000 years.

The immense size of the domain of the Chinese civilization held back its advance to the outside world for thousands of years. Geographically, the boundless seas on its eastern coast and the towering mountains on its western borders had served to discourage travellers from venturing into the unknown. The adequate living and thriving space within the national territory also contributed to the self-sustaining nature of the Chinese civilization, marked by a complacency of maintaining an independent existence, without being bothered by busy outside world.

However, civilization had to advance and following the movement of men and history. Thus, when the ancient Chinese learned to make bronze and iron tools, they established contact with the nomadic horsemen travelling on the Eurasian Steppe—and through them, with the European inhabitants living on the coast of the Baltic Sea and Black Sea, for the first time in history. Such contacts then spread onto the ancient nations of Central Asia, leading to the opening of the Silk Road and more traffic links with the European continent.

Since then, the Chinese had maintained contact with other parts of the world, as was then known to them. In the history of China, it had never succumbed to any external culture, nor ever rejected any external culture. While continuing to call for preservation of its traditional heritage, dating from the prehistoric Yao and Shun period, the Chinese nation had never held on to any monolithic symbol described as their sole cultural emblem, or stubbornly resisted the introduction of any culture from the outside. As an example, Buddhism—as one of the three pillars of the traditional Chinese culture, beside Confucianism and Taoism, was originally a culture introduced from abroad. Through the centuries, it had first clashed and then intermingled with the other indigenous cultures to continue its growth in China, while leading to the emergence of such new ramified cultures as the Xuan sect of the Wei and Jin dynasties, the Chan sect of the Tang Dynasty, the Li school of the Song and Ming dynasties and finally the Esoteric sect of Buddhism. Such a cohesive character of Chinese culture enabled it to absorb the better qualities of other cultures and continue to survive through the ages, as one of the leading civilizations in the world. This was, indeed, the essence of the lasting vitality of Chinese culture, and the basic reason for its continuation on the globe.

Chinese culture went through drastic changes during the last three hundred years—at first under the pressure of the joint power of Christian culture and modern sciences. It was such a powerful pressure that had, since the seventeenth century, pushed China, persistently albeit hazardously, into the world market and the global strategic scenario, manipulated by the politicians of Europe. Powerless to resist such a historic course, China was forced to accept humiliating treaties imposed on it, thereby sinking into the depths of national crisis, which lasted a whole century when the fate of the Chinese nation and culture hung in the balance.

China's entry into the global trend of modernization had not been spontaneous, and its acceptance of the Western culture was not voluntary: hence, its movements were hesitant and sluggish. Such a mentality was shared even by pioneer reformists Lin Zexu and Kang Youwei. Since obstinate boycott of Western culture had been proved by history as leading only to a doomed outcome, the disaster-battered China was compelled to compromise with the demand for reform, under the best possible condition of "preserving the Chinese theories as the basic principles, while adopting the Western theories as working methods." Later, this principle was completely reversed by the radical reformers—after the

Revolution of 1911 and the anti-restoration campaign—who went to the other extreme and called for a complete divorce from the traditional Chinese culture—in order to realize a complete Westernization and a complete reform. The ensuing controversies on such issues as the choice of new or old literature, the clash between Eastern and Western cultures and the dispute between science and idealism all indicated the dawning of a stormy cultural revolution—an inevitable and irresistible historic impact, which people must accept and try to explore the best possible outcome it might bring.

Where is the future of Chinese culture? The answer had to come through a revolution that would free China from her thousand-year-old shackles of feudalism, crush the burdens imposed on it by foreign powers and introduce China to the trend of the modern civilization. A cultural revolution, which obeys, yet transcends a political revolution, is a transformation that goes deeper into the mentality and psychology of the people. As such, it should be seen as the continuation of a political revolution. In fact, the formulation of any type of culture was not based merely on the difference of epoch or nationality, but also on the cohesive power in the mentality of a particular nation. Therefore, to view the cultural differences only in the light of the change of epoch —neglecting the difference of mentality—would lead to blind imitation of a foreign culture, imposing more external cultural force than the people could possibly accept, psychologically. Such a forcibly imported culture could not hope to survive. Similarly, if attention was paid only to the ethnic difference, overstressing the traditional bondage of mentality, then it would create more ground for the cultural conservatives to reject reform and lead to continued cultural isolation and backwardness.

Overemphasis on the epochal distinction of culture may cause people to overlook the hindrance from traditional force, which would inevitably persist in the course of progressive reform. A nation's traditional culture would not totally vanish at the moment when a reform takes place. The cultural revolution must go much deeper into the mind and seek to set it free, so that the people may have a broader world outlook in their pursuit of democracy and sciences. China—as not only a part of the Orient but also a part of the world—should leave its past sharp clashes with the West to the memory of history, and try to establish more extensive and more sincere linkage with the Western world, because only in this way can China rebuild its culture upon more solid foundations.

Index

abacus 139
Abdul Razzak 194
Abraham Lincoln 325
Accounts of Paintings 279
Adventures of Tom Sawyer, The 358
Aleksander Ostrovsky 352, 357
Aleksander Pushkin 357
Alexander the Great 35
Alexander Wylie 302, 305, 315, 316, 385
Alexandre Dumas 343, 351, 354, 355
Alexandre le Blond 284
Alexandria 50, 51, 69
Alexis Carrel 327
Alighieri Dante 356
All Men Are Brothers 382
All Quiet on the Western Front 356
Alphonse Daudet 355
Alt-Kutscha (Ancient Kuqa) 69
An Lushan 88
An Qing 109
An Shigao 101
Analects of Confucius, The 268, 381, 382

anarchism 328
ancient nude art 63
Andersson 10, 13
Andreyev 354
Anglo-Chinese Garden 291
Anton Chekhov 344, 352, 357
Approach to Historic Research on Social Science 367
Arab medical expertise 152
Arab music and dances 152
Arab pharmacopoeia 152
Arabian maps and navigation manuals 151
Archaeology in the CCCP 116
Aristotle 294
Arnold Toynbee 368
Art of Chess 97
Arthur Schopenhauer 361
Arthur Waley 382
Asia Minor 69
Asian Plateau Exploration Team 64
Asian Steppe 22
Asoka 47, 48, 61
Astrolabium 235
Athanasius Kircher 8
Attiret 282, 285, 291

Auguste Comet   361, 363
Augustus De Morgan   302
Aunty Gongsun   94
Autocracy   266
Auzout   245
Axum   43

B. Karlgren   382
Bactria   33
Bai Juyi   88, 217, 382
Bai Mingda   83
Bai Zhitong   83
Baimasi (White Horse) Temple   49, 56
Baimasi Pagoda   126
Bamboo Annals, The   20
Ban Chao   41, 52
Ban Gu   52
Bao Xuan   208
Baochuan (Treasure Boat) Fleet   188, 191, 192, 193, 197
Basil   136
Beauties   51
Begram   51
Beijing Astronomical Observatory   245
Beijing Opera   387
Ben Cao Shi Yi (Materia Medica Addenda)   120
Benjamin Kidd   323
Benoist   284, 285, 286
Bernard Shaw   356, 389
Bernardus Rhodes   249
Bernini   264
Bertolt Brecht   389
Bertrand Russell   359, 360

Bible   219, 234
bili   80, 81
Biography of King Mu, the Son of Heaven   19, 20, 28
blue-floral-patterned porcelain   195, 196, 198, 211
blue-white floral patterned porcelain   211
Book of Changes   9, 110, 111, 268, 270, 293, 294, 295, 381
Book of History   159, 381
Book of Huainanzi   7
Book of Master Baopu, The   208
Book of Sir Marco Polo, the Venetian, The   141
Book of Songs, The   382
Book of Spirits and Ghosts   113
Book of Stories   222
Boro   158
Böttger   213
Bouvet   295, 296
Brahman art   71
Brahman dance   94
bronze mirrors   139
Budagaya   126
Buddhabhadra   109
Buddhism   48, 49
Buddhism-preaching dramas   89
Buddhist art   56, 58
Buddhist art of nude   64
Buddhist Art of Gandhara, The   65
Buddhist pagodas   127
Buddhist paintings   57, 69

Buddhist relics 48
Buddhist scripture 101
Bureau of Calendar Reform
   238, 240
Byron 353
Byzantine 99
Byzantine dances 87
Byzantine silk industry 206

C.H. Brewitt-Taylor 382
Cai Huang 107
Cai Lun 215
Cai Yin 49
Cai Yuanpei 343, 349, 361,
   372
calendar reform 239, 243,
   244
Canon Law 231
Cao Buxing 57
Cao Cao 112, 114
Cao Miaoda 83
Cao Qinghua 358
Cao Xueqin 249
Cao Yin 249
Cao Zhi 51
Cao Zhongda 58
Captain's Daughter, The 357
Cassini 245, 256
Castiglione 280, 281, 282,
   284, 285, 287
Chang'an 102, 103
Chang'e 62
Chao Wujiu 97
Character of Races, The 365
Charaka 124
Charles Darwin 319, 320,
   327, 361, 362, 384

Charles Dickens 343, 355
Charles Kingsley 356
Charles Seignobos 367
Chavannes 382
Chekhov 354
Chen Duxiu 341, 342, 343,
   347
Chen Mei 282
Chen Tang 64
Cheng Dawei 236
Cheng Dayue 278
China Monumentis qua Sacris
   qua Profanis Illustrata 8
China's Autocracy 275
China's glass-making industry
   28
Chinese arts 289
Chinese astronomy 239
Chinese bronze culture 16
Chinese chess 97, 98
Chinese Civilization 3, 8
Chinese culture 87
Chinese garden design 289,
   290
Chinese paintings 277, 278,
   281, 283
Chinese porcelain 163, 164,
   166, 210, 211, 213, 289
Chinese puppet shows 96
Chinese qigong 94
Chinese relics 51
Chinese-Roman culture 51
Chinese sericulture 205
Chinese ships 47
Chinese silk 22, 23, 24, 25,
   39, 40, 50, 56, 160, 161, 163,
   203, 289

Chongzhen Calender 239
Christmas Carol, A 355
Christopher Clavius 235
Christopher Columbus 176
Chroniques d'Angleterre 225
Cimabue 277
Civilization of China, The 381
Claudus de Visdelou 296
Clavius' *Epitome Arithmeticae Practicae* 236
Clavius' Sphere of Earth 233
Clearing away Heresies 242
Collected Literary Works of Master Jingxiu 139
Collection of Ink Paintings 278
Communist Manifesto 347, 348
compass 386
Compendium of Materia Medica 383, 384
Confucius 268, 270, 274, 275, 293, 294
Confucius Sinarum Philosophus 267, 268, 270
Congling range 25, 26, 28, 31, 34, 40, 41, 50, 54, 170, 201
Constantinople 47
Continuation of Qi Xie Records, A 113
Copernicus 303, 316
Couplet 245, 268, 270, 292, 293
Cultural Theories on Sociolo-gy, The 363

D.L. Mongant 116
Da Ce (Grand Survey) 237
Da Qin 52
Da Tang Xi Yu Ji (Records of the Western Regions in the Tang Dynasty) 106
Da Tong Calendar 243
"Da Yan" calendar 123
Da Yuan Yi Tong Zhi (Unified Map of the Great Yuan Dynasty) 151
Da Zang Jing (Tripitaka) 108
Dai Kui 57
Dai Zheng 282
damask 23, 24
Daniel Defoe 355
Daniel Hanbury 384
Dao De Jing (Canon of the Dao and Its Virtue) 107
Dao Xing Jing 102
Dao Yi Zhi Lue 182, 185, 186
David Copperfield 355
Dayan (Big Goose) Pagoda 127
Dayuan 33
De Augmentis Scientiarum 236
De Bello Gothico 206
De Bello Tartarieo 292, 293
Derby porcelain 214
Description geographique, historique, chronologique, politique et physique de l'Em-

pire de la Chine et de la Tartarie Chinoise 269, 273, 297
Designs for Chinese Buildings, Furniture, Dresses, Machines and Utensils 290
Dewey 359, 360, 361, 367
Dharmaraksha 102
Di Renjie 98
Didacus de Pantoja 238
Ding Guanpeng 282
diplomatic relations with China 47
Directive of 1656 257, 258
Doctrine of the Mean, The 380
Doll's House, A 343, 351
Domingo Navarrete 258
Dominicus Parrenin 248, 251
Donglin party 235
Dr. Davidson Black 375, 376
Dr. James Legge 380
Dr. Martin 309, 313
Dr. Radakrisinan 108
Dr. Sun Yat-sen 324, 325, 326, 327, 328
Dream of Red Mansions, A 249
Dream of the Red Chamber 383
drum music 82
Du Hai Fang Cheng (Navigation Directory) 192
Du Halde 269, 273, 297
Du You 78, 96

Dunhuang Grottoes 62, 129
Dutreil de Rhins 64
Early Chinese Culture, An 10
East-West communications 31
East-West cultural exchange 53
East-West exchange 46
East-West trade 37, 41, 43, 51, 54
Eastern-Western Monthly Magazine 298
Ecce Homo 362
Elements of Algebra 302
Ellen C. Semple 366
Ellsworth Huntington 365, 366
Emile Zola 355
Emmanuel Diaz 238
Emms Read 384
Emperor Jingzong 99
Emperor Jones, The 352
Emperor Kangxi 242-54, 256, 259, 260, 261, 262, 265, 268, 269, 271, 272, 294, 295, 296, 303, 309
Emperor Qianlong 282, 283, 284, 286, 287, 291
Emperor Taizong 99, 107, 125
Emperor Xuanzong 86, 88, 91, 95, 99, 125
Empress Wu Zetian 91, 97, 98
Encyclopaedia 297
Enemy of the People, An 351

Engels   362
Erich Remarque   356
Erlitou culture   14
Ernest Hemingway   359
Er Ya (Literary Expositor)   6
Essai sur les moeurs et l'espir-it des nations   266
Essays on Oriental Garden-ing   291
Ethnic Character and Ethnic Health   365
Euclid's *Elements of Geometry* 233, 235, 247, 302
Eugene O'Neill   352, 359
Eurasian Steppe   21, 60
European chess   97
European porcelain indus-try   212
Evolution and Ethics   319, 320
Excerpts of Music   252

Fa Xian   101, 103, 104
Fan Shouyi   261-65, 283
Fan Yang   95
Fathers and Sons   357
Fayuan Zhulin   93
Fei Xiaotong   364
Fei Xin   197
Feng Zikai   349
Feodor Dostoyevsky   357
Ferdinandus Verbiest   243, 244, 245, 257
Flavio Gioja   222
Forty-two Chapters of Scrip-ture   101
Francis Galton   364, 365

Francois Quesnay   267, 275
French King Louis IX   145
Friedrich Engels   347
Friedrich Nietzsche   361, 362
Fuxi   294

Galileo   240
Gan Yanshou   64
Gan Ying   41, 43
Gandhara art   66, 67, 68, 71
Ganges Valley   34
Gao Han   362
Gao Shiqi   249
Ge Hong   208, 209
Ge Xuan   208
Ge Zhi Hui Bian (Chinese Scientific Magazine)   307
Ge Zhi Qi Meng (An Introduc-tion to Sciences)   307
General Doctrines of the *Book of Changes*   296
Geng Jizhi   357, 358
Genghis Khan   133, 134, 135, 136, 172, 273, 274
Geographia   40
Geography   159, 163
Georg Wilhelm Hegel   362
George Byron   342
Gerhart Hauptmann   356
Germinal   355
Gilded Age, The   358
Giles   381
Giotto   277
glass-making industry   27, 116, 118, 119
"Glass Route"   117
Golden Horde   137, 138

Gou Shi　113
Government Inspector, The 357
Graeco-Roman culture　62, 64
Graeco-Roman fine art　65
Graeco-Roman genre　69
Great Khan Kublai　32, 33, 49, 61, 64, 137, 150, 169, 171, 172
Great Learning, The　267, 380
Great Yuezhi　50, 101
Greek culture　64, 65
Gregor Mandel　364
Grünwedel　69, 339, 340
Gu Kaizhi　57
Guang Hui Bureau　152
Gulliver's Travels　355
gunpowder　223, 386
Guo Moruo　344, 355, 356, 358
Guo Que　188
Guo Shoujing　150
Gürkhan　132, 133
Gustave Flaubert　355
Gutenberg　216, 219
Guy de Maupassant　354
Guyuk Khan　146, 147

Hai Di Bu (Notes of the Sea)　192
Hai Guo Tu Zhi (Illustrated Record of Maritime Nations)　299, 300, 301
Hai Yao Ben Cao (Overseas Materia Medica)　121

Hamlet　355
Han Emperor Wudi　32
Han Shu (History of the Han Dynasty)　64, 75, 215
Hans Andersen　356
Hans Driesch　359
Harriet Stowe　351
He Bingsong　367
He Chou　120
Heinrich Heine　356
Henrik Ibsen　343, 351, 352, 353, 356
Henry Wadsworth Longfellow　359
Henry Yule　141
Heraclitus　21
Herbert Spencer　319, 320
Hereditary Talents　365
Hexi Corridor　22, 33, 47, 55, 71, 82, 131, 135
Hezan Khan　142
Hinayama scriptures　108
Histoire de l'Empereur de la Chine　268
Historia Mongolorum quos nos Tartaros appellamus　144
Historical Literature (Jami at-Tawarikh)　142
Historie de l'Empereur de la Chine　269
History of Chinese Literature, A　381
History of Mongolia　159
History of the Han Dynasty　35, 52
History of the Kingdom of China　194

History of the Later Han Dynasty 37, 43
History of the Sui Dynasty 94, 122
Hong Jun   175
Hong Shen   352
Hong Zun   98
Hongshan culture   63
Honore de Balzac   355
Hou Yi   62
Hu Ben Cao (Hu Materia Medica)   121
Hu Shih   320, 341, 342, 343, 360, 361, 372
Hu Teng (Jumping) Dance 88
Hu Xuan (Whirling) Dance 88
Hua Hengfang   304, 305, 314, 315, 316
Hua Tuo   124
Hua Xia nation   18, 19, 21
Huang Di (Yellow Emperor)   49
Hui Hui Prescriptions   152
"Hui Hui" (Muslim) Calendar   150
Hui Sheng   55
Hulagu   169
Huntuo dance   91
Huo Han Shu (History of the Eastern Han Dynasty)   6

Ibn Battutah   156, 162, 168, 177, 178, 179, 187
Ibn Faqih   162
Ibn Sina   152

Identification of Materials 305, 316
Idrisi   159, 161, 166
Ignatius Sickelparth   282, 285
Il-Khanate Astronomical Table   141, 150
Immanuel Kant   361
Immensee   356
Indian acrobatics and magic   92
India and China   108
Indian Art Museum in Berlin   67
Indian Buddhist circles   108
Indian Buddhist temples   66
Indian calendar   123
Indian chess   96, 97
Indian culture   63
Indian emigrants   48
Indian medicine   124
Indian nude art   68
Indian Power Dance   87
Indian Prince Kumara   107
Indian puppet art   96
Indian stupa   126
Indian-style music   82
Indian yoga   94
Indus Valley   33, 34, 64, 80
Isaiah Bowman   366
Islamic Calendar   243
Issac Newton   256, 266, 303, 316
Ivan Goncharov   357
Ivan Turgenev   357

Jabir Ibn Hayyan   209

Jack London   359
Jacobus Rho   240, 241, 248
Jamal al-Din ibn Mahammad
   al-Najjari   150, 151
Jean de Wavrin   225
Jean Francois Foucquet   296
Jean-Francois Gerbillon   248,
   253, 257
Jean Jacques Rousseau   323,
   324
Jean Morales   293
Ji Junxiang   273
Jia Dan   155
Jia Lanpo   376
Jiao Bingzhen   279, 282
Jichuo   18
Jin Tingbiao   282
Jing Bao   175
Jingde Conuty Annals   219
Jingdezhen porcelain   165
Joachim Bouvet   248, 257,
   268, 293, 294
Joannes Adam Schall von Bell
   240-44, 252, 257
Joannes Bapt Régis   254,
   256, 296
Joannes Terrenz   248
Johann von Goethe   356
Johann von Schiller   356
Johannes Kepler   316
John Fryer   307, 316, 318,
   321
John Galsworthy   355
John Herschel   315
John Locke   266
John Marshall   65
John of Plano Carpini   140,

144
John Steinbeck   359
Jonathan Swift   355
Joseph Needham   220, 386
Juan Gonzalez de Mendoza
   194

Kabul   51
*Kai Yuan Zan Jing (Kai Yuan
   Classic on Astrology)*   123
Kang Tai   44, 45
Kang Youwei   317, 395
Kangju   33, 49
Kangxi Atlas   255, 256
Kangxi Yongnian Calendar
   245
Karasuc culture   17
Karl Marx   347, 362
Kew Garden   289, 290
Keyserling   378, 379
Khan Ogdai   136, 143
Kiangnan Machine Building
   Works   314, 316
King Coal   358
King Mu of the Zhou Dynasty
   19, 20, 27
Kipchak Steppe   138
Kizir Grottoes   67
Kizir mural paintings   68
konghou   75, 76, 77
Kumarajiva   102, 109, 110,
   112
Kumtura Grottoes   67

L'Assommoir   355
L'Orphelin de la Chine   272,
   273

La Dame aux camélias 351
La Theorie et Pratique du Jardinage 284
langgan 26, 27
Lao Zi 49, 107
Law of Nations, The 298
Laws of Nature 275
Le Coq 339, 340
Le Jarden Anglo-Chinois 291
Legge 381
Lei Yao (Summary of Books) 97
Leibniz 269, 270, 271, 272, 293, 294, 295
Lenin 362, 379
Leo Tolstoy 351, 357
Leonid Andreev 344, 357
Lettres philosophiques 266, 267
Li Dazhao 345, 347
Li Duan 88
Li Hongzhang 369
Li Huo Lun (On Truth and Doubts) 50
Li Ji (The Book of Rites) 4, 381
Li Shanlan 302, 303, 306, 309, 314, 315, 316
Li Shizhen 383
Li Susha 120
Li Tianjing 239
Li Xun 121
Li Yannian 81
Li Zhizao 235, 236, 238, 239
Liang Qichao 311, 319, 322, 324, 328, 367, 379, 380
Liang Shumin 380

"Lin De" calendar 122
Lin Fengmian 351
Lin Shu 342, 343, 354
Lin Yutang 383
Lin Zexu 298, 299, 301, 302, 395
Liu Che 35
Liu Dabai 343
Liu Haisu 350, 391
Liu Xiaosun 122
Liu Yanshi 88
Liu Yin 139
Liu Yuxi 124
Liu Zhuo 122
Long Old Road in China, The 340
longevity drug 125
Longquan porcelain 164
Longshan culture 15, 30
Loulan 61, 62
Lü Lü Zheng Yi (Definitions of Music) 252
Lu Rong 189
Lu Xun 343, 344, 353, 354
Ludovicus Le Comte 268, 290
Ludwig Bachkofer 12
lunar calendar 122
Luo Fumin 282
Luoyang 103
Lyell 316

Ma Huan 197
Ma Junwu 320, 321
Ma Ming 89
Machang culture 15
magnetic compass 220

Mahayana Buddhism 110
Mahayana scriptures 102, 108
Maitreya 111
Majiayao culture 15
Man Shu (Book of the Barbarians) 115
Mangu Khan 147
Manuscript of St. Mark 207
Mao Dun 352, 354, 357
Mao Yuanyi 192
Marco Polo 133, 162, 168-75, 179, 265
mariner's compass 220, 221, 222
Mark Twain 358
Martin Luther 219
Martino Martini 257, 292
Master Lü's Spring and Autumn Annals 5
Materia Medica et Dieta 128
Mathematical Collections of Zeguxizhai Studio 303
Matteo Ricci 216, 229, 230, 231, 232, 235, 237, 252, 256, 260, 261, 278, 292, 302
Maxim Gorky 352, 357, 358
May Fourth Movement 341, 344, 345
Mean, The 268
Mechanics 303
"Medici" blue-floral porcelain 212
Medieval Technology 116
Meeting with Maitreya 89
Mei Lanfang 387, 388, 389
Meissen porcelain 213

Mencius 268, 381
Meng Qi Bu Bi Tan (A Supplement to Dream Stream Essays) 79
metal movable type 219
Michael Ruggieri 231, 261, 292
Michelangelo 264
Mickiewicz 354
Middle Kingdom 3, 4
Miguel de Cervantes 356
Mikhail Lermontov 357
Mogao Grottoes 59
Monk Yixing 123
Mou Rong 50
movable type printing 140, 216, 219
Ms. Qiu Jin 329
music of four categories 81
Must, A 242

Nana 355
Nanshao Fengsheng Yue (Holy Music of Nanshao) 77, 80
National Development Strategy 325
Natural History 205
New Culture Movement 341, 348, 386
New History, The 367
New Youth 341, 342, 343, 347
Nian Xiyao 287
Nicolaus Longobardi 238, 239
Night Inn 352
Nikolai Gogol 344, 357

nine-volume calendar 124
"Nishang Yuyi Qu" (Song of Rainbow Dress and Plume Gown) 86
northern Iran route 34
Northern Zhou Emperor Wudi 83
Notes on China 230
Notes Recollected 93, 94
Notre Dame de Paris 354
Nouveaux memoires sur l'etat present de la Chine 268
Novissima Sinica (Contemporary China) 269, 270
Novum Organum 236
Novus Atlas Sinensis 293

Oedipus Egyptiacus 8
Oil! 358
Old Metaphors in Buddhist Scriptures 113
On Groundless Prediction of Fortunes 244
On the Origin of Species by Means of Natural Selection 320, 384
On the Truth of Calendar 244
On Winning Friends 234
Opium War 288
Orient 341
Origin of Species, The 319
Oscar Wilde 352, 356
Outline of Global Geography, An 301
Outlines of Astronomy 303, 315, 317

overseas trade route 42

Pan Guangdan 364, 365
panling puppet show 96
paper-making 215, 216, 217, 386
Paris Astronomical Observatory 245
Parthia 33, 35, 36, 49
Pearl S. Buck 382
Pei Wenzhong 375
Peking Man 375, 376, 377
Pelliot 337, 382, 390
Periodic Table of Chemical Elements 304
Periplus of the Erythraean Sea, The 24, 50, 118, 186, 203
Persian artwork 59
Persian brocade 73
Persian King Darius the Great 22, 31
Persian monopoly 41
Persian porcelain 212
Petofi 353, 354
Petrus Jartoux 254, 256
Philosophiae Naturalis Principia Mathematica 316
Philosophy of History 362
Physics et Mystica 207
Picard 245
Pickwick Papers, The 355
Ping Zhou Ke Tan (Pingzhou Table Talk) 220
pipa 78, 79, 80
Plato 294
Pliny the Elder 205

polo   99
Pompeii wall paintings   69
populism   329
Porcelain Route   166
Port Alexandria   36
Posthumous Fortune   113
Prince Gong   308, 309
Princess Wusun   79
Principle of Geology   315, 316, 318
Principles of Sociology, The   320
printing idustry   218
Procopius   206
puppet shows   95
Pushkin   353

Qi Baishi   391
Qian Jin Yao Fang (The Thousand Golden Formulae)   121
Qian Jin Yi Fang (Supplement to the Thousand Golden Formulae)   121
Qianxun Pagoda   127
Qin Jing   49
Qing Yuan Xu Zhi   182
Qiuci   54
Qiuci art   68
Qiuci culture   90
Qiuci grottoes   70
Qiuci music   80, 82
Qiuci music band   85
Qu Qiubai   357, 358
Qu Taisu   233, 234

Rabban mar Sauma   148
Rabindranath Tagore   359
Raphael   264
Ras Dedin   159
Records of the Western Regions in the Tang Dynasty   107
Records on Translated Scripture of the Zhenyuan Era   108
Register of New Instruments for the Heavenly Observatory   245
Rémusat   383
Renaissance   219
Resurrection   351, 357
Return of the Native, The   355
Rihla (Travel Stories)   178
Rites Issue   258, 265, 266, 293, 294, 330
Robert Louis Stevenson   355
Robinson Crusoe   355
rococo   architecture   284, 288, 291
rococo design   291
rococo-style building design   285
rococo trend   283, 290
Romain Rolland   352, 355
Roman Empire   36, 37, 43, 44, 46
Roman glassware   117, 118
Roman Pope Clement V   146
Roman products   51
Romance of the Three Kingdoms, The   382
Rome   39, 41, 45

Romeo and Juliet   355
Rouran   53
Rubaiyat   344
Rudolf Steiner   362
running sand   6
Rural China   364

S. Fourmont   296
Samarkand   135
Sanchi   126
Sanskrit dramas   89
Sanskrit scripture   49
Sassanian-Persian art style   71, 72
Sassanian-Persian glassware   73
Sassanian relics   73
Schopenhauer and Nietzsche   362
Science and Civilization in China, The   386
Science of Survey   235
Science of Vision   287
Scythian   21
Scythian zoomorphic design   29
Se people   6, 21, 24, 64
Se traders   22
Se tribes   31
sea trade route   44
Secular History   139
Seima culture   16
700-year-history of translation   109
Shang bronze   14, 15, 17
Shang culture   13, 14
Shangshu (Book of History)   26
Shanhaijing (Classic of Mountains and Rivers)   5, 20, 62
Shaolin Temple   87
Shen Kuo   79, 220, 221
Shen Xian Zhuan (The Biography of Immortals)   208
Shen Yiguan   235
Sheng Shi Wei Yan (Warning to a Prosperous Society)   321
Shi Ji (Records of the Historian)   32, 75, 382
Shosoin Museum   74, 98
Shou Shi (Time-Telling) Calendar   150
Shu Jing (Book of History)   296
Shu Yuan Za Ji   189
Shuanglu (game)   98
Shun Feng Xiang Song (Bon Voyage)   192
Sienkiewicz   353, 354
silk trade   21, 36, 38, 41
Silk Road   36, 37, 39, 41, 42, 332
Sima Qian   32
Sinicae Historiae Decus Prima   293
Sino-Graeco-style   61
Sino-Indian cultural exchange   104
Sino-Indo-Burma Route   35
Sino-Indo Snow Mountain Route   34
Sino-Iranian cultural cooperation   140

Sino-Western mixed art style 281
Sinology 293, 296, 297
Sir Jean Chardin's Travel in Persia 212
Skullcap of Adult Sinanthropus Pekinensis, The 376
Socialism 328
Song Shi (History of the Song Dynasty) 159, 167
southern Iran route 34
southern trade route 55
Spencer 324
Spring and Autumn Annals, The 381
Steam Engine 305
Stefan Zweig 356
Stein 61, 62, 65, 72, 332, 334-40, 382, 390
Stories from Ancient Yunnan 48
Storm, The 352, 357
Story of an Innocent Soul 113
Strange Case of Dr. Jekyll and Mr. Hyde 355
Study of History 368
Study of Sociology 320
Study on the Consanguinity of the Chinese Opera Performers, A 364
Study on the Making and Distribution of Wealth, A 276
Study on Truthfulness of Zuozhuan (Zuoqiu Ming's Chronicles), The 382
Su Manshu 342

Suan Fa Tong Zong (Systematic Treatise on Arithmetic) 236, 295
sugar refining 128
Sui Emperor Yangdi 93
Supplements to the Translated History of the Yuan Dynasty 175
Sven Hedin 332, 333, 338
Sword Dance 94

Table of Economy 275
Tai Xi Shui Fa (Western Hydraulic Engineering) 236
Tan Sitong 318
Tang Dynasty music and dance 87
Tang-Sanskrit Dictionary 127
Taoist ideology 7
tea 139, 143
Tess of the D'Urbervilles 355
The Jungle 358
The Silk Road 333
The Tempest 355
Theodor Storm 356
Theodore Dreiser 359
Theory of Mechanics 305
Theory of Western Civilization 323
thin water 6
Thomas Hardy 343, 355
Thomas Henry Huxley 319
Thomas Morgan 364
Thousand-Buddha Caves 334, 335
Three People's Principles

325
Timur 196
Tomas Pereira 250, 251, 252, 253, 257
Tong Dian (Encyclopaedia) 39, 78
Tong Meng Hui (Chinese Revolutionary League) 329
Tong Wen Suan Zhi (Mathematical Handbook) 236
Tongguan Kiln 164
Tongwen Institute 304, 308, 309, 311
Tour of Ten Continents, The 27
Tractados historicos, politicos, eticosy religioses de la monarquia de China 258
Travels of Ibn Battutah 180
Travels of Marco Polo, A Visiting Official of the Yuan Dynasty 168-73, 175, 176, 179
Treasure Island 355
Trial of Boris, The 23
Trip to the Orient 144
Tripitaka 111
Tripolije culture 12
Tujue 55
Turgot 276
Turpan grottoes 69

Uber die Chine-sischen Garden 291
Uncle Tom's Cabin 351
Upton Sinclair 352, 358
Utensils 290

"utopian" society 346

Vengeance of Zhao's Orphan, The 273
Vicente Blasco Ibanez 356
Victor Hugo 342, 354
Voltaire 266, 267, 272-75, 293

Wai Tai Mi Yao (Medical Secrets Held by an Official) 121
Walter Whitman 359
Wandering Lake, The 333
Wang Dayuan 168, 180, 182-87, 195
Wang Fuzhi 318, 319
Wang Guangqi 346, 349
Wang Guowei 361, 362
Wang Kangnian 175
Wang Xuance 125, 128
Wang Xun 150
Wang Yan 113
Wang Youxue 282
Wang Yuanlu 333-37
Wang Zhaojun Bianwen 113
Wang Zhen 219
Wang Zinian 93, 94
Warner 340
Washington Irving 358
Wei Boyang 207, 208, 209, 385
Wei Lie (Memorable Things of the Wei Kingdom) 45
Wei Shu (History of the Wei Dynasty) 119
Wei Xie 57

Wei Yi   175
Wei Yuan   299, 300, 301
Western art style   285
Western calendar system 240, 241, 244
Western culture   229, 231, 233
Western garden design   289
Western Interpretation of the Four Books   267
Western medicine   249
Western music   250, 252
Western paintings   277, 278, 280
Western Regions   33, 41, 49
Western sciences   235
Westernization group   309, 310, 311
William Chambers   288, 290, 291
William James   360, 361
William Rubruck   144, 145, 147
William Shakespeare   352, 355
Williams Chambers   288
woodblock printing   139, 217, 218, 219
Work-Study Mutual-Aid Group   346
Wu Bei Zhi (Treatise on Armament Technology)   192
Wu Daozi   58
Wu Jun   113
Wu Mengfei   349
Wu Mingxuan   244
Wu Pu   192

Wu Yue   329
Wu Zixu Bianwen   113
Wutasi Temple   126

Xi Jing Za Ji (Miscellaneous Records of the West Capital)   116
Xia culture   13
Xia Nai   55
Xiang Mo Bian Wen (Colloquial Scripts Based on Subduing of Demon)   112
Xiao Youmei   349
Xiaoyan (Small Goose) Pagoda   127
Xin Xiu Ben Cao (Revised Materia Medica)   120, 128
Xiongnu   31, 33, 36, 41, 54, 64
Xiongnu Steppe Empire   53
Xiwangmu (Western Queen Mother)   5, 6, 7, 19, 20, 62
Xiyu acrobatics   94
Xiyu culture   82
Xiyu Garrison Command   36
Xiyu music and dance   74, 81, 82, 85, 86
Xu Beihong   350, 391
Xu Guangqi   235, 236, 237, 239, 241, 257, 302
Xu Jianyin   314, 315
Xu Jishe   301
Xu Shou   302, 303, 304, 305, 307, 314, 315
Xu Xilin   329
Xu Zang Jing (Continuation of Tripitaka)   108

Xuan Zhuang   103-08, 110, 111, 206
Xuan Zhuang Pagoda   127

Yan Fu   319, 320, 343
Yan Zhitui   113
Yan Zhu   97
Yan Zong   110
Yang Chunren   352
Yang Guangxian   243, 244
Yang Tingbi   158
Yang Xianyi   381
Yang Yuhuan   88
Yangshao culture   10, 11
Ye Xianggao   235
Yelu Chucai   150
Yelu Dashi   131, 132
Yi Yan (Suggestions of Change)   321
Ying Ya Sheng Lan (Reflections of Overseas Tours)   197
Yogacara Treatise   111
Yong Le Da Dian (Great Encyclopaedia of the Yongle Reign)   173
Yongnian Calendar   241
Yongning Temple Pagoda   126
Yuan Rong Jiao Yi (Study of Circles and Volumes)   235
Yuan Shao   114
Yuan Shi (History of the Yuan Dynasty)   173
Yuan Weizhi   217
Yuanmingyuan   283, 285, 286, 287, 288, 290

Yuanmingyuan in Pictures   291
Yuezhi   31, 41, 42, 45
Yutian   48, 49, 54

Zadig   272
Zaitun culture   12
Zhan Tianyou   369
Zhang Daqian   392
Zhang Gui   47
Zhang Heng   92
Zhang Huang   234
Zhang Qian   32, 33, 35, 81
Zhang Sengyao   57
Zhang Weibang   282
Zhao, the King of Hell   352
Zhao Yuanyi   314
Zhejiang kilns   164
Zheng Boqi   352
Zheng Guanying   321, 322
Zheng He   165, 186, 188, 189, 190, 191, 193, 194, 195, 196
Zheng Yin   208
Zheng Zhenduo   357
Zhiloujiachen   101, 109
Zhong Xi Wen Jian Lu (Sino-Western Information Review)   175
Zhou Bi   235
Zhou Yi Can Tong Qi (Kinship of the Three and Book of Changes)   207, 385
Zhou Zuoren   343, 353
Zhu Shixing   102
Zhu Tian Jiang (On the Celestial System)   317
Zhu Yin   44

Zhu Yu   220
Zhuan Ji Bai Yu Jing (A Hundred Metaphors in Buddhist Scriptures)   112
Zhushu Jinian (The Bamboo Annals)   20
Zij Assorted Calendar   150

图书在版编目（CIP）数据

中外文化因缘：英文/沈福伟著.—北京：
外文出版社,1995
（中国知识丛书）
ISBN 7－119－00431－X

Ⅰ.中… Ⅱ.沈… Ⅲ.文化交流,中、外－文化史－英文
Ⅳ.K203

中国版本图书馆 CIP 数据核字（95）第 10206 号

责任编辑　吴灿飞

中外文化因缘

沈福伟　著

*

©外文出版社
外文出版社出版
（中国北京百万庄大街 24 号）
邮政编码 100037
北京外文印刷厂印刷
中国国际图书贸易总公司发行
（中国北京车公庄西路 35 号）
北京邮政信箱第 399 号　邮政编码 100044
1996 年(大 32 开)第 1 版
1997 年第 1 版第 2 次印刷
（英）
ISBN 7－119－00431－X/K·121(外)
04500
11－E－2987P